CHRISTIANITY THROUGH THE CENTURIES

Christianity Through the Centuries

A History of the Christian Church

by

EARLE E. CAIRNS

Chairman of the Department of History
Wheaton College

ZONDERVAN PUBLISHING HOUSE

GRAND RAPIDS, MICHIGAN

To
Helen and Bruce

PREFACE

The invitation from the Zondervan Publishing House to write a church history led the writer to think about the advisability of such a task when there are already so many books in the field. Examination of the available texts, however, reveals that no church history text without a particular denominational or theological interpretation is available to the student who wishes to know and to understand the significant material of church history. Either the author's Presbyterian, Methodist, Episcopalian, Congregational, or other denominational viewpoint pervades his book, or, if the text is free from denominational interpretation, it often follows a particular theological approach, such as that of Calvin, Arminius, or Pelagius; or, far more serious, it interprets church history from the viewpoint of the liberal theologian. There seems to be room in the field for a text in which a conservative, interdenominational theological position is taken. Such a work seems to be what the numerous Bible institutes and colleges desire.

In this book the author seeks to present persons, places, dates, events, ideas and trends or movements in their proper perspective. There is no attempt to make the text encyclopedic. Some of the details often discussed in church history texts, those which only serve to confuse the student, are omitted in favor of those which are more interesting and significant in the course of Christian history. Attention is given to the impact of Christianity upon its day as well as to the development of doctrines and institutions. The presentation of basic knowledge is coupled with an endeavor to promote clear understanding by clarity of organization and definite outline.

The interpretation is that of conservative Christianity, permeated with a Christian philosophy of history. At the same time the author has attempted to orient church history to its environment of secular history. Church historians have written of Christianity too often without relating it to its secular background. The writer is convinced that one can never understand Christianity effectively without having some conception of the political, economic, social, intellectual and aesthetic movements of each era of its history. Because all human events must occur in time and space, there is some justification for such consideration.

The use of both primary and secondary source materials during the study of the various eras of Christianity is essential to a better understanding of church history. For that reason, both bibliographies and footnotes cite readily available sources that are relevant to the matters under discussion. A bibliography is given at the end of each chapter, at the beginning of discussions of the three major eras of church history and in the introduction to the book. Simple charts have been added where they can contribute to a real understanding of the development of Christianity. The dates of a person's life, after the first mention of the name, are usually those given in *Webster's Biographical Dictionary* (Springfield, Mass.: G. & C. Merriam Co., 1943).

The author wishes to acknowledge his indebtedness to his able teachers and to the writers whose works in the field of church history he has read. The reading of the entire manuscript by his wife and the reading of parts by colleagues of the English Department of Wheaton College contributed greatly to its value. Morris Nelson of Moody Bible Institute and the author's colleague, Dr. Ernest Larson, gave helpful suggestions. The writer is grateful to Dr. V. Raymond Edman, President of Wheaton College, whose encouragement made the book a possibility. The careful typing of the manuscript by Miss Joyce Block helped greatly in the completion of the work.

This book is put forth with a sincere prayer that many might become conscious of their spiritual ancestry and be constrained to praise God in life, word and deed.

E. E. CAIRNS
Wheaton, Illinois

January 15, 1954

Mem. 3 groups c̄ major headings

CONTENTS

ix

590-1054- Rise of Papal Power

MODERN CHURCH HISTORY
1517 and After

DIAGRAMS

MAPS

PICTURES

All pictures courtesy of Religious News Service

INTRODUCTION

Curiosity concerning the past has characterized man from the time of such an antiquary as Nabonidus of Chaldea to the present-day archaeologist and historian. Christians have a special interest in history because the very foundations of the faith which they profess are rooted in history. God became man and lived in time and space in the person of Christ. Church history is thus a matter of profound interest to the Christian who desires to be enlightened concerning his spiritual ancestry.

I. The Definition of Church History

The English word for history came from the Greek word *historia*, which is derived from the Greek verb *historeo*. This word was used by the Attic Greeks and originally meant to learn by inquiry or investigation. It denoted the activities of one seeking knowledge. The word is used by Paul in Galatians 1:18 to describe his interview with Peter in Jerusalem. Like any true historian, he sought to learn about Christianity by a process of inquiry.

The Greeks subsequently began to use the word *historikos* for history. It differed from the word *historia* in that it indicated the *product* of inquiry, the record: whereas the other indicated the *process* by which the record is made. The former meaning — history as product — is the most used by modern historians.

The German word *geschichte*, a form of the verb *geschehen*, which means to happen, refers to history as *event* rather than to history as a process or a product.

From this discussion the student will see that one may use the word *history* with reference to event, process, or product. The crowning of Charlemagne in 800 as emperor of the Romans was an historic event. The historian's study of the sources to ascertain the facts of the event is process, and the account of those facts is history as product. History as event is absolute and cannot be changed once it happens, but history as process and product is relative and subject to change.

History may be defined as the interpreted record of the socially significant human past, based upon organized data collected by the scientific method from archaeological, literary or living sources. The church historian must be just as impartial in his collection of the data of history as the secular historian is, even though the church historian recognizes the fact that neither of them will be neutral to the data but each will approach the material with a framework of interpretation.

Church history, then, is the interpreted record of the origin, progress and impact of Christianity upon human society, based upon organized data gathered by scientific method from archaeological, documentary or living sources. It is the interpreted, organized story of the redemption of man and the earth. Only if this definition is fulfilled will the Christian student of history have an accurate record of the story of the Faith which he professes. The children of light in this instance must not lag behind the children of darkness.

II. The Writing of Church History

A. *The Scientific Element.*

Church history will have a scientific element in that the historian of the Church uses the scientific method also. The historian uses the scientific work of the archaeologist, who makes available information from the material remains of the past which he has unearthed. Study of the art of the catacombs of Rome has taught us much about the Early Church. The writer of church history will also make use of the techniques of literary criticism to evaluate the documents of the history of the Church. He will have a decided preference for original sources whether they be those of the archaeologist, the document, or the living person who took part in the event. All of this material and the evaluation of it will give him information concerning the important questions of historical method — who, what, when and where. The last two questions are important to the historian because historical events are conditioned by time and place.

B. *The Philosophic Element.*

The problem of the meaning of history faces the writer of history once he has ascertained his facts. This is the point at which history has a philosophic element. Historians tend to fall into three classifications in their pursuit of meaning in history.

1. One group may be classed as *pessimists.* Seeing history only "under the sun," they often adopt a materialistic approach to reality. They are obsessed with the failure of man in history. Oswald Spengler's *The Decline of the West* (New York: Alfred A. Knopf, 1939) is an illustration of this approach to history.

Spengler is concerned with civilizations rather than with nations. Each civilization, he maintains, goes through a cycle of birth, adolescence, maturity, decay and death. Western civilization, the most recent of civilizations, is in its period of decay. It will soon die, and along with it will die Christianity. Obsessed with man's failure, such men as Spengler can see no progress in history. Their views may be symbolized by a series of identical circles superimposed upon each other.

2. A second group may be called *optimists*. Their view of history can be symbolized by an ascending graph or successively rising levels of a spiral. Most optimistic interpreters are humanists: they see man as the main and determinative factor in history. They also usually accept biological and social evolution. The work of Arnold Toynbee, a great modern philosopher of history, serves to illustrate this philosophy of history. Toynbee agrees with Spengler that one should study the history of civilizations; but, unlike Spengler, he believes that each civilization makes progress toward its goal — the earth as a province of the kingdom of God. In spite of his more spiritual approach to history, he accepts modern Biblical criticism and the theory of evolution.

Another optimist, Hegel, the famous German philosopher of the nineteenth century, looks upon history as the unfolding of the Absolute Spirit in the development of human freedom. Progress is by a process in which successive series of contradictions are reconciled until the Absolute is fully manifested in history.

Another nineteenth century thinker, Karl Marx, also belongs to the optimistic school. Borrowing Hegel's logic, he disavows Hegel's view of reality. Marx teaches that matter in flux is the only reality, and that all human institutions, including religion, are determined by the economic processes of production. He maintains that a series of class struggles will end with the victory of the workers and the establishment of a classless society. Notice that Marx emphasizes man's power to redeem himself and his world in the same way that Toynbee and Hegel do.

3. The third group of interpreters, in which the writer places himself, may be described as *pessimistic optimists*. This group agrees with the pessimists in emphasizing the failure of unregenerate man; but in the light of divine revelation and grace, it is optimistic concerning man's future. The pessimistic op-

timists approach history as Biblical theists and seek to find the glory of God in the historic process. History becomes a process of conflict between good and evil, God and the Devil, in which man is helpless apart from the grace of God. The work of Christ upon the Cross is the final guarantee of the eventual victory of the divine plan for man and the earth.

The City of God, a defense and explanation of Christianity by Augustine, one of the Church Fathers, is an excellent illustration of this approach, although many Christians do not agree with Augustine's equation of the millennium with the present period of the Church. The grandeur of Augustine's conception grows out of its ascription of *creation* to the sovereign God of creation. The *compass* or scope of Augustine's view of history includes the whole of the human race in contrast with the favored German nation of Hegel or the favored working class of Marx. Augustine argues that the *course* of human history proceeds to and from the Cross; and the grace flowing therefrom is seen as operative within the Christian Church, the invisible Body of Christ. Christians, with divine grace to strengthen them, engage on the side of God in the conflict with evil until history reaches its cataclysmic *consummation* with the return of Christ.

Among contemporary writings that set forth a Christian approach to history, Herbert Butterfield's *Christianity and History* (New York: Charles Scribner's Sons, 1950) is one of the most helpful. The accompanying diagram is designed to aid the student in the application of the Christian approach to church history.

C. *The Artistic Element.*

Finally, the maker of history as record must seek to be as artistic as possible in his presentation of the facts. Modern historians have not stressed an interesting literary presentation of history as much as they should have.

III. The Value of Church History

Church history is only a dreary academic exercise in the remembering of facts unless some thought is given to the matter of its value to the Christian. The ancient historians had a much higher appreciation of the pragmatic, didactic and moral values of history than many modern historians have. The student who is conscious of the values to be achieved in the study of the

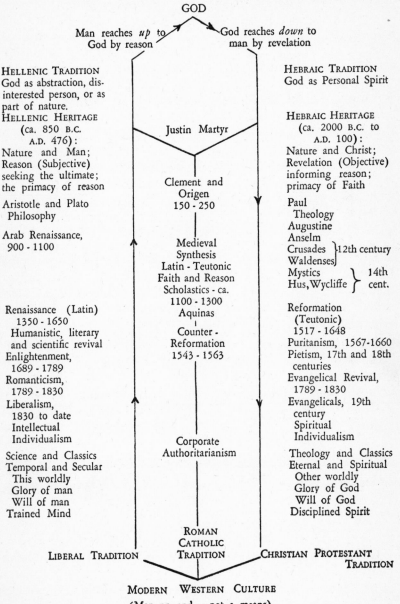

GOD

Man reaches *up* to
God by reason

God reaches *down* to
man by revelation

HELLENIC TRADITION
God as abstraction, dis-
interested person, or as
part of nature.
HELLENIC HERITAGE
(ca. 850 B.C.
A.D. 476):
Nature and Man;
Reason (Subjective)
seeking the ultimate;
the primacy of reason

Aristotle and Plato
Philosophy

Arab Renaissance,
900 - 1100

Renaissance (Latin)
1350 - 1650
Humanistic, literary
and scientific revival
Enlightenment,
1689 - 1789
Romanticism,
1789 - 1830
Liberalism,
1830 to date
Intellectual
Individualism

Science and Classics
Temporal and Secular
This worldly
Glory of man
Will of man
Trained Mind

Justin Martyr

Clement and
Origen
150 - 250

Medieval
Synthesis
Latin - Teutonic
Faith and Reason
Scholastics - ca.
1100 - 1300
Aquinas
|
Counter -
Reformation
1543 - 1563

Corporate
Authoritarianism

HEBRAIC TRADITION
God as Personal Spirit

HEBRAIC HERITAGE
(ca. 2000 B.C. to
A.D. 100):
Nature and Christ;
Revelation (Objective)
informing reason;
primacy of Faith

Paul
Theology
Augustine
Anselm
Crusades ⎱12th century
Waldenses⎰
Mystics ⎱ 14th
Hus, Wycliffe ⎰ cent.

Reformation
(Teutonic)
1517 - 1648
Puritanism, 1567-1660
Pietism, 17th and 18th
centuries
Evangelical Revival,
1789 - 1830
Evangelicals, 19th
century
Spiritual
Individualism

Theology and Classics
Eternal and Spiritual
Other worldly
Glory of God
Will of God
Disciplined Spirit

ROMAN
CATHOLIC
TRADITION

LIBERAL TRADITION

CHRISTIAN PROTESTANT
TRADITION

MODERN WESTERN CULTURE
(Man an end — not a means)

history of the Christian Church has a powerful motivation to a real interest in this particular area of human history.

A. *Church History as a Synthesis.*

One of the primary values of church history is that it links the past factual data of the Christian Gospel with the future proclamation and application of that Gospel in a present synthesis that creates understanding of our great heritage and inspiration for its further proclamation and application. Church history shows the Spirit of God in action through the Church during the ages of its existence. Exegetical theology is linked in a meaningful pattern with practical theology as the student sees how systematic theology has made an impact upon previous human thought and action. '

B. *Church History as an Explanation of the Present.*

Church history has great value as an explanation of the present. We can understand the present much better if we have some knowledge of its roots in the past. The answer to the puzzling query concerning the presence of over two hundred and fifty religious groups in the United States is to be found in church history. The principle of separation found a place early in the history of the Church which the Reformation was to accentuate. It is interesting to trace the Protestant Episcopal Church back to England and to note the origin of the Anglican Church in the struggle of the royal power with the papacy. The Methodist is interested in the beginnings of his church in the Wesleyan revival which finally brought separation of Methodism from the Anglican Church. Those of the Reformed or Presbyterian faith will take delight in tracing the origin of their church to Switzerland.

Different beliefs and liturgical practices become more understandable in the light of past history. Methodists kneel at the rail for communion because for many years the Methodists constituted a church within the Anglican Church, and Wesley, who was reluctant to break with the Anglican Church, followed its liturgical customs. In contrast, Presbyterians are served the Communion in their seats. The difference in Methodist and Presbyterian theology becomes much plainer when one studies the views of Calvin and Arminius.

Present-day problems of the Church are often illuminated by study of the past. The refusal of most modern dictatorial rulers to permit their people to have any private interests separate from their public life in the state is more easily understood if one remembers that the Roman emperors did not think that one could have a private religion without endangering the existence of the state. The relationship between the Church and state has again become a real problem in Russia, China and the Russian satellite states, and it is to be expected that these states will persecute Christianity just as Decius and Diocletian did in their day. The danger inherent in the union of the Church and state through the state support for parochial schools and through the sending of envoys to the Vatican is illuminated by the slow decline of spirituality in the Church and the interference with the Church by the temporal power beginning with the control of the Council of Nicaea by Constantine in 325.

C. *Church History as a Guide.*

The correction of existing evils within the Church or the avoidance of error and false practice is another value of the study of the past of the Church. The present is usually the product of the past and the seed of the future. Paul reminds us in I Corinthians 10:6, 11 that the events of the past are to help us avoid the evil and emulate the good. Study of the hierarchal medieval Roman Catholic Church will point out the danger in the modern ecclesiasticism that seems to be creeping into Protestantism. New sects will often be revealed as old heresies in a new guise. Christian Science can be understood better after a study of Gnosticism in the Early Church and the ideas of the Cathari in medieval times. Ignorance of the Bible and the history of the Church is a major reason why many advocate false theologies or bad practices.

D. *Church History as a Motivating Force.*

Church history also offers edification, inspiration or enthusiasm that will stimulate high spiritual life. Paul believed that knowledge of the past would give hope to the Christian life (Rom. 15:4). No one can study the brave stand of Ambrose of Milan, in refusing Emperor Theodosius the Communion until he repented of his massacre of the Thessalonian crowd, without being encouraged to stand for Christ against evil in high political or ecclesiastical circles. The industry and drive which enabled Wesley to preach over ten thousand sermons during his life and to travel thousands of miles on horseback is bound to be a rebuke and a challenge to Christians who have much better means for travel and study than Wesley had, but who do not make adequate use of them. One may not agree with Rauschenbusch's theology, but one cannot help but be inspired by his passion to apply the Gospel to social problems. The story of Carey's life was and is an inspiration to missionary service. The biographical aspect of church history is bound to bring inspiration and challenge to the student.

There is also edification in the process of becoming aware of one's spiritual ancestry. There is as much need for the Christian to become aware of his spiritual genealogy as there is for the citizen to study the history of his land in order that he might become an intelligent citizen. In showing the genetic development of Christianity, church history is to the New Testament what the New Testament is to the Old Testament. The Christian ought to be as aware of the main outlines of the growth and development of Christianity as he is of Biblical truth. Then he will have a sense of being a part of the Body of Christ, which includes a Paul, a Bernard of Clairvaux, an Augustine, a Luther, a Wesley or a Booth. The sense of unity that comes from a knowledge of the continuity of history will lead to spiritual enrichment.

One who is fearful for the future of the Church in countries where it is now persecuted will become more hopeful as he realizes the indestructible character of the Church in past ages. Neither external persecution nor internal unfaithful officialdom or false theology could stand against the perennial power of renewal that is revealed in the history of revival in the Church. Even secular historians give credit to the Wesleyan revival as the agency which saved England from the equivalent of the French Revolution. The study of church history offers a stabilizing influence in an age of secularism, for one sees the power of God operating in past history.

E. *Church History as a Practical Tool.*

The reading of the history of the Church has many practical values for the Christian worker, be he evangelist, pastor or teacher. The writer has derived pleasure from seeing how much more intelligible systematic theology has become to the student who has studied its historical development. The doctrines of the Trinity, of Christ and of sin, and soteriology will never be properly understood unless one is aware of the history of the period from the Council of Nicaea to the Council of Constantinople in 681.

An abundance of illustrative material for his sermons also awaits the efforts of the diligent student of church history who intends to preach. Is he seeking to warn of the dangers of a blind mysticism which puts Christian illumination on a level with the inspiration of the Bible? Then let him study the mystical movements of the Middle Ages or early Quakerism. If he seeks to warn of the dangers of an orthodoxy unaccompanied by a study and application of the teachings of the Bible, then let him give attention to the period of cold orthodoxy in Lutheranism after 1648, which created a reaction known as Pietism, a movement which stressed earnest study of the Bible and practical piety in daily life.

F. *Church History as a Liberalizing Force.*

Finally, church history has a cultural value. The history of Western civilization is incomplete and unintelligible without some understanding of the role of the Christian religion in the development of that civilization. The history of man can never be divorced from the history of his religious life. The efforts of despots throughout the ages to eliminate religion have always resulted in the substitution of some false religion for the Christian religion. Both Hitler and Stalin gave to their systems of statism a religious element by their respective emphasis upon race and class.

The man who has studied the history of the Church will never again be denominationally provincial. He will sense the unity of the true Body of Christ throughout the ages. He will also be humble as he encounters the giants of his spiritual past and realizes how much he owes to them. He will become more tolerant of those who differ with him on non-essentials but who, with him, accept the great basic doctrines of the Faith, such as the vicarious death and resurrection of Christ, which were emphasized by Paul in I Corinthians 15:3, 4.

IV. The Organization of Church History

A. *Branches of Church History.*

For the sake of convenience, church history can be organized under the following topics.

1. The *political* element involves the relations between the Church and the state, and the secular environment of the Church. No one can understand the reversal of policy in France involved in the change from the situation created by the Civil Constitution of the Clergy of 1791 to the situation created by the Con-

cordat of Napoleon in 1801, unless he has some knowledge of how Napoleon destroyed the democratic element in the French Revolution and set up a new authoritarian system in which the Church (Roman Catholic) was only to play a part because it was the religion of "the majority of Frenchmen." An understanding of the political, social, economic and aesthetic forces at work in history is essential if one is going to interpret church history properly. Such background will be provided at the points where it is appropriate.

2. The *propagation* of the Christian faith cannot be ignored. This involves study of foreign missions, home missions and city missions, and the story of any special technique by which the Gospel has been carried to others. The story of missions has its heroes and martyrs and is an integral part of the story of the Church. The essential person-to-person nature of the spread of Christianity and the unlimited possibilities for a Church faithful to its Lord is shown in a study of the propagation of the faith.

3. This propagation has many times brought *persecution* to the Church. This persecution was begun by the political-ecclesiastical Jewish state; was organized on an imperial basis by Decius and Diocletian; was often made a part of Moslem policy; and has been revived by the modern secular totalitarian state. Study of persecution reveals the truth of Tertullian's dictum that the blood of the martyr is often the seed of the Church. This branch of church history, far from leading to discouragement, shows rather that the Church has made its greatest advances in periods of persecution or immediately thereafter.

4. *Polity* is another branch of church history. It is the study of the government of the Church. It necessitates consideration of the government of the Church by bishops (episcopacy), elders (presbyterianism), the congregation in a system of direct rather than representative democracy (congregationalism), or modifications of these three systems. Consideration of the position of the minister and the growth of the distinction between clergy and laity is also a part of this topic. Discipline and forms of worship (liturgy) are related to polity.

5. *Polemics*, which concerns the struggle of the Church to fight heresy and to think out its own position, is an important aspect of the development of the Church. It involves study of the opposing heresies and of the formulation of dogma, creeds

and Christian literature in answer to heresies. The literature of the Church Fathers is a particularly rich field for the study of polemics — whether that literature be the writings of Justin Martyr, answering the contention that the state must be all in life, or of Irenaeus, exposing the heresies of the various types of Gnosticism. Most theological systems have been born in a period of struggle to meet existing needs. The eras between 325 and 451 and between 1517 and 1648 specially involve the problem of polemics. Calvin developed his system of theology in an attempt to provide a Scriptural theology that would avoid the errors of Romanism.

6. Still another branch of our study may be called *praxis.* It is the consideration of the practical outworking in life of the Christian faith. The home life, charitable work and the influence of Christianity upon the life of the day are parts of this branch of church history.

7. Christianity could not continue to grow unless it gave attention to the problem of *presentation* or propaganda. Presentation involves study of the educational system of the Church, its hymnology, liturgy, architecture, art and preaching.

Each of these branches will be discussed in the eras in which each is most important, but not all will be developed in detail in each of the periods. Each can be the center of fascinating studies that the individual can carry on for himself once he has the necessary general background.

B. *Periods of Church History.*

The student must remember that history is "a seamless garment." By this Maitland meant that history is a continuous stream of events within the framework of time and space. For that reason periodization of church history is merely an artificial device to cut the data of history into easily handled segments and to aid the student in remembering the essential facts. The people of the Roman Empire did not go to sleep one night in the ancient era and wake up the next morning in the Middle Ages. There is instead a gradual transition from a view of life and human activity that characterizes one era of history to a view that characterizes another. Because the division of history into periods does aid the memory, does help one to deal with one segment at a•time and does present the view of life in that period, it is worthwhile to organize history chronologically. The following chronology will help the reader to grasp the plan of this book.

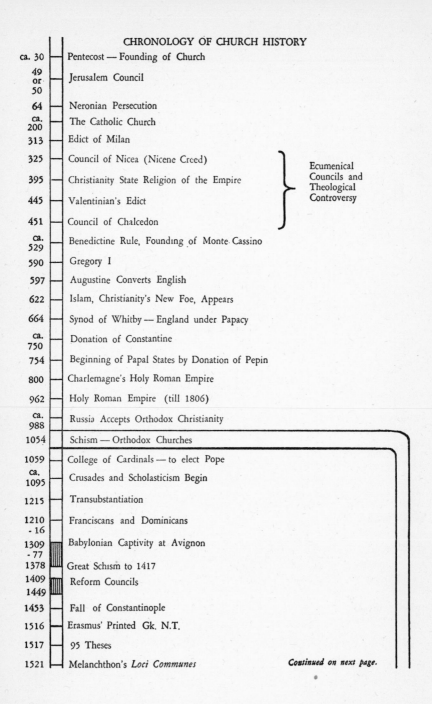

CHRONOLOGY OF CHURCH HISTORY

ca. 30	Pentecost — Founding of Church
49 or 50	Jerusalem Council
64	Neronian Persecution
ca. 200	The Catholic Church
313	Edict of Milan
325	Council of Nicea (Nicene Creed)
395	Christianity State Religion of the Empire
445	Valentinian's Edict
451	Council of Chalcedon
ca. 529	Benedictine Rule, Founding of Monte Cassino
590	Gregory I
597	Augustine Converts English
622	Islam, Christianity's New Foe, Appears
664	Synod of Whitby — England under Papacy
ca. 750	Donation of Constantine
754	Beginning of Papal States by Donation of Pepin
800	Charlemagne's Holy Roman Empire
962	Holy Roman Empire (till 1806)
ca. 988	Russia Accepts Orthodox Christianity
1054	Schism — Orthodox Churches
1059	College of Cardinals — to elect Pope
ca. 1095	Crusades and Scholasticism Begin
1215	Transubstantiation
1210 - 16	Franciscans and Dominicans
1309 - 77	Babylonian Captivity at Avignon
1378	Great Schism to 1417
1409 1449	Reform Councils
1453	Fall of Constantinople
1516	Erasmus' Printed Gk. N.T.
1517	95 Theses
1521	Melanchthon's *Loci Communes*

Ecumenical Councils and Theological Controversy

Continued on next page.

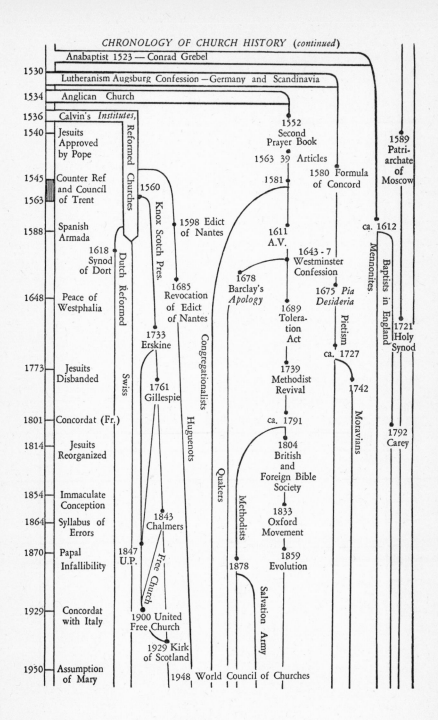

INTRODUCTION

ANCIENT CHURCH HISTORY, 5 B.C.–A.D. 590

The first period of church history is one in which the growth of the Apostolic Church into the Old Catholic Imperial Church and the beginning of the Roman Catholic system can be traced. The center of activity was the Mediterranean basin which included parts of Asia, Africa and Europe. The Church operated within the cultural environment of Greco-Roman civilization and the political environment of the Roman Empire.

1. The Spread of Christianity in the Empire to 100.

In this section attention will be given to the environment in which Christianity emerged. The foundation of the Church in Christ's life, death and resurrection and its founding among the Jews is important to an understanding of the genesis of Christianity. The gradual growth of Christianity within the swaddling bands of Judaism and the bursting of those bands at the Council of Jerusalem preceded the carrying of the Gospel to the Gentiles by Paul and others and the emergence of Christianity as a sect distinct from Judaism. Attention is also called to the leading role of the apostles in this period.

2. The Struggle of the Old Catholic Imperial Church for Survival, 100–313.

In this period the Church was concerned with continued existence in the face of opposition from without — persecution by the Roman state. Martyrs and apologists were the answer of the Church to this *external* problem. The Church also had to deal with the *internal* problem of heresy at the same time, and the polemical writers of the Church provided the answers to heresy.

3. The Supremacy of the Old Catholic Imperial Church, 313–590.

The Church faced the problems that arose out of its reconciliation with the state under Constantine and its union with the state in the time of Theodosius. Soon it found itself being dominated by the state. The Roman emperors demanded a unified dogma in order to have a unified state to save Greco-Roman culture. But the Christians had not had time to work out such a body of dogma in the period of the persecution. There followed then a long period of creedal controversy. The writings of the more scientifically minded Greek and Latin Fathers were a natural outcome of the theological disputes. Monasticism arose, partly as a reaction from and partly as a protest against the increasing worldliness of the organized and visible church. During this period the office of bishop was strengthened and the Roman bishop grew in power. As the period comes to an end, the Old Catholic Imperial Church has virtually become the Roman Catholic Church.

MEDIEVAL CHURCH HISTORY, 590–1517

The scene of action in this period moved from Southern Europe to North and Western Europe — the Atlantic seaboard. The medieval Church, faced with the migrating hordes of Teutonic tribes, sought to win them to Christianity and to integrate Greco-Roman culture and Christianity with Teutonic institutions. In so doing the medieval Church still further centralized its organization under papal supremacy and developed the sacramental-hierarchal system characteristic of the Roman Catholic Church.

4. The Rise of the Empire and Latin-Teutonic Christianity, 590–800.

Gregory I, the first pope with papal authority, although he never claimed the name, worked hard at the task of evangelizing the hordes of Teutonic invaders within the Roman Empire. The Eastern Church in this period faced the threat of a rival religion, Islam, which took away much of its territory in Asia and Africa. Gradually the alliance between the pope and the Teutons took place in the organization of the Teutonic successor to the old Roman Empire, the Carolingian Empire of Charlemagne.

5. Ebb and Flow in Relationships between Church and State, 800–1054.

The first great schism within the Church occurred during this period. The Greek Orthodox Church after 1054 went its own way with the static theology created by John of Damascus in the eighth century. The Western Church during this time became feudalized and tried without much success to work out a policy of relations between the Roman Church and the state acceptable to the pope and emperor. At the same time the Cluniac reformers aimed at the correction of evils within the Roman Church.

6. The Supremacy of the Papacy, 1054–1305.

The medieval Roman Catholic Church reached the peak of its power under the leadership of Gregory VII (Hildebrand) and Innocent III, and successfully enforced its claims to supremacy over the state by the humiliation of the most powerful sovereigns of Europe. The Crusades brought prestige to the pope; monks and friars spread the Roman faith and reclaimed dissenters. The Greek learning of Aristotle, brought to Europe by the Arabs of Spain, was integrated with Christianity by Thomas Aquinas in an intellectual cathedral that has become the authoritative expression of Roman theology. The Gothic cathedral expressed the supernatural, otherworldly outlook of the era and provided a "Bible in stone" for the faithful. The Roman Church was to tumble from this peak of power in the next era.

7. Medieval Sunset and Modern Sunrise, 1305–1517.

Internal attempts to reform a corrupt papacy were made by mystics, who sought to personalize a religion too institutionalized. Attempts at reform were also made by early reformers, such as John Wycliffe and John Hus, and by reform councils. An expanding geographical world, a new secular intellectual outlook in the Renaissance, the rising nation-states and an emerging middle class were *external* forces that would not long brook a decadent and corrupt Church. The refusal by the Roman Church to accept internal reform made the Reformation a probability.

MODERN CHURCH HISTORY, 1517 AND AFTER

This era was ushered in by a schism that resulted in the origin of the Protestant state-churches and the world-wide spread of the Christian faith by the great missionary wave of the nineteenth century. The scene of action was no longer the Mediterranean Sea or the Atlantic Ocean but the world.

8. Reformation and Counter Reformation, 1517–1648.

The forces of revolt held back by the Roman Church in the previous period broke forth in this period, and new national Protestant churches emerged — Lutheran, Anglican, Calvinistic. As a result, the papacy was forced to consider reformation. In the Counter Reformation movements of the Council of Trent, the Jesuits and the Inquisition, the papacy was able to halt the spread of Protestantism in Europe. Only after the Treaty of Westphalia (1648), which ended the bitter Thirty Year's War, did the two movements settle down to consolidate their gains.

9. Rationalism, Revivalism and Denominationalism, 1648–1789.

During this period the Calvinistic views of the Reformation were brought to North America by the Puritans. England passed on to the Continent a rationalism that had its religious expression in Deism. On the other hand, Pietism on the Continent proved to be the answer to cold orthodoxy. It expressed itself in England in the Quaker and Wesleyan movements.

10. Revivalism, Missions and Modernism, 1789–1914.

During the early part of the nineteenth century there was a revival of Catholicism. This was matched by a Protestant revival that created a surge of missionary endeavor abroad and that brought social reform at home in European countries. Later in the period the eroding forces of rationalism and evolution led to a "break with the Bible" that expressed itself in religious liberalism.

11. The Church and Twentieth Century Problems.

Totalitarian Roman Catholicism in this period is facing a terrific battle with the secular totalitarian state. Protestantism faces both the totalitarian state and an aggressive Roman Church. The Barthian movement has largely displaced the sentimental liberalism of the early part of the twentieth century. The movement for an ecumenical Church is gaining in strength and reunion is taking place quite frequently. The tendencies toward centralization of authority and toward new absolutist theologies seem to be the major answers the Protestant Church is offering to totalitarianism.

V. GENERAL BIBLIOGRAPHY

This bibliography is confined to the more general literature of church history that should be available to the teacher or student who desires to have the basic bibliography in the field. These books are likely to be found in the average college or public library.

A. *Bibliography of Church History.*

A *Guide to Historical Literature* (New York: The Macmillan Co., 1931) by George M. Dutcher and others is a selected, classified and critical bibliography that covers the whole field of history. There is a useful section dealing with church history.

Shirley J. Case has edited A *Bibliographical Guide to the History of Christianity* (Chicago: The University of Chicago Press, 1931), which is the most inclusive bibliography for the average student of church history. It should be supplemented by relevant bibliographical articles in the periodical *Church History* for books published since 1931.

B. *General Source Collections.*

Henry Bettenson has compiled and edited *Documents of the Christian Church* (New York: Oxford University Press, 1947). This book is the best single-volume collection of primary materials. It includes an excellent selection of documents for the period up to the Reformation, but it shows a preference for the documents of Anglican church history from then to the present. This little work makes an excellent supplementary volume to be used with a regular text.

Documents Illustrative of the History of the Church (London: Society for Promoting Christian Knowledge, 3 vols., 1920-1941) by Beresford J. Kidd contains more documents than Bettenson's work, but it ends at 1500.

Source Book and Bibliographical Guide for American Church History (Menasha, Wisconsin: George Banta Publishing Co., 1921) by Peter G. Mode includes bibliography as well as the most important documents needed to illustrate American church history.

Creeds of Christendom (New York: Charles Scribner's Sons, 3 vols., 6th ed., 1890) by Philip Schaff is an excellent work for a study of the creeds and confessions of the Church. Volume I deals with the history of the creeds; Volume II gives the ecumenical, Roman Catholic and Greek Orthodox creeds; Volume III consists of the Protestant creeds and confessions.

Source works that cover a definite period, such as ancient, medieval or modern church history, will be listed at the end of the first chapter beginning the discussion of that period. Others will be cited at the end of relevant chapters.

C. *History of Church History.*

A *History of Historical Writings* (Norman, Oklahoma: University of Oklahoma Press, 1937) by Harry E. Barnes includes good evaluations of the various writers of church history.

Peter Guilday has edited *Church Historians* (New York: P. J. Kennedy, 1926), a work that has some good essays by Roman Catholic writers concerning church historians who may be classed as writers of source works.

D. *Periodicals.*

The Catholic Historical Review (Washington: Catholic University of America, 1915–) is the official organ of the American Catholic Historical Association. It gives the results of the work of Roman Catholic church historians.

The files of *Church History* (Chicago: The American Society of Church History, 1932–) are rich with bibliographical and special topical articles of value to the teacher of church history.

E. *Encyclopedias.*

The following encyclopedias are useful reference tools for the student of church history: *Encyclopedia of Religion and Ethics* (New York: Charles Scribner's Sons, 13 vols., 1908–26) edited by James Hastings; *Catholic Encyclopedia* (New York: Encyclopedia Press, 17 vols., 1907–22) edited by C. G. Herbermann and others; *New Schaff-Herzog Encyclopedia of Religious Knowledge* (New York: Funk and Wagnalls, 1908–12) edited by S. M. Jackson and others. Unfortunately, there is no definitely conservative encyclopedia that covers the whole field of church history.

F. *Atlases.*

William R. Shepherd's *Historical Atlas* (New York: Henry Holt & Co., 3d. rev. ed., 1923) is out of print, but it is probably the best general historical atlas relative to church history.

G. *Outlines of Church History.*

The outlines by Richard Cameron entitled *Outlines of the Early and Medieval History of the Christian Church* (Boston, 1943) and *Outlines of the Reformation and Modern History of the Christian Church* (Boston, 1941) contain fine bibliographies and organize church history chronologically and topically with references to relevant pages in the best texts. They are especially useful to the teacher.

Topical Outline Studies in Ecclesiastical History (Milwaukee: Houtkamp and Cannon, 1901) by Henry M. Dosker is another useful outline.

A Guide to the Study of Church History (New York: George H. Doran Co., 1914) by William J. McGlothin includes most of the essential factual material in outline form and will prove to be most useful to the teacher.

H. *Church History Texts.*

C. P. S. Clarke in his *A Short History of the Christian Church* (London: Longmans, Green & Co., 1929) presents church history from the Anglican viewpoint.

George P. Fisher's *History of the Christian Church* (New York: Charles Scribner's Sons, 1887) has long been a favorite of many teachers, is well organized but has none of the history of the Church in the twentieth century.

The Story of the Church (Philadelphia: The Muhlenberg Press, rev. ed., 1947) by Charles M. Jacobs is little more than an outline, but it would be most useful to a Lutheran layman seeking information on the growth of his church.

A History of the Christian Church (Grand Rapids: Wm. B. Eerdmans Publishing Co., 1945) by D. H. Kromminga is primarily for high school students as the sub-title indicates, but it has some useful syntheses of ideas.

A History of Christianity (New York: Harper & Brothers, 1953) by the eminent scholar, Kenneth J. Latourette, is a detailed one-volume general church history with selected, critical bibliographies of value to the teacher.

Arthur W. Nagler's *The Church in History* (New York: The Abingdon Press, 1929) is written from a liberal and Methodist viewpoint, but it has a fine general chronological treatment of church history. Following this, there are several chapters that trace specific topics.

Albert H. Newman in his *A Manual of Church History* (Chicago: American Baptist Publication Society, 2 vols., rev. ed., 1931-33) sets forth the Baptist viewpoint clearly, but he devotes too much of the first volume to the apostolic period. This has somewhat marred the balanced treatment.

Robert H. Nicholas in *The Growth of the Christian Church* (Philadelphia: The Westminster Press, 1930) treats church history from the viewpoint of the Presbyterian denominations. His treatment is rather sketchy in many places.

Lars P. Qualben in his *A History of the Christian Church* (New York: Thomas Nelson & Sons, 1933) emphasizes the Lutheran approach to church history. While the organization is not always clear, the book has many excellent features, such as bibliographies at the end of each chapter, helpful maps and many excellent charts and graphs. The treatment also gives full attention to the Biblical viewpoint.

Henry K. Rowe's *History of the Christian People* (New York: The Macmillan Co., 1931) follows the liberal point of view, but it is useful for the excellent background material which it presents.

Philip Schaff's *History of the Christian Church* (New York: Charles Scribner's Sons, 8 vols., 1882–1910) is the work of the acknowledged dean of American church historians of the past and present generations. It is an interesting and accurate portrayal of the drama of church history to the end of the Reformation. The reprinting of this work by the Wm. B. Eerdmans Publishing Company is a real service to church historians.

A *History of the Christian Church* (New York: Charles Scribner's Sons, 1918) by Williston Walker has long been used as a text for the church history course in seminaries. While it follows a liberal interpretation, it has an excellent presentation of the basic factual material of church history.

I. *History of Doctrine.*

The author has found A *History of Christian Thought* (Philadelphia: United Lutheran Publications, 2 vols., 1943–46) by Juergen L. Neve and Otto W. Heick, to be a most useful treatment of the history of doctrine, although it is primarily from the Lutheran viewpoint. There are several older works, such as those by G. P. Fisher, A. Harnack, G. Sheldon, and others, that are still useful.

J. *History of Missions.*

The Progress of Worldwide Missions (New York: Harper & Brothers, 4th rev. ed., 1939) by Robert Glover is an excellent little manual to supplement the necessarily brief treatment that missionary history is given in a church history text.

Kenneth S. Latourette's A *History of the Expansion of Christianity* (New York: Harper & Brothers, 7 vols., 1937-45) is the most inclusive history of missions available and is written by an acknowledged authority in the field. Dr. Latourette, however, subscribes to a philosophy of history that envisages the gradual evolutionary conquest of the world by Christianity.

K. *Christian Literature.*

George I. Hurst's A*n Outline of the History of Christian Literature* (New York: The Macmillan Co., 1926) contains listings of the important writings of the great figures of the Church with a statement concerning the nature of each writing.

L. *Christian Art and Architecture.*

Art Through the Ages (New York: Harcourt Brace & Co., rev. ed., 1936) by Helen Gardner is a useful volume to the layman for understanding the development of Christian art and architecture in the various periods.

This general bibliography, which is selective and critical, will be supplemented by the citation of primary and secondary works at the end of each chapter. The student should find much pleasure and profit in the use of the source works cited.

ANCIENT CHURCH HISTORY, 5 B.C. – A.D. 590

I. The Spread of Christianity in the Empire to 100

II. The Struggle of the Old Catholic Imperial Church for Survival, 100–313

III. The Supremacy of the Old Catholic Imperial Church, 313–590

Chapter I

THE FULNESS OF THE TIME

In Galatians 4:4, Paul calls attention to the historical era of providential preparation that preceded the coming of Christ to earth in human form: "When the fulness of the time was come, God sent forth his Son . . . ." Mark also emphasizes the coming of Christ when all was made ready on this earth (Mark 1:15). Consideration of the events that preceded the appearance of Christ upon this earth lead the sober student of history to acknowledge the truth of the statements of Paul and Mark.

In most discussions of this subject it has been forgotten that not only Jew but also Greek and Roman contributed to the religious preparation for the appearance of Christ. Greek and Roman contribution, it is true, was negative, but it still aided in bringing historical development to the point where Christ could make the maximum impact upon history in a way not possible before or since the time of His birth. The discussion of the preparation for Christ's coming will be organized under the political, intellectual and religious contributions of the great peoples of the first century preceding the Christian Era.

I. POLITICAL CONTRIBUTIONS

The political contribution to history preceding the coming of Christ was primarily the work of the Romans. This people, who followed the way of idolatry, mystery religions and emperor worship, were thus used by God to bring about the fulfillment of the will of the God of whom they were ignorant.

A. *A Sense of the Unity of Mankind.*

The Romans, as no other people up to their time, developed a sense of the unity of mankind under a universal law. This sense of the solidarity of man within the Empire created an environment favorable to the reception of a Gospel that proclaimed the unity of the human race in the fact that all men are under the penalty of sin and in the fact that all are offered a salvation which makes them a part of a universal organism, the Christian Church, Christ's body.

No empire of the ancient Near East, not even the empire of Alexander, had succeeded in bringing to men a sense of their unity in a political organization. Political unity was to be the peculiar task of Rome. The application of the Roman law to citizens in all parts of the Empire was daily pressed upon the Romans and the subjects of the Empire by the impartial justice of Roman courts. This Roman law grew out of the customary law of the early monarchy. During the early republic, in the fifth century before Christ, this law was codified in the Twelve Tables, which became an essential part of the education of every Roman boy. The realization that great principles of Roman law were also a part of the laws of all the nations of men grew upon the Romans as the *praetor peregrinus,* who was charged with the task of dealing with court cases in which foreigners were involved, became acquainted with the national legal systems of these foreigners. Thus the code of the Twelve Tables, based upon Roman custom, was enriched by the laws of other nations. Philosophically inclined Romans explained these similarities by borrowing the Greek concept of a universal law whose principles were written into man's nature and could be discovered by rational processes.

A further step in the fostering of the idea of unity was the granting of Roman citizenship to non-Romans. This process was started in the period preceding the birth of Christ and was completed when Caracalla in 212 admitted all freemen in the Roman Empire to Roman citizenship. Because the Roman Empire included all of the Mediterranean world that counted in the history of that day, for all practical purposes, all men were under one system of law and citizens of one kingdom.

Roman law, with its emphasis upon the dignity of the individual and his right to justice and Roman citizenship and with its tendency to fuse men of different races into one political organization, anticipated a Gospel that proclaimed the unity of the race both in setting forth the penalty for sin and the Saviour from sin. Paul reminded the people of the Philippian church that they were members of a heavenly commonwealth (Philippians 3:20).

[38]

B. Peace.

Free movement about the Mediterranean world would have been most difficult for the messengers of the Gospel before the reign of Augustus Caesar (27 B.C.–A.D. 14). The division of the ancient world into small jealous units, city states or tribes, hindered travel and the spread of ideas. With the extension of Roman imperial power during the period of empire building, a period of peaceful development occurred in the countries surrounding the Mediterranean. Pompey had swept the pirates from the Mediterranean, and Roman soldiers kept the peace upon the roads of Asia, Africa and Europe. This relatively peaceful world made it easy for the early Christians to move from place to place so that they could preach the Gospel to all men everywhere.

C. Roman Roads.

The Romans developed an excellent system of roads radiating out from the golden milestone in the Roman forum to all parts of the Empire. The main roads were built of concrete to serve for ages. They went straight over hill and dale to the farthermost point of the Empire. Some of them are still in use at the present time. A study of the journeys of Paul will leave the impression that he made great use of the excellent road system to get from strategic center to strategic center of the Roman Empire. If the great empire builder, the Emperor Trajan, had a vision of Roman imperialism, Paul as a builder of Christ's empire, the Church, had a vision of Christian imperialism that embraced not only the Roman Empire but the whole world. Roman roads and strategic cities located on these roads were an indispensable aid in the realization of this vision.

D. The Roman Army.

The role of the Roman army in the development of the ideal of a universal organization and in the spread of the Gospel should not be ignored. The Romans adopted the custom of using provincials in the army as the supply of Roman citizens declined because of war and easy living. These provincials were brought into contact with Roman culture and helped to spread its ideas throughout the ancient world. Moreover, some of these men became converts to Christianity and spread the Gospel to areas where they were assigned for military duty. It is probable that the earliest introduction of Christianity to Britain was a result of the efforts of Christian soldiers who were stationed there.

Consideration of such factors as those that have been discussed leads one to the conclusion that the Roman Empire provided a political environment favorable to the spread of Christianity in the days of its infancy. Even the Church of the Middle Ages was never able to rid itself of the glory of imperial Rome and sought to perpetuate its ideals in an ecclesiastical system.

II. Intellectual Contributions

Great as the preparation by Rome for the coming of Christianity was, it was overshadowed by the intellectual environment that the Greek mind provided. The city of Rome may be associated with Christianity's political environment, but it was Athens which helped to provide an intellectual environment that aided the propagation of the Gospel. The Romans may have been the political conquerors of the Greeks, but, as Horace indicated in his poetry, the Greeks conquered the Romans culturally. The practical Roman may have built good roads, mighty bridges and fine public buildings, but the Greek reared lofty edifices of the mind. Under Greek influence the plain rural culture of the early Republic gave way to the intellectual culture of the Empire.

A. *Universal Language.*

The universal Gospel was in need of a universal language if it was to make maximum impact upon the world. Men have sought since the Tower of Babel to create a universal language so that they might communicate their ideas freely to one another. Just as English has become in the modern world and Latin became in the medieval scholarly world, so Greek had become in the ancient world, by the time the Roman Empire appeared, the universal tongue. Most cultured Romans knew both Greek and Latin.

The process by which Greek became the vernacular of the world is of interest. The Attic dialect used by the Athenians came into wide usage in the fifth century B.C. with the growth of the Athenian Empire. Even though the Empire was destroyed by the end of the fifth century, the dialect of Athens, which was that of classical Greek literature, became the language that Alexander, his soldiers and the merchants of the Hellenistic world between 338 and 146 B.C. modified, enriched and spread throughout the Mediterranean world.

It was this dialect of the common man, known as Koine and

differing from classical Greek, through which Christians were able to make contact with the peoples of the ancient world, and in which they were to write their New Testament, and the Jews of Alexandria to write their Old Testament, the Septuagint. Not until recently was it known that the Greek of the New Testament was the Greek of the common man of Christ's day, because of the difference between it and the Greek of the classics. One German theologian even went so far as to say that the Greek of the New Testament was a special Greek given by the Holy Ghost for the writing of the New Testament. Adolf Deissman made the discovery near the end of the last century that the Greek of the New Testament was the same as the Greek used by the ordinary man of the first century in the papyri records of his business and the documents essential to his daily life. Since that time such scholars as Moulton and Milligan have put Deissman's discovery on a sound scientific foundation by comparative study of the vocabulary of the papyri and that of the New Testament. This discovery has fostered the rise of numerous modern speech translations. If the Gospel was written in the tongue of the common man in the period of its inception, the translators reason, it should be put in the vernacular of the common man of our day.

B. Greek Culture.

Greek philosophy may be considered as negative preparation for the coming of Christianity. Whoever came to know its tenets, whether Greek or Roman, soon found that this intellectual discipline made his polytheistic religion so rationally unintelligible that he turned away from it to philosophy. But philosophy failed to satisfy his spiritual needs, so he either became a skeptic or sought comfort in the mystery religions of the Roman Empire. At the time of Christ's advent, philosophy had declined from the peak reached by Plato to a system of selfish individualistic thought, such as Stoicism or Epicureanism. Moreover, philosophy could only seek for God and posit Him as an intellectual abstraction; it could never reveal a personal God of love. This bankruptcy of philosophy by the time of the coming of Christ disposed men's minds toward a more spiritual approach to life. Christianity alone was capable of filling the vacuum in the spiritual life of the day.

Another way in which the great Greek philosophers served Christianity was to call the attention of the Greeks of their day to a reality that transcended the temporal and relative world in which they lived. Both Socrates and Plato in the fifth century before Christ taught that this present temporal world of the senses is but a shadow of the real world in which the highest ideals are such intellectual abstractions as the good, the beautiful and the true. They insisted that reality was not temporal and material but spiritual and eternal. Their search for truth never led them to a personal God, but it demonstrated the best that man can do in seeking God through the intellect. Christianity offered to such people as accepted Socrates' and Plato's philosophy the historical revelation of the Good, the Beautiful and the True in the person of the God-man, Christ.

Greek literature and history also convince the reader that the Greeks were concerned about questions of right and wrong and man's eternal future. Aeschylus in his drama, *Agamemnon,* comes close to the Biblical dictum, "Be sure your sin will find you out" (Numbers 32:23), in his insistence that Agamemnon's troubles are the result of his wrongdoing. However, the Greek never saw sin as more than a mechanical and contractual matter. It was never a personal matter that affronted God and injured others.

At the time when Christ came, men realized, as never before, the insufficiency of human reason and polytheism. The individualistic philosophies of Epicurus and Zeno and the mystery religions all testify to man's desire for a more personal relationship to God. Christianity came with the offer of this personal relationship and found that Greek culture, because of its own inadequacy, had created many hungry hearts.

III. Religious Contributions

Religious contributions to the "fulness of time" include those of the Greek and Roman as well as those of the Jew. But however great may have been the contributions of Athens and Rome to Christianity by way of environment, the contributions of the Jew stand forth as the heredity of Christianity. Christianity may have developed in the political milieu of Rome and may have had to face the intellectual environment created by the Greek mind, but its relationship to Judaism was much more intimate. Judaism may be thought of as the stalk on which the rose of Christianity was to bloom.

A. *Roman Religion.*

Roman conquests led to a loss of belief by many peoples in

their gods because the gods had not been able to keep them from defeat by the Romans. Such people were left with a spiritual vacuum that could not be filled satisfactorily by the religions of the day.

Then, too, the substitutes that Rome had to offer for the lost religions could do no more than make people realize their need of a more spiritual religion. The cult of Roman emperor worship, which made its appearance early in the Christian Era, made an appeal to people only as a means of making the concept of the Roman Empire tangible.

The various mystery religions seemed to offer more than this in the way of spiritual and emotional aid, and in them Christianity was to find its greatest rival. The worship of Cybele, the great earth mother, was brought to Rome from Phrygia. The worship of this goddess of fertility had in it rites, such as the drama of the death and resurrection of Cybele's consort, Attis, that seemed to meet the emotional needs of men. The worship of Isis, imported from Egypt, was similar to that of Cybele with its emphasis upon death and resurrection. Mithraism, an import from Persia, made a special appeal to the soldiers of the Roman Empire. It had a December festival, an evil one, a miraculously born savior — Mithra, a dead and resurrected god — and chapels and worship.

All of these religions emphasized the savior-god. The worship of Cybele called for the sacrifice of a bull and the baptism of worshipers with the bull's blood. Mithraism involved, among other things, sacrificial meals. Because of the influence of these religions, there seemed little odd in the demands of Christianity upon the individual. When many found that the bloody sacrifices of these religions could do nothing for them, they were led by the Holy Spirit to accept the reality offered to them in Christianity.[1]

[1] Some scholars in recent times have attempted to find in the mystery religions one of the main sources of Christianity. According to them, Paul developed the simple ethical religion of Jesus into a mystery religion. But it must be remembered that the Church early fought these religions and refused to have anything to do with them (I Corinthians 8:5). Such action was in marked contrast to the Roman tendency to syncretism. As long as a Roman citizen fulfilled the obligations of emperor worship, he was free to follow other religions if he so desired. Furthermore, it was because the Christians refused to mix Christianity with any other religion that they were severely persecuted by the Roman state. One has only to read the various apologies to realize that it was the exclusive claims of Christianity upon the life of the individual that brought severe persecution. The pagan Roman world was quick to realize that this new religion, unlike others, was uncompromising in its ethic and its theology. When one bears these things in mind, it is easy to see how impossible it would have been for Paul to synthesize Christianity with any religion prevailing in that day.

B. Greek Religion.

The Greek people also contributed in a religious way to making the world ready to accept the new Christian religion when it appeared. The advent of materialistic Greek philosophy in the sixth century before Christ destroyed the faith of the Greek peoples in the old polytheistic worship that is described in Homer's *Illiad* and *Odyssey*. Although elements of this worship lived on in the mechanical state worship, it soon lost its vitality.

The people then turned to philosophy; but it, too, soon lost its vigor. Philosophy became a system of pragmatic individualism under the successors of the Sophists or a system of subjective individualism, such as is seen in the teachings of Zeno the Stoic and Epicurus. Lucretius, the poetic exponent of Epicurus' philosophy, founded his teaching of disregard for the supernatural upon a materialistic metaphysic that considered even the spirit of man as merely a finer type of atom. Stoicism did consider the supernatural, but its god was so closely identified with creation that it was pantheistic. While Stoicism taught the fatherhood of God and the brotherhood of man, and held to a highly desirable code of ethics, it left man by rational processes to work out his own obedience to the natural laws that he was to discover with his unaided reason.

Both the Greek and Roman systems of philosophy and religion thus made a negative contribution to the coming of Christianity by destroying the old polytheistic religions and by showing the inability of human reason to reach God. And the mystery religions, to which many turned, accustomed the people to think in terms of sin and redemption. Thus when Christianity appeared, people within the Roman Empire were more receptive to a religion that seemed to offer a spiritual approach to life.

C. Jewish Religion.

The Jewish people in contrast to the Greeks did not seek to discover God by processes of human reason. They assumed His existence and granted to Him readily the worship that they felt was His due. They were influenced toward this course by the fact that God sought them and revealed Himself to them in history by His appearances to Abraham and the other great leaders of the race. Jerusalem became the symbol of a positive religious preparation for the coming of Christianity. Salvation was to be, indeed, "of the Jews," as Christ told the woman at the well (John 4:22). From this tiny captive nation, situated on the crossroads of Asia, Africa and Europe, a Saviour was to come. Judaism provided the heredity of Christianity and, for a time, even gave the infant religion shelter.

1. Judaism existed in striking contrast to the generality of pagan religions by its emphasis upon a sound spiritual monotheism. Never again after the return from the Babylonian captivity did the Jews lapse into idolatry. The message of God through Moses to them was allegiance to the one true God of all the earth. The gods of the pagan were merely idols which the Jewish prophets condemned in no uncertain terms. This lofty monotheism was spread by numerous synagogues scattered throughout the Mediterranean area during the three centuries preceding the coming of Christ.

2. The Jews offered to the world the hope of a coming Messiah who would bring righteousness to this earth. This Messianic hope was in sharp contrast with the nationalistic aspiration that Horace depicted in the poem in which he described an ideal Roman ruler who was to come — the son to be born to Augustus. The hope of a Messiah had been popularized in the Roman world by its steady proclamation by the Jews. Even the disciples after the death and resurrection of Christ were still looking for a Messianic kingdom upon earth (Acts 1:6). Certainly the wise men who appeared in Jerusalem shortly after the birth of Christ had gained some knowledge of this hope. The expectancy of many Christians today regarding the coming of Christ helps one to realize the atmosphere of expectancy in the Jewish world concerning the coming of the Messiah.

3. In the moral part of the Jewish law, Judaism also offered to the world the purest ethical system in existence. The high standard of the Ten Commandments was in sharp contrast with the prevailing ethical systems of the day and the still more corrupt practice of those moral systems by those who professed them. To the Jews sin was not the external, mechanical, contractual failure of the Greeks and Romans, but it was a violation of the known will of God, a violation which expressed itself in an impure heart and then in overt external acts of sin. This moral and spiritual approach of the Old Testament made for a doctrine of sin and redemption that really met the prob-

lem of sin. Salvation came of God and was not to be found in rationalistic systems of ethics or subjective mystery religions.

4. The Jewish people still further prepared the way for the coming of Christianity by providing the infant Church with a sacred book, the Old Testament. Even a casual study of the New Testament will reveal Christ's and the apostles' deep indebtedness to the Old Testament and their reverence for it as the Word of God to man. Many Gentiles also read it and became familiar with the tenets of the Jewish faith. This fact is indicated by accounts of the numerous proselytes to Judaism. Many of these proselytes were able to move from Judaism to Christianity because of the Old Testament, the sacred book of the newborn Church. Many religions, Mohammedanism for example, look to their founder for their sacred Book, but Christ left no sacred writings for the Church. The books of the Old Testament and the books of the New Testament, given under the inspiration of the Holy Spirit, were to be the living literature of the Church.

5. The Jews also provided an institution that many Christians forget was most useful in the rise and development of early Christianity. This institution was the Jewish synagogue. Born of necessity during the enforced absence of the Jews from the temple at Jerusalem during the Babylonian captivity, the synagogue became an integral part of Jewish life. Through it Jews and also many Gentiles were made familiar with a higher approach to life. It was also the place to which Paul first went to preach in all the cities he reached in the course of his missionary journeys. It became the preaching house of early Christianity. There is also some cogency in the argument that the system of government practiced in the early Church owed a good deal to its Jewish antecedents in the synagogue. The elders and deacons of the Early Church are reminiscent of similar officers in the Jewish synagogue. Judaism was indeed the *paidagogos* to lead men to Christ (Galatians 3:23-25).

The matters that have been discussed show how favored Christianity was, both as to time and region, in the period of its emergence. At no other time in the world's history before the coming of Christ was such a large region under one law and government. The Mediterranean world also had one culture centering in Rome. One common tongue made it possible to give the Gospel to most of the people of the Empire in a tongue common to them and to the preacher. Palestine, the birthplace of the new religion, had a strategic location in this world. Paul was right in emphasizing that Christianity was not something "done in a corner" (Acts 26:26), because Palestine was an important crossroads linking the continents of Asia and Africa with Europe by a land route. Many of the most important battles of ancient history were fought for possession of this strategic area. In the period of its birth and during the first three centuries of its existence, conditions were more favorable for the spread of Christianity throughout the Mediterranean world than at any other time in the ancient or medieval eras. Such is also the opinion of the world's leading scholar of missions.[2]

Negatively, through the contribution of the Greek and Roman world, and positively, through Judaism, the world was prepared for "the fulness of the time" when God sent forth his Son to bring redemption to a war-torn and sin-weary humanity. It is significant that of all the religions practiced in the Roman Empire at the time of Christ's birth only Judaism and Christianity have been successful in surviving the changing course of human history.

BIBLIOGRAPHY

Any standard edition of the Old Testament and the Apocrypha constitutes the main source material for Judaism.

The set by George Howe and Gustave A. Harrer, *Greek Literature in Translation* (New York: Harper & Brothers, 1924) and *Roman Literature in Translation* (New York: Harper & Brothers, 1924) contains excellent selections of source material relevant to the theme of the chapter.

David Breed's *A History of the Preparation of the World for Christianity* (New York: Revell Co., 2d. ed., 1893) is a good discussion of the general theme of the chapter.

Emil Schurer's *History of the Jewish People in the Time of Jesus Christ* (New York: Charles Scribner's Sons, 5 vols., 2d. ed., 1891) is still an excellent work concerning the Jewish heredity of Christianity.

Jack Finegan in his *Light from the Ancient Past* (Princeton: Princeton University Press, 1946) provides the archaeological background for Judaism and early Christianity.

James H. Breasted in his *Ancient Times* (New York: Ginn & Co., 2d. ed., 1935) gives

Albert A. Trever's *History of Ancient Civilization* (New York: Harcourt, Brace & Co., a brief and excellent survey of the history of the ancient Near East. His discussions of Greek and Roman history are weaker.

2 vols., 1936-39) is an excellent survey of ancient history with enough detail for a complete discussion of most topics concerning the Near East, Greece and Rome in ancient times.

Hellenic History (New York: The Macmillan Co., 1948) by George W. Botsford and Charles A. Robinson and *A History of Rome to 565 A.D.* (New York: The Macmillan Co., 1943) by Arthur E. Boak will suffice to give recent and authoritative information on most phases of Greek or Roman history.

2 Kenneth S. Latourette, *A History of the Expansion of Christianity. Volume I, The First Five Centuries* (New York: Harper & Brothers, 1937), p. 8.

CHRISTIANITY THROUGH THE CENTURIES

BIBLIOGRAPHY FOR ANCIENT CHURCH HISTORY

The student of *ancient* church history will find useful source materials not only in the compilations by Bettenson and Kidd noted in the General Bibliography (p. 30) but also in the work by Joseph C. Ayer, Jr., *A Source Book for Ancient Church History* (New York: Charles Scribner's Sons, 1913). This work, which has an explanatory preface to each document, is particularly useful for the period between 100 and 590.

History of the Christian Church (New York: The Macmillan Co., 1913) by Philip Schaff can always be consulted with profit for the details of ancient church history.

The Student will find *The History of the Christian Church from the Earliest Times to A.D. 461* (Cambridge: Deighton, Bell & Co., Ltd., 6th ed., 1947) by Frederick Foakes Jackson a useful volume for ancient church history.

B. J. Kidd in his *A History of the Christian Church to A.D. 461* (Oxford: Clarendon Press, 3 vols., 1922) gives full references to sources and detailed background material.

The liberal Roman Catholic viewpoint is presented by Louis Duchesne in his *Early History of the Christian Church* (London: John Murray, 3 vols., 1909-24).

The more recent set by Hans Lietzmann, *A History of the Early Church* (New York: Charles Scribner's Sons, 4 vols., 3 vols. trans. by B. L. Woolf, 1938-50) can be consulted with profit for more detailed information on certain points.

Charles S. Cochrane in his *Christianity and Classical Culture* (New York: Oxford University Press, 1944) has given an excellent interpretation of the intellectual struggle of Christianity with classicism.

Ralph Stob's *Christianity and Classical Civilization* (Grand Rapids: Wm. B. Eerdmans Publishing Co., 1950) is an able presentation of the relationship between Christianity and its classical environment.

Chapter II

UPON THIS ROCK

Christ is the Rock upon which the Church is founded. Through Him comes faith in God for salvation from sin; and from Him comes love to the human heart, which makes men view personality as sacred because God is the Creator of both man's physical and spiritual being and because He is the basis for hope concerning the future.

I. The Historicity of Christ

The values of Christianity have their beginnings, from the subjective human side, in temporal history. Because these values are inextricably linked with the person, life and death of Christ, some consideration must be given to the evidence for the historical existence of Christ. Many have denied the fact that Christ was manifested in human history (John 1:14).[1] It is fortunate that there is extra-Biblical historical evidence for the historical existence of Christ.

A. Pagan Testimony.

Tacitus, the dean of Roman historians, links the name and origin of Christians with "Christus," who in the reign of Tiberius "suffered death by the sentence of the Procurator, Pontius Pilate."[2]

Pliny, who was propraetor of Bithynia and Pontus in Asia Minor, wrote to the Emperor Trajan about 112 for advice as to how he should deal with the Christians. His epistle gives valuable extra-Biblical information concerning Christ. He paid high tribute to the moral integrity of the Christians by writing of their unwillingness to commit theft or adultery, to falsify their word, or to repudiate a trust given to them. He went on to say that they "sing a song to Christ as to a God."[3]

[1] Shirley J. Case, *The Historicity of Jesus* (Chicago: The University of Chicago Press, 2d. ed., 1928), pp. 39-61.
[2] Tacitus, *Annals*, XV, 44.
[3] Pliny, *Epistles*, X:xcvi.

Another rather satirical and, for that reason, valuable witness is Lucian, who wrote a satire upon Christians and their faith about 170. Lucian described Christ as the one "who was crucified in Palestine" because he began "this new cult." He wrote that Christ had taught the Christians to believe that they were brothers and should observe His laws. He also ridiculed them for "worshipping that crucified sophist."[4]

These testimonies are highly valuable historical evidence, coming as they did from cultured Romans who despised the Christians and were hostile towards them. On the basis of these testimonies, apart from the Bible, which is also an historical work, one can conclude that there is valid evidence for the historical existence of Christ.

B. Jewish Testimony.

Josephus, the wealthy Jew who tried to justify Judaism to the cultured Romans by his writings, also mentions Christ. He wrote of James, "the brother of Jesus, the so-called Christ."[5] In another passage, which is often condemned as an interpolation by Christians, but which many still think is authentic, Josephus wrote of Christ as "a wise man" condemned to die on the Cross by Pilate.[6] Even granting some interpolation by Christians, most scholars agree that this basic information just mentioned is most likely a part of the original text. Certainly Josephus was not a friend of Christianity, and thus his mention of Christ has more historic value.

II. The Character of Christ

The Bible does give some indications as to Christ's personality and character. Even a casual reading of the Gospels leaves a powerful impression of His originality. Where Jewish and modern authorities quote others as authorities for various statements, Christ simply uttered the words, "I say." Statements following the use of this phrase and like phrases in the Gospels indicate the creativity and originality of Christ's thought, which astonished the people of His day (Mark 1:22, Luke 4:32).

Christ's sincerity also stands out in the Biblical records. He was the only human being who had nothing to hide, and so He could be completely Himself.

The Gospels also give an impression of balance in His char-

---

[4] Lucian, *The Passing of Peregrinus*, 1, 11, 13.
[5] Flavius Josephus, *Antiquities of the Jews*, XX: ix: 1.
[6] *Ibid.*, XVIII: iii: 3.

acter. Boldness of character usually is associated with Peter; love with John; and meekness with Andrew. No one facet of character is in excess in Christ; rather the records reveal a balance and unity of character. This balance, originality and transparency can only be adequately explained by the historical account of the Virgin Birth of Christ.[7]

III. THE WORK OF CHRIST

The transcendent importance of the personality of Christ must never be disassociated from His work. This work was both active and passive. During His three-year ministry Christ gave evidence of a righteousness demanded by the law which was in addition to His intrinsic righteousness as the Son of God. This extrinsic, earned righteousness qualified Him to die for men who could never earn such a righteousness and who needed a righteous Substitute if their sins were to be forgiven by God. This active work had its counterpart in His passive work, His voluntary death on the Cross (Philippians 2:5-8). These two historic phases of the work of Christ are summed up in His statement concerning His mission of service and suffering (Mark 10:45).

A. *The Ministry of Christ.*

Except for the description of Christ's visit to Jerusalem with His parents at the age of twelve (Luke 2:41-50) and a few scattered references to His mother and brothers, little is known of Christ's many years of residence in Nazareth. Most likely He was given a Biblical education at home and in the synagogue school for children. He also learned the trade of His father because every Jewish child was given instruction in some manual trade. Since Nazareth was on one of the main trade routes, Christ would have opportunity to observe the life of the outside world as it passed through Nazareth. His parables and sermons show that He was a keen observer of nature. He knew God both from God's revelation of Himself in nature as well as from the Old Testament. During these years He developed physically, socially, mentally and spiritually (Luke 2:52) in preparation for the great work ahead.

Christ's ministry was preceded by the brief ministry of his forerunner, John the Baptist. His first public appearance at the beginning of His ministry was associated with His bap-

[7] J. Gresham Machen, *The Virgin Birth of Christ* (New York: Harper & Brothers, 2d. ed., 1932). This is the best conservative and scholarly work on this subject.

tism by John. The careful student of the ministry of Jesus will notice that after this event He usually worked in Jewish centers throughout His ministry. This policy was in keeping with His own assertion that He came to help "the lost sheep of the house of Israel" (Matthew 15:24).

After His temptation in the wilderness, Christ chose some of the disciples who were to continue His work under the leadership of the Holy Spirit after His resurrection and ascension. A visit to Cana marked the occasion of His first miracle, the turning of water into wine. This was followed by a brief visit to Jerusalem, during which He cleansed the temple and had His momentous interview with Nicodemus. This interview revealed the spiritual nature of His ministry (John 3:3, 5, 7). He returned to Galilee by way of Samaria, where His interview with the woman of Samaria (John 4) demonstrated that His ministry was not going to be limited by national or sex barriers even though His mission was primarily to the Jews.

After His rejection in Nazareth, Christ made Capernaum the base for the Galilean ministry, and this ministry constituted the greatest portion of His earthly service to men. From here He made three tours of Galilee. The first tour, mainly in Eastern Galilee, was marked by healing of the paralytic, the lame man and many others, as well as by the raising from the dead of the widow's son at Nain and the completion of the task of choosing His disciples. The miracles were matched by the superb presentation of the principles which He declared should govern human conduct. These principles are contained in the Sermon on the Mount. The theme of the Sermon is that true religion is of the spirit rather than of external acts demanded by the law.

The high point of Christ's second tour of southern Galilee was His parabolic teaching concerning His kingdom (Matthew 13). Additional miracles, such as the healing of the Gadarene demoniac and the daughter of Jairus, testified to His power to back up His words with deeds. The third tour was a continuation of this work of teaching, preaching and healing.

The three tours of Galilee were followed by brief periods of retirement during which Christ's main emphasis seemed to be instruction for His disciples. Nevertheless, He still found time to meet the needs of those who came to Him, for He fed the five thousand during His first retirement. He also demonstrated His Lordship of nature by walking on the Sea of Galilee, which miracle impressed upon His disciples the reality of His claims to be the Son of God. He brought healing, during the second withdrawal, to the daughter of the SyroPhoenician woman who demonstrated remarkable faith in Christ. The third retirement was a still further revelation of His power to heal and bless.

The extended ministry in Galilee was followed by a short ministry in Jerusalem at the Feast of Tabernacles, during which Christ faced and met boldly the rising opposition from religious leaders — the Pharisees and the Sadducees. Because of this opposition, Christ withdrew east of the Jordan to Perea, where He taught and healed. This Perean ministry was succeeded by the short ministry of the last week in Jerusalem, during which He publicly met the rising antagonism of the Jewish national and ecclesiastical leaders. He rebuked their mechanical and external approach to religion in His parabolic teaching. The sad weekend, during which He gave His life on the Cross, ended His active ministry to the world. After His glorious resurrection—an established historical fact based on documentary evidence in the New Testament — He appeared only to His own followers. The culmination of His ministry came with His ascension into heaven in the presence of His disciples. This ascension was prefaced by His promises to send the Holy Spirit in His place and to return again to this earth.

The Christian Church is fortunate to possess four accounts of this ministry of Christ upon earth. Each of the authors presents his account from a different viewpoint. Matthew emphasizes Christ's kingly activity as the promised Messiah who fulfilled the Old Testament prophecies. He does this by the constant use of the phrase, "that it might be fulfilled which was spoken by the prophet." Mark, who wrote to appeal to Roman mind, stressed the pragmatic side of Christ's ministry. The sense of action and power is heightened by his constant use of the Greek word translated variously as "straightway" or "immediately." Luke the historian (Luke 1:1-4) gives us the human side of the ministry of Christ. John presents Christ as the Son of God with power to bring blessing to those who accept him by faith (John 1:12; 20:30-31).

B. *The Mission of Christ.*

The active phase of the ministry of Christ, which extended

[53]

over three years, was but preparatory to the passive phase of His work, His suffering upon the Cross. His suffering and death was the great event foretold by the prophets (Isaiah 53) which was to bring about the final defeat of all the forces of evil and to release to those who accept Him all the spiritual power of His work on the Cross (Ephesians 1:19-23; 3:20). It was for this important temporal and eternal purpose that He came to earth. The Gospels emphasize this fact by the sense of climax in such references as Matthew 16:21, Mark 8:31 and Luke 9:44.

C. *The Message of Christ.*

Although the Cross was the primary mission of Christ upon earth, it was not His main message, nor was it considered as an end in itself. Any careful study of the Gospels will reveal that the kingdom was the primary message of the teaching of Christ. Two phrases were used by Christ: "the kingdom of God" and "the kingdom of heaven." The latter designation was used mostly by Matthew. The meaning of these terms has led to much controversy in the Christian Church.

Both of the major interpretations of these phrases accept the fact that the kingdom of God refers to the rule of God over all beings in the universe who give to Him a voluntary allegiance. This kingdom, which is spiritual and which embraces time and eternity, is entered by human beings subsequent to a spiritual rebirth (John 3:3, 5, 7; Matthew 6:33). Never is there suggestion of evil in this realm in which Christ Himself will finally become subject to the Father (I Corinthians 15:24-28). Both groups believe that in the present this kingdom is ethical and spiritual and linked with the Church. Both think that its full eschatological realization is yet future.

Discussion of the phrase "kingdom of heaven" brings a division of opinion. Some claim that the two phrases are synonyms for each other. Others feel that they refer to two separate realms although there is a measure of overlapping. The major reason for making a distinction between the two arises out of the fact that Christ used and interpreted the parables of the tares and dragnet in describing the kingdom of heaven, but He never used them in describing the kingdom of God. Since these two parables posit a mixture of good and evil men in the kingdom of heaven, and since all references to the kingdom of God refer only to those voluntarily subject to the will of God, many feel that there must be some distinction between the two terms, and that they cannot, therefore, be used as synonyms for each other.

Those who hold that the two terms are synonymous and may be equated with the Church think that the kingdom will be realized by an evolutionary historical process in which the Church does the work of preparing the way for a kingdom which Christ shall receive at His return. Social action to create a better environment for men is an important part of their plan. Christianity is often interpreted in ethical terms at the expense of the atoning work of the Cross. Augustine's equation of the term with the Church age has given much support to this view, which is held by the liberals.

Others, who do not subscribe to the above interpretation, but who think that the two terms are synonymous, believe that the final realization of the kingdom is yet future and that it will be consummated supernaturally and cataclysmically at the return of Christ. They do not accept the evolutionary approach of the previous group. They are usually known as amillennialists. They do not accept the idea of a millennial kingdom of Christ.

The premillennialists, who hold that the two terms are not identical, believe that the kingdom of heaven is linked with Christ's rule on this earth, and they identify the kingdom of God with the eternal rule of God the Father. During the present period of the Church, the kingdom of heaven is equivalent to Christendom, which consists of a mixture of Christians, professing Christians, unbelievers and Jews. At the return of Christ the kingdom of heaven will be purged of unbelieving Jews and Gentiles and will be ruled for a thousand years by Christ and His Church. This will be the kingdom foretold by the prophets in which Israel was to be blessed in the land of Palestine. After a short rebellion, led by Satan, following his release from his imprisonment of one thousand years during the millennium, Christ will hand His authority over to God, and the pure part of the kingdom of heaven will be finally merged with the kingdom of God.

It will be readily seen that those who hold to this viewpoint admit an overlapping of the two kingdoms in that believers are subjects of both, but they cannot admit that the two kingdoms are identical because of the mixture of good and evil beings in the kingdom of heaven. This mixture is never associated in

Scripture with the kingdom of God. The following diagram will serve to illustrate the premillennial view.

Whether one believes that the two phrases are synonymous or are not identical, is not so important an issue as the agree-

THE PREMILLENNIAL VIEW OF THE KINGDOM OF GOD

ment of Evangelicals concerning certain points about which there can be no disagreement if one rightly interprets the Scriptures. Christ taught that the kingdom will never be realized by an historical evolutionary process in which the Church by social action prepares the world for His coming. The Scriptures plainly teach that the future eschatological, as distinguished from the present ethical and spiritual phase of the kingdom, will be realized supernaturally and cataclysmically at the coming of Christ rather than as a result of the work of the Church. Hence, the primary task of the Church is not world conversion by preaching and social action, but the evangelization of the world by the proclamation of the Gospel, so that those who are to make up the true Church may have an opportunity to respond to that message as the Holy Spirit brings conviction to their hearts. This is the specific task of the Church in this period of human history, but it does not preclude making Christianity practical in daily life in society by the Christian who is also a citizen.

D. *The Miracles of Christ.*

Christ's miracles were numerous and constituted an important part of His ministry. They were to reveal the glory of God and to show that Christ was the Son of God (John 3:2), in order

[56]

that belief might follow. They are variously called power, works, wonders or signs. Rationalists and empiricists have denied their possibility and have sought to explain them by natural law or to explain them away as myths. The latter necessarily involves a denial of the records as historical. Miracles may be defined as phenomena not explicable by known natural law which are wrought by a special intervention of Deity for moral purposes.

The possibility and probability of miracles is demonstrated by the existence of historical records that give accounts of such miracles as historical facts. The person and work of Christ received authentication in the eyes of many in His day because of the miracles which He wrought.

E. The Meaning of Christ.

Men have held many different views of this amazing Person, Christ, who is brought before us so graphically in the Gospels. During the great periods of theological controversy, between 325 and 451 and between 1517 and 1648, men sought to interpret Christ primarily in terms of creeds. The mystics have thought of Him as the Christ of immediate personal experience. Others in the late eighteenth and early nineteenth centuries spoke of Him as the Christ of history and sought to explain away the supernatural so that they might think of Christ as only an unusual man. The true Christian has always thought of Him as the Christ of God.

The historical significance of Christ is revealed in the development of a new value placed upon human personality. The Greeks insisted upon the dignity of human personality because man was a rational being, but the Church has always insisted that human personality has dignity because man is a potential or actual son of God through faith in Christ. The Christian conception has resulted in the humanizing of life. Class and racial barriers have been set aside in the Church and social reform has brought about better conditions of life for all men. It was the Evangelicals who were leaders in social reform in nineteenth century England. Above all, the emphasis upon an inner ethical code for conduct rather than external rules is a result of the contact of human personality with the Christ of Calvary.

Christ's character, work, teachings, and, above all, His death and resurrection mark the beginning of Christianity. Many religions could exist without their human founders, but the removal of Christ from Christianity would leave a lifeless, empty shell. Christ gave to His Church its two ordinances, the apostles, its basic message of the kingdom of God, its primary discipline (Matthew 16:16-19; 18:15-20) and the Holy Spirit to be the One to work through the Church in the evangelization of the world. He left no basic organization nor well-defined system of doctrine. These were to be worked out by the apostles, including Paul, under the guidance of the Holy Spirit Whom Christ sent to the earth to minister in His absence. The true Church, with Christ as the Foundation and the Holy Spirit as the Founder, was to march forward triumphantly, exalting its crucified, risen and ascended Lord from the day of Pentecost to the present.

BIBLIOGRAPHY

The Gospels are the primary sources for the study of Christ in history. The use of a harmony of the Gospels is an invaluable aid to a systematic, chronological study of the life of Christ. *A Harmony of the Gospels for Students of the Life of Christ* (New York: Harper & Brothers, 1922) by Archibald T. Robertson is the best for the reader of the English Bible.

Shirley J. Case in his little volume, *The Historicity of Jesus* (Chicago: University of Chicago Press, 2d. ed., 1928), has ably criticized the evidence of those who deny the historicity of Christ and has presented positive evidence to demonstrate His historical existence.

The little manual by Philip Vollmer, *The Modern Student's Life of Christ* (New York: Fleming H. Revell Co., 1912), is a useful companion volume to illuminate the study of the harmony of the Gospels.

The Life and Times of Jesus the Messiah (New York: Longmans, Green & Co., 3d. ed., 1900) by Alfred Edersheim is still an excellent work on the life of Christ. It throws much light on the historical background of Christ's day.

The work by David Smith, *The Days of His Flesh* (London: Hodder & Stoughton, Ltd., 1924) is one of the best of recent works on the life of Christ despite the author's inclusion of many liberal interpretations.

A. T. Robertson gives a fairly extensive bibliography for study of the life of Christ on pages 89 to 133 of his *Syllabus for New Testament Study* (London: Hodder & Stoughton, Ltd., 5th ed., 1923).

Chapter III

TO THE JEW FIRST

That Christ was the Foundation rather than the Founder of the Church is evident from His use of the future tense in Matthew 16:18 in the statement, "Upon this rock I *will* build my church." Luke claimed that he was informing us in his Gospel concerning "all that Jesus began both to do and to teach" (Acts 1:1); while in the Acts he recorded the account of the founding and early spread of the Christian Church by the apostles under the leadership of the Holy Spirit. Even the disciples misunderstood the spiritual nature of Christ's mission because they wanted to know whether, after His resurrection, He would restore the Messianic kingdom (Acts 1:6). Christ, instead, told them that, after they were empowered by the Holy Spirit, their task was to witness to Him "in Jerusalem, and in all Judea, and in Samaria, and unto the uttermost part of the earth" (Acts 1:8).

It will be noticed that Christ gave priority to the proclamation to the Jew. Even a casual study of the Acts will reveal that this is the order followed by the Early Church. The Gospel was first proclaimed in Jerusalem by Peter on the day of Pentecost; then it was carried by the Christian Jews to other cities of Judea and Samaria. Consequently, the Early Church was primarily Jewish and existed within Judaism. The development of Christianity within Judaism and its progress to Antioch is described by Luke in the first twelve chapters of the Acts.

I. The Founding of the Church in Jerusalem

That the very center of bitterest enmity to Christ should have become the city where the Christian religion first emerged seems paradoxical; but such was the case. From 30 to approximately 44 the church in Jerusalem held a leading position in the early Christian community.

The Holy Spirit was given the position of prominence in

the founding of the Christian Church. This was in accord with Christ's promises in the last weeks of His life that He would send "another Comforter" who should give leadership to the Church after His ascension. A careful study of John 14:16-18; 15:26-27, and 16:7-15 will make the function of the Holy Spirit in the Early Church quite clear. In fact, the foci of the book of Acts are the resurrection of Christ, as the subject of apostolic preaching, and the Holy Spirit as the Empowerer and Guide of the Christian community from the day of Pentecost. The Holy Spirit became the Agent of the Trinity in mediating the work of redemption to men.

Jews from all parts of the Mediterranean world were present at Jerusalem to observe the Feast of Pentecost at the time of the founding of the Church (Acts 2:5-11). The supernatural manifestation of divine power in the speaking with tongues, which occurred in connection with the origin of the Church and the coming of the Holy Spirit, brought to the Jews present the declaration of God's wonderful works in their own tongue (Acts 2:11). Peter made this the occasion for the first and possibly the most fruitful sermon ever preached, the declaration of Christ's Messiahship and saving grace. At least three thousand accepted the word which he declared and were baptized (Acts 2:41). In this manner that spiritual entity or organism, the invisible Church, the Body of the resurrected Christ, came into being.

Growth was rapid. Others were added daily to the number of the original three thousand until the number soon reached five thousand (Acts 4:4). Multitudes were later mentioned as becoming a part of the Church (Acts 5:14). It is rather interesting that many of these were Hellenistic Jews (Acts 6:1) of the dispersion who were in Jerusalem to celebrate the great festivals associated with the Passover and Pentecost. Not even the priests were immune from the contagion of the new faith. "A great company of the priests" (Acts 6:7) was mentioned as among the members of the early church in Jerusalem. Perhaps some of them had seen the rending of the great veil of the temple, which had accompanied the death of Christ, and this, coupled with the preaching of the apostles, had caused them to give willing allegiance to Christ.

Such rapid growth was not without much opposition on the part of the Jews. Quickly the ecclesiastical authorities realized that Christianity offered a threat to their prerogatives as interpreters and priests of the law, and they rallied their forces to combat Christianity. Persecution came first from a politico-ecclesiastical body, the Sanhedrin, which, with Roman permission, supervised the civil and religious life of the state. Peter and John were hailed before that august body at least twice and forbidden to preach the Gospel, but they refused to accede to the request. Later persecution became primarily political. Herod killed James and imprisoned Peter (Acts 12) in this period of persecution.

This early persecution provided Christianity with its first martyr, Stephen. He had been one of the most outstanding of the seven men chosen to administer the charitable funds of the Jerusalem church. False witnesses, who could not gainsay the spirit and logic with which he spoke, had him hailed before the Sanhedrin to answer for his offense. After a thrilling discourse in which he arraigned the Jewish leaders for their rejection of Christ, he was taken out and stoned to death. The death of this, the first martyr of the Christian faith, was a valuable factor in the spread and growth of Christianity. Saul, later to be Paul the Apostle, kept the outer garments of those who stoned Stephen. There is little doubt but that Stephen's bravery and his forgiving spirit in the face of a cruel death made an impact upon the heart of Saul. The words of Christ to him in Acts 9:5, "It is hard for thee to kick against the pricks," would seem to indicate that. The persecution that followed was most severe and was the means of scattering the infant church so that the message could be carried to other parts of the country (Acts 8:4).

However, not all converts to Christianity had an undivided heart. Ananias and Sapphira became the first objects of discipline in the Jerusalem church because of their sin of deceit. Swift and terrible, such discipline was exercised through the apostles who were the leaders of this early organization.

The account of the visitation of discipline upon this guilty pair raises the question whether or not the early church in Jerusalem practiced Communism. A young Communist tried hard on one occasion to demonstrate to the writer that they did practice Communism. Passages, such as Acts 2:44-45 and 4:32, seem to suggest the practice of a Utopian type of socialism based upon the favorite socialistic maxim, "From each according to his ability to each according to his need." But it will be noticed in the first place that this was a *temporary* measure possibly designed to meet the needs of the many from outside Jerusalem who would be desirous of instruction in the new faith before they returned to their homes. The fact that this was *voluntary* is much more important. Peter clearly stated in Acts 5:3-4 that Ananias and Sapphira had liberty either to hold or to sell their property. Common sharing was a purely voluntary matter. The Bible cannot be used as a Scriptural warrant for Communism in our day.

But early Christianity did promote great social change in certain areas. The early Jerusalem church insisted upon the spiritual equality of the sexes and gave much consideration to the women of the church. Dorcas' leadership in the promotion of charitable works was noted by Luke (Acts 9:36). The creation of a group of men to take care of the needy was another remarkable social phenomenon which occurred in the early years of the birth of the Church. Charity was to be handled by an organized body, the forerunner of the deacons. In this way the apostles were left free to give their whole time to spiritual leadership. Necessity, because of the rapid growth, and possibly imitation of the practices of the Jewish synagogue, led to the multiplication of offices and officials early in the history of the Church. Sometime later elders were added to the number of officials so that finally apostles, elders and deacons shared the responsibility of leadership in the Jerusalem church.

The nature of the preaching of the leaders of the early Jerusalem church stands out in the account of the rise of Christianity. Peter's sermon (Acts 2:14-36) is the first sermon by an apostle. It will be noticed that Peter appealed to the prophets of the Old Testament who foretold a suffering Messiah. He then advanced the idea that Christ was this Messiah because He had been raised from the dead by God. Consequently, He was able to bring salvation to those who would accept Him by faith. The main arguments of early sermons by the apostles are summarized in Acts 17:2-3. The necessity of Christ's death for sin was foretold in the prophets, and the resurrection of Christ was proof that he was the Messiah who could save men. Paul also followed this same technique (I Corinthians 15:3-4). The resurrected, crucified Christ was the content of their preaching either to Jews or, later, to Gentiles. The Church today would do well to study the message of the Early Church.

The Jewish church in Jerusalem, whose history has just been

[62]

described, soon lost its place of leadership in Christianity to other churches. The decision at the council in Jerusalem not to bind the Gentiles to obedience to the law opened the way for spiritual emancipation of the Gentile churches from Jewish control. During the siege of Jerusalem in 70 by Titus, the members of the Church were forced to flee from Jerusalem to Pella across the Jordan. Jerusalem was no longer looked upon as the center of Christianity after the destruction of the temple and the flight of this Jewish church, and the spiritual leadership of the Christian Church was centered in other cities, such as Antioch. This removed the possible danger that Christianity might never outgrow the swaddling clothes of Judaism.

II. The Church in Palestine

Interest in the activities of the church in Jerusalem holds the attention of the readers of Luke's history of the Early Church up to the end of chapter seven of the Acts. The center of interest widens to include Judea and Samaria in chapters eight to twelve. Christianity was carried to people of other races.

Philip's visit to Samaria (Acts 8:5-25) brought the Gospel to a people who were not of pure Jewish blood. The Samaritans were the descendants of those of the ten tribes who were not carried away to Assyria after the fall of Samaria and the settlers whom the Assyrians brought in from other parts of their empire in 721 B.C. The Jews and Samaritans became bitter enemies from that time. Peter and John were asked to come down to Samaria to help Philip when the work grew so rapidly that he found himself unable to meet all the demands. This revival was the first breach in the racial barrier to the spread of the Gospel. Philip was led by the Holy Spirit after the completion of his work in Samaria to preach the Gospel to an Ethiopian eunuch who was a high official in the government of Ethiopia.

Peter, who had been the first to preach the Gospel to the Jews, was also the first to bring the Gospel officially to the Gentiles. After a vision, which made clear to him that the Gentiles also had a right to the Gospel, he went to the home of Cornelius, the Roman centurion, and was amazed when the same manifestations which had occurred upon the day of Pentecost occurred in the home of Cornelius (Acts 10-11). He was willing from that time on to have the Gentiles hear the word of grace. The Ethiopian eunuch and Cornelius were the first

Gentiles to have the privilege of receiving the message of Christ's saving grace.

Although those who had been forced out of Jerusalem preached only to the Jews at first (Acts 11:20), it was not long before a large Gentile church sprang up in Antioch. Here the name Christian, first given in ridicule by the witty Antiochians, originated and became the honored designation of the followers of Christ. It was at Antioch where Paul began his active public ministry among the Gentiles and from whence he started on the missionary journeys which were to carry him to his goal, the city of Rome. The church at Antioch was so large that it was able to give relief to the Jewish churches when they faced famine.

But the task of carrying the Gospel to Gentiles in "the uttermost parts" was still to be done. That task, begun by Paul, is still the unfinished mission of the Church of Christ.

BIBLIOGRAPHY

Chapters one to twelve of the Book of Acts constitute the primary material for this period. A good commentary on the Book of Acts will be useful in the interpretation and understanding of this source material.

The work by Beresford J. Kidd, *A History of the Church to A.D. 461* (Oxford: Clarendon Press, 2 vols., 1922), with its full reference to sources will prove to be a useful and authoritative guide to information concerning this early period.

The work by George T. Purves, *Christianity in the Apostolic Age* (New York: Charles Scribner's Sons, 1902), is also a brief and useful manual.

Philip Schaff's *History of the Apostolic Church* (New York: Charles Scribner's Sons, 1869) is still an excellent volume for this period.

Chapter IV

ALSO TO THE GREEK

The Early Jewish-Christian Church was slow to apprehend the universal character of Christianity even though Peter had been instrumental in giving the Gospel to the first Gentile converts. It was Paul who was to have by revelation of God the largeness of vision to see the need of the Gentile world and to spend his life carrying the Gospel to that world. As no other in the Early Church Paul realized the universal character of Christianity and dedicated himself to the propagation of it to the ends of the Roman Empire (Romans 11:13; 15:16). One might well wonder whether he did not have in his mind the slogan "The Roman Empire for Christ" as he slowly made his way westward with the message of the Cross (Romans 15:15, 16, 18-28; Acts 9:15; 22:21). He did not spare himself in achieving this end, but he did not neglect his own people, the Jews. This is evidenced by his seeking out the Jewish synagogue first in every town to which he came and by proclaiming the Gospel to the Jews and Gentile proselytes as long as they would listen to him.

I. Paul's Environment

Paul was conscious of three temporal loyalties during the course of his life. He had as a young man the training accorded only to promising young Jews and had sat at the feet of the great Jewish teacher, Gamaliel. Few could boast of having more training than Paul had, so far as Jewish religious education was concerned, and few had profited as thoroughly from their training as Paul had (Philippians 3:4-6). He was also a citizen of Tarsus, the leading city of Cilicia, "no mean city" (Acts 21:39). He was also a freeborn Roman citizen (Acts 22:28), and he did not hesitate to make use of the privileges of a Roman citizen when such privileges would help in the carrying out of his mission for Christ (Acts 16:37; 25:11). Judaism was his religious environment prior to his conversion;

[65]

Tarsus with its great university and intellectual atmosphere, the scene of his earlier years; and the Roman Empire was the political milieu in which he lived and did his work.

This political environment did not seem to be too promising a one for the proclamation of the Gospel. Caesar Augustus had brought about the downfall of the Republic, except as a political form, when he set up a dyarchy in 27 B.C. in which he nominally shared control of the state with the senate. Unfortunately, his successors had neither the ability nor the character of Augustus, and they were guilty of misrule. Caligula (37-41) was insane during part of his reign, and Nero (54-68), under whom Paul was martyred and the Church endured its first persecution, was a cruel and bloody man who did not hesitate to kill members of his own family. However, Claudius (41-54) was an excellent administrator, and the Empire was fairly stable during his reign. It was in his reign that Paul made most of his missionary journeys.

The social and moral situation was much more unpromising than the political. Booty from the Empire created a wealthy upper class of new aristocrats who had slaves and wealth to pander to their every legitimate and illegitimate desire. This class was somewhat contemptuous of the new religion and saw in its appeal to the poorer classes a threat to their superior position in society. But even some of this class were won by the preaching of the Gospel when Paul was a prisoner in Rome (Philippians 1:13).

Paul also faced the rivalry of competing systems of religion. The Romans were somewhat eclectic in their religious outlook and were willing to give toleration to any faith that would not prevent its worshipers from taking part in the state system of worship, which combined emperor worship with the old republican state worship and claimed the allegiance of all people in the Empire except the Jews, who were exempt by law from its rites. Christians could not, of course, do this and so they faced the problem of opposition from the state. The more subjective mystery religions of Mithra, Cybele, and Isis claimed the allegiance of many others in the Empire. Judaism, as Christianity was distinguished from it as a separate sect, offered increasing opposition.

Roman intellectuals accepted philosophical systems, such as Stoicism, Epicureanism and Neo-Pythagoreanism, that suggested philosophical contemplation as the way to salvation. Stoicism with its pantheistic view of God, its conception of natural ethical laws to be discovered by reason, and its doctrine of the fatherhood of God and the brotherhood of man seemed to provide a philosophical foundation for the Roman Empire. Some of the emperors, such as Marcus Aurelius (161–180), found its ethical standards appealing.

It was this confused religious scene that Paul had to face with the simple redemptive Gospel of the death of Christ.

II. Paul's Work

Paul's genius was so many-sided that it is necessary to give consideration to his work under different categories. Each of the discussions will emphasize the magnitude of the task that God gave to him and the devotion with which he worked to accomplish the appointed task.

A. *The Propagator of the Gospel.*

Paul was a wise as well as devoted missionary, and his life illustrates the use of principles that have served many well in seeking to carry out Christ's great commission to the Church. A consideration of the maps of his journeys reveals the advance of the Gospel under his preaching along a great semicircle reaching from Antioch to Rome. Paul adopted as a basic principle the expansion of the Gospel to the West, and it must have been with delight that he first caught sight of his goal, Rome, even if it was as a prisoner of the Roman government.

Paul also thought in terms of areas that could be reached from strategic centers. He always started his work in a new area in the most strategic city and used the converts to carry the message to the surrounding towns and countryside. Because of this practice it is not likely that he visited Colosse (Colossians 2:1), but rather that the strong church in that town was founded by those whom he sent from Ephesus.

He began his work in strategic Roman centers by going first to the synagogue, where he proclaimed his message so long as he was well received. When opposition arose, he turned to a direct proclamation of the Gospel to the Gentiles in any place that he found suitable. His principle was to preach to the Gentile after he had given the message to the Jew. This principle may be seen by a study of accounts of the journeys recorded in Acts.

[67]

After founding a church, Paul would organize it with elders and deacons so that the work might continue after his departure. He sought to build on solid foundations.

His desire not to be a burden to the infant churches led him to assume the responsibility of supporting himself while he preached in a new area. He worked at his trade of tentmaking while he preached to the people in Corinth (Acts 18:1-4; cf. I Thessalonians 2:9). He did not make this a rule for others but felt that it was a necessity for his work.

His dependence upon the Holy Spirit's guidance in his work is clearly evident in both the Acts and his Epistles (Acts 13:2, 4; 16:6-7). He did not wish to go to any place unless there was clear evidence that it was the field in which God would have him labor. He sought to reach the areas untouched by others so that he might be a pioneer of the Gospel (Romans 15:20). This pioneering spirit was productive in that it resulted in his carrying the Gospel from Antioch to Rome and, possibly, as far west as Spain during his lifetime.

These principles that the apostle followed served him well in the development of churches that were organized centers for the continued preaching of the Gospel. He did not leave them without continued help, for he made a practice of revisiting the churches that he founded in order to encourage and to strengthen them (Acts 15:36). One does not wonder at the rapid growth of Christianity under such sane, yet, inspired leadership.

B. Paul's Publications.

Paul made a practice of keeping in touch with the local situation in each church through visitors from that church (I Corinthians 1:11) or through the reports of agents whom he sent to visit the churches (I Thessalonians 3:6). Whenever the local situation seemed to demand it, he wrote letters under the guidance of the Holy Spirit to deal with particular problems. He wrote twice to the Thessalonian church to clear up misunderstanding concerning the doctrine of the second coming of Christ. The Corinthian church faced the problems of a church in a large pagan city, and Paul addressed his first letter to the solution of their problems. Questions concerning human and spiritual wisdom peculiar to a church in a cultured Greek city (I Corinthians 1-4), the problem of morality in a pagan environment (Chapter 5), lawsuits between Christians before pagan judges (6), marriage problems (7), and the problem of social intercourse with pagan idolaters (8–10) were some of the matters with which Paul had to deal by correspondence. His Second Epistle to the Corinthians grew out of the need to assert his apostleship so that his authority to act as stated in the first letter would be confirmed. The letter to the Galatians was made necessary by the problem of the relation of the Jewish law to Christianity so that faith rather than the works of law might be seen as the actuating principle of Christianity. The letter to the Romans is a systematic exposition and explanation of his Gospel. The four Epistles written during his imprisonment in Rome were occasioned by the special problems in the churches of Ephesus, Colosse and Philippi. The personal Epistle to Philemon is concerned with the problem of the Christian master and the slave who became a Christian. The three pastoral letters to Timothy and Titus are concerned with the problems facing a young pastor.

It will be noticed that each of these letters grew out of a definite historical crisis in one of Paul's beloved churches. The greatness of these "tracts for the times" is revealed by the fact that the principles that Paul developed to meet emergencies in first century churches are still relevant to the Church in modern times. Human beings face similar problems, and similar principles are useful even if the temporal and spatial environment is different. The Epistles are always of value to any church in the solution of its problems. Paul always balanced theological formulas by practical application.

C. The Principles of Paul's Theology.

No historical discussion of Paul can afford to ignore the basic doctrines that are developed in his letters, particularly in the letter to the Roman church. Christ left no well-defined body of dogma. The formulation of this was to be the work of Paul, guided by the Holy Spirit. This body of dogma was not, however, in contrast to the teachings of Christ, but rather, it grew out of the teachings and death of Christ.[1]

The essence of the Pauline Gospel may be simply summarized. Paul realized that happiness and usefulness are basic goals to which all men aspire. Happiness and usefulness in this and

[1] Floyd V. Filson, *One Lord One Faith* (Philadelphia: The Westminster Press, 1943). This work asserts the essential oneness of the Gospel that Paul preached with the teachings of Christ. It answers those who claim that Paul transformed the simple ethical message of Christ into a species of mystery religion.

the next life are dependent upon the achievement of God's favor. God's favor can only be granted to the man who does God's will. Paul and his Jewish compatriots believed that observance of the law of Moses, which was an expression of God's holiness, should guarantee a happy and useful life. However, Paul found to his sorrow that the works of the law only result in the knowledge of sin and leave man helpless to fulfill the will of God as expressed in that law (Romans 7). The experience of the Damascus road revealed to Paul that not the law but the Cross of Christ is the starting point for spiritual life. Christ, who had kept the Jewish law perfectly, could as perfect man and God offer Himself on the Cross on behalf of sinful man and assume the burden of man's sin (Galatians 3:10, 13). Men need only accept by faith (Romans 5:1) the work that Christ has done for them.

Paul's ethical system grew out of this personal union of the believer with Christ by faith. This vertical relationship is to be balanced by a horizontal relationship in which one is united with fellow believers by Christian love expressed in a moral life (I John 3:23; Ephesians 1:15). Neither the legalism of Judaism, nor the rationalism of Stoicism, but Christian love is to be the spring of Christian conduct. The mystic union of the believer with his Lord is to be the source of love. This life of love involves separation from personal defilement growing out of idol worship, sex impurity, or drunkenness — the major sins of heathendom. It results, positively, in loving service to others and steadfastness in the matter of personal integrity.

Such a system of ethics did not mean repudiation of the Jewish moral law but rather it meant its fulfillment on the higher level of love in the family, household and the state. The high ethical standards of the Christians impressed their pagan neighbors with the greatness of the Christian faith. Paul's own life of selfless service was a revelation to both Jew and Gentile of what God could do in the development of a Christian personality devoted to service for the glory of God and the good of man.[2]

Paul's philosophy of history is closely related to his ethical and theological views. He rejected the cyclic theory of history, which was so characteristic of the ancient world, and the modern theory of indefinite evolutionary progress, in favor of a

[2] Morton S. Enslin, *The Ethics of Paul* (New York: Harper & Brothers, 1930). The writer has found this a most useful book for the study of Paul's ethical system, though Enslin's liberal bias is at times apparent.

cataclysmic supernatural view of history that takes into account unregenerate man's failure and God's power to fulfill His divine plan. This view is not limited to nations but encompasses the human race. According to it progress can come only through spiritual conflict in which man is given strength through the grace of God. Ultimately God will be Victor over all the forces of evil which were provisionally defeated upon the Cross of Calvary by Christ (Romans 11:36; Ephesians 1:10; Weymouth Translation).

D. Paul as a Polemicist.

Paul was never content merely to present Christianity; threats to the purity of Christian doctrine arrayed him in the lists against the foe. By voice and pen he fought for purity of Christian doctrine in his day. No deficient view of the person or work of Christ escaped his castigation, nor did he fail to try to win the erring one back to the faith.

The problem of the scope and means of salvation was the first difficulty to which Paul addressed himself during the Jerusalem Council at the end of his first missionary journey. The Church, born in the bosom of Judaism, had developed into two groups. One narrow reactionary group of Jewish Christians with a Pharisaic background believed that Gentiles as well as Jews must keep the law of Moses for salvation. They wanted to make Christianity a particularistic sect of Judaism. The other group realized that salvation came by faith in Christ alone and was universal.

The visit of Judaizers to Antioch, ostensibly with authority from James to preach the former view (Acts 15:24), was the occasion for the meeting at Jerusalem in 49 or 50 to settle this problem. Commissioned by the church at Antioch (Acts 15:2) and assured by revelation (Galatians 2:2), Paul and Barnabas made their way to Jerusalem to the first and, possibly, the most important church council in church history.

They described their activities to a general public meeting of the church (Acts 15:4-5), after which they met with the apostles and elders in a special private meeting to discuss the problem in detail and to try to work out a solution (Acts 15:6; Galatians 2:2-10).[3] This private meeting seems to have been

---

[3] The author follows the line of reasoning that links the Jerusalem visit of Gal. 2:1-10 with that of the Jerusalem Council. This view is ably presented by William J. Conybeare and John P. Howson, *The Life and Epistles of St. Paul* (New York: Charles Scribner's Sons, 1897).

followed by another meeting of the whole church in which a decision was reached that was agreeable to all those present (Acts 15:7-29). The commendation of Paul's work among the Gentiles (Acts 15:25-26; Galatians 2:10) and the freeing of the Gentiles from keeping the Jewish law (Acts 15:19) were the immediate results of the conference. Minor demands to conciliate Jewish believers, such as refraining from eating blood or things strangled, were stated. Gentile converts were also asked to avoid the sins of idolatry and immorality—sins which would be a special temptation to converts from a sinful pagan environment (Acts 15:20-21). It will be clearly seen that these requests had nothing to do with the basic principle of how man is justified. They were designed simply to facilitate good relations between Jewish and Gentile converts to Christianity.

The happenings at the Jerusalem Council revealed Paul's doggedness where a matter of principle was concerned. Not for one moment would he consider the circumcision of Titus at the Council (Galatians 2:3), but at the beginning of his second journey, when Timothy became his helper, he had Timothy circumcised (Acts 16:1-3) in order that the lack of this rite might not be a barrier in the presentation of the Gospel. Paul was willing to make harmless concessions, such as this one, in order to facilitate his work; but he would not permit Titus to be circumcised at Jerusalem because Gentile freedom from observance of the Jewish ritual law was the principle for which he was fighting.

The liberation of Christianity from observance of the ceremonial Jewish law was the long range result of the Council. Henceforth, faith is the only means by which salvation comes to man. Because this faith is universal, Christianity is freed from the danger of becoming only a sect of Judaism. The new law of love, which leads to the keeping of the Jewish moral law out of love to God rather than out of a sense of duty, becomes the basis for Christian ethics. It is also interesting to note the democratic fashion in which the Church met its great problem. The decision was made by the Church and its leaders under the guidance of the Holy Spirit. Jewish Christians, who had been saved by faith, were left free to observe the law of Moses as a voluntary task if they so desired.

Christianity must never forget the lesson of the Jerusalem Council. If it does, it will lose that which makes it vital. The same problem was faced by the Reformers, who saw that the Roman church was demanding man-made works in addition to faith as the condition for salvation. Modern liberals with their emphasis upon pleasing God by ethical deeds make the same error. The problem of the Jerusalem Council is a perennial problem, and the principles which were victorious there are principles which have relevance throughout the history of the Church.

Paul also faced the challenge of Greek rationalism when he fought an incipient Gnosticism in the Church. Some men sought to make the means of salvation *intellectual* as the Jewish Christians had sought to make them *legalistic*. Gnosticism developed with particular danger in the Colossian church.

The Gnostics held to a dualistic philosophy that made a sharp distinction between spirit as good and matter as evil. According to them, the link between pure spirit and evil matter is a hierarchy of celestial beings. Christ is considered as one of this hierarchy. Angels are to receive worship because they have a part in this hierarchy (Colossians 2:8, 18-19). Salvation is to be achieved mainly by ascetic acts to deny the desires of the material and evil body (Colossians 2:14-17, 20-23) and by a special gnosis or knowledge accessible only to the elite among Christians. Faith is relegated to a subordinate position in this system that panders to human pride.[4]

Paul answered this heresy by unqualifiedly asserting the all-sufficiency of Christ as Creator and Redeemer (Colossians 1: 13-20). Christ is the full manifestation of God and is in no way inferior to God (Colossians 1:19; 2:9). Only in this doctrine did Paul feel that man had any assurance of a Saviour adequate to meet the problem of sin.

Gnosticism was the first heresy to be met by the Church, but it was by no means the last. Error is perennial and usually springs from the same causes in every age. Man's pride in reason and his rationalizing tendency can still lead to heresy as it did in the Colossian church. Retention of the religious heritage of the pre-Christian period in the individual life may lead to a mixture of truth and error with dire consequences for salvation. That was the mistake made by the Judaizers. Misuse or overemphasis of some Scripture may lead to error. Sometimes a leader with mistaken enthusiasm, who seeks to protect the truth, may subvert it. Such was the case of Montanus in the second century.

[4] For more about Gnosticism, see Chapter VIII, pp. 105-107.

With such faith and courage and a sound approach to his task as he had, it is little wonder that Paul was able to carry the message of salvation to the Gentile nations of the Roman Empire and to start Christian culture on its triumphant westward march across Europe. He was the unique interpreter of the meaning of Christ's life and death in terms of salvation for sinful man. He kept the faith free from admixture of legalism and rationalism. He worked out the details of organization in the Christian churches and was in constant correspondence with them to help them solve their problems in a Christian manner. As no one else did, Paul realized the cosmic significance of Christ for time and eternity; and, as the "Apostle of the Nations" (Romans 11:13; 15:16), he interpreted Him to the Gentile world.

BIBLIOGRAPHY

The primary Biblical sources for Paul's life and work are integrated in an interesting fashion in Ernest D. Burton's *The Records and Letters of the Apostolic Age* (New York: Charles Scribner's Sons, 1895).

The work by William J. Conybeare and John S. Howson, *The Life and Epistles of St. Paul,* is still a standard classic of Paul's life and work, though in some areas it must be supplemented by more recent works.

The Life and Letters of St. Paul (London: Hodder & Stoughton, 1919) by David Smith is a helpful volume for the study of Paul's life.

J. Gresham Machen has ably presented proof that Paul's message was not derived from the pagan mystery religions in his book, *The Origin of Paul's Religion* (New York: The Macmillan Co., 1923).

The Religion of Jesus and The Faith of Paul (New York: George H. Doran Co., n.d.) by Gustav Deissmann presents Paul's theology as an outgrowth of his experience of God's revelation and his consciousness of the indwelling Christ.

James S. Stewart in his book, *A Man in Christ* (London: Hodder & Stoughton, 1935), has a similar emphasis.

The Pauline Theology (New York: Charles Scribner's Sons, 1892) by George B. Stevens is an able outline of the Biblical theology of Paul, but care should be exercised in its use because of the deficiencies in Stevens' theology at some points.

Chapter V

THE BOOKS AND THE PARCHMENTS

The New Testament is not an isolated mountain peak of religious literature; it is rather the highest peak of a mountain range of religious literature produced by the Early Church. Its basic literary forms — gospels, acts, epistles and apocalypse — became the models upon which the early Fathers of the Church based their writings. One is not so much amazed at the large number of books in the New Testament as one is at the small number in view of the abundance of religious literature in the Early Church. Luke hints at the numerous Gospels that were in circulation in the day when he took pen in hand to give his Spirit-inspired account of the life of Christ (Luke 1:1).

The writings of the Fathers do much to fill the gap in historical knowledge between the New Testament period and the latter part of the fourth century. The leading men of the Church, by pen as well as by voice, formulated apologetic and polemical literature as they faced external persecution and internal heresy. Creeds were formed to give accurate statements of faith. Hence, the Fathers are of tremendous value in the study of the development of Christian life and thought in this period. This literature is far from dull, and the reading of it will repay the serious student with inspiration as well as with knowledge.

The name "Father of the Church" has its origin in the use of the name "Father," which was given to bishops, especially in the West, to express affectionate loyalty. It was increasingly used from the third century on to describe the orthodox champions of the Church and exponents of its faith. These men were usually bishops. Patrology or patristics is the name of the study of the life and works of these men, most of whom lived in the period between the end of the apostolic age and the Council of Chalcedon (451). The diagram on page 76 will give some

[75]

THE CHURCH FATHERS

West   *East*

FIRST CENTURY (96 - ca. 150) APOSTOLIC FATHERS — TO EDIFY —
TYPOLOGICAL INTERPRETATION.

Clement of Rome

Ignatius
Polycarp
Pseudo - Barnabas
The Epistle to Diognetus
The Second Epistle of Clement
Papias
Shepherd of Hermas (apocalyptic)
Didache (catechetical manual)

SECOND CENTURY (125 - 190) APOLOGISTS — TO DEFEND CHRISTIANITY
(Defenders)

Tertullian

Aristides
Justin Martyr
Tatian
Athenagoras
Theophilus

THIRD CENTURY (190 - 250) POLEMICISTS — TO FIGHT FALSE DOCTRINE

Practical (*polity*)
Irenaeus - Gnostics
Tertullian - Trinity
Cyprian - Episcopacy of
    Rome

Speculative (*theology*) Alexandria
Pantaenus
Clement
Origen - *Hexapla* (text of Old Testament)
   De Principiis (first systematic theology;
   used allegory)

FOURTH CENTURY (325 - 460) GOLDEN AGE OF SCIENTIFIC BIBLE STUDY

Dogmatic — Creed
Jerome — translator of
    Bible
Ambrose — preacher
Augustine — philosophy
    of history in *City of*
    of God; theologian.

Alexandrian School
(Allegorical)
Athanasius
Basil of Caesarea

Antiochene School
(Grammatico-historical)
Chrysostom-preacher
   (Christian conduct)
Theodore (use of
   context)

[76]

indication of who they were, their period, their major works and the most important characteristics of their writings.

There is now reasonable assurance that the writings of the New Testament were completed just before the end of the first century after Christ. Men who knew the apostles and apostolic doctrine continued the task of writing Christian literature. These men are known as the Apostolic Fathers. Most of the literary works of these men were produced between 95 and 150.

Certain well-defined characteristics appear in their writings. Their utterances are informal, simple statements of sincere faith and piety and show little evidence of the philosophical training in pagan philosophy that one notices in the writings of Origen or Clement of Alexandria. The Apostolic Fathers had a great reverence for the Old Testament and they leaned heavily upon it for support of their ideas. For this reason one notes in some cases an almost excessive use of typological interpretation. Christianity is declared to be the fulfillment of Old Testament prophecies and types. These men were also acquainted with the literary forms of the New Testament and used them as models for their work. Edification of the Church stands out above all else as the major objective of their writings.

I. EPISTOLARY LITERATURE

A. *Clement of Rome* (*ca.* 30–100).

About the year 95 a serious disturbance occurred in the church at Corinth. Two years later, Clement, the leading elder in the church at Rome, wrote his first epistle to the Corinthian church to urge the Christians who were in revolt against the elders to end their disturbance and to be in subjection to these elders (1:1; 14:1-2; 46; 47:3-6). This epistle has been assigned the most prominent place among the writings of the Apostolic Fathers in recent times because it is the earliest Christian writing apart from the books of the New Testament.

After an introduction in which he calls to their remembrance the fine spirit of their church in former times (chapters 1–3), Clement launches into a series of exhortations concerning such Christian virtues as love, penitence and humility in order to inspire obedience to his later admonitions (4–38). These exhortations, based upon the citation of numerous examples from the Old Testament, are divided by a short parenthesis (24–26) concerning the certainty of future resurrection. It is interesting to note that Clement uses the pagan story of the Phoenix in

Chapter 25 as an illustration of the resurrection. More direct attention is given to the troubles at Corinth in Chapters 39 to 59:2. The heart of his argument appears in Chapters 42–44 and centers around the fact that the elders and deacons were provided for by the apostles, who in turn were sent out by Christ, and Christ was sent out by the Father. Clement then urges obedience to these democratically appointed leaders (44: 3). This section is followed by a long prayer (59:3–Chapter 61) in which his intense desire for the unity of the church is clear. A final exhortation to unity (62–65) concludes the work.

This letter is valuable for its information concerning the exalted position of the bishops or elders in the Church at the end of the first century. Obedience to the bishop is to be the practical guarantee of Christian unity. Clement's letter is also interesting because of its profuse quotations (about 150) from the Old Testament. Moreover, it contains a widely quoted reference to Paul's career (5:5-7). The theory of two imprisonments at Rome and a period of release in the interim is built mainly upon this reference.

B. *Ignatius* (1st–2d c.).

Another Apostolic Father is Ignatius, bishop of Antioch in Syria, who was arrested by the authorities because of his Christian testimony and sent to Rome to be killed by beasts in the imperial games. Allowed to have visitors from the churches of the towns along the way, before his martyrdom he addressed letters of thanks to these churches for their kindness to him. The letter to the Romans is primarily a plea that they should make no efforts to save him from his martyrdom in Rome. Ignatius welcomed his coming martyrdom and sought to prevent any action that might hinder him from becoming "pure bread of Christ" by the grinding of the teeth of the beasts (2:2; 4:1-2). These seven letters must have been written about 110.

In his letters Ignatius seeks to warn those churches which he had visited on the way to Rome, about the heresies that threaten the peace and unity of these churches. He opposes Gnostic and Docetic tendencies. The Docetists sought to keep Christ a purely spiritual being, free of any contamination by material body. This led them to deny the reality of Christ's material body and to state that only a phantom suffered on the Cross (Epistle to Smyrna, Chapter 1). Ignatius insists upon the revelation of Christ in the flesh as an antidote to this false teaching (Chapter 1, and Trallians, 9–10).

This early Church Father also lays great emphasis upon subjection to the bishop as the way to achieve unity and to avoid the growth of heresy. There is considerable evidence in his letters that by this time one of the elders in each church had become a monarchal bishop to whom fellow elders were obedient.[1] Ignatius compares obedience of the elders to the bishop with the accord of the strings of a harp (Ephesians 4:1) and urged all Christians to obey the monarchal bishop and the elders (20:2). He is the first to place the office of the bishop in contrast with the office of the presbyter and to subordinate the presbyters or elders to the monarchal bishop and the members of the church to both. The hierarchy of authority in the Church is, according to him, bishop, presbyter and deacon. However, Ignatius does not exalt the bishop of Rome as superior to other bishops. The only superiority is that of the bishop in each church above the presbyters.

C. Polycarp (ca. 70–155).

Polycarp, the writer of a letter to the Philippians that is reminiscent of Paul's letter to that church, had special opportunities to know the mind of the disciples because he had been a disciple of John. Bishop of Smyrna for many years, he was martyred in 155 by being stabbed to death and his body burned at the stake. During his trial before the Roman proconsul he said that he could not speak evil of Christ whom he had served eighty-six years and who had given him nothing but good.

Polycarp wrote his letter in answer to one from the Philippians in 110. In his letter Polycarp does not exercise much originality for he quotes often, directly and indirectly, from the Old and New Testaments and gives much information that he has derived from the apostles, especially John. He is, however, a valuable second century witness to the life and belief of the Early Church. He exhorts the Philippians to virtuous living, good works and steadfastness even to death, if necessary, because they had been saved by faith in Christ. About sixty New Testament quotations, of which thirty-four are from Paul's writings, show his acquaintance with Paul's Epistle to the Philippians and other epistles as well as with the other writings of the New Testament. Polycarp was not interested in church polity, as Ignatius was,

[1] See Ephesians (not to be confused with the Ephesians of the Bible) 2:2; 3:2; 4:1-2; 5:1-2; 6:1; 20:2; Magnesians 3:1; 4:1; 6:1-2; 7:1; 13:1-2; Trallians 2:1; 3:1-2; 7:1-2; 13:2; Philadelphians 1:1; 3:2; 8:1-2.

but was interested in strengthening the practical daily life of Christians.

D. *The Epistle of Barnabas.*

This letter is often known as *Pseudo-Barnabas* because it was evidently written by someone other than the Barnabas of the New Testament. Evidence within the epistle itself would confirm this view, although many of the Fathers of the Church associate it with the Barnabas of the New Testament. It is believed that the letter was written about 130 by some Christian from Alexandria.

The letter was intended to help converts from paganism whom some Jewish Christians were trying to persuade that the law of Moses should be observed because it was still, so they thought, in force. The writer disposes of this claim in the first seventeen chapters by showing that the life and death of Christ are completely adequate for salvation and that Christians are not bound to observe the law. The Mosaic covenant has ended with the death of Christ. The last four chapters present the contrast between two ways of life, "The Way of Light" and "The Way of the Black One." The reader is urged to follow the first way of life. These two ways are reminiscent of the two ways of *The Didache,* with which they probably had a close relationship.

The writer of this letter uses Old Testament (119 quotations) typology to the point where it becomes allegory.[2] He allegorizes the 318 servants of Abraham (9:8) into a reference to Christ's death on the Cross on the basis that the Greek letter for 300 is cross-shaped and the Greek numerals for eighteen are the first two letters of the name Jesus. He was very proud of this unique interpretation (9:9) of Genesis 14:14. He constantly goes beyond legitimate typology to allegory in order to derive the meaning he wants from the Old Testament Scriptures. This practice, derived from Philo of Alexandria, who sought to reconcile Greek philosophy and the Old Testament by it, was later developed into an organized method of interpretation by Origen. It has done much harm to sound interpretation of the Bible.

E. *The Epistle to Diognetus.*

The tutor of Marcus Aurelius, whose name was Diognetus, may be the man to whom this letter was written by some anony-

---

[2] Allegory is the seeking of a symbolic, hidden meaning by reading into the literal meaning of the Scripture meanings in accord with moral or philosophical preconceptions. It distorts the meaning intended by the writer for the people to whom he was writing into what the interpreter wants to find in the Scripture.

mous writer in the late second or early third century. It is ranked among the writings of the Apostolic Fathers only by custom because its nature is apologetic, and it could well be considered as one of the apologetic writings.

The writer presents a rational defense of Christianity by showing the folly of idolatry (chapters 1–2), the inadequacy of Judaism (3–4), the superiority of Christianity in its beliefs, the character it builds and the benefits which it offers to the convert (5–12). He also likens the role of Christians in the world to that of the soul in the body in a series of interesting comparisons (6).

F. The Second Epistle of Clement to the Corinthians.

This work is usually considered with the writings of the Apostolic Fathers, although it is not a letter but a sermon or homily (19:1) and was not written by Clement. It was written about 150.

The writer is interested in a sound view of Christ, a belief in the resurrection of the body and purity of life on the part of the Christian. After a preliminary assertion of the utility of salvation (chapters 1–4), he urges the Christian to enter the conflict against the world (5–7) by practicing Christian virtues (8–17) and working out the salvation that has become his through Christ (18–20). The letter is an interesting illustration of the content of preaching during the second century.

G. Papias.

The *Interpretations of the Sayings of the Lord* was written about the middle of the second century by Papias, the bishop of Hierapolis in Phrygia, in order to record the information that he had received from older Christians who had known the apostles. It is possible that Papias had been a disciple of John. The document deals with the life and words of Christ. Although it has disappeared, fragments of it are available in the writings of Eusebius and Irenaeus. The fragment preserved in Irenaeus' writings[3] gives clear evidence of Papias' strong millennial views. The section preserved by Eusebius[4] throws interesting light on the origin of the Gospels. He states that Mark was the interpreter of Peter and that Matthew wrote his work in the Hebrew language. These little excerpts are tantalizing to the student who realizes the light that his complete work

---

[3] Irenaeus, *Against Heresies*, V:xxxiii:3-4; V:xxxvi:1-2.
[4] Eusebius, *Church History*, III:xxxix:3-5, 15-16.

would throw on the beliefs, life and literature of the New Testament.

II. Apocalyptic Literature

The Shepherd of Hermas, modeled after the Book of Revelation, was probably written about 150 by Hermas, who was considered by the writer of the Muratorian Canon to be the brother of Pius, the bishop of Rome between 140 and 155.[5] The author's use of vision and allegory reminds one of John Bunyan's work, but, unfortunately, Hermas had little of the ability which that Puritan writer had.

Although the work is written in the form of a revelation abounding in symbols and visions, its aim is both moral and practical. The writer had been the slave of Rhoda, a Christian lady of Rome. She had freed him, and he had become a prosperous farmer. But in the process he had neglected his own family, and his family consequently fell into vile sin. He and his wife repented and confessed their faith, but his children turned against the faith. Then he lost all his possessions. Out of this experience came this work which is designed to call sinners to repentance. Repentance and holy living are the keynotes of the work (Mandate 4, Chapter 2). The messages of the work are given to Hermas by a woman and an angel. The first section consists of five visions that emphasize the need of repentance in symbols. This is followed by twelve mandates or commandments depicting the code of ethics which the repentant one should follow in order to be pleasing to God. The final section is made up of ten similitudes or parables in which the main theme is the significance of repentance in life. The writer of *The Shepherd* is much concerned with the individual in relation to the Christian society, the Church.

III. Catechetical Literature

The little book, the *Didache* (the *Teaching of the Twelve Apostles*), came to light in 1873 or 1875 when a man named Bryennios discovered it in an ecclesiastical library in Constantinople and published it in 1883. This manual of church instruction was most likely composed about the middle of the second century in the form in which it has come down to us. However, many contend for a date at the end of the first cen-

---

[5] The Muratorian Canon is a mutilated fragment containing a list of New Testament scriptures, probably those recognized as canonical by the Roman church toward the end of the second century.

tury because of the resemblance of much in it to the practices of the New Testament.

Even the casual reader can pick out the clearly defined four parts of the work. The first section, which closely resembles the two ways of life in the *Pseudo-Barnabas*, consists of a discussion of the Ways of Life and Death (chapters 1–6). Here the ethical action consistent with a Christian life is set forth in contrast with the deeds of those who follow the Way of Death. The writer then discusses such liturgical problems as baptism, fasting and the communion (7–10). Instruction on how to distinguish false prophets from true, how to find worthy officials and other disciplinary matters forms the burden of the third section (11–15). The document wryly points out the false prophet as one who seeks food and lodging without giving anything in return to the church in the form of spiritual inspiration. The need for a watchful and consistent life in view of the coming of the Lord is the burden of the last chapter. This discussion should make clear the importance of the *Didache* as a picture of life in the Early Church between 95 and 150.

The diligent reader of the literature that has been discussed will find much reward in the way of knowledge and inspiration. It seems somewhat of a pity that these writings of edification should have been neglected by the Church throughout the ages.

BIBLIOGRAPHY

The two little volumes of the writings of the Apostolic Fathers by Kirsopp Lake in the Loeb Classical Library series (New York: G. P. Putnam's Sons, 1930) contain a good translation of the Fathers' writings on the right-hand page and the original text on the left-hand page. This is one of the best translations of these primary sources.

There are many excellent introductions to the writings and lives of the Fathers. The work by the Roman Catholic, J. Tixeront, *A Handbook of Patrology*, translated by S. A. Raemers (St. Louis: B. Herder Book Co., 1947), contains good introductions to and analyses of these writings.

Edgar Goodspeed in his *A History of Early Christian Literature* (Chicago: The University of Chicago Press, 1942), writes illuminating introductions to and discussions of the nature and value of the writings of the Fathers.

Many will find the little manual by Henry B. Swete, *Patristic Study* (New York: Longmans, Green & Co., 3d ed., 1904), useful in providing a historical background.

The student will find pages 211 to 290 of volume one of Albert Newman's *A Manual of Church History* (Philadelphia: The American Baptist Publication Society, rev. and enl. ed., 1933) helpful for its presentation of the theology of these writers as well as for introductions to their writings.

Chapter VI

WITH THE BISHOPS AND DEACONS

The Christian is a part of an organism and of an organization. As a member of the invisible Church, which is made up of those who yield control of their lives by faith to Christ, he becomes conscious of being a part of an *organism,* the Church, which is the living Body of Christ (I Corinthians 12). As a member of the visible church with its machinery to make it function smoothly, he is aware of belonging to an *organization.* The development of the Church as an organization was left to the apostles to work out under the guidance of the Holy Spirit. Any large corporate body must of necessity have leadership, and, as it grows, the division of functions and consequent specialization of leadership must come if it is to function effectively. A liturgy to guide the worship of the Church in an orderly fashion (I Corinthians 14:40) is another logical outcome of the growth of the Church as an organization. The eventual aim of the Church as a worshipping organism is the achievement of quality of life.

I. THE GOVERNMENT OF THE CHURCH

The origin of church polity is to be credited to Christ because He chose the twelve apostles who were to be the leaders of the infant Church. The apostles took the initiative in the development of other offices in the Church when they were so directed by the Holy Spirit. This does not by any means imply a pyramidal hierarchy, such as the Roman Catholic Church has developed, because the new officials were to be chosen by the people, to be ordained by the apostles and to have special spiritual qualifications that involved leadership by the Holy Spirit. Thus there was an inward call by the Holy Spirit to the office, an external call by the democratic vote of the church and the ordaining to office by the apostles. There was to be no special class of priests set apart to minister a sacerdotal

[84]

system of salvation, because both the officials of the Church and members were priests with the right of direct access to God through Christ (Ephesians 2:18).

These officials may be divided into two classes. The *charismatic officials* (Greek *charisma* means gift) were chosen by Christ and endowed with special spiritual gifts (Ephesians 4: 11-12; I Corinthians 12–14). Their function was primarily inspirational. The *administrative* officials constituted the second class. Their functions were mainly administrative; although after the death of the apostles, the elders took over many spiritual responsibilities. These officials were chosen by the congregation after prayer for the guidance of the Holy Spirit.

A. *Charismatic Officials.*

These men, whose main responsibilities were the guarding of the truth of the Gospel and its initial proclamation, were specially selected by Christ through the Holy Spirit to exercise leadership within the Church. There were four or five such offices designated by Paul — apostles, prophets, evangelists, pastors and/or teachers. Many think that pastor and teacher may be designations for the same man.

The apostles were men who had been witnesses to Christ's life, death and particularly His resurrection (Acts 1:22; cf. I Corinthians 1:1; 15:8), and who had been personally called by Christ. Paul based his apostleship on a direct call from the living Christ. These men, who were the first officials of the Early Church, had combined in their work all of the functions later carried on by various officials when the apostles were unable to take care of the needs of the rapidly expanding Early Church.

Peter is the dominant figure among the apostles in the first twelve chapters of Luke's record of the history of the Early Church. Not only did he make the first official proclamation to the Jews in Jerusalem on the day of Pentecost, but he also first introduced the Gospel among the Gentiles by his preaching to the household of Cornelius. Despite this leadership, nothing of the hierarchal, authoritarian concept of the medieval Roman Catholic Church is to be seen in the New Testament account of his activities. Tradition dating from the Early Church fixes Rome as the place of Peter's death. One rather interesting tradition describes Peter's escape from prison in Rome and flight from the city. Confronted by Christ, Peter asks Him where

He was going. Christ replies that He is going to Rome to be crucified again. Smitten with remorse, Peter hastens back to the city, where he is crucified at his own request, according to one tradition, with his head down because he did not feel worthy to die in the same way his Lord had died.

James, the brother of Christ (Galatians 1:19), ranked next to Peter as the leader of the church in Jerusalem. His prominence in the church is clearly evident from his position of leadership at the Jerusalem Council. While closer to the legalism of Judaism than most of the leaders of the early Jerusalem church, he occupied a mediatorial position between Jewish and Gentile Christians at the Jerusalem Council. He had such a desire for holiness and a devout life of prayer that, according to tradition, his knees became calloused like those of a camel because of his constant kneeling. He was martyred by being clubbed after he had been thrown down from the pinnacle of the temple. All the while he uttered words of forgiveness similar to those used by Stephen.[1]

John is ranked along with Peter as a leader in the Early Church. Tradition associates his later labors with the city of Ephesus. He was banished by Domitian to the island of Patmos, a solitary barren rock island off the western coast of Asia Minor. Here he wrote the Book of Revelation. After the death of Domitian, he was allowed to return to Ephesus, where he remained, ministering to the churches of Asia until his death at the advanced age of ninety. His Gospel, his three epistles and Revelation are a rich part of the literary heritage of the Church in the New Testament.

Peter's brother Andrew preached in sections of the Near East. He was martyred because he had been instrumental in the conversion of the wife and brother of the Roman proconsul. The proconsul ordered him to be crucified on the peculiarly shaped cross that has since been known by his name.

Little is known of Philip's later life except that he most likely died a natural death at Hierapolis after the destruction of Jerusalem. James the Less, the son of Alphaeus, worked in Palestine and later in Egypt where he was finally crucified. Tradition concerning the death of Judas Thaddaeus is divided between assigning his labors to Persia, where he was martyred, and designating the Near East as the scene of his labors and his natural death. Matthias, who took the place of Judas, labored

[1] Eusebius, *Church History*, II:23.

in Ethiopia and was there martyred, according to one account. Simon Zelotes was also martyred. Tradition is not clear concerning the mode of martyrdom of Bartholomew, but his name is linked with the proclamation of the Gospel in India by one tradition. Matthew was supposed to have also labored in Ethiopia. The name of the most skeptical of the disciples, Thomas, is associated with labor in Parthia, but other accounts link his work and martyrdom with India. The silence of the New Testament and even tradition concerning these men[2] is remarkable compared with the later medieval tendency to glorify the death of the notable men of the Church.

Prophets appeared to be among the more influential leaders of the New Testament Church. They exercised the function of forthtelling or preaching the Gospel (Acts 13:1; 15:32) as well as foretelling or predicting the future. Agabus is credited with having successfully predicted a coming famine and Paul's imprisonment at the hands of the Jews (Acts 11:28; 21:10-14). Evidently the Early Church was plagued with many who falsely pretended to be prophets because the *Didache* gives clear instruction as to how to distinguish the false prophet from the genuine prophet (10:7; 11:7-12).

Philip exercised the gift of evangelism (Acts 21:8), but little is known of this office and its specific functions. Perhaps it had special reference to work of the itinerant missionary whose main task was to proclaim the Gospel in new, hitherto-untouched areas.

There is also the problem concerning whether the separate offices of pastor and teacher existed in two persons or were simply designations for two functions that one man specially gifted by God was to fill. The New Testament is less obscure concerning the test of a genuine teacher. No one who denied the personal advent of Christ into the world as man in human flesh could be a true teacher, according to John (II John 7-11). The character of a true teacher is pointed out in the *Didache* (11:1-2).

B. Administrative Officials.

All of the officials who have been discussed were specially appointed to their offices by God rather than man. There was another class of officials who were democratically chosen by the congregation. Their task was to carry out governmental

2 *Ibid.*, III:1.

[87]

functions within a given church. Unlike the apostles and other charismatic officials, these men, and in some cases women, worked and exercised their authority in the local church or congregation rather than in the Church of Christ as a whole. These offices grew by division of function and specialization as necessity dictated aid to the overworked apostles faced with the problem of a growing Church. Perhaps the example of the synagogue with its elders who presided over local affairs may have been a factor in the creation of these offices.

The office of the elder or presbyter ranked highest in the local congregation. Those who hold to a threefold organization in the Church contend that the names elder (*presbuteros*) and bishop (*episkopos*) are not synonymous terms but represent the separate offices of bishop and presbyter. The New Testament, however, is quite clear in its association of these two names with the same office (Acts 20:17, 28; Philippians 1:1; Titus 1: 5, 7). The growth of the office of the monarchal bishop did not come until after the end of the apostolic age in the second century.

The qualifications of an elder are clearly outlined at least twice in the New Testament (I Timothy 3:1-7; Titus 1:5-9). Elders must be men of good reputation among the members of the church and outsiders. Conduct of public worship seems to have been one of their main functions (I Timothy 5:17; Titus 1:9) along with the responsibility for the good government and orderly discipline of the church.

The deacons had a subordinate position to the elders, but those who filled the office faced the same rigid qualifications for office that the elders had to meet (Acts 6:3; I Timothy 3: 8-13). The procedure for democratic election was also prescribed by the apostles in Jerusalem (Acts 6:3, 5). The dispensing of charity by the church was the major task of the deacons. Later, they aided the elders by giving the elements of the communion to the people.

Women seem to have been admitted to this office in apostolic times, for Paul mentions Phoebe the deaconess with approval (Romans 16:1). The daughters of Philip the evangelist also fulfilled the functions of a prophet (Acts 21:9), but Paul is specific in his assertion that women could not be teachers in the church (I Timothy 2:12; I Corinthians 14:34).

The emergence of a set of officials for the congregation and the definition of their qualifications and duties were completed by the end of the first century. With salvation by faith in Christ as its Gospel, a growing literature written by the apostles and a form of organization to meet its needs, Christianity grew rapidly in the late first and early second centuries.

II. THE WORSHIP OF THE EARLY CHURCH

The question of a dignified orderly form of worship seems to have been a matter of some concern from the time of the apostles. Paul had to urge the Corinthian church to conduct its worship in an orderly dignified manner (I Corinthians 14: 40). Christ stated the essence of true worship when He declared that because God was a spirit, true worship was a matter of the spirit (John 4:24). Worship is really the upward reach of the human spirit through religious exercises that bring the soul into the presence of God.

The early Christians did not think of a church as a place of worship according to the common usage of the word today. A church signified a body of people in personal relationship with Christ. Such a group met in homes (Acts 12:12; Romans 16:5, 23; Colossians 4:15; Philemon 1-4), the temple (Acts 5:12), public auditoriums of schools (Acts 19:9) and in the synagogues so long as they were permitted to do so (Acts 14:1, 3; 17:1; 18:4). The place was not as important as the matter of meeting for fellowship with one another and for worship of God.

During the first century two services were held on the first day of the week. That day was adopted as the day of worship because it was the day on which Christ rose from the dead (Acts 20:7; I Corinthians 16:2; Revelation 1:10). The morning service most likely included the reading of Scripture (Colossians 3:16), exhortation by the leading elder, prayers and singing (Ephesians 5:19). The love feast (I Corinthians 11:20-22) or *agape* preceded the Communion during the evening service. By the end of the first century the love feast was generally dropped and the Communion celebrated during the morning service of worship. Pliny described the Christians to Trajan as those who met before daybreak, sang hymns and took vows to lead an ethical life.[3]

Information concerning the order of worship in the middle part of the second century is much more complete, and is to be

---

[3] Pliny, *Epistles*, X:xcvi:7 in Henry Bettenson, ed., *Documents of the Christian Church* (New York: Oxford University Press, 1947), p. 6.

found in the *First Apology* of Justin Martyr and the *Didache*.[4] The service, which was held on "the day of the sun," started with reading of the "memoirs of the apostles" or "the writings of the prophets" for a period "as long as time permits." An exhortation or homily, based on the reading, was then given by the "president." The congregation then stood for prayer. The celebration of the Lord's Supper followed the kiss of peace. The elements of bread and "water and wine" were dedicated by thanksgiving and prayers to which the people responded by an "Amen." The deacons then distributed the elements to the people. After the service they also took them to the homes of those unable to be present at the meeting. They finally took up a collection for aid to widows and orphans, the sick, prisoners and strangers. The meeting was then dismissed, and all made their way to their homes.

The Lord's Supper and baptism were the two sacraments that the Early Church used because they had been instituted by Christ. Immersion seems to have been widely practiced in the first century, but, according to the *Didache*, baptism could be performed by pouring water over the head of the one being baptized if no stream of running water or large amount of water were available.[5] Only such as were baptized could partake of the Communion.

III. THE LIFE OF THE CHURCH

The Early Church had no benevolent welfare state to give aid to the poor and sick. A church took that responsibility upon itself. The money collected from those able to give in the offering following the celebration of the Communion was dispensed to meet such needs. Paul also mentioned the practice of collecting the gifts of the faithful each Sunday (I Corinthians 16:1-2). The deacons would then use it to care for those who were in need. The women of the churches also aided in this charitable work by making clothes for those with such a need (Acts 9:36-41).

The Church did not attack the institution of slavery directly; nor was the ownership of slaves forbidden to Christians. However, Christianity soon undercut the institution of slavery by bidding the Christian master and slave to remember that they were brother Christians. Paul's tactful letter to Philemon, the

[4] *Didache*, XIV, IX, X; *Apology*, lxv-lxvii in Bettenson, *op. cit.*, pp. 93-05.
[5] *Didache*, VII:1-3.

leader of the church in Colosse, leaves one with the impression that Philemon as a sincere Christian would most likely give Onesimus his freedom.

The Early Church insisted upon separation from the pagan practices of Roman society, but it did not insist upon separation from pagan neighbors in harmless social relationships. In fact, Paul by inference made provision for such social mingling so long as it did not involve the compromise or sacrifice of Christian principles (I Corinthians 10:20-33). He did, however, urge complete separation from any practice that might be related to idolatry or pagan immorality. The Christian should follow the principles of doing nothing that would harm the body that Christ owned (I Corinthians 6:12); of doing nothing that would harm others or lead other weak Christians astray (I Corinthians 8:13; 10:24); of avoiding all that would not bring glory to God (I Corinthians 6:20; 10:31). These principles precluded attendance at pagan theaters, stadiums, games or temples.

Despite this attitude of moral and spiritual separation, the Christians were willing, were even urged by Paul, to fulfill their civic obligations of obedience to and respect for civil authority, payment of taxes and prayers for those in authority (Romans 13:7; I Timothy 2:1-2). They made excellent citizens so long as they were not asked to violate the precepts of God, the higher authority to whom their primary allegiance was due.

The purity of life, love and courage of the Early Church in standing and dying for principle made such an impact upon the pagan society of imperial Rome that it was only three centuries after the death of Christ that Constantine gave official recognition to the importance of Christianity in the state by calling and presiding over the Council of Nicaea.

BIBLIOGRAPHY

P. Schaff, in his *History of the Apostolic Church* (New York: Charles Scribner's Sons, 1869), pp. 433-492, 545-586, has excellent discussions of the topics considered in this chapter.

The Struggle of the Old Catholic Imperial Church for Survival, 100–313

Chapter VII

CHRIST OR CAESAR

Christianity has always faced both external and internal problems in every period of its history. The Church had to face the serious *internal* problem of *heresy* and deal with it between 100 and 313 and, at the same time, had to solve the *external* problem of *persecution* from the Roman state.

Many have a confused idea of the number, duration, scope and intensity of the persecutions which the Church suffered. Before 250 persecution was mainly local, sporadic and more often the result of mob action than the result of definite civil policy. After that date, however, persecution became at times the studied policy of the Roman imperial government, and hence, widespread and violent. During that time Tertullian's idea that the blood of the martyrs is the seed of the Church became a terrible reality to many Christians. The Church continued to develop in spite of or, perhaps, partly because of persecution until at the end of the period it won freedom of worship under Constantine.

I. Causes of Persecution

A. *Political.*

The Church endured little persecution so long as it was looked upon by the authorities as a part of Judaism, which was a *religio licita,* or legal sect. But as soon as Christianity was distinguished from Judaism as a separate sect and might be classed as a secret society, it came under the ban of the Roman state, which would brook no rival for the allegiance of its subjects. It then became a *religio illicita,* an illegal religion, which was considered a threat to the safety of the Roman state.

The people in positions of leadership in the Roman Empire believed that the Roman state was the highest good. Even religion could only be tolerated as it contributed to the stability

[95]

of the state. Since the rapidly growing Christian religion was exclusive in its claims upon the moral and spiritual loyalty of those who accepted Christ, when a choice had to be made between loyalty to Christ and loyalty to Caesar, Caesar was bound to take second place. This was conceived by the Roman leaders, bent on preserving classical culture within the framework of the Roman imperial state, as disloyalty to the state, and they thought of the Christians as those who were trying to set up a state within a state. Either the universal state or the universal Church, the Body of Christ, must give way.

Many Christian practices seemed to confirm the Roman authorities in their suspicions of the basic disloyalty of the Christians to the state. The Christians consistently refused to offer incense on the altars devoted to the genius of the Roman emperor with whom the welfare of the state was inextricably mingled in the minds of the people during the imperial period from Caesar Augustus to Constantine. If one would sacrifice on these altars, one could then practice a second private religion. The Christians would not make such sacrifices, and, consequently, it was thought that they were disloyal. The Christians also held most of their meetings at night and in secret. To the Roman authority this could mean nothing else than the hatching of a conspiracy against the safety of the state.

B. Religious.

In addition to the basic political cause for persecution, there was a religious reason. Roman religion was mechanical and external. It had its altars, idols, priests, processionals, rites and practices that the people could see. The Romans were not averse to adding a new idol to the group in the Pantheon so long as that deity was subordinate to the prior claims of the Roman state religion. The Christians had no idols and little visible paraphanalia of worship. Their worship was spiritual and internal. When they stood and prayed with eyes closed, there was no visible object to which those prayers were addressed. This could mean nothing else but atheism to the Romans, who were accustomed to symbolic material manifestations of their god.

The secrecy of the meetings of the Christians also brought moral charges against them. Public rumor made them guilty of incest, cannibalism and unnatural practices. Misunderstanding concerning the meaning of "eating and drinking" the elements representing Christ's body and blood easily led to the rumor that the Christians killed and ate infants in sacrifice to their God. Word of "the kiss of peace" was easily twisted into charges of incest and other types of immoral conduct repugnant to the cultured Roman mind. It made little difference that there was no truth in these rumors.[1]

C. Social.

Social problems also made their contribution to the cause of Roman persecution of the Church. The Christians, who had great appeal for the lower classes and slaves, were hated by the influential aristocratic leaders of society. These leaders looked down upon them with contempt but were fearful of their influence upon the lower class. The Christians upheld the equality of all men (Colossians 3:11); paganism insisted upon an aristocratic structure for society in which the privileged few were served by the lower class and slaves. Christians separated themselves from pagan gatherings at temples, theaters and places of recreation. This nonconformity to accepted social patterns brought down upon them the dislike that the nonconformist always faces in any period of history. The purity of their lives was a silent rebuke to the scandalous lives that people of the upper class were leading. The Christians' nonconformity to existing social patterns led the pagans to believe that they were a danger to society and to characterize them as "haters of mankind" who might incite the masses to revolt.

D. Economic.

It must not be forgotten that economic considerations played a part in the persecution of the Christians. The opposition that Paul received from the idol makers of Ephesus, who were more concerned over the danger of Christianity to their craft than to the damage it might cause Diana worship (Acts 19:27), is a clue to the feelings of those vested interests whose livelihood was threatened by the spread of Christianity. Priests, idol makers, soothsayers, painters, architects and sculptors would hardly be enthusiastic about a religion that was threatening their means of livelihood.

The year 250, when persecution became general and violent instead of local and spasmodic, was, according to the reckoning of the Romans, about one thousand years after the founding of Rome. Since plague, famine and civic unrest plagued the Empire at this time, popular opinion ascribed these troubles

[1] Justin Martyr, *Dialog*, 10.

to the presence of Christianity within the Empire and to the consequent forsaking of the older gods. There is always a good deal of superstition concerning the end of a millennium, and the Romans were no better in this regard than people in the Middle Ages just before 1000. Persecution of the Christians seemed a logical way for the Romans to overcome their troubles.

All of these considerations combined to justify the persecution of the Christians in the minds of the authorities. Not all were present in each case, but the exclusiveness of the claims of the Christian religion upon the life of the Christian conflicted with pagan syncretism and the demand for exclusive loyalty to the Roman state in most instances. Persecution followed naturally as a part of imperial policy to preserve the integrity of the Roman state. Christianity was not a licensed religion with a legal right to existence.

II. Persecution of the Church

Persecution of the Christians was both ecclesiastical and political. The Jews were the persecutors during the infancy of the Church in Jerusalem. Only in the reign of Nero (54–68) did persecution begin to come from the Roman state. Even these persecutions were local and sporadic until 250, when they became general and violent, beginning with that under Decius.

A. Persecution to 250.

Nero has the dubious distinction of being the first Roman emperor to persecute the Christian Church. Tacitus records the rumor that Nero had ordered the fire that destroyed part of the city of Rome. This rumor was so widely accepted by the people that Nero had to find a scapegoat. He diverted feeling against himself to the Christians by accusing them of arson and by engaging in a saturnalia of destruction of the Christians. Apparently the persecution was confined to Rome and its environs.[2]

Persecution broke out a second time in 90 during the reign of the despotic Domitian. The Jews had refused to pay a poll tax levied for the support of Capitolinus Jupiter. Because the Christians were still associated with the Jews, they also suffered the effects of the Emperor's wrath. It was during this persecution that the Apostle John was exiled to the Isle of Patmos where he wrote the Book of Revelation.

---

[2] Tacitus, *Annals*, XV:44 in Henry Bettenson, ed., *Documents of the Christian Church* (New York: Oxford University Press, 1947), pp. 3-5.

The first organized persecution, which resulted from definite governmental policy, took place in Bithynia during the governorship of Pliny the Younger about 112. Pliny wrote a rather interesting letter to Emperor Trajan, in which he gave information about the Christians, outlined his policy and asked Trajan for his judgment concerning the matter. He wrote that "the contagion of this superstition" (Christianity) had spread in the villages and rural areas as well as in the larger cities to such an extent that the temples had been almost deserted and the sellers of sacrificial animals impoverished. Pliny went on to inform Trajan of his procedure in treating Christians. When someone informed upon a Christian, Pliny brought the Christian before his tribunal and asked him if he were a Christian. If he still admitted the charge after three such questions, he was sentenced to death. In his answer Trajan assured Pliny that he was following the correct procedure. No Christians were to be sought out; but if someone reported that a certain individual was a Christian, the Christian was to be punished unless he recanted and worshiped the gods of the Romans.[3] It was during this persecution that Ignatius lost his life.

Another persecution took place at Smyrna about the middle of the second century. It was at this time that Polycarp was martyred as an enraged mob brought the Christians before the authorities.

Local calamity, such as the fire in Rome, or the activity of a conscientious governor were the causes of persecution up to the reign of Marcus Aurelius (161–180). Marcus Aurelius was a devout Stoic who had been biased against Christianity by his teacher Fronto. Inclined to ascribe the natural and man-made calamities of his reign to the growth of Christianity, he gave orders for persecution of the Christians. Justin Martyr, the great apologetic writer, suffered martyrdom in Rome during this persecution.

B. Persecution After 250.

The Emperor Decius took the imperial throne about the time Rome was reaching the end of the first millennium of her history and at a time when the Empire was reeling under natural calamities and internal and external attacks upon its stability. He decided that if classical culture were to be saved it would have to be with a strong arm. The Christians were picked out

[3] Pliny, *Epistles*, X:xcvi-xcvii in Bettenson, op. cit., pp. 5-7.

[99]

as a peculiar threat to the state because of their rapid increase in numbers and their seeming attempt to set up a state within a state.

Decius issued an edict in 250 that demanded, at the least, an annual offering of sacrifice at the Romans altars to the gods and the genius of the emperor. Those who offered such sacrifices were given a certificate called a *libellus*.[4] The Church was later agitated by the problem of how to deal with those who denied their Christian faith to get such certificates. Fortunately for the Church, the persecution only lasted until the death of Decius in the next year.

Although there were periods of state persecution by order of the emperors, no major persecution occurred after that of Decius until the reign of Diocletian. Diocletian was a strong military leader who came to the imperial throne at the end of a century that was marked by political disorder in the Roman Empire. He decided that only a strong monarchy could save the Empire and its classical culture. In 285 he ended the dyarchy of the principate, created by Caesar Augustus in 27 B.C., by which the emperor and senate had shared authority. A powerful, orientalized monarchy seemed in his opinion to offer the only alternative to chaos. In such a despotic Empire there was no place for democratic elements in government or for the toleration of faiths hostile to the state religion. It was out of this historical situation that the most severe persecution that the Christians ever endured came.

The first edicts calling for persecution of the Christians came in March, 303. Diocletian ordered the cessation of meetings of the Christians, the destruction of the churches, the deposition of officers of the church, the imprisonment of those who persisted in their testimony to Christ and the destruction of the Scriptures by fire. This last order was to give the Church trouble later on when the Donatist controversy broke out in North Africa over how the traditores, those who had given up copies of the Scriptures to persecutors, were to be treated when they asked to be readmitted to the Church after the persecution was over. A later edict ordered the Christians to sacrifice to the pagan gods upon pain of death if they refused to do so.[5] Eu-

4 Bettenson, *op. cit.*, p. 19.
5 Bettenson, *op. cit.*, p. 21; Eusebius, *Church History*, VIII:2-12.

sebius points out that prisons became so crowded with Christian leaders and their congregations that there was not even enough room for criminals.[6] Christians were punished by loss of property, exile, imprisonment, or execution by the sword or wild beasts. The more fortunate were sent to the Roman equivalent of a totalitarian labor camp where they were worked to death in the mines. The pace of the persecution slackened when Diocletian abdicated and retired in 305.

After other periods of persecution Galerius issued an edict from his deathbed in 311 that gave toleration to Christianity, provided the Christians did not violate the peace of the Empire. Persecution did not cease completely until the reign of Constantine, who issued the Edict of Milan in 313. This edict brought freedom of worship not only to Christianity but to all religions.[7] Because Constantine believed that "the worship of God" should be the "first and chiefest care" of the ruler, he thought that there could be no alternative to freedom of religion as the policy of the Empire. Perhaps the tradition that he had had a vision of the Cross, which gave him the assurance of victory over his rivals, had something to do with his tolerant policy. Certainly he was ahead of his times, for not until the modern period has freedom of religion become a settled policy, even of democratic states. From that time on, Christians had freedom to worship and to propagandize others in order to win them for Christ.

In our day, this same issue of Church and state has again been revived, and in many countries Christians are only tolerated under law. In other countries they face persecution from a state that will brook no rival. The early struggle of the Church with persecution helps to point up the importance of the modern concept of the separation of the Church and state. Only where people are permitted to have private interests apart from public interests can there be religious freedom.

III. Results of Persecution

The rapid spread of Christianity, even during the periods of heaviest persecution, proved that indeed the blood of the martyrs was the seed of the Church. During the apostolic period Christianity had been largely an urban movement. The num-

---

[6] Eusebius, *op. cit.*, VIII:vi:9
[7] Bettenson, *op. cit.*, pp. 22-23.

ber of active believers in Jerusalem after the resurrection was estimated at approximately five hundred by Paul (I Corinthians 15:6). Pliny's letter proved that Christianity was strong in Asia Minor shortly after the beginning of the second century. During the first century it had been confined largely to the Eastern section of the Empire, with the Jews being given the first chance to accept Christianity as the Christian reached new cities. During the second century expansion was rapid among the Greek-speaking Gentile population of the Empire. Christians could be found in all parts of the Empire by 200. The emphasis during the third century was upon the spread of the Gospel to the Latins of the Western section of the Empire. A powerful church with Carthage as its intellectual center grew up in North Africa. The church in Alexandria became the chief church of the churches of Egypt. Estimates of the size of the Church by 250 vary between five and twelve per cent of the population of the Empire.

Persecution, however, did create internal problems that had to be solved. Two severe controversies broke out in North Africa and Rome concerning the manner of treatment which those who had offered sacrifices at pagan altars in the Decian persecution and those who had given up the Scriptures in the Diocletian persecution should receive from the Church when they repented. Some desired to exclude them from any fellowship with the Church; others would receive them after a period of probation. The Donatist controversy, which grew out of the Diocletian persecution, was not settled by the time of Constantine (see Chapter VIII, page 112).

The Diocletian persecution forced upon the Church the problem of the canon of the New Testament (see Chapter X, page 127). If possession of letters might mean death, the Christians wanted to be sure that the books which they would not give up on pain of death were really canonical books. This consideration contributed to the final decisions as to what literature was canonical.

The era of persecution is interesting for the light it throws upon the perennial problem of the relation of the Church to the state. Christianity claimed the exclusive loyalty of its followers in moral and spiritual matters. The Christian was to be obedient to the state so long as it did not ask him to violate his moral and spiritual allegiance to God. Christians who live in states where Christianity is now persecuted may take the history of early persecution as a guide. The problem of obedience to Christ or Caesar is perennial in the history of the Church.

BIBLIOGRAPHY

The compilation by Joseph Ayer, Jr., *A Source Book for Ancient Church History* (New York: Charles Scribner's Sons, 1913), contains much primary material concerning the causes of and the story of the major persecutions.

Persecutions in the Early Church (London: C. H. Kelly, 1906) by Herbert B. Workman is a useful work for the student of the history of persecution of the Church.

Early Church History to A.D. 313 (London: The Macmillan Co., 3 vols., 1909) by M. Gwatkin will be found helpful for the period from 100 to 313.

Chapter VIII

FABLES OR SOUND DOCTRINE

The Christians of the second and third centuries had to fight what every strategist tries to avoid — a war on two fronts. While the Church was fighting to preserve its existence in the face of attempts by the Roman state to abolish it, at the same time it was fighting to preserve purity of doctrine within the Church. Converts to the Christian faith either came from a background of Jewish legalism or from the intellectual environment of Greek philosophy. Many of these converts, until the Church could instruct them properly, tended to carry their old ideas over into their new environment. Others tried to make Christianity appear intellectually respectable to the upper classes in the state. The threat of legalistic or philosophical perversions of Christianity was a very real one in the Church during this era. In some instances overzealous leaders developed a particular interpretation to correct real or fancied evils in the Church and got many to follow their heretical ideas until heresies finally resulted in schisms and from schisms came new sects.

I. LEGALISTIC HERESIES

One would have thought that the decision at the Jerusalem Council to free the Gentiles from the ceremonial and ritualistic demands of the Jewish law as requirements for salvation would have been final. However, groups of Ebionites persisted in Palestine and nearby countries for over two centuries after the suppression by the Roman authorities of the rebellion of Jews under Bar Cocheba between 132 and 135. These people emphasized the unity of God and His creatorship of the universe. They believed that the Jewish law was the highest expression of His will and that it was still binding upon man. They believed that Jesus was not God but became the Messiah by virtue of his complete fulfillment of the law. They upheld, there-

[104]

fore, the teachings of Peter and James, but they disliked the writings of Paul. Some of the more moderate members of the sect believed that the law was binding only upon Jewish Christians; others insisted that Gentile as well as Jewish Christians were still bound by the law of Moses and that there was no salvation apart from circumcision and the law of Moses. After the destruction of Jerusalem by the Romans in 135 they ceased to have much influence, but their existence and beliefs showed that the Church had repeatedly to fight for the principle that faith in Christ alone justifies the individual before God.

II. Philosophical Heresies

A far greater threat to the doctrinal purity of the Christian faith came from Greek philosophy. Many more Gentiles than Jews were won to Christianity. Among these there were many philosophers who wanted to make Christianity a system of philosophy.

A. Gnosticism.

Gnosticism, the greatest of the philosophical threats, was at its peak of power about 150. Its roots reached back into New Testament times. Paul seems to have been fighting an incipient form of Gnosticism in his letter to the Colossians. Christian tradition related the origin of Gnosticism to the Simon Magus[1] whom Peter had to rebuke so severely.

Gnosticism sprang from the natural human desire to create a theodicy, an explanation of the origin of evil. The Gnostics, because they associated matter with evil, sought a way to create a philosophical system in which God as spirit could be freed from association with evil and in which man could be related on the spiritual side of his nature to Deity. It was also a logical or rational system that illustrated the human tendency to seek answers to the great questions of the origin of man. It sought to do this by synthesizing Christianity and Hellenistic philosophy. The Gnostics, like the Greeks of the first two chapters of I Corinthians, sought by human wisdom to understand the ways of God with man and to avoid what seemed to them to be the stigma of the Cross. It took all of the intellectual skill and spiritual power of the polemicist Irenaeus and the development of a rule of faith and a canon of Scripture by the Church to overcome the threat to Christianity in this movement. If the

---

[1] Irenaeus, *Adversus Haereses*, I:xxiii:1-5. Cf. Acts 8:9-24.

Gnostics had succeeded, Christianity would have been simply another philosophical mystery religion of the ancient world.

Dualism was one of the main tenets of Gnosticism. The Gnostics insisted upon a clear separation between the worlds of the material and the spiritual because to them matter was always associated with evil and spirit with good. Hence God could not have been the creator of this material world.

The gap between God and the world of matter was bridged by the idea of a demiurge who was one of a series of emanations from the high god of Gnosticism. These emanations were beings with less of spirit and increasingly more of matter. The demiurge, as one of these emanations, had enough of spirit in him to have creative power and enough of matter to create the material world. This demiurge the Gnostics identified with the Jehovah of the Old Testament, whom they heartily disliked.

To explain Christ they adopted a doctrine known as Docetism. The name comes from a Greek word *dokeo* meaning to seem. Because matter was evil, Christ could not be associated with a human body despite the Bible to the contrary. Christ as absolute spiritual good could not unite with matter. The man Jesus was either a phantom with the seeming appearance of a material body (Docetism), or Christ came upon the human body of Jesus only for a short time — between the baptism of the man Jesus and the beginning of his suffering upon the Cross. Then Christ left the man Jesus to die upon the Cross. It was the task of Christ to teach a special gnosis or knowledge that would help man to save himself by an intellectual process.

Salvation, which was only for the soul or spiritual part of man, might begin with faith but the special gnosis, which Christ imparted to the elite, would be far more beneficial, according to the Gnostic, in the process of the salvation of his soul. Since the body was material and was destined to be cast off, it might be kept under by strict ascetic practices or be given over to libertinism. Only the pneumatic Gnostics, those possessing the esoteric gnosis, and the psychic group, those having faith but no access to the gnosis, would get to heaven. The hylic would never enjoy the heavenly state, for they were destined to eternal loss.

This description of the major tenets held in common by the Gnostics should not mislead one as to the existence of numerous Gnostic sects with special doctrines of their own. Even a casual reading of the first few books of Irenaeus' *Against Heresies* will show the reader how numerous were the groups and how varied their ideas. Saturninus headed a Syrian school of Gnosticism; in Egypt, Basilides led another school. Marcion and his followers seem to have been the most influential of the Gnostic groups.

Marcion left his native Pontus about 138 and went to Rome, where he became influential in the Roman church. He felt that Judaism was evil and, therefore, he hated the Jewish Scriptures and the Jehovah described therein. He set up his own canon of Scripture, which included the Gospel of Luke, the Acts and ten of the letters of the New Testament associated with the name of Paul. Although his business made him wealthy enough to be a real help to the Roman church, he was expelled for holding to these ideas.

A critique of Gnosticism from a Scriptural viewpoint will soon make it clear that the Church was wise to fight this doctrine. It posited two gods, the evil one of the Old Testament to create and the good one to redeem. Consequently, it pandered to anti-Semitism in the Church. It also rejected the reality of the deity of the human Christ whom John claimed dwelt among us to reveal the glory of God. Little wonder that Paul asserted the fulness of God in Christ in his letter to the Colossian church (Colossians 1:19; 2:9). Gnosticism also pandered to spiritual pride with its suggestion that only an aristocratic elite would ever enjoy the pleasures of dwelling with Deity in heaven. It had no place for the human body in the future life. In this respect it resembled the thinking of Greek mythology and philosophy which also had no future for the human body beyond this life. Its asceticism was a contributing factor to the medieval ascetic movement which we know as monasticism.

It did, however, contribute unwittingly to the advancement of the Church. When Marcion formed his canon of New Testament Scriptures, the Church was forced in self-defense to give attention to the problem of what books were to be considered canonical and thus authoritative for doctrine and life. The development of a short creed to test orthodoxy was speeded up to meet a practical need. The bishop's prestige was enhanced by emphasis upon his office as a center of unity for the faithful against heresy. This in turn led to the later rise to prominence of the Roman bishop.

B. *Manicheanism.*

Manicheanism, which was somewhat similar to Gnosticism, was founded by a man named Mani or Manichaeus (ca. 216–276) of Mesopotamia, who developed his peculiar philosophical system about the middle of the third century. Mani worked a curious combination of Christian thought, and Zoroastrianism and other oriental religious ideas into a thoroughgoing dualistic philosophy. Mani believed in two opposing and eternal principles. Pure primitive man, characterized by the possession of pure light, came into being by emanation from the mother of life who in turn was a higher emanation from the ruler of the kingdom of light. Opposed to the king of light was the king of darkness, who managed to trick primitive man so that man lost part of his light and became a being with mingled light and matter. Man's soul linked him with the kingdom of light, but his body brought him into bondage to the kingdom of darkness. Salvation was a matter of liberating the light in his soul from its thralldom to the matter of his body. This liberation could be accomplished by exposure to the light, Christ. The elite or perfect ones constituted the priestly caste for this group. They lived ascetic lives and performed certain rites essential to the release of light. The auditors or hearers shared in the holiness of this elect group by supplying their physical needs. In this way the hearers might also participate in salvation.

Manicheanism laid so much stress on the ascetic life that it looked upon the sex instinct as evil and emphasized the superiority of the unmarried state. Manicheanism may also have aided in the rise of the conception in the Church of a priestly class apart from the rest of the believers, who were considered as uninitiated laymen.

Manicheanism had much influence for a long time after the death of Mani in Persia. So great a thinker as Augustine, during the years he was seeking for truth, was a disciple of the Manicheans for twelve years. After his conversion, Augustine devoted much energy to refuting it.

C. *Neoplatonism.*

Too often the average person thinks of mysticism only in connection with the medieval mystics. The fact is that there have been mystical tendencies in the Church throughout the ages.

Mysticism may be thought of as existing in three forms.

There may be an *epistemological* type of mysticism in which the emphasis is upon how man comes to know God. Those devoted to this type of mysticism think that all our knowledge of God is immediate and comes directly to us by intuition or spiritual illumination. Reason and, in some cases, even the Bible are subordinated to the inner light. Most medieval mystics, the Roman Catholic Quietists of the seventeenth century and the Quakers held to this view. Others emphasize a *metaphysical* type of mysticism in which the spirit of man is thought to be absorbed mystically into the divine being in occasional experiences here and now. Following the extinction of his separate personality by death, man's spirit becomes a part of the divine being. The Neoplatonists, some of the more extreme mystics of the Middle Ages, and Buddhists held to this type of mysticism. The Bible in contrast emphasizes an *ethical and spiritual* type of mysticism in which the individual is related to God through his identification with Christ and the indwelling Holy Spirit.[2]

Neoplatonism is a good illustration of the ontological type of mystical philosophy. It originated in Alexandria as the brain child of Ammonius Saccas, who was born of Christian parents. Origen, the Christian Church Father, and a man named Plotinus studied under Saccas. Plotinus (205?–270) then became the real leader and taught this doctrine in a school at Rome during the third quarter of the third century. The work of producing the literary statement of Neoplatonism was done by Porphory (233–300) from the collected writings of Plotinus. The resulting compilation, known as the *Enneads,* has been preserved.

The Neoplatonists thought of absolute Being as the transcendent source of all that is and from which all was created by a process of overflow. This overflow or emanation finally resulted in the creation of man as a reasoning soul and body. The goal of the universe was reabsorption into the divine essence from which all had come. The senses may be freed from the physical present by the contemplation of works of nature and art; reason gains freedom by the manifestation of love. Philosophy contributes most to this process as one engages in the life of contemplation and by mystical intuition seeks to know God and to be absorbed into the One from

[2] Arthur C. McGiffert, *A History of Christian Thought* (New York: Charles Scribner's Sons, 1946), Vol. 1, pp. 28-29.

whence all has come. The experience of ecstasy was the highest state one could enjoy in this life.

The Emperor Julian, who was known as "the Apostate," embraced this rival of Christianity and during his short reign from 361 to 363 tried to make it the religion of the Empire. Augustine embraced it for a time during the period of his quest for truth. The movement no doubt contributed to the rise of mysticism in Christianity, and it offered an attractive substitute for Christianity to the pagan unwilling to face the high ethical and spiritual demands of the Christian religion.

III. THEOLOGICAL ERRORS

Certain views may be thought of as misinterpretations of the meaning of Christianity, overemphases or as movements of protest. They were, however, harmful to Christianity, and some of the energy that might have gone into the work of evangelization had to be directed to the task of refutation of these errors. Montanism and Monarchianism are examples of two such errors.

A. *Montanism.*

Montanism emerged in Phrygia about 135 to 160 as an attempt on the part of Montanus to meet the problems of formalism in the Church and the dependence of the Church upon human leadership instead of upon the guidance of the Holy Spirit. He was opposed to the rise to prominence of the bishop in the local church. This attempt to combat formalism and human organization led him to a reassertion of the doctrines of the Holy Spirit and the Second Advent. Unfortunately, as so often happens in such movements, he swung to the opposite extreme and developed fanatical misinterpretations of Scripture.

In the development of his peculiar doctrine concerning inspiration, Montanus contended that inspiration was immediate and continuous and that he was the paraclete or advocate through whom the Holy Spirit spoke to the Church as He, the Spirit, had spoken through Paul and the other apostles. Montanus also had an extravagant eschatology. He believed that the heavenly kingdom of Christ would soon be set up at Pepuza in Phrygia and that he would have a prominent place in that kingdom. In order that they might be prepared for that coming, he and his followers practiced strict asceticism. There was to be no second marriage if a mate died; many fasts were to be observed; and dry foods were to be eaten.[3]

3 Eusebius, *Church History*, V:16.

The Church reacted against these extravagances by condemnation of the movement. The Council at Constantinople in 381 declared that the Montanists should be looked upon as pagans. But Tertullian, one of the greatest of the Church Fathers, found the doctrines of the group appealing and became a Montanist. The movement was strongest in Carthage and Eastern lands. It represented the perennial protest that occurs in the Church when there is overelaboration of machinery and lack of dependence on the Spirit of God. Unfortunately, these movements tend to depart from the Scriptures in their enthusiasm for the type of reform they desire. The Montanist movement was and is a warning to the Church not to forget that its organization and its formulation of doctrine must never be divorced from the satisfaction of the emotional side of man's nature and the human craving for immediate spiritual contact with God.

B. *Monarchianism.*

If Montanus was overzealous in his presentation of the doctrines of the Holy Spirit and inspiration, the Monarchians may be said to have erred because of their excessive zeal in emphasizing the unity of God in opposition to any attempt to conceive of God as three separate personalities. They were concerned with an assertion of monotheism but ended up with an ancient form of Unitarianism, which denied the real deity of Christ.

During the third century a man named Paul of Samosata was bishop of Antioch. In addition to this office he held an important political post in the government of Zenobia, Queen of Palmyra. He often played the demagogue in the Antioch church by preaching to the gallery with violent bodily gestures and asking for applause and for the waving of handkerchiefs. On occasion he had a female choir sing hymns praising him. Because he neither inherited a fortune nor was engaged in business, there was some suspicion as to the sources of his large fortune. This able but unscrupulous man taught that Christ was not divine but was merely a good man who, by righteousness and by the penetration of his being by the divine Logos, achieved divinity and saviourhood. This attempt, by Paul and others, to uphold monotheism robbed the Christian of a divine Saviour and was the equivalent in the ancient Church of modern Unitarianism. The doctrine set forth by Paul of Samosata became known as Dynamic Monarchianism.

The leader of another type of Monarchianism was a man named Sabellius, who decided that he wished to avoid any danger of tritheism. About 200 he formulated the teaching that goes by his name. He taught a trinity of manifestation of forms rather than of essence. God was manifested as Father in Old Testament times, later as the Son to redeem man and as the Holy Spirit after the resurrection of Christ. Thus there were not three persons in the Godhead but three manifestations. His view may be illustrated by the relationships which a man may have. In one relationship he is son; in another, brother; and in a third, father. In all of these relationships there is but one real personality. This view, known as Modal Monarchianism, denied separate personality to Christ.

IV. Ecclesiastical Schisms

A. Easter Controversy.

Certain schisms concerning matters of discipline and ritual also developed in the Church during its infancy. The Easter controversy arose about the middle of the second century over the question of what was the proper date to celebrate Easter. The Church in the East held that Easter should be celebrated on the fourteenth day of Nisan, the date of the Passover according to the Jewish calendar, no matter what day of the week it fell upon. Polycarp of Asia was opposed in this view by the Roman bishop Anicetus, who believed that Easter should be celebrated on the Sunday nearest to the fourteenth of Nisan. The Eastern and Western segments of the Church could not arrive at any agreement until the Council of Nicaea in 325, when the viewpoint of the Western Church was adopted.

B. Donatism.

The Donatist controversy developed after 300 as a result of the persecution of the Church by Diocletian. Most of the controversy was centered in North Africa. In 311 a churchman named Donatus wanted to exclude Caecilian, who was accused of being a traditor, from his office as bishop of Carthage because Caecilian had been ordained by Felix, and Felix had been a traditor during the Diocletian persecution. Donatus argued that the failure to remain true during the persecution invalidated the power of Felix to ordain because he had thus committed

CHRISTIAN MARTYRS IN THE AMPHITHEATER

AUGUSTINE, BISHOP OF HIPPO

an unpardonable sin. Donatus and his group elected Majorinus as bishop, and, after the death of Majorinus, Donatus became bishop. When Constantine gave money for the African church, the Donatists complained because they received none. A synod held at Rome decided that the validity of a sacrament does not depend on the character of the one administering the sacrament. Hence the Donatists had no right to any of the aid. Another council of Western bishops, held at Arles in 314, again decided against the Donatist position. This controversy became a matter of some concern to Augustine, and, as a result of his concern, he wrote much on the question of the authority of the Church.

It may be said in conclusion that the results of the controversies, errors and heresies were not always destructive. The Church was forced to develop an authoritative canon of Scripture and a creed that summarized the essential teachings of the Bible. The necessity of answering the false theologies stimulated the rise of Christian theology. The position of the bishop was strengthened by the emphasis upon his office as a rallying point against heresy or error. False teachings that arise through the attempts of ambitious men to assert their authority, or through overemphasis and consequent misinterpretation of certain Scriptures, or through loveless treatment shown to an erring minority by the Church — these did not finally weaken the Church but forced it to think out its belief and to develop organization.

BIBLIOGRAPHY

Any one of the many good histories of doctrine may be consulted with profit for more information on the doctrines discussed.

Although *History of Christian Doctrine* (New York: Charles Scribner's Sons, 1896) by George P. Fisher is old, it contains much useful material.

The work by Juergen L. Neve and O. W. Heick, *A History of Christian Thought* (Philadelphia: The Muhlenberg Press, 2 vols., 1946) is very useful.

McGiffert's work, cited in this chapter, contains many stimulating interpretations despite its liberal bias.

Chapter IX

EARNESTLY CONTENDING FOR THE FAITH

During the second and third centuries the Church expressed its emerging self-consciousness in a new literary output — the writings of the Apologists and the Polemicists. Justin Martyr was the greatest of the former group; Irenaeus, the outstanding man of the latter group. These men faced a hostile government which they tried to win with the arguments of their literary productions. The Apologists tried to convince the leaders of the state that the Christians had done nothing to deserve the persecutions being inflicted upon them, and the Polemicists, such as Irenaeus, tried to meet the challenge of heretical movements. Whereas the Apostolic Fathers wrote only to and for Christians, these writers wrote to and for the leaders of the Roman state or to heretics in an effort to win them back to the truth of the Scriptures by literary argument.

I. THE APOLOGISTS

The Apologists had a negative and positive aim in their writings. Negatively, they sought to refute the false charges of atheism, cannibalism, incest, indolence and anti-social action that pagan neighbors and writers, such as Celsus, leveled against them. Positively, they developed a constructive approach by showing that, in contrast with Christianity, Judaism, pagan religions and state worship were foolish and sinful.

Their writings, known as apologies, made a rational appeal to the pagan leaders and aimed to create an intelligent understanding of Christianity and to remove legal disabilities from it. One of their major arguments was that since the false charges could not be substantiated, the Christians were entitled to civil tolerance under the laws of the Roman state.

These men, writing as philosophers rather than theologians, pictured Christianity as the oldest religion and philosophy because such writings as the Pentateuch were written before the Trojan wars, and because whatever truth could be found in Greek thought was borrowed from Christianity or Judaism. Much was made of the pure life of Christ and the fulfillment of Old Testament prophecies concerning Him as proofs of the fact that Christianity was the highest philosophy. Trained for the most part in Greek philosophy before their acceptance of Christianity, these writers looked upon Greek philosophy as a means to lead men to Christ.

A. *Eastern Apologists.*

Shortly before or after 140, Aristides, a Christian philosopher of the city of Athens, directed an apology to the Emperor Antonius Pius. Dr. Rendel Harris discovered a complete Syriac version of this work in 1889 in the Monastery of St. Catherine's on Mount Sinai. The first fourteen chapters compare Christian, Chaldean, Greek, Egyptian and Jewish methods of worship to prove the superiority of the Christian form of worship. The last three chapters give a clear picture of early Christian customs and ethics.

Justin Martyr (ca. 100–165) was the foremost Apologist of the second century. Born of pagan parents near the Biblical town of Shechem, he early became a wandering philosopher in search of truth. He tried Stoic philosophy, the noble idealism of Plato, which was marred for him by the exorbitant fees demanded by the peripatetic successors of Plato, and the numerical philosophy of Pythagoras. Not until one day, when he was walking along the seashore and an old man directed him to the Scriptures as the true philosophy, did Justin find the peace which he craved (*Dialogue with Trypho,* Chapters 2–8).

Shortly after 150 he addressed his first *Apology* to Emperor Antoninus Pius, the noble Stoic Emperor Marcus Aurelius, and the senate and Roman people. In it he urges the emperors to examine the charges against the Christians (Chapters 1–3) and to free them from legal disabilities if they are innocent. He proves that the Christians are not atheists or idolaters (4–13). The major section of the work (14–60) is devoted to a discussion of the morals, dogmas and Founder of Christianity. He seeks to show that Christ's superior life and morality had been foretold in the Old Testament prophecies. Persecution and error he attributes to the work of demons. The last chapters (61–67) are given over to an exposition of the worship of the Christians.

He argues that since examination would show that the Christians were blameless concerning the charges against them, they should have freedom from persecution.

The so-called second *Apology* is in the nature of an appendix to the first *Apology*. In it Justin cites illustrations of cruelty and injustice to Christians and, after a comparision of Christ and Socrates, points out that the good in men is due to Christ.

In the *Dialogue with Trypho* Justin endeavors to convince the Jews of the Messiahship of Jesus Christ. He allegorizes Scripture and emphasizes prophecy in this attempt. The first eight chapters of the work are autobiographical and constitute an excellent source of information concerning the life of this great writer. The largest section (Chapters 9–142) is a development of three ideas: the relation of the decline of the law of the old covenant to the rise of the Gospel; the linking of the Logos, Christ, with God; and the calling of the Gentiles as the people of God.

Tatian, the widely travelled Eastern scholar who was converted in Rome by Justin, wrote a work known as *Address to the Greeks* about the middle of the second century. It is a denunciation of Greek pretensions to cultural leadership couched in apologetic form. Its main interest, for us, is in the fact that it is addressed to a whole people, the Greeks. Tatian argues that since Christianity is superior to Greek religion and thought, Christians should be given fair treatment. The second section (Chapters 5–30) is devoted to a comparison of Christian teachings with Greek mythology and philosophy. In the next section he asserts that Christianity is far more ancient than Greek thought and religion because Moses antedated the Trojan wars (31–41). He also gives an interesting discussion of the Greek statuary that he had seen (33–34) in the city of Rome. In addition to being author of the *Address*, Tatian was the compiler of the *Diatessaron*, the earliest harmony of the Gospels.

Athenagoras was a professor of Athens who had been converted by reading the Scriptures. About 180 he wrote a work called *Supplication for the Christians*. After stating the charges against the Christians in the introductory chapters, he refutes the charge of atheism made against the Christians by showing that the pagan gods are merely human creations (Chapters 4-30) and that the pagan gods are guilty of the same immoralities as their human followers (31-34). Because the Christians are not guilty of incest nor of eating their children in sacrificial feasts (35-36), he concludes in the final chapter that the emperor should grant them clemency.

Theophilus of Antioch, who also was converted by the reading of the Scriptures, sometime after 180 wrote the *Apology to Autolycus.* Autolycus was apparently a learned pagan magistrate whom Theophilus hoped to win to Christianity by rational arguments. In the first book Theophilus discusses the nature and superiority of God. In the second book he compares the weaknesses of the pagan religion to the strength of Christianity. In the final book he answers the objections of Autolycus to the Christian faith.

B. Western Apologists.

The Western apologetic writers laid a greater emphasis upon the distinctiveness and finality of Christianity than they did upon the similarities between the Christian faith and the pagan religions.

Tertullian was the outstanding Apologist of the Western Church. Shortly before 160 he was born into the home of a Roman centurion on duty in Carthage. Trained in both Greek and Latin, he was at home in the classics. He became a proficient lawyer and taught public speaking and practiced law in Rome, where he was converted to Christianity. His fiery nature and fighting spirit inclined him toward the puritan approach to life of Montanism, and he became a Montanist about 202. His logical Latin mind was devoted to the development of a sound western theology and the defeat of all false philosophical and pagan forces opposed to Christianity.[1]

In the *Apologeticus,* addressed to the Roman governor of his province, he refutes the old charges against the Christians and argues that they are loyal citizens of the Empire. He points out that persecution is a failure anyway because the Christians multiply every time the authorities try to down them by persecution.[2] Revealing the influence of his legal training, he argues that the state is persecuting the Church upon dubious legal grounds because the associations, doctrines and morals of the Christians are of a higher caliber than those of their pagan neighbors.

[1] Henry Bettenson, *Documents of the Christian Church* (New York: Oxford University Press, 1947), pp. 9-10.
[2] *Apology*, Ch. 50; see also Chs. 32 and 37 for his insistence on the loyalty of Christians to the state despite their rapid growth. It is in Ch. 50 that his famous saying, "The blood of Christians is seed," occurs.

It has often been asserted that the attempt to win the favor of the pagan world by this moral-rational approach led to a syncretism that made Christianity only another, although superior philosophy. The fact is that while the apologies are philosophical in form, they are basically Christian in content. This can be verified by even a casual reading of the actual works of these men. The apologies are valuable to us for the light they throw upon Christian thought in the middle of the second century. Whether they accomplished the purpose their authors intended for them, the ending of the persecution of the Christian Church, is open to question.

II. THE POLEMICISTS

While the Apologists of the second century sought to give a rational explanation and justification of Christianity to the authorities, the Polemicists of the late second and the early third centuries endeavored to meet the challenge of false teaching by heretics with an aggressive condemnation of these false teachings and teachers. One notes again the difference in the approach used by the Eastern and Western churchmen in meeting the problems of heresy and the theological formulation of Christian truth. The Eastern mind busied itself with speculative theology and gave most attention to metaphysical problems; the Western mind was more concerned with aberrations of the polity of the Church and endeavored to formulate a sound practical answer to the questions involved in this problem.

The Apologists, who had been newly converted from paganism, wrote concerning the external threat to the safety of the Church, namely, persecution; the Polemicists, who had had a background of Christian culture, were concerned with heresy, an internal threat to the peace and purity of the Church. The Polemicists, unlike the Apologists, who had laid much stress upon the Old Testament prophecies, emphasized the New Testament as a source for Christian doctrine. The Polemicists sought to condemn by argument the false teachings which they opposed; the Apologists sought to explain Christianity to their pagan neighbors and rulers. The Apostolic Fathers had merely sought to edify the Christian Church.

A. *Irenaeus, the Anti-Gnostic Polemicist.*

Irenaeus, who was born in Smyrna shortly before the middle of the second century, had been influenced by Polycarp's preaching while Polycarp was bishop of Smyrna. From there Irenaeus went to Gaul, where he became bishop about 180. He was a successful missionary bishop, but his greatest work was done in the field of polemical writing against Gnosticism.

His work, *Adversus Haereses,* an attempt to refute Gnostic doctrines by use of the Scriptures and the development of a body of related tradition, was written between 182 and 188. Book I, which is primarily historical, is our best source of knowledge concerning the teachings of the Gnostics. It was a philosophic polemic against Valentinian, the leader of the Egyptian school of Gnosticism. In Book II he insists upon the unity of God in opposition to the Gnostic idea of the demiurge as distinct from God. The more negative approach of the first two books gives way to a positive exposition of the Christian position in the last three books. Gnosticism is refuted by the Scriptures and relevant tradition in Book III; Marcion is condemned in Book IV by the citation of the words of Christ that are in opposition to Marcion's position; and the final book is a vindication of the doctrine of the Resurrection, which the Gnostics opposed because, according to their views, it associates the evil material body with spirit.

It should be noted that in Book III Irenaeus emphasizes the organic unity of the Church through the succession of leaders from Christ. He was conscious of the unity that could be achieved by a closely knit Church and felt that such a Church could easily resist the blandishments of heretical ideas and their teachers.

B. The Alexandrian School.

Soon after the middle of the second century a catechetical school to instruct converts from paganism to Christianity was opened in Alexandria. Its earliest leader was Pantaenus, an able convert from, according to some, Stoicism. Clement and then Origen succeeded him as leaders of that influential school of Christian thought. The men of the Alexandrian school were anxious to develop a system of theology that by the use of philosophy would give a systematic exposition of Christianity. They had been trained in the classical literature and philosophy of the past and thought that it could be used in the formulation of Christian theology.

Instead of emphasizing a grammatico-historical interpretation of the Bible, they developed an allegorical system of interpretation that has plagued Christianity since that time. This type of interpretation is based on the supposition that Scripture has more than one meaning. Using the analogy of man's body, soul and spirit, they argued that Scripture had a literal, historical meaning which corresponded to the human body; that it had a hidden moral meaning which corresponded to the soul; and that it had a deeper, underlying spiritual meaning which only the more spiritually advanced Christians could understand. This system of interpretation grew out of the technique employed by Philo, the Alexandrian Jew, who tried to link Judaism and Greek philosophy by finding hidden meanings in the language of the Old Testament that could be related to Greek philosophy. Instead of being concerned with the meaning of the writer of Scripture for those to whom he was writing and its application to present circumstances, the men of the Alexandrian school were ever seeking hidden meanings. This method of interpretation has done much harm to the cause of correct interpretation of the Scriptures and has resulted in absurd and, often, unscriptural theological ideas.

Clement, not to be confused with Clement of Rome, one of the Apostolic Fathers, was born about 150 in Athens of pagan parents. He traveled widely and studied philosophy under many masters before he began to study with Pantaenus. From around 190 he was associated with Pantaenus as leader of the school at Alexandria and from 200 to 202 he was head of the school until persecution forced him to leave.

Clement had the ideal of a Christian philosopher as his goal. Greek philosophy was to be related to Christianity so that one could see that Christianity was the great and final philosophy. He was widely read in Greek pagan literature and quoted something like five hundred authors in his works.

His *Protrepticus* or *Address* is an apologetic missionary document written about 190 to show the superiority of Christianity as the true philosophy so that pagans might be influenced to accept it. Another work, the *Paedagogus* or the *Tutor,* is a moral treatise of instructions for young Christians. Christ is presented as the true teacher who has given rules for the Christian life. The *Stromata* or *Miscellanies* reveals Clement's wide acquaintance with the pagan literature of his day. In Book I Christianity is presented as the true knowledge and the Christian as the true Gnostic. Clement believed that Greek philosophy borrowed what truth it had from the Old Testament, and that it was a preparation for the Gospel.[3] In Book II he shows that Christian morality is superior to pagan morality. Book III is an exposition concerning Christian marriage. In Books VII and VIII, which are the most interesting, he pictures the development of the religious life of the Christian.

There is no doubt that Clement favored Greek learning, but any careful study of his works leaves one with the impression that for him the Bible comes first in the life of the Christian. At the same time, since all truth belongs to God, what truth there is in Greek learning should be brought into the service of God. The danger in this position is that one may imperceptibly synthesize Christianity and Greek learning until Christianity is only a syncretism of Greek philosophy and Biblical teaching.

Clement's pupil and successor to leadership of the catechetical school was Origen (ca. 185-254). Origen took over the care of a family of six at the age of sixteen when his father Leonidas was martyred. According to one account, he wished to be martyred with his father, but his mother hid his clothes so that he had to stay home. He was so capable and learned, that in 203, at the age of eighteen, he was chosen to be Clement's successor as leader of the school, a position that he held until 232. A wealthy man named Ambrose whom he had converted from Gnosticism became Origen's friend and arranged for the publication of his many works. According to one estimate, Origen was the author of six thousand scrolls. In spite of his exalted position and wealthy friend, Origen lived a simple ascetic life that involved sleeping on bare boards.[4]

Origen may be compared with Augustine in the scope of his work. The earliest beginnings of textual criticism of the Scriptures can be traced to the *Hexapla* in which several Hebrew and Greek versions of the Scriptures are arranged in parallel columns.[5] In this work Origen sought to establish a text that Christians could be assured was a correct representation of the original. This interest in the text led him to do more exegetical work than anyone did before the Reformation. Another work, *Against Celsus*, is an answer to the charges that the Platonist Celsus had made against the Christians. Origen deals with Celsus' charges concerning the irrationality of Christians and

[3] Clement, *Stromata* I:v, also in Bettenson, *op. cit.*, p. 10. See Eusebius, *Church History*, VI:13 for a description of this work.
[4] Eusebius, *Church History*, VI, 1-8.
[5] Eusebius, *op. cit.*, VI, 16.

the lack of apparent historical foundations for Christianity by emphasizing the change in conduct that Christianity produces in contrast with paganism; the open-minded investigations of truth by Christians; and the purity and influence both of Christ, the leader of the Christians, and His followers.

Perhaps Origen's greatest contribution to Christian literature is his work entitled *De Principiis* (230), which has come down to us only in a Latin version by Rufinus. This work is the first Christian treatise of systematic theology. In the fourth book of this work, Origen develops his allegorical system of interpretation at great length. Unfortunately, he thought of Christ as "eternally generated" by the Father but subordinate to Him. He also held the ideas of the pre-existence of the soul and the final restoration of all spirits.

C. The Carthaginian School.

The Western or Latin mind was more interested in practical matters of church organization, government and doctrines relating to the Church than in the speculative type of theology that attracted such a scholar as Origen, for example. This difference of viewpoint can be seen by contrasting the work of Origen with that of Tertullian and Cyprian of North Africa.

Tertullian wrote widely and well, though often intolerantly, on many different subjects. His *Apologeticus*, in which he defends the Christian against false charges and persecution, has already been discussed (see p. 117). He also wrote on practical as well as apologetic matters. In special pamphlets he urged simplicity of dress and ornament for women and urged Christians to separate themselves from pagan amusements, immorality and idolatry. These practical works seem to have been an outcome of his Montanist puritanism.

It is his work as a theologian, however, that is most outstanding. He was the founder of Latin theology and was the first to state the theological doctrine of the Trinity and to make use of that term to describe that doctrine. He did this in *Adversus Praxean*, written about 215. He seems to emphasize the distinction that must be made between the persons of the Father and the Son. In *De Anima*, regarding the soul, he emphasized the traducian doctrine of the transmission of the soul from the parents to the child in the reproductive process. He laid great emphasis upon the rite of baptism in his *De Baptismate* and believed that post-baptismal sins were mortal sins. It is, however, his use of the words "trinity" and "substance" for the essence of the Godhead and his developments of that doctrine in *Against Praxeas* (Chs. 2-3) that stands out as his greatest contribution to Christian theology.

Cyprian was born of well-to-do pagan parents shortly after 200 in the same city as Tertullian and was given a good education in rhetoric and the law. He became a successful rhetoric teacher but did not find the satisfaction his soul craved until he became a Christian about 246. Less than five years after his conversion he became the bishop of Carthage, a position that he held for nine years until his martyrdom about 258. He was a great organizer and administrator.

Though he looked up to Tertullian as his master, according to Jerome, he was calm where Tertullian was passionate. His most important work was the *De Unitate Catholicae Ecclesiae,* which was directed against the schismatic followers of Novatian, who seemed bent upon the destruction of the unity of the Church. Cyprian makes a clear distinction between bishop and elder and emphasizes the bishop as the center of unity in the Church and a guarantee against schism. While he does not assert the supremacy of Peter's episcopal see in Rome, he does assert the primacy of Peter in tracing the line of apostolic succession down through the early history of the Church. If one can say that Tertullian helped to formulate the doctrine of the Trinity and gave a name to that doctrine, one can also say that Cyprian gave the earliest formulation of the doctrines of apostolic succession and the primacy of the Roman bishop in the Church.

BIBLIOGRAPHY

The student will find most of the bibliography cited at the end of Chapter V useful for this era also.

Handbook of the Early Christian Fathers (London: Williams & Norgate, 1920) by Ernest Leigh-Bennet contains good biographical material and discussions of the works and theological ideas of the leading Church Fathers in this period.

Volume I of Frederick W. Farrar's work entitled *Lives of the Fathers* (New York: The Macmillan Co., 2 vols., 1889) is a useful work on the lives and work of the leading Fathers of this period.

Chapter X

THE CHURCH CLOSES RANKS

During the period between 100 and 313 the Church was forced to give consideration to how it could best meet the external persecution from the Roman state and the internal problem of heretical teaching and consequent schism. It sought to close its ranks by the development of a canon of the New Testament, which gave it an authoritative *book* for faith and practice; by the creation of a creed, which gave it an authoritative statement of *belief;* and by obedience to the monarchal bishops, among whom the Roman bishop took a place of leadership. The last gave it a *bond* of unity.

I. THE MONARCHAL BISHOP

Practical and theoretical necessities led to the exaltation of one bishop's position in each church until people came to think of him and to acknowledge him as superior to the other elders with whom his office had been associated in New Testament times. The need of leadership in meeting the problems of persecution and heresy was a practical need that dictated an expansion of the bishop's power. The development of the doctrine of apostolic succession and the increasing exaltation of the Lord's Supper were important factors in his rise to power. It was but a short step to the recognition that the monarchal bishops of some churches were more important than others. The exaltation of the monarchal bishop by the middle of the second century soon led to recognition of the special honor due to the monarchal bishop of the church in Rome.

Several considerations brought extra prestige to the bishop of Rome. The first and most important argument that had been advanced since early in the history of the Church was the argument that Christ gave to Peter, presumably the first bishop of Rome, a position of supremacy among the apostles by His supposed designation of Peter as the rock upon which He would build His Church (Matthew 16:18). According to Matthew 16:19, Christ also gave Peter the keys to the kingdom and later specially commissioned him to feed His sheep (John 21:15-19).

It should be borne in mind that in the account in Matthew, Christ uses two words for rock, and it is by no means clear that the rock upon which He said He would build His Church is Peter the rock. Christ called Peter a *petros* or stone, but he speaks of the rock upon which He will build His Church as *petra,* a living rock. The word "rock" that is applied to Peter is masculine in gender, but the "rock" upon which Christ said He would build His Church is feminine in gender. There is good reason to believe that the correct interpretation is that Christ was by the word "rock" referring to Peter's confession of Him as "the Christ, the Son of the living God."

One cannot help but remember, too, that Christ told Peter he would fail Him in the crisis in the garden, that Satan would defeat Him (Luke 22:31-32), and that Christ had to urge upon him the care of His flock after the resurrection and His forgiveness of Peter for betraying Him. One also notices that powers similar to those mentioned in connection with Peter in Matthew 16:19 were also conferred upon the other apostles equally with Peter (John 20:19-23). Peter himself in his first letter makes it abundantly clear that not he but Christ was the foundation of the Church (I Peter 2:6-8). Paul had no conception of Peter's superior position, for he did not hesitate to rebuke him when Peter temporized and cooperated with the Judaizers in Galatia.

In spite of these facts, the Roman Church has insisted from earliest times that Christ gave to Peter a special rank as the first bishop of Rome and the leader of the apostles. Cyprian did the most to advance this position by his assertion of the superiority of the Roman see to the other ecclesiastical seats of authority.[1]

Extra prestige would accrue to the Roman bishop because Rome was linked with many apostolic traditions. Both Peter and Paul had suffered martyrdom in Rome for their faith. Because both were outstanding leaders of the Early Church, it was not strange that the church and bishop of the church in Rome would have added prestige. The church at Rome had been the center of the earliest persecution by the Roman state under Nero in 64. The

[1] Henry Bettenson, *Documents of the Christian Church* (New York: Oxford University Press, 1947), pp. 101-104.

longest and possibly the most important of Paul's letters had been addressed to this church. It was one of the largest and wealthiest of the Christian churches by 100. The historical prestige of Rome as the capital of the Empire led to a natural exaltation of the position of the church in the capital city. It had a reputation for unswerving orthodoxy in facing heresy and schism. Had not Clement, one of its early leaders, written to the church in Corinth to urge upon that church a unity which centered in the person of the bishop? Many Western Church Fathers, such as Clement, Ignatius, Irenaeus and Cyprian, had urged the importance of the position of bishop and, in the case of Cyprian, that of the bishop of Rome. Though all bishops were equal, special honor should be paid to the Roman bishop in charge of the see of St. Peter. Though all bishops were in the line of apostolic succession of bishops from Christ Himself, Rome deserved special honor, it was believed, because its bishop was in the line of succession from Peter.

It must be remembered that some of the five important bishops of the Church lost their seat of authority for various reasons. After 135, with the destruction of Jerusalem by the Romans, the bishop of Jerusalem ceased to count as a rival to the bishop of Rome. The bishop of Ephesus lost prestige as Asia was torn by the Montanist schism in the second century and as the bishop of Rome near the end of the century excommunicated the bishop of Ephesus and the churches of Asia.

By the end of the period three things concerning the Old Catholic Church became clear-cut realities. The doctrine of apostolic succession, which linked each bishop in an unbroken line with Christ through the apostles, was accepted. In each church one bishop stood out among his fellow elders as a monarchal bishop. The Roman bishop came to be recognized as the first among equals because of the importance of the weight of tradition associated with his see. This primacy was later to be developed into supremacy of the Roman bishop as pope of the Church.

II. THE DEVELOPMENT OF THE RULE OF FAITH

The role of the bishop as a bond of unity in the Church was reinforced by the development of a creed. A creed is a statement of faith for public use; it contains articles needful for salvation and the theological well-being of the Church. Creeds have been used to test orthodoxy, to recognize fellow believers and to serve as a convenient summary of the essential doctrines of faith. They presuppose a living faith of which they are the intellectual expression. Denominational creeds appeared during the Reformation period. Conciliar or universal creeds made by representatives of the whole Church emerged during the period of theological controversy between 313 and 451. The earliest type of creed was the baptismal creed of which the Apostles' Creed may serve as an example.[2] It must always be remembered that creeds are relative and limited expressions of the divine and absolute rule of faith and practice within the Scriptures.

The Apostles' Creed is the oldest summary of the essential doctrines of Scripture that we have. Statements in the New Testament that savor of a creed are found in Romans 10:9-10; I Corinthians 15:4; I Timothy 3:16. Some think the Apostles' Creed grew out of the brief statement of Peter concerning Christ in Matthew 16:16 and that it was used as a baptismal formula from very early times. The oldest form, similar to the one used by Rufinus about 400, appeared in Rome about 340. This creed, which is definitely Trinitarian, gives attention to the person and work of each of the three Persons of the Trinity. It emphasizes the universal nature of the corporate Church and, after linking salvation with Christ, has an explicit eschatology centering in the resurrection of the believer and his goal of eternal life. Many churches still find the Apostles' Creed useful as a convenient summary of the main points of the Christian faith.

III. THE NEW TESTAMENT CANON

To the authoritative bond in the bishop and to the authoritative belief of the creed, the canon, a listing of the volumes belonging to an authoritative book, came as a reinforcement. People often err by thinking of the canon as a list of authoritative books coming directly from heaven or by thinking that the canon was set by church councils. Such was not the case, for the various church councils that pronounced upon the subject of the canon of the New Testament were merely stating publicly, as we shall see later, what had been widely accepted by the consciousness of the Church for sometime. The development of the canon was a slow process substantially completed by 175 except for a few books whose authorship was disputed.

Certain practical reasons made it essential that the Church

---

[2] Philip Schaff, *The Creeds of Christendom* (New York: Charles Scribner's Sons, 3 vols., 6th ed., 1890) Vol. I, Ch. 1. This is an excellent introduction to the whole topic of creeds of the Church.

develop the list of books that should comprise the New Testament. Heretics, such as Marcion, were setting up their own canon of Scripture and were leading people astray. In persecution men were not willing to risk their lives for a book unless they were sure it was an integral part of the canon of Scripture. Because the apostles were slowly passing from the scene, there was need for some records that could be recognized as authoritative.

The major test of the right of a book to be in the canon was whether it had the marks of apostolicity. Was it written by an apostle or one who was closely associated with the apostles, such as Mark, the writer of the Gospel of Mark, with the aid of the Apostle Peter? The capacity of the book to edify when read publicly and its agreement with the rule of faith served as tests also. In the final analysis, it was the historical verification of apostolic authorship or influence and the universal consciousness of the Church, guided by the Holy Spirit, that resulted in the final decision concerning what books should be considered canonical and worthy of inclusion in what we know as the New Testament.

Apparently the Epistles of Paul were first collected by leaders in the church of Ephesus. This collection was followed by the collection of the Gospels sometime after the beginning of the second century. By A.D. 180 at least twenty of the present books of the New Testament were accepted on the same level as the books of the Old Testament. James, II Peter, II and III John, Jude, Hebrews and Revelation were among the books whose place in the canon was still under consideration.[3] The delay in placing these was caused primarily by an uncertainty concerning questions of authorship. Athanasius, however, in his Easter letter of 367 to the churches under his jurisdiction as the bishop of Alexandria listed the same twenty-seven books that we now have in the New Testament as canonical. Later councils, such as that at Chalcedon in 451, merely approved and gave uniform expression to what was already an accomplished fact generally accepted by the Church for a long period of time. The slowness with which the Church accepted Hebrews and Revelation as canonical is indicative of the care and devotion with which it dealt with this question.

[3] Eusebius, *Church History,* III, 25.

MEDIEVAL FRENCH MONASTERY

POPE INNOCENT III

POPE GREGORY VII

THOMAS AQUINAS

IV. Liturgy

Emphasis upon the monarchal bishop who, it was believed, derived his authority by apostolic succession, led many to think of him as a center of unity, the depository of truth and the dispenser of the means of the grace of God through the sacraments. Many converts from the mystery religions may also have aided in the development of the concept of the separation of the clergy and laity as they emphasized the holiness of the bishop's position. The Lord's Supper and Baptism came to be rites that could only be performed adequately by an accredited minister. As the idea of the Communion as a sacrifice to God developed, it enhanced the superior sanctity of the bishop as compared with the rank and file of the ordinary church members.

Baptism as an act of initiation into the Christian Church was usually performed at Easter or Pentecost. At first apparently faith in Christ and the desire for baptism were the only requirements, but by the end of the second century a probationary period as a catechumen was added to test the reality of the experience of the convert. During this period of probation the catechumen attended services in the narthex of the church building and was not allowed to worship in the nave. Baptism was normally by immersion; on occasion affusion or pouring was practiced. Infant baptism and clinical baptism, the baptism of the sick, developed in this period. The Church increasingly hedged the two sacraments of the Lord's Supper and Baptism around with requirements and rites which a priest alone could perform.

The emergence of a cycle of feasts in the church year may be noted in this era. Easter, originating in the application of the Jewish Passover to the resurrection of Christ, seems to have been the earliest of the festivals. Not until about 350 was Christmas adopted as a Christian festival and purged of its pagan elements. Lent, a forty-day period of penitence and restraint upon bodily appetites preceding Easter, had been accepted as a part of the churches' cycle of worship before the adoption of Christmas.

The Christians met during times of persecution before 313 in the catacombs of Rome and there often made themselves places for interment of their dead as well as places of worship. These places were made up of miles of underground passages, anywhere from 20 to 50 feet below the surface of the ground.

Evidences of Christian art, such as symbols of the fish, dove and figures associated with Christianity, have been found in some of the graves.[4] Near the end of the period the Christians began to build churches patterned after the Roman basilica. The basilica-church was an oblong building with a porch or narthex at the west end where the catechumens worshiped, a semicircular apse at the east end where the altar and bishop's seat was placed, and a long central nave with aisles at either side. Usually these churches were fairly simple during this period, but they became increasingly ornate after 313 as the Church found itself in favor with the state.

Pagans still looked upon worshipers in the churches or catacombs as anti-social because the Christians, urged by writers, such as Tertullian, avoided the worldly amusements of their day and refused to become involved in political life. Apart from this, the Christians were willing to play their part in society when they could do so without denying their Lord. Their love for one another, revealed in a pure and happy family life and philanthropic activity for the needy, made an impression upon their pagan neighbors. The emperors of the Roman state, finding that they could not stamp out Christianity, finally realized that they had to come to terms with it. Despite external problems, created by persecution by the state, and the internal threat of dissension and schism because of heresy, the Church came through all its difficulties with flying colors. Its closer association with the Roman state during the period between 313 and 590 was to bring into it many flaws that had not been problems during the periods of persecution.

BIBLIOGRAPHY

The Creeds of Christendom by Philip Schaff is still the best work to consult for the historical background and the text of the various creeds.

The Bible in the Church (London: The Macmillan Co., 1913) by Brooke F. Westcott has an excellent chronological and topical discussion of the growth of the canon.

Alexander Souter in *The Text and Canon of the New Testament* (New York: Charles Scribner's Sons, 1923) has a briefer but excellent historical treatment that includes quotations from many of the relevant documents.

Oscar Hardman in *A History of Christian Worship* (London: Hodder & Stoughton, Ltd., 1937) has helpful chapters on the liturgy and worship of each important era of church history.

[4] Jack Finegan, *Light From the Ancient Past* (Princeton: Princeton University Press, 1946) pp. 353-398.

The Supremacy of the Old Catholic Imperial Church, 313–590

Chapter XI

THE CHURCH FACES THE EMPIRE AND
THE BARBARIANS

Between 375 and 1066, during the period of the so-called
Dark Ages, in which the mass movement of the barbarian Teutonic tribes took place in Western Europe, the Church faced
a twofold problem. The decline of the Roman Empire placed
before her the task of conserving the Helleno-Hebraic culture,
which was threatened with destruction. The monasteries, centers
where manuscripts were carefully preserved and copied, were
a great aid in her fulfillment of this function. Confronting her
also was the task of giving the Gospel to the peoples making
up the masses of wandering barbarians. This she did, and succeeded in the mighty task of winning the Teutonic tribes to the
Christian faith. But in the process of conserving culture and
converting the barbarians, the Church lost much of her spiritual
force because of the overelaboration of needed organization to
meet these herculean tasks. Secularization and the voice of the
state in affairs of the Church were a part of the price she had
to pay for her success.

I. THE CHURCH AND THE STATE

If one is to understand relationships between the Church and
state after the granting of freedom of religion by Constantine,
it is necessary to give some attention to the political problems
that the Emperor faced at this time. The anarchy of the century
of revolution, which wrecked the Roman Republic between 133
and 31 B.C., had been ended by the powerful principate that
Augustus created after he destroyed Antony's army. But the
principate, in which the emperor as princeps shared authority
with the senate, proved to be too weak to meet the challenge
of internal decay and barbarians on the borders of the Empire,
and the prosperity and peace of the early era of the principate
gave way to another century of revolution between 192 and

284. Diocletian in 285 reorganized the Empire along more autocratic lines, copied from oriental despotisms, in an attempt to create security for Greco-Roman culture. Because Christianity seemed to threaten this culture, he made an unsuccessful attempt to wipe it out between 303 and 305. His more astute successor, Constantine, realized that if the state could not wipe out Christianity by force, it might make use of the Church as an ally to save classical culture.[1] The process by which the Church and state came to terms began with Constantine's winning complete control in the state. Although he officially shared authority with Coemperor Licinius between 311 and 324, he made most of the real decisions in matters of state.

Constantine was the illegitimate son of the Roman military leader Constantius and a beautiful Christian Oriental freedwoman, named Helena. When his enemies seemed about to overwhelm him in 312, he had a vision of a cross in the sky with the words "in this sign conquer" in Latin. Taking it as a favorable omen, he went on to defeat his enemies at the battle of the Milvian bridge over the Tiber River. Though the vision may have occurred, it is likely that Constantine's favoritism to the Church was a matter of expediency. The Church might serve as a new center of unity and save classical culture and the Empire. The fact that he delayed baptism till shortly before his death and kept the position of *Pontifex Maximus*, chief priest of the pagan state religion, would seem to support this view. Moreover, his execution of the young men who might have had a claim to his throne was not in keeping with the conduct of a sincere Christian. Perhaps there was a mixture of superstition and expediency in his policy.

Whether or not this interpretation of his motives be correct, Constantine embarked on a policy of favoring the Christian Church. In 313 he and Licinius granted it freedom of worship by the Edict of Milan. During the next few years Constantine issued edicts that brought about the restoration of confiscated property to the Church, the subsidization of the Church by the state, the exemption of the clergy from public service, a ban on soothsaying and the setting apart of the "Day of the Sun" (Sunday) as a day of rest and worship.[2] He even assumed a

[1] This viewpoint is ably developed with an abundance of illustrative material by Charles N. Cochrane in his excellent book, *Christianity and Classical Culture* (New York: Oxford University Press, 1944).

[2] Henry Bettenson, *Documents of the Christian Church* (New York: Oxford University Press, 1947), pp. 23-27.

position of theological leadership at the Council of Nicaea in 325 when he proposed to arbitrate the Arian controversy. Even though the number of Christians could not have been above one-tenth of the population of the Empire at this time, they exercised an influence in the state far in excess of their numbers.

The sons of Constantine continued his policy of favoring the Church and even went beyond it to such an extent that they forced paganism onto the defensive by such procedures as edicts banning pagan sacrifices and attendance at pagan temples. Just when it looked as if Christianity would shortly become the state religion, it received a set back by the accession of Julian the Apostate to the imperial throne. Julian had been forced to accept Christianity outwardly, but the death of his relatives at the hands of the Christian ruler and his study of philosophy at Athens inclined him to become a follower of Neoplatonism. He took away from the Christian Church her privileges and restored full freedom of worship. Every facility was given to aid the spread of pagan philosophy and religion. Fortunately for the Church, his reign was short, and the setback to the development of the Church only temporary.[3]

Later rulers continued the process of granting privileges to the Church until Christianity finally became the state religion. The Emperor Gratian renounced the title of *Pontifex Maximus*. Theodosius I in 380 issued an edict that made Christianity the exclusive religion of the state. Any who would dare to hold to any other form of worship would suffer punishment from the state.[4] By 395 Christianity was finally recognized as the official and only religion of the Roman state. Justinian in 529 struck paganism a further blow by ordering the closing of the school of philosophy at Athens.

Looking back at the steps by which Christianity, a despised sect with small numbers, became the official religion of the mighty Roman Empire, one might well believe, with the advantage of the perspective of time, that this victorious march was detrimental to the Church. It is true that Christianity had raised the moral tone of society so that the dignity of women was given more recognition in society, gladiatorial shows were eliminated, slaves were given milder treatment, Roman legislation became more just, and the spread of missionary work was speeded up; but the Church also found that, while there were

[3] *Ibid.*, pp. 28-30.
[4] *Ibid.*, pp. 31-32.

BARBARIAN INVASIONS
AND GERMANIC STATES IN A.D. 526

advantages to close association with the state, there were also marked disadvantages. The government in return for position, protection and aid demanded the right to interfere in spiritual and theological matters. Constantine at Nicaea in 325 arrogated to himself the right to arbitrate the dispute in the Church, even though he was only the temporal ruler of the Empire. The long vexatious problem of the struggle between the Church and state had its beginnings in this era. Unfortunately, the Church, when it gained the power, too often became as arrogant a persecutor of paganism as the pagan religious authorities had ever been of the Christians. It would appear on balance that the rapprochement between Church and state brought more drawbacks than blessings to the Christian Church.

II. The Church and the Barbarians

It was well that the Church had been able to come to terms with the Empire in the early part of the fourth century because the latter part of the century brought a new problem to the fore, the problem of how to win to Christianity the masses of people who started the migrations in Europe that were to continue until the eleventh century. There were mass migrations of Teutonic and Mongol peoples into, in and from Europe between 375 and 1066.

A. *The Spread of the Barbarians.*

Barbarian Goths first appeared on the Danube frontier of the Empire in the latter part of the fourth century, and, pressed by Mongol tribes behind them, they asked permission of the Roman authorities to move into the Empire. The battle of Adrianople between them and the Romans in 378 resulted in the death of the Emperor Valens and the influx of the Visigoths (West Goths) into the Eastern section of the Empire. Nearly a quarter of a million crossed the river boundary after that battle and started their migrations within the Empire. After sacking Rome in 410, they finally founded a kingdom about 426 in Spain. They were followed by the Vandals from east of the Rhine who finally settled in North Africa. The Ostrogoths, coming later, took over the leadership of the bankrupt Roman Empire for a time. The Teutonic Lombards, Burgundians and Franks crossed the Rhine and settled during the fifth century in the area of what is now modern France. In the same century the Church in the West had also to face the temporary, yet terrible, threat created by the invasion of Europe by the Mongol horde of Huns under the leadership of Attila. The Huns were only driven back by the victory at Chalons in 451. Just as the Church seemed to be winning many of the Teutonic peoples to Christianity, new threats from Mohammedanism and the Lombards became a reality in the seventh century.

The greatness of the civilization that Western Europe was to develop was not so much due to the irruption of fresh, vigorous barbarians into the Empire as it was to the successful conversion of these barbarians to Christianity by the Church.

B. *The Evangelization of the Barbarians.*

Missionary work among the Goths began before the Visigoths poured over the Danube into the Roman Empire. Ulfilas (ca. 311–381), an Arian Christian, felt the call to missionary work among these people. Consecrated bishop of the Gothic Christians, he went to live among them. His work was so successful that, when the Goths came into the Roman Empire, many of them came as Christians. As the first outstanding missionary translator he reduced the language of the Goths to writing, after creating an alphabet, and gave them the Scriptures in their own tongue. Because the Goths were so warlike, he felt justified in not translating the books of Kings and Samuel into their language. The Goths were thus won to the Arian form of Christianity which Ulfilas professed. This fact was later to give the Church in the West the difficult task not only of converting many tribes from paganism but also of converting the Visigoths of Spain from Arianism to orthodox Christianity.

The Teutonic invaders from across the Rhine presented a more immediate and pressing problem for the Western Church. Martin of Tours (311–396), now the patron saint of France, felt called to preach to the Burgundians who had settled in Southern Gaul. Adopting rather rough and ready pioneering tactics in carrying the Gospel to these people, he organized his soldier monks into bands and led them in the destruction of the groves where the people worshiped their pagan gods. His work did not have the impact upon subsequent history which that of Augustine had because the Burgundians were brought under the sway of their Frankish cousins who also settled in Gaul.

Gregory of Tours in his interesting *History of the Franks* describes the settlement, history and conversion of the Franks. Near the end of the fifth century, Clovis, king of the Franks, married Clotilda, a Christian princess of Burgundy. Clotilda's influence combined with what Clovis believed was divine aid in battle led to his conversion in 496.[5] When he became a Christian, the mass of his people also accepted Christianity.

Whether all conversions were genuine or not, the formal acceptance of Christianity by Clovis was to have far-reaching effects upon the future history of the Church. All of the Franks, who dominated Gaul, the area of modern France, were now within the Christian Church. Gaul became a base from which missionaries could go into Arian Spain to win the Arian Goths, who had settled there, back to Christianity of the orthodox persuasion. Most important of all, the Frankish monarchy became the ardent supporter of the papacy during the early Middle Ages. Frankish kings crossed the Alps many times to save the Roman bishop from his enemies in Italy.

The British Isles were also won for Christianity in this period. We do not have much information about the introduction of Christianity to Celtic Britain, but it is more than likely that it was planted there by Roman soldiers and merchants. We do know that Celtic bishops represented the British church at the Council of Arles in 314. Pelagius, Augustine's opponent, also came from the British church and began to teach the heresy known by his name on the continent about 429. This primitive Celtic church in Britain did not recognize either the jurisdiction or the primacy of the Roman bishop. It also followed the practice of the Eastern Church in determining the date of Easter. There were other differences of a minor character. This Celtic church was left defenseless when the Roman armies were withdrawn from Britain at the beginning of the fifth century to meet the threat of the barbarians on the eastern frontier of the Empire. The Celtic peoples were exterminated or driven into the western and northern hills by the pagan Angles, Saxons and Jutes.

Patrick (ca. 389–493), the patron saint of Ireland, was taken from Britain to Ireland by pirates at the age of sixteen. He lived there, tending flocks, for six years. Upon his return to his homeland he felt called to labor among the people of Ireland as a missionary. From 432 to 461 he worked among the Celts of Ireland and, despite the efforts of the priests of the Druid religion, managed to make the island a strong center of Celtic Christianity. During the time of the Dark Ages in Europe, Ire-

[5] Frederic A. Ogg, *A Source Book of Medieval History* (New York: American Book Company, 1907), pp. 53-54.

land was a center of culture from which missionaries and scholars were sent to work upon the Continent. It was from Ireland that Columba set forth to win the Scots to Christianity.

Columba (521–597) was the apostle of Scotland as Patrick had been the apostle of Ireland. In 563, on the island of Iona, he founded a monastery that became a center for the evangelization of Scotland. It was from here that Aidan in the next century set out to carry the Gospel to the Teutonic invaders of Northumbria. The Celtic church in Ireland and Scotland was above all a missionary church.

At the end of the period under discussion Celtic Christianity had been victorious in Scotland and Ireland. It had been all but exterminated in England. The Celtic Christians and the Roman Christians were to become rivals for the allegiance of the Anglo-Saxons, whom both groups helped to win to Christianity.

By 590 the Church had successfully met the challenge of the Roman state. It had also done its part in converting the Teutonic invaders of the Empire to Christianity and in passing on to them the elements of Greco-Roman culture. But in the process, masses of pagans had been won to the Christian religion too quickly for the Church to train them and to guide them through a period of probation. Many of them brought old patterns of life and customs with them into the Church. Saint worship was substituted for the old hero worship. Many ritualistic practices that savored of paganism found an open door into the Church. The Church in attempting to meet the need of the barbarians was itself partially paganized.

BIBLIOGRAPHY

The Conversion of Europe (London: Longmans, Green & Co., 1917) by Charles G. Robinson gives interesting and scholarly accounts of the work of the men cited in this chapter.

Chapter XII

CREEDAL DEVELOPMENT IN THE CONCILIAR ERA

There have been two great eras of theological controversy in the history of the Church. The great creeds of Protestantism were hammered out in the period of theological dispute at the time of the Reformation. The earlier period of theological controversy occurred between 325 and 451, when universal or ecumenical councils of leaders of the Church were held to resolve conflict. These councils brought about such great universal formulations of the Christian Church as the Nicene and Athanasian creeds. It was the era when the main dogmas of the Christian Church were developed. The unfavorable connotation conveyed by the world "dogma" in a day of doctrinal laxity, such as the present, should not obscure the value to the Church of dogma. The word "dogma" came through the Latin from the Greek word *dogma,* which was derived from the verb *dokeo.* This word meant to think. The dogmas or doctrines formulated in this period were the result of intense thought and searching of the soul in order to interpret correctly the meaning of the Scriptures on the disputed points and to avoid the erroneous opinions (*doxai*) of the philosophers.

The era is also an excellent illustration of how intense zeal for a doctrine may unwittingly lead an individual or church into error unless there is a balanced study of the Bible. Just as Sabellius was led to a denial of the essential Trinity by his attempt to safeguard the unity of the Godhead, so Arius became involved in an anti-Scriptural approach to the relation of Christ to the Father in his attempt to escape what he thought was the danger of polytheism.

One might wonder why controversy over theological questions came so late in the history of the ancient Church, but, in the era of persecution, allegiance to Christ and the Scriptures took precedence over the meaning of particular doctrines. The

[141]

threat from the state forced the Church to internal unity in order to present a united front. Then, too, Constantine's attempt to unify the Empire in order to save classical civilization meant that the Church must have a unified body of dogma if it were to be the cement to hold the body politic together. One Empire must have one dogma.

The method adopted by the Church to resolve the vital differences of opinion concerning the meaning of the Scriptures was the ecumenical or universal council, usually called and presided over by the Roman emperor. There were seven councils that were representative of the whole Christian Church.[1] Great Church leaders from all part of the Empire represented their respective localities and gave their assistance in the working out of solutions to the theological problems that dominated the thinking of Christians in this era.

I. Theology — the Relationships of the Persons in the Trinity

A. *The Relationship of the Son to the Father.*

The problem of the relationship between God the Father and His Son Jesus Christ became an acute problem in the Church soon after the cessation of persecution. In Western Europe, Tertullian, for example, insisted upon the unity of essence in three personalities as the correct interpretation of the Trinity. Hence the dispute centered in the Eastern section of the Empire. It must be remembered that the Church has always had to fight Unitarian conceptions of Christ. Modern Unitarianism has had its forerunners in Arianism and sixteenth century Socinianism.

In 318 or 319, Alexander, the bishop of Alexandria, discussed with his presbyters "The Unity of the Trinity." One of the presbyters, Arius, an ascetic scholar and popular preacher, attacked the sermon because he believed that it failed to uphold a distinction among the persons in the Godhead. In his desire to avoid a polytheistic conception of God, Arius took a position that did injustice to the true deity of Christ.

---

[1] Nicaea (325) — to settle the Arian dispute.
Constantinople (381) — to assert the personality of the Holy Spirit and the humanity of Christ.
Ephesus (431) — to emphasize the unity of Christ's personality.
Chalcedon (451) — to state the relationship between the two natures of Christ.
Constantinople (553) — to deal with the Monophysite dispute.
Constantinople (680) — to condemn the Monothelites.
Nicaea (787) — to deal with problems raised by the image controversy.
Manual of Councils of the Holy Catholic Church (Edinburgh: John Grant, 2 vols., 1909) by Edward G. Landon contains descriptions of the problems, personnel and main discussions of the councils. See Map on page 190 for the cities named.

The issue was soteriological in nature. Could Christ save man if He were a demi-god, less than true God, and of a similar or different essence from the Father as Eusebius and Arius respectively asserted? Just what was His relationship to the Father? The controversy became so bitter that Alexander had Arius condemned by a synod. Arius then fled to the friendly palace of Eusebius, the bishop of Nicomedia, who had been his schoolmate. Since the dispute centered in Asia Minor, it threatened the unity of the Empire as well as that of the Church. Constantine tried to settle the dispute by letters to the bishop of Alexandria and Arius, but the dispute had gone beyond the power even of a letter from the Emperor. Constantine then called a council of the bishops of the Church to work out a solution to the dispute. This council met at Nicaea from June 19 to August 25, 325. Three hundred and eighteen leaders were present, but less than ten were from the Western section of the Empire. The Emperor presided over the council and paid its expenses. For the first time the Church found itself dominated by the political leadership of the head of the state. The perennial problem of the relationship between the Church and state emerged clearly here, but the bishops were too busy dealing with theological heresy to think of that particular problem.

Three views were put forth at the council. Arius, who was backed by Eusebius of Nicomedia (to be distinguished from Eusebius of Caesarea) and a minority of those present, insisted that Christ had not existed from all eternity but had a beginning by the creative act of God prior to time. He believed that Christ was of a *different* (*heteros*) essence or substance than the Father. Because of the virtue of His life and His obedience to God's will, Christ was to be considered divine. But Arius believed that Christ was a being, created out of nothing, subordinate to the Father and of a different essence from the Father. He was not coequal, coeternal or consubstantial with the Father. To Arius He was divine but not deity.[2]

Athanasius became the chief exponent of what became the orthodox view. His wealthy parents had provided for his theological education in the famous catechetical school of Alexandria.

[2] Beresford J. Kidd, *Documents Illustrative of the History of the Church* (London: Society for Promoting Christian Knowledge, 3 vols., 1920-1941), Vol. II, pp. 6-10; Joseph Ayer, Jr., *A Source Book for Ancient Church History* (New York: Charles Scribner's Sons, 1913), pp. 297-356. The pages in Ayer contain most of the documents of importance for an understanding of the Arian heresy. See also Socrates, *Ecclesiastical History*, I:v-ix; Eusebius, *Life of Constantine*, I: lxi-lxxiii.

His work *De Incarnatione* presented his idea of the doctrine of Christ. At the council this young man, slightly over thirty, insisted that Christ had existed from all eternity with the Father and was of the same essence (*homoousios*) as the Father, although He was a distinct personality. He insisted upon these things because he believed that, if Christ were less than He had stated Him to be, He could not be the Saviour of men. The question of man's eternal salvation was involved in the relationship of the Father and the Son according to Athanasius. He held that Christ was coequal, coeternal and consubstantial with the Father, and for these views he suffered exile five times before his death.

The largest party was led by the gentle scholar and church historian, Eusebius of Caesarea, whose dislike of controversy led him to propose a view that he hoped would be an acceptable compromise. He proposed a moderate view which would combine the best ideas of Arius and Athanasius. Over two hundred of those present followed his views at first. He taught that Christ was not created out of nothing as Arius had insisted, but that He was begotten of the Father before time in eternity. Christ was of a like (*homoi*) or similar essence to the Father. His creed became the basis of the creed that was finally drawn at Nicaea, but that one differed from his in its insistence upon the unity of essence or substance of the Father and the Son.[3]

Orthodoxy gained a temporary victory at Nicaea by the assertion of the eternity of Christ and the identity of His substance with that of the Father. However, the creed formulated here must not be confused with the Nicene Creed used by the Church today, although that creed grew out of the formulation at Nicaea. The creed of 325 stops with the phrase "And in the Holy Spirit" and is followed by a section condemning Arius' views.[4]

Between 325 and 361 under Constantine and his sons orthodoxy had to face a reaction that led to its defeat and the temporary victory of Arianism. A second reaction against orthodoxy, with orthodoxy's final victory in 381, came between 361 and 381. Theodosius defined as the faith of true Christians the views formulated by the orthodox at Nicaea, but the years between 325 and 381 were marked by bitterness and contention. The Council of Constantinople in 381 stated in Canon 1 of its de-

[3] Kidd, *op. cit.*, Vol. II, pp. 21-25. This letter from Eusebius to his people includes both his creed and the one formulated at Nicaea.

[4] Henry Bettenson, *Documents of the Christian Church* (New York: Oxford University Press, 1947), p. 36.

cisions that the faith of the 318 fathers at Nicaea "shall not be set aside but shall remain dominant." This decision was approved at Chalcedon in 451. Thus it is the creed accepted at Constantinople in 381 that is today known as the Nicene Creed and is used in the Church.[5] Between 381 and 590 the Church busied itself with the task of bringing Christianity to the Teutonic tribes and winning the Arian tribes back to orthodox Christianity.

We can be thankful that the orthodox party was finally triumphant at Constantinople in 381 when we consider the havoc wrought in the Church by Unitarian ideas. Arianism, to which Modernism and Unitarianism are both related, was rejected as unorthodox doctrine, and the true deity of Christ was made an article of Christian faith. Though the decision at Nicaea became a factor in the eventual split between the Eastern and Western Churches, that must not blind us to the value of that decision for our faith. Nicaea cost the Church its independence, however, for the Church became imperial from this time and was increasingly dominated by the emperor. The Church in the West was able to rise above this domination, but the Church in the East never freed itself from domination by the political power of the state.

B. The Relationship of the Holy Spirit to the Father.

Macedonius, bishop of Constantinople between 341 and 360, taught that the Holy Spirit was "a minister and a servant" on a level with the angels. He believed that the Holy Spirit was a creature subordinate to the Father and Son. This was a denial of the true deity of the Holy Spirit and would be as harmful to the conception of the Holy Spirit as the views of Arius were to the conception of Christ. The ecumenical Council of Constantinople condemned the views of Macedonius in 381. When the creed of Constantinople, our Nicene Creed, was recited at the third Council of Toledo in 589 the words "and the Son" (*filioque*) were added to the statement "that proceedeth from the Father" which is concerned with the relationship between the Holy Spirit and the Father and the Son. The Western churches since then have insisted upon the true deity and the personality of the Holy Spirit as coequal, coeternal and consubstantial with the Father and the Son.[6]

[5] Bettenson, *op cit.*, p. 37; Canon 1 of the Council of Constantinople is given in Ayer, *op cit.*, p. 353, and Philip Schaff, *Creeds of Christendom* (New York: Charles Scribner's Sons, 3 vols., 6th ed., 1890), Vol. I, pp. 24-34; Vol. II, pp. 57-61.

[6] Bettenson, *op. cit.*, pp. 36-37, footnote 6.

II. CHRISTOLOGY — CONTROVERSIES CONCERNING THE RELATIONSHIP BETWEEN THE NATURES OF CHRIST

The settlement of the theological question concerning the relationship of the Son to the Father at Nicaea raised new problems concerning the relationship between the human and divine natures of Christ. Before the orthodox doctrine of the relationship of the two natures was finally formulated, many scenes of passion and violence occurred. In general, those theologians linked with Alexandria emphasized the deity of Christ; those with Antioch, His humanity.

A view of the two natures of Christ that did injustice to Christ's true manhood was developed by Apollinaris, a converted teacher of rhetoric and bishop of Laodicea. Apollinaris developed his peculiar doctrine concerning the natures of Christ when he was about sixty. Until that time he had been a good friend of Athanasius and had been one of the leading champions of orthodoxy. In an attempt to avoid the undue separation of the human and divine natures of Christ, Apollinaris taught that Christ had a true body and soul, but that the spirit in man was replaced in Christ by the logos. The logos as the divine element actively dominated the passive element, the body and soul, in the person of Christ. He stressed the deity of Christ but minimized His true manhood. His view was officially condemned at the ecumenical Council of Constantinople in 381.[7]

In contrasts to the view of Apollinaris was the view developed by Nestorius, a scholarly monk who became patriarch at Constantinople in 428. Nestorius disliked the use of the term *theotokos* (God-bearer) as a name for the Virgin Mary because it seemed to exalt her unduly. He offered the word *Christotokos* as an alternative, arguing that Mary was only the mother of the human side of Christ. By so arguing he made Christ out to be a man in whom, in Siamese twin fashion, the divine and human natures were combined in a mechanical union rather than in an organic union of natures. Christ was in effect only a perfect man who was morally linked to deity. He was a God-bearer rather than the God-man. Leaders of the Church gathered at Ephesus in 431 and condemned this doctrine, but the followers of Nestorius continued their work in the Eastern section of the Empire and carried the Gospel as they conceived it to Persia, India and even China.[8]

[7] *Ibid.*, pp. 63-64; Kidd, *op. cit.*, Vol. II, pp. 84-86, 103, 108, 114, 147.
[8] Bettenson, *op. cit.*, pp. 65-68; Ayer, *op. cit.*, pp. 504-511.

In reaction to views of such men as Nestorius, emphasis was again laid upon the divine nature of Christ to the neglect of His human nature. Eutyches, a monk of Constantinople, insisted that after the Incarnation the two natures of Christ, the human and the divine, were fused into one nature, the divine. This view, known as Eutychianism, resulted in the loss of the true humanity of Christ. It was condemned in a long letter, known as the *Tome,* by Leo I, the bishop of Rome between 440 and 461, and the Council of Chalcedon held in 451. The Council of Chalcedon went on to promulgate a Christology that would be in accord with the Scriptures. The Council held that Christ was "complete in Godhead and complete in manhood, truly God and truly man," having "two natures, without confusion, without change, without division, without separation." These two natures were brought together harmoniously in one Person with one essence by the Incarnation. This formulation has been the view of the orthodox on this point since the time of the Council.[9]

The views of Eutyches were revived in the Monophysite controversy which disturbed the peace of the Eastern Empire until the middle of the sixth century. Some groups still hold to this view in Abyssinia, Syria and Egypt.

The settlement of the relation between the human and divine natures of Christ was followed by discussion of the relationship of the wills of Christ. Did He have both a divine and human will? If so, were they equal or was one subordinate to the other? This dispute was finally settled at the Council of Constantinople (680–681) with the assertion that the two wills of Christ exist in Him in a harmonious unity in which the human will is subject to the divine will.

The settlement of these various issues in the Eastern Church left the Eastern section of Christianity with little further contribution to make to the main stream of Christianity. Except for the word of John of Damascus in the eighth century, Eastern theology remained stagnant until modern times.

III. ANTHROPOLOGY — THE MANNER OF MAN'S SALVATION

The student will have observed that the heresies and controversies so far discussed were problems mainly in the Eastern wing of the Church. Theology and Christology were not grave problems in the West where such leaders as Tertullian had led the Church to the orthodox view of the relationship of Christ to

9 Bettenson, *op. cit.,* pp. 68-73; Ayer, *op. cit.,* pp. 511-529.

the Father and of His two natures to each other. The Western Church was not as concerned with speculative metaphysical theology as the more rationalistic Greek thinkers of the Eastern Church were. Instead, the thinkers of the Church in the West were concerned with more practical problems. This distinction becomes quite clear to any student of ancient history. The Greek mind made its contribution in the field of thought; whereas the more practical Roman mind was concerned with matters of practice in the Church. For example, Augustine and Pelagius were concerned with the problem of how man is saved. Was man to be saved by the divine power only, or was there a place in the process of salvation for the human will?

Pelagius (ca. 360-420), a British monk and theologian, came to Rome about 400 where, with the help of Coelestius, he preached his idea of how man is saved. He met Augustine in Africa about 410 and soon found that Augustine would have no part of his ideas. He was banished from Rome in 418. Pelagius, the cool, calm Anglo-Saxon, had known nothing of the struggle of soul through which Augustine had gone before he was saved. Hence, Pelagius was more willing to give the human will a place in the process of salvation. But Augustine had found his will helpless to extricate him from the morass of sin in which he found himself because of his sinful nature.

Pelagius believed that each man is created free as Adam was and that each man has the power to choose good or evil. Each soul is a separate creation of God and, therefore, uncontaminated by the sin of Adam. The universality of sin in the world is explained by the weakness of human flesh rather than by the corruption of the human will by original sin. Man does not inherit original sin from his first ancestor, although the sins of individuals of the past generation do weaken the flesh of the present generation so that sins are committed unless the individual wills to cooperate with God in the process of salvation. The human will is free to cooperate with God in the attainment of holiness and can make use of such aids to grace as the Bible, reason and the example of Christ. Because there is no original sin, infant baptism is not an essential element in salvation.[10]

Augustine, the great bishop of Hippo, opposed what he believed was a denial of the grace of God by insisting that regeneration is exclusively the work of the Holy Spirit. Man was

[10] Bettenson, *op. cit.*, pp. 74-76; Kidd, *op. cit.*, Vol. II, pp. 235-236, 246-247.

originally made in the image of God and free to choose good and evil, but Adam's sin bound all men, because Adam was the head of the race. Man's will is entirely corrupted by the Fall so that he must be considered totally depraved and unable to exercise his will in regard to the matter of salvation. Augustine believed that all inherit sin through Adam and that no one, therefore, can escape original sin. Man's will is so bound that he can do nothing to bring about His salvation. Salvation can come only to the elect through the grace of God in Christ. God must energize the human will to accept His proffered grace, which is only for those whom He has elected to salvation.[11]

Pelagius' views were condemned at the Council of Ephesus in 431, but neither the Eastern nor Western churches ever fully accepted Augustine's views. John Cassianus, a monk, endeavored to find a compromise position by which the human and divine will could cooperate in salvation. He taught that all men are sinful because of the fall, and that their wills are weakened but not totally corrupted. Man's partially free will can cooperate with divine grace in the process of salvation. He feared that the doctrines of election and irresistible grace taught by Augustine might lead to ethical irresponsibility. The view of Cassianus was condemned at the Synod of Orange in 529[12] in favor of a moderate Augustinian view.

The problem raised by Pelagius and Augustine has, however, been perennial in the Christian Church. Modernism in our day is only a resurgence of the Pelagian idea that man can achieve salvation by cooperation with the divine will through his own efforts. The problem is whether Christianity is a matter of morals or religion; man's free will or God's grace; character development by culture or by a conversion that makes such development possible; a matter of man's rational powers or God's revelation. The Church has always been closer to Augustine's view than to that of Pelagius or John Cassianus, although the views of the medieval Church on this point were similar to those of the Semi-Pelagians who followed John Cassianus.

Most of the major controversies were ended by 451, but they left a definite impact upon the Christian Church. The unity of the Church was preserved but at the expense of the freedom of spirit that was so characteristic of the Early Church. Christians were now in possession of authoritative statements as to

11 Bettenson, *op. cit.*, pp. 76-83.
12 Kidd, *op. cit.*, Vol. II, pp. 334-337.

the sense in which the Scriptures were to be interpreted on major doctrinal issues. But there were also some disadvantages that must be considered. The emphasis upon the theological led to a danger that men might be orthodox in faith but not live up to the ethical implications of that faith. Creed and conduct must always go hand in hand. It was also sad that many Christians felt that the Church could resort to violence and persecution in its attempt to keep the faith pure. The emperor as an arbiter of the differing viewpoints at councils was able to assert the power of the state in religious matters and end the separation of the Church and state. But we can be grateful to those who risked life as well as position to get the Church to accept doctrines that are true to the Scriptures and we can unite in praise to God for His providential guidance in all these matters.

BIBLIOGRAPHY

The books mentioned in the bibliography for Chapter VIII will be found useful references for the material discussed in this chapter.

Volumes I and II of Philip Schaff's *Creeds of Christendom* (New York: Charles Scribner's Sons, 3 vols., 6th ed., 1890) contain discussions of the rise of the creeds as well as the relevant documents.

Newman gives a good discussion of the controversies mentioned in his *A Manual of Church History* (Chicago: American Baptist Publication Society, 2 vols., rev. ed., 1931-33), Vol. I, pp. 320-392.

Chapter XIII

THE GOLDEN AGE OF CHURCH FATHERS

The Church Fathers who have been discussed thus far were known as the Ante-Nicene Fathers, whether they were Apostolic Fathers, Apologists or Polemicists, because the active period of their work came before that great watershed of church history, the Council of Nicaea. Between the Councils of Nicaea (325) and Chalcedon (451) several of the most able Fathers of the Christian Church did their greatest work. They endeavored to study the Scriptures along more scientific lines in order to develop their theological meaning. Because of the sheer weight of his work and his influence upon the Church of his day, Augustine was the greatest of these fathers.

I. EASTERN POST-NICENE FATHERS

The Fathers of the Eastern wing of the Church belonged to what have been called the Alexandrian and Antiochene schools of interpretation. Such men as Chrysostom or Theodore of Mopsuestia followed the Antiochene or Syrian school of interpretation, emphasizing a grammatico-historical study of the Scriptures in order to discover the meaning that the sacred writer had for those to whom he was writing. They avoided the allegorizing tendency practiced by the men of the Alexandrian school, who were still under the influence of Origen.

A. *Chrysostom — Expositor and Orator.*

John, who was called Chrysostom shortly after his death because his eloquence was literally that of one who deserved the name "golden-mouthed," was born about 345 into a wealthy aristocratic family of Antioch. His mother Anthusa reminds one of Augustine's mother because, though she was widowed at the age of twenty, she refused to remarry in order that she might devote all her time to her son's education. Chrysostom was a student of the sophist Libanius who had been a friend of the

Emperor Julian. This man gave him a good training in the Greek classics and the rhetoric that laid the foundation for his excellent speaking ability. For a time he practiced law, but after his baptism in 368 he became a monk. After his mother's death in 374, he practiced a severely ascetic life until 380. During this time he lived in a cave on a mountain near Antioch. Ill health stopped this severe regimen. Ordained in 386, he preached some of his best sermons in Antioch until 398. In that year he was made a patriarch of Constantinople, which position he held until Empress Eudoxia finally banished him in 404 because he had denounced her for her extravagant dress and for placing a silver statue of herself near St. Sophia where he preached. He died in exile in 407.

Chrysostom lived a pure simple life that was a rebuke to his highly placed wealthy parishoners in Constantinople. Extremely ascetic in his insistence upon simplicity of life and inclined to mysticism, he did not always possess tact; but he did have a courteous, affectionate, kindly nature. Though he was a giant in moral and spiritual stature, he was short and thin. His emaciated but pleasant face, wrinkled forehead, bald head and piercing bright eyes made a lasting impression upon his auditors.

Perhaps some years of study under Diodorus of Tarsus had something to do with his ability as an expositor. About 640 of his homilies are still extant, and even a reading of the cold print gives one some idea of his oratorical ability. Most of his homilies or sermons are expositions of Paul's Epistles. Not knowing Hebrew, he could not make a critical investigation of the Old Testament Scriptures, but he kept the importance of the context in mind and sought to discover the literal meaning of the writer and to make a practical application of that meaning to the problems of the people of his day. These practical moral applications of the Gospel were given with great moral earnestness. He taught that there must be no divorce of morals and religion; the Cross and ethics must go hand in hand. It is little wonder that he was and still is hailed as the greatest pulpit orator the Eastern Church ever had.[1]

[1] Translations of his homilies may be studied in Beresford J. Kidd, *Documents Illustrative of the History of the Church* (London: Society for Promoting Christian Knowledge, 3 vols., 1920-1941), Vol. II, p. 102f., and in Vols. X to XIV of Philip Schaff, *A Select Library of the Nicene and Post-Nicene Fathers of the Christian Church* (New York: The Christian Literature Co, 1889, First Series).

B. *Theodore — Exegete.*

Another noted Church Father is Theodore of Mopsuestia (ca. 350–ca. 428). He, too, studied the Scriptures — for fourteen years — under Diodorus of Tarsus. This good education was made possible by his birth into a wealthy family. He was ordained a presbyter in Antioch in 383 and became the bishop of Mopsuestia in Cilicia about 392.

Theodore has been rightly called "the prince of ancient exegetes." He opposed the allegorical system of interpretation and insisted upon a thorough understanding of the grammar of the text and the historical background of the text in order to discover the meaning of the writer. He also gave careful attention to the text in its immediate and more remote context. This type of study made him an able commentator and theologian. He wrote commentaries on such books of the Bible as Colossians and the letters to the Thessalonians. Both he and Chrysostom had a healthy influence upon the interpretation of the Bible in their day. Their work was a marked contrast to the strained interpretations of Scripture that resulted from the use of the allegorical method of interpretation.

C. *Eusebius — Church Historian.*

One of the most widely studied Church Fathers is Eusebius of Caesarea (ca. 260–340), who has as much right to the title of Father of Church History as Herodotus has to the title Father of History. After having had a good education under Dorotheus at Caesarea, he helped his friend Pamphilus build up his library in that city. Eusebius was an assiduous student and read everything he could obtain that might help him in his research. He excerpted widely from both profane and sacred literature. Much literature of his day that might otherwise have been lost has been preserved because these excerpts were quoted in his works.

Eusebius' personality was one that fitted him for such scholarly pursuits. He was of a gentle and agreeable disposition and disliked the quarrels engendered by the Arian heresy. He was given a place of honor at the right hand of Constantine at the Council of Nicaea and, like him, preferred a compromise between the parties of Athanasius and Arius.

His greatest work is the *Ecclesiastical History*, a survey of the history of the Church from apostolic times until 324. His purpose was to make a record of the past trials of the Church at the end of its long period of struggle and the beginning of its era of prosperity. The work is especially valuable today because Eusebius had access to the fine library at Caesarea and the imperial archives. He made a great effort to be honest and objective in his use of the best and most reliable of the primary sources that were available to him. In his critical use of many reliable documents Eusebius anticipated something of the careful scientific study which the modern historian does in evaluating the sources of his knowledge. It is little wonder that Eusebius is our best source of knowledge concerning the history of the Church during the first three centuries of its existence, but scholars regret that he did not make careful footnotes of his sources of knowledge after the manner of the modern historian. Sometimes, too, his work becomes little more than a collection of facts and extracts with no orderly view of cause and effect. Despite these defects and the monotonous rambling and desultory style, the work has been of inestimable value to the Church all through the ages.

Eusebius wrote the *Chronicle,* a universal history from the time of Abraham until 323, which provided the conventional chronological framework for medieval history. His *Life of Constantine* was written somewhat as an appendix to his *History* and is an excellent, though somewhat laudatory, source of information concerning the doings of Constantine as they were related to the Church.

The historical work of Eusebius was continued by two successors who did not always measure up to the high standard of reliability set by him. It must be said, however, that these laymen, Socrates and Sozomen, both trained for the legal profession, showed a lack of bigotry even in dealing with those who were opposed to them. Socrates' work carries the story of Christianity from 323 to 439 in an attempt to complete the task begun by Eusebius. Sozomen was much more credulous than Socrates and often plagiarized his work. He also often digressed in favor of asceticism. His work covers the period from 323 to 423. Together with Eusebius these men are the chief ecclesiastical authorities for the history of the ancient Church.

II. Western Post-Nicene Fathers

The Fathers of the Western Church in this period excelled in different fields from those of the East. The translation of the Scriptures and the writings of pagan philosophers, and the writing of theological treatises were important parts of their work.

The practical bent of the Latin in contrast with the interest in speculation of the Greek may be seen in the work of Jerome, Ambrose and Augustine.

A. *Jerome — Commentator and Translator.*

Jerome (ca. 340–420), a native of Venetia, was baptized in 360 and for several years was a wandering student in Rome and the cities of Gaul. During the next decade he visited Antioch and followed the monastic life while he learned Hebrew. He became secretary to Damasus, bishop of Rome in 382, and Damasus suggested to him that he might profitably make a new translation of the Bible.[2] In 386 Jerome went to Palestine and there, through the generosity of Paula, a wealthy Roman lady whom he had taught Hebrew, he lived in a monastic retreat at Bethlehem.

Jerome's greatest work was a Latin translation of the Bible known as the Vulgate. By 388 he had completed the revision of the Latin New Testament by carefully checking it with the Greek. He went back of the Greek of the Septuagint version of the Old Testament to make a translation into Latin from Hebrew of the Old Testament. Jerome's version of the Bible has been widely used by the Western Church and has been, until recently, the only official Bible of the Roman Catholic Church since the Council of Trent.

Jerome was also an able commentator and wrote many commentaries which are still helpful today. His early love for and knowledge of the classics was a help in the interpretation of the Scriptures, although in later years he disavowed classical learning. He wrote a fine work, *De Viris Illustribus*, after the model of ancient biographers, which contains brief biographical and bibliographical sketches of leading Christian writers and their works from the time of the apostles until his day. His love of the ascetic life caused him to champion it with his pen, and the later medieval popularity of the ascetic life in the West owed much to the writings of Jerome on this subject.

B. *Ambrose — Administrator and Preacher.*

Ambrose (ca. 340–397) demonstrated his ability in the fields of church administration, preaching and theology. His father had held the high position of prefect of Gaul, and his family,

[2] Kidd, *op. cit.*, Vol. II, pp. 176-177.

high in imperial circles in Rome, educated him in law for a political career. He soon rose to the position of imperial governor of the area around the city of Milan. Upon the death of the bishop of Milan in 374 the people unanimously wanted him to take that position. Believing this to be the call of God, he gave up his high position, distributed his money to the poor, became a bishop, and began an intensive study of the Scriptures and theology.

Ambrose proved to be a fearless and able administrator of the affairs of the Church. He spoke against the powerful Arian groups and did not even hesitate to oppose the Emperor Theodosius. Theodosius had gathered the people of Thessalonica, who had been guilty of revolt, into the circus in that city and had ordered their massacre. When he came to church to take the Communion, Ambrose refused him admission to the Lord's Supper until he humbly and publicly repented of this deed.[3] Ambrose wanted to make the state and its rulers respect the Church so that it might not transgress upon the rightful claims of the Church in the spiritual realm.

Even though his practical expositions of Scripture were marred by his use of the allegorical method, Ambrose was an able preacher. His preaching in the cathedral at Milan was instrumental in bringing Augustine to a knowledge of Christianity that later resulted in his salvation. Apparently he introduced the singing of hymns and antiphonal psalmody into the Western Church. He also became a theologian of no mean ability, although he had not studied theology until his consecration as bishop.

C. *Augustine — Philosopher and Theologian.*

Although Jerome and Ambrose were honored with the title of doctor by the medieval church, their fame is small compared to the reputation of Augustine. Both Protestantism and Roman Catholicism pay tribute to the contribution of Augustine to the cause of Christianity. He was an able polemicist, a good preacher, a fine episcopal administrator, a superb theologian and the creator of a Christian philosophy of history that is still valid in its essentials. Living at a time when the old classical civilization seemed to be doomed to fall before the barbarians, Augus-

---

[3] Kidd, *op. cit.*, Vol. II, pp. 146-147.

tine stood between two worlds, the classical and the new medieval. He insisted that men must look forward to the "City of God," a spiritual civilization, because the old classical civilization was passing.

Augustine was born in 354 into the home of a Roman official in the North African town of Tagaste. His mother, Monica, devoted her life to his upbringing and conversion to the Christian faith. He received his early education in the local school, where he learned Latin to the accompaniment of many beatings and hated Greek so much that he never learned to use it proficiently. He was sent to school in nearby Madaura and from there to Carthage to study rhetoric. Freed from the restraint of home, Augustine followed the pattern of many students of his day and indulged his passions by an illegitimate union with a concubine. His son Adeodatus was born of this union in 372. Two years later he adopted Manichean teaching in his search for truth, but, finding it insufficient, he turned to philosophy after a reading of Cicero's *Hortensius* and the Neoplatonic teachings. He taught rhetoric in his hometown and Carthage until he went to Milan in 384.

In 386 the crisis of conversion came in his life. Meditating upon his spiritual need one day in a garden, he heard a voice next door saying "Take up and read." Augustine opened his Bible to Romans 13:13-14, and the reading brought the light to his soul which he had been unable to find either in Manicheanism or Neoplatonism. He dismissed his concubine and gave up his profession of rhetoric. His mother, who had prayed long for his conversion, died shortly after his baptism. Returning to Carthage, he was ordained priest in 391. Five years later he was consecrated bishop of Hippo. From that time until his death in 430 he gave his life to episcopal administration, studying and writing. He is acclaimed as the greatest of the Fathers of the Church.[4]

Perhaps the most widely known work from the pen of Augustine is his *Confessions,* one of the great autobiographical works of all time. In the course of this work he laid bare his soul. Books I to VII describe his life before conversion; Book VIII

---

[4] Augustine, *Confessions,* Books I-X These books give the story of his life until shortly after his conversion. The account of his conversion is given in VIII:xii:29.

describes the events surrounding his conversion; and the next two books recount the events after his conversion, including the death of his mother and his return to North Africa. Books XI to XIII are a commentary on the first chapters of Genesis in which Augustine often resorts to allegory.

Christians throughout the ages have found spiritual blessing in the reading of this work which Augustine wrote to God to praise Him for the grace that He had extended to such a sinner as he. The book contains the often quoted "Thou madest us for thyself, and our heart is restless, until it repose in thee" in the very first paragraph. The sense of his sin and the power of evil revealed by his passionate immoral life caused him to cry out, "Give me chastity and continency, only not yet." That need was finally met by his experience of the grace of God.[5]

Augustine wrote another autobiographical work, *Retractiones* (Revisions), shortly before his death. He discusses his works in chronological order and points out wherein his mind has changed over the years. He particularly regrets his early connection with pagan philosophy because it can never bring man to the truth as it is in Christianity.[6]

Augustine also wrote philosophical works in dialogue form. *Contra Academicos* is the most interesting of these works. In it he tries to demonstrate that man can never achieve more than probable truth through philosophical study and that certainty only comes by the revelation in the Bible.

His *De Doctrina Christiana* is the most important of his exegetical works. It is a small manual dealing with his views on hermeneutics or the science of interpretation. In it he developed the great principle of the analogy of faith. He meant by it that no teaching contrary to the general tenor of the Scriptures should be developed from any particular passage. Failure to keep this in mind has led many into fields of error and, often, heresy. With this principle in mind he wrote many exegetical commentaries on the Old and New Testaments.

Augustine also wrote theological treatises of which his *De Trinitate*, concerning the Trinity, is the most significant. The

[5] Augustine, *Confessions*, VIII:vii:17.

[6] Meredith F. Eller, "The *Retractiones* of Saint Augustine," *Church History*, XXXII:3: 172ff. (Sept., 1949). This article discusses the value of this work in some detail.

first seven books of the work are devoted to a Scriptural exposition of that doctrine. His little work, *Enchiridion ad Laurentium*, is a small manual of his theological views. This little work, coupled with his *Retractiones*, will give the reader a clear picture in small compass of the theological views of Augustine. He also wrote many polemical works to defend the faith from the false teachings and heresies of the Manicheans, the Donatists, and particularly the Pelagians. His *De Haeresibus* is a history of heresies.

He wrote several practical and pastoral works and many letters of which we have over two hundred still available. These works and letters deal with the many practical problems which a church administrator or pastor faces over the years of his ministry.

His greatest apologetical work and, in the minds of many, his greatest work, upon which his enduring fame rests, is the treatise, *De Civitate Dei*, popularly known as the *City of God*. Augustine himself was of the opinion that it was his great work.[7] Shocked by the sack of Rome by Alaric in 410, the Romans made the charge that this disaster had come upon them because they had forsaken the old classical Roman religion and had adopted Christianity. Augustine set out to answer this charge at the request of his friend Marcellinus. Books I to X constitute the apologetic part of this work. He tries to demonstrate in Books I to V that the prosperity of the state is not dependent upon the old polytheistic worship because the Romans had catastrophes long before the advent of Christianity, and what success they have had is due to the providence of the God of whom they have been ignorant. In the next five books Augustine demonstrates that the worship of the Roman gods is not necessary in order to attain eternal blessing. Neither in the temporal nor spiritual realms can the gods aid their devotees, but Christianity can give them and has given them what temporal blessings they have enjoyed.

Augustine's philosophy of history, the first real philosophy of history ever to be developed, is to be found in Books XI to XXII of this great work. The origin of the two cities is discussed in Books XI to XIV. The central idea of the work is developed in Chapter 28 of Book XIV. The first city, the City of God, consisted of all human and celestial beings united in love to

[7] *Retractiones,* II:43.

God and seeking His glory alone. The City of Earth is composed of those beings who, loving only self, seek their own glory and good. The supreme dividing principle is that of love. Augustine never had the Roman Empire or the Church of Rome in mind when he spoke of these two cities. His outlook was much more universal and opposed to the prevailing cyclical view of history. In Books XV to XVIII he traces the growth and progress of the two cities through Biblical and secular history. The remaining books give an account of the destiny of the two cities. After judgment the members of the City of God share in eternal happiness and those of the City of Earth in eternal punishment. Augustine does not take into account the place of the Jew in the future and believes that the present age of the Church is the millennium. He asserts that the dualism of the two cities is only temporal and permissive and will be ended by the act of God. Though the work is heavy and tedious, a careful student will have a better grasp of the plan and purpose of God after reading it.

The development of a Christian interpretation of history must be considered as one of the abiding contributions made by this great Christian scholar. Neither Greek nor Roman historians had been able to achieve any such universal grasp of man's history. Augustine exalts the spiritual over the temporal in his assertion of the sovereignty of the God who became the *Creator* of history in time. God is Lord over history and is not bound up in history as the philosopher Hegel taught. All that comes into being does so as a result of His will and action. Even before creation God had a plan in mind for His creation. This plan will be partially realized in time in the struggle between the two cities on earth, and finally realized outside of history by the supernatural power of God. Augustine also had a wider *compass* to his view of history than any man before him. He saw history as universal and unitary in that all men were included in it. Herodotus, in writing of the Persian War, limited his work to the struggle between the Greeks and the Persians. Augustine instead asserted the solidarity of the human race. Moreover, he believed that progress was primarily along moral and spiritual lines and was the result of *conflict* with evil, a conflict in which man had God's grace on his side. The *consummation* of this conflict would dissolve the temporal dualism of the struggling cities in the final victory of the City of God. In this way Augustine avoided the error of Marx and others who try to make the temporal relative scene of history absolute and eternal by finding solutions to man's problems in temporal history. The end or goal of history, for Augustine, is outside of history, in the hands of an eternal God. This inspiring philosophy sustained the Church through the dark half-millennium before 1000.

Augustine is looked upon by Protestants as one who was a forerunner of Reformation ideas in his emphasis upon salvation from original and actual sin as a result of the grace of a sovereign God who irresistibly saves those whom He has elected. But, in his discussion of how man is saved, Augustine so emphasized the Church as a visible institution with the true creed, sacraments and ministry that the Roman Church looks upon him as the father of Roman ecclesiasticism. It should be remembered that he made these emphases to defeat the claims of the Pelagians on the one hand and the Donatists on the other. His insistence upon consideration of the whole tenor of Scripture in interpreting a part of Scripture has been a principle of lasting value in the Church.

In spite of these abiding values Augustine brought some errors into the stream of Christian thought. He helped to develop the doctrine of purgatory with all its attendant evils. He so emphasized the value of the two sacraments that the doctrine of baptismal regeneration and sacramental grace were logical outcomes of his views. His interpretation of the millennium as the era between the Incarnation and Second Advent of Christ in which the Church would conquer the world led to the Roman emphasis upon the Church of Rome as the universal Church destined to bring all within its fold.

These emphases of Augustine should not blind one to his significance for the Christian Church. The Reformers found Augustine an invaluable ally in their belief that man bound by sin needs salvation by God's grace through faith alone. Between Paul and Luther the Church had no one of greater moral and spiritual stature than Augustine.

BIBLIOGRAPHY

Many of the bibliographical items enumerated in the bibliography for Chapter V may be profitably consulted for information concerning the Fathers of this period.

Ernest Leigh-Bennett in his *Handbook of the Early Christian Fathers* (London: Williams & Norgate, 1920) has excellent chapters on most of the Fathers discussed in this chapter.

The writer found *Augustine's Quest of Wisdom* (Milwaukee: The Bruce Publishing Co., 1945) by Vernon J. Bourke a helpful, scholarly and detailed account of Augustine's life and work. One should remember that the author approaches the great Father from the Roman Catholic viewpoint.

Volume II of *Lives of the Fathers* (New York: The Macmillan Co., 2 vols., 1889) by Frederick W. Farrar has lengthy accounts of the life and work of Jerome, Chrysostom and Augustine.

Chapter XIV

THE CHRISTIANITY OF THE CLOISTERS

Throughout history men have renounced society in times of social crisis and have retired into solitude to work out their own salvation apart from the society which they believe to be decadent and doomed. During the period of the gradual internal decay of the Roman Empire monasticism made a powerful appeal to many, who promptly renounced society for the cloister. This movement had its origins in the fourth century, and laymen in increasing numbers retired from the world from that time on. By the end of the sixth century monasticism had deep roots in the Western as well as in the Eastern sections of the Church. A second era of greatness for monasticism occurred in the monastic reforms of the tenth and eleventh centuries. The era of friars in the thirteenth century was a third period. And the emergence of the Jesuits in the Counter Reformation of the sixteenth century constituted the final period in which monasticism deeply affected the Church. The movement still has an important place within the life of the Roman Catholic Church.

I. The Causes of Monasticism

Several influences contributed to the rise of monasticism within the ancient Church. One of the most important of these influences was a philosophical influence. The dualistic view of flesh and spirit, with its tendency to consider flesh evil and spirit good — so characteristic of the Orient — influenced Christianity through the Gnostic and Neoplatonic movements. Retirement from the world would, it was thought, help the individual to crucify the flesh and to develop the spiritual life by meditation and ascetic acts.

One should also remember that some Scriptures seem to support the idea of separation from the world. Paul's apparent advocacy of the celibate life in Chapter 7 of I Corinthians is a case in point. The Early Church Fathers, such as Origen, Cyprian, Tertullian and Jerome, urged celibacy as the correct interpretation of such Scriptures.

Certain psychological tendencies strengthened the desire for a monastic life. In periods of crisis there is always a tendency to retreat from the harsh realities about one. The late second and third centuries saw the beginning of civil disorder which was to become so prevalent in the later history of the Empire. Many left society for the monastery as a means of escape from harsh reality and the moral contamination of the times. With the union of the Church and state the possibility of martyrdom was lessened, but those who desired martyrdom as a pledge of their faith could find a psychological substitute in the ascetic practices of monasticism. Monasticism also offered a more individualistic approach to God than the formal corporate worship of the times.

History also played a part in the decision of many to accept the life of the cloister. The increasing number of barbarians crowding into the Church brought many semi-pagan practices within the Church against which puritanical souls revolted. The increasing moral deterioration, especially of the upper classes in Roman society, caused many to despair of social reform. Monasticism became a haven for those in revolt against the growing decadence of the times. It was a living criticism of the society of the day.

Geography merits some consideration as a factor responsible for the rise of monasticism. It would have been much more difficult to carry on the monastic life in areas where the climate was much more severe than in Egypt, where the monastic life had its beginnings. The warm dry climate and the multitude of caves in the hills along the banks of the Nile were conducive to separation of the individual from society. Small gardens, along with the resources of food provided by the nearby Nile, made securing of food by the individual fairly easy. Nearness to the desolate forbidding scenery of the desert stimulated meditation.

II. THE DEVELOPMENT OF MONASTICISM

Monasticism went through four stages during the period of its emergence in Western civilization. At first, ascetic practices were carried on by many within the Church. Many later withdrew from society to live as anchorites or hermits. The holiness of these hermits attracted others, who would then take up residence in nearby caves and look to them for leadership. A cloister for common exercises might be built. In the final stage organized communal life within a monastery appeared. This process had its beginnings in the East in the fourth century from whence it spread to the Church in the West.

A. In the East.

Anthony (ca. 250–356) is usually regarded as the founder of Monasticism. At the age of twenty he sold all his possessions, gave the money to the poor, and retired to a solitary cave to lead a life of meditation. His life of holiness gave him such a reputation that others also went to live near him in numerous caves that were not far from his habitation. He never organized these followers into a community; rather, each practiced the ascetic life of a hermit in his own cave.[1]

Not all of the hermit monks were as sane as Anthony and his followers. One, known as Saint Simeon Stylites (386–460), after having lived buried up to his neck in the ground for several months, decided to achieve holiness by becoming an ecclesiastical "pole sitter." He spent thirty years upon the top of a sixty foot pillar near Antioch. Others, known as the Bosci, lived in the field and grazed grass after the manner of cattle. A certain Ammoun had a particular reputation for sanctity because he had never undressed or bathed after he became a hermit. Another wandered naked in the vicinity of Mt. Sinai for fifty years. These, however, were only the fanatic fringe of the movement and were to be found in the East more than in the West.

The communal or social type of monasticism, often called cenobite monasticism, also made its appearance first in Egypt. Pachomius (292–346), a discharged soldier, after living twelve years with a hermit, organized the first monastery on the island of Tabenna in the Nile river about 340. He soon had seven thousand monks under his direct control in Egypt and Syria. Simplicity of life, work, devotion and obedience were the keynotes of his organization.[2]

Basil of Caesarea (ca. 330–379) did much to popularize the communal type of monastic organization. Having had an excellent education in Athens and Constantinople, at the age of

---

[1] Athanasius, *Life of Anthony* in *A Select Library of Nicene and Post-Nicene Fathers of the Christian Church* (New York: The Christian Literature Company, 1892, 2nd series) Vol. IV, pp. 195-221.

[2] Joseph Ayer, Jr., *A Source Book for Ancient Church History* (New York: Charles Scribner's Sons, 1913), pp. 402-405; Sozomen, *Ecclesiastical History*, III:xiv.

twenty-seven he gave up worldly advancement for the ascetic life. He was made a bishop of a large area in Cappadocia in 370, a post which he held until his death. He gave a more utilitarian and social expression to the monastic spirit by insisting that the monks under his rule work, pray, read the Bible and perform good deeds. He discouraged extreme asceticism. The monasticism of the Church in Eastern Europe today owes much to the rule that he developed for the guidance of his monks.[3] More and more people were swept into the movement until there were nearly a hundred monasteries in Europe at the accession of Justinian to the throne of the Eastern Empire.

B. In the West.

Monasticism in the West differed considerably from that in the East. The colder climate made communal organization much more essential in order that warm buildings and food for the winter season might be provided. Monasticism was also much more practical in its expression. It rejected idleness and deplored purely ascetic acts. Work as well as devotion was emphasized.

Athanasius is traditionally credited with the introduction of monasticism to the West during one of his periodic exiles from Constantinople. Pilgrims to Palestine came in contact with it there and in Syria and were attracted to it. Martin of Tours, Jerome, Augustine and Ambrose wrote in favor of it and helped to popularize it within the Roman Empire. Jerome's writings on asceticism ranked next to the Bible and Benedict's Rule in the medieval monk's library.

The greatest leader of Western monasticism was Benedict of Nursia (ca. 480–543). Shocked by the vice of Rome, he retired to live as a hermit in a cave in the mountains east of Rome about 500. In 529 he founded the monastery of Monte Cassino, which survived until World War II when it was destroyed by bombardment. Soon several monasteries were under his control and following his plan of organization, work and worship, that is, his Rule. Each monastery was considered as a self-sufficient, self-supporting unit or garrison of the soldiers of Christ. The day was divided into periods in which worship and work played an important part. The regulations that he drew up provided little meat for the monks but allowed plenty of fish, oil, butter, bread, vegetables and fruit in their diet. This Rule, which em-

[3] Ayer, *op. cit.*, pp. 405-406.

phasized poverty, chastity and obedience, was one of the most important in the Middle Ages.[4] It was carried to England, Germany and France by the seventh century and became almost universal in the time of Charlemagne.

III. EVALUATION OF MONASTICISM

Casual students of church history often dismiss the work of the monk as of little value or evince a hostility that does not take into account the contribution made by the monk in his own day, a contribution that still affects modern civilization.

The local monastery often served as the medieval equivalent of a modern experimental farm in demonstrating better methods of agriculture. The monks cleared the forests, drained the marshes, made roads and improved seeds and breeds of livestock. Nearby farmers often emulated the better techniques which they saw the monks using.

Monasteries helped to keep scholarship alive during the Dark Ages between 500 and 1000 when urban life practically disappeared as the barbarians took over the Roman Empire. Monastery schools provided education on the lower levels for those nearby who were desirous to learn. Monks busied themselves copying precious manuscripts which were thus preserved for posterity. In the middle of the sixth century, Cassiodorus, a high government official under the Ostrogoths, retired from government service to devote himself to the task of collecting, translating and copying Greek works of literature. He was aided in this task by the monks of a monastery that he founded. The Book of Kells, a lovely illuminated manuscript of the Gospels in Latin, done about the seventh century by Irish monks, is an example of the beauty of the monks' work. Monks, such as Bede, Einhard and Matthew Paris, wrote historical records, which are primary sources of information concerning the history of the period.

Monks became the missionaries of the medieval Church. They went out as fearless soldiers of the Cross to found new monasteries, and these became centers from which whole tribes were won to Christianity. Columba, a monk from Ireland, won the Scots, and one of his followers, Aidan, won the people of northern England. Unfortunately, much of their missionary work was marred by their mass methods of conversion. If a ruler

4 Henry Bettenson, *Documents of the Christian Church* (New York: Oxford University Press, 1947) pp. 164-181.

accepted Christianity, he and his people were baptized whether or not they fully understood the meaning of the act or the implications of Christianity for their lives.

The monasteries provided a refuge for the outcast of society who were in need of help. Those in need of hospitalization would usually find loving care in the monastery. The weary traveler could be sure of food and bed in the hospice of the monastery. Those who tired of the worldliness of their day could find in the monastery a refuge from the cares of life. Some of the best leaders of the medieval Church, such as Gregory VII, came from monasteries.

But there is also a debit sheet which must be considered in any evaluation of early medieval monasticism. Too many of the best men and women of the Empire were drained off into the monasteries, and their abilities were lost to the world which was so badly in need of such leaders. Moreover, the celibate life kept these able men and women from marriage and the rearing of able children. This led to one standard of morality for the monks (celibacy) and another for the ordinary individual.

Too often monasticism merely pandered to spiritual pride as monks became proud of ascetic acts performed to benefit their own souls. As the monasteries became wealthy, because of community thrift and ownership, laziness and avarice and gluttony crept in.

Monasticism aided in the rapid development of a hierarchal centralized organization in the Church because the monks were bound in obedience to superiors who in turn owed their allegiance to the pope. We can but deplore these tendencies while at the same time we admire the fine contributions that the monks made to medieval life.

BIBLIOGRAPHY

The student will find a good discussion of monasticism in Ian Hannah's *Christian Monasticism* (New York: The Macmillan Co., 1925).

Chapter XV

HIERARCHAL AND LITURGICAL DEVELOPMENTS

Between 313 and 590 the Old Catholic Church, in which each bishop had been an equal, became the Roman Catholic Church, in which the bishop of Rome won primacy over other bishops. The ritual of the Church also became much more elaborate.

I. THE DOMINANCE OF THE ROMAN BISHOP

The bishop in the Early Church was considered as one of many bishops who were equal to each other in rank, power and function. Between 313 and 590 the Roman bishop came to be acknowledged as the first among equals. But, beginning with Gregory's accession to the episcopal throne in 590, the Roman bishop began to claim his supremacy over other bishops. The need for efficiency and coordination led naturally to centralization of power. The bishop was also considered as the guarantor of orthodox doctrine. In addition, some of the Roman bishops of this period were strong men who missed no opportunity to increase their power.[1]

Historical events during this era conspired to enhance the reputation of the bishop of Rome. Rome had been the traditional center of authority for the Roman world for half a millennium and was the largest city in the West. After Constantine moved the capital of the Empire to Constantinople in 330, the center of political gravity shifted from Rome to that city. This left the Roman bishop as the single strongest individual in Rome for great periods of time, and the people of that area came to look to him for temporal as well as spiritual leadership whenever a crisis faced them. He was a tower of strength during the sacking of Rome in 410 by Alaric and his Visigothic followers, and his clever diplomacy had at least been able to save

[1] See Chapter X for additional discussion of factors responsible for the rise of the bishop of Rome.

the city from the torch. The emperor at Constantinople seemed to be remote from Rome and its problems, but the bishop was near at hand to exercise effective authority in meeting political as well as spiritual crises. When the imperial throne in the West fell into the hands of the barbarians after 476, and other Italian cities became the seat of temporal power, the people of Italy came to look to the Roman bishop for political as well as spiritual leadership.

The Petrine theory based on such Scriptures as Matthew 16: 16-18, was generally accepted by 590. According to this theory, Peter had been given "ecclesiastical primogeniture" over his fellow apostles, and his superior position had been passed on from him to his successors, the bishops of Rome, by apostolic succession.

The bishop of Rome had also developed a reputation for orthodoxy. Such great theologians as Cyprian, Tertullian and Augustine were outstanding men of the Western Church under the leadership of the bishop of Rome. The domains of the bishop had never suffered from heretical disputes, such as had divided the East — for example, those of Arius. Indeed, the bishop of Rome had held synods in which he had been able to develop clearly what was to be the orthodox position. At the meeting at Arles in 314 he had been able to deal effectively with the Donatist problem which was causing the Church so much trouble in North Africa.

Of the five great metropolitan church leaders — in Jerusalem, Antioch, Alexandria, Constantinople and Rome — only the patriarch of Constantinople and the bishop of Rome lived in cities of world consequence by 590. The bishop of Jerusalem lost prestige after the Jewish rebellion against Rome during the second century. Alexandria and Antioch rapidly declined in importance and were lost to Christendom when they were overrun by the Mohammedan hordes in the seventh century. The bishop of Rome and of Constantinople were left as the two most prominent clerical leaders by 590. The Council of Constantinople in 381 recognized the primacy of the Roman see. The patriarch of Constantinople was given "the primacy of honor next after the Bishop of Rome," according to the third canon of the Council of Constantinople.[2] This was a practical recognition of the primacy of the Roman bishop by a group

[2] Henry Bettenson, *Documents of the Christian Church* (New York: Oxford University Press, 1947), pp. 115-116.

of leading clerics of the Church. The Emperor Valentinian III, in an edict issued in 445, recognized the primacy of the bishops of Rome in spiritual affairs. What that bishop would enact was to be "law for all."[3] Thus both ecclesiastical and temporal authorities in the fourth and fifth centuries recognized the claims of the bishop of Rome to primacy in the Church.

The effective missionary work of monks loyal to Rome also enhanced the authority of the Roman bishop. Clovis, the leader of the Franks, was won to Christianity in 496 and became a loyal supporter of the authority of the bishop of Rome. Gregory I sent Augustine to England, and that monk and his successors were able to bring Britain under the sway of Rome. Wherever missionary monks went, they insisted upon their converts yielding allegiance to the bishop of Rome.

Above all, the Roman church was blessed with many able bishops during this era, and these men let no chance to strengthen their power slip from them unused. Damasus I (366–384) was apparently the first bishop of Rome to describe his see as the "apostolic see." The Vulgate translation of the Bible, which Jerome began at Damasus' request while he was his secretary, added to the prestige of the occupants of the episcopal chair in Rome. Jerome's high opinion of the authority of his employer can be read in a letter that he wrote to Damasus in which he categorically states that the chair of Peter is the rock on which the Church was built.[4]

Leo I, who occupied the episcopal throne in Rome between 440 and 461, was the ablest occupant of that chair until Gregory I took that position in 590. His abilities won for him the name "great." He was the first to be called *papas* from which our word "pope" is derived. In 452 he was able to persuade Attila the Hun to let the city of Rome alone. Again in 455, when Gaiseric and his Vandal followers from North Africa came to sack Rome, Leo persuaded them to save the city from fire and pillage; he had to agree, however, that the city would be given over to a two-week period of sacking by the Vandals. Gaiseric kept his word, and the Romans looked up to Leo as the one who had saved their city from complete destruction. His posi-

[3] *Ibid.*, pp. 32-33.
[4] *Ibid.*, p. 113.

tion was further strengthened when Valentinian III recognized his spiritual supremacy in the West by an edict in 445. Leo insisted that appeals from the church courts of bishops should be brought to his court and that his decision should be final. He defined orthodoxy and wrote against the heresy of the Manicheans and the Donatists.[5] Even if we do not consider Leo as the first pope, it is fair to say that he made the claims of and exercised the power of many later incumbents of the Roman bishopric. Perhaps such power was useful in this early period in dealing with the barbarians, but later it led to corruption within the Roman church itself.

II. The Growth of the Liturgy

The practical union of the Church and state under Constantine and his successors led to the secularization of the Church. The patriarch of Constantinople came under the control of the emperor, and the Eastern Church became a department of the state. The influx of pagans into the Church through the mass conversion movements of the era contributed to the paganization of worship as the Church tried to make these barbarian converts at home within its fold. This influx of pagans, many of whom did not become more than nominal Christians, caused the Church to call upon the state to help enforce discipline by the use of its temporal power to punish ecclesiastical offenses. In 529 Justinian, emperor of the Eastern Empire, ordered the closing of the Academy at Athens. Up until that time pagan Greek philosophy had been taught there. Discipline became lax within the Church because its resources were overtaxed in handling the many barbarians who had only been partially converted from paganism.

The influx of barbarians and the growth of episcopal power also brought changes in the worship of the Church. If the barbarians who had been used to worshiping images were to find any real help in the Church, many church leaders believed that it would be necessary to materialize the liturgy to make God seem more accessible to these worshipers. The veneration of angels, saints, relics, pictures and statues was a logical outcome of this attitude. Connection with the monarchic state also led to a change from a simple democratic worship to a more

[5] Beresford J. Kidd, *Documents Illustrative of the History of the Church* (London: Society for Promoting Christian Knowledge, 3 vols., 1920-1941), Vol. II, pp. 311-319.

aristocratic, colorful form of liturgy with a sharply drawn distinction between the clergy and the laity.

Sunday became one of the major days in the church calendar after Constantine decided that it was to be a day of civic as well as religious worship. The festival of Christmas became a regular practice about the middle of the fourth century with the adoption of the December date that had been previously used by the worshipers of Mithra. The Feast of Epiphany, which celebrated the coming of the Magi to see Christ, was also brought into the church calendar. Accretions from the Jewish sacred year, the gospel history and the lives of saints and martyrs led to a steady expansion of the number of holy days in the church calendar.

There was also an increase in the number of ceremonies that could be ranked as sacraments. Augustine was inclined to believe that marriage should be regarded as a sacrament. Cyprian held that penance was vital to the Christian life. With the increased gap between the clergy and laity it was almost necessary to consider ordination in the light of a sacrament. Confirmation and extreme unction came to be looked on as having sacramental value about 400. The early theological development of the doctrine of original sin contributed to the importance of infant baptism. In the beginning of the third century, Cyprian considered infant baptism as an accepted fact. Augustine especially emphasized the importance of baptism. The Lord's Supper occupied the central place in the thinking of the worshiper and the order of the liturgy. In fact, it was in process of becoming a sacrifice as well as a sacrament. Cyprian thought that the priest acted in Christ's place at Communion, and that he offered "a true and full sacrifice to God the Father."[6] The Canon of the Mass, which Gregory I altered slightly, emphasized the sacrificial nature of the Communion service.[7] By the end of the sixth century all of the seven acts which the Roman Catholic Church regards as sacraments were in use and had an exalted position in worship. Sacerdotalism, the belief that the substance of the ordinance is efficacious through the priestly celebrant, steadily gained ground. This led to an increasing emphasis upon the separation of the clergy and the laity.

The veneration of Mary, the mother of Jesus, which was to

[6] Cyprian, Epistles, LXII:14.
[7] Frederick J. Foakes Jackson, An Introduction to the History of Christianity A.D. 590-1314 (New York: The Macmillan Co., 1928), pp. 25-27.

lead to the adoption of the doctrines of her immaculate conception in 1854 and her miraculous assumption to heaven in 1950, developed rapidly by 590. The false interpretation of Scripture and the mass of miracles associated with Mary in the apocryphal gospels created great reverence for her. The Nestorian and other Christological controversies of the fourth century resulted in the acceptance of her as the "Mother of God" and entitled her to special honors in the liturgy.

Clement and Tertullian had ascribed eternal virginity to Mary. Augustine believed that the mother of the sinless Christ had never committed actual sin. Monasticism, with its emphasis upon virginity, strengthened the idea of the veneration of Mary. These and other considerations led the Roman Church to give special honor to Mary. What at first was merely acknowledgment of her exalted position as Christ's mother soon became belief in her intercessory powers because it was thought that the Son would be glad to listen to the requests of His mother.

The prayer of Ephraim Syrus about 380 is the first record of a formal invocation to her. By the middle of the fifth century she was placed at the head of all the saints. Festivals associated with her also sprang up in the fifth century. The Feast of the Annunciation on March 25, which celebrated the angelic announcement of the birth of a son to her; Candlemas on February 2, the celebration of her purification after the birth of Christ; and the Assumption on August 15, which considered her as one who ascended to heaven without death, were the principal festivals. In the sixth century Justinian asked her intercession on behalf of his Empire. By 590 she had a unique position in the worship of the Roman Church.

The veneration of saints grew out of the natural desire of the Church to honor those who had been martyrs in the days when the Church had been severely persecuted by the state. Furthermore, the pagans had been accustomed to the veneration of their heroes, and when so many pagans came into the Church, it was almost natural for them to substitute the saints for their heroes and to give them semidivine honors. Up to 300, celebrations at the grave involved only prayers for the repose of the soul of the saint, but by 590 prayer *for* them had become prayer to God *through* them. Churches and chapels were built over their graves; festivals associated with their death gained a place in the church calendar; and legends of miracles associated with them developed rapidly. The traffic in relics, such as bodies, teeth, hair, or bones, became such a problem that it was ordered stopped in 381.

The use of images and pictures in worship expanded rapidly as more and more untutored barbarians came into the Church. Both images and pictures materialized the invisible reality of deity for these worshipers. They also had a decorative function in beautifying a church. The Fathers of the Church tried to make a distinction between service to these images, which was a part of the liturgy, and the worship of God, but it is doubtful whether this subtle distinction prevented the ordinary worshiper from offering to them the worship which the Fathers would reserve for God alone.

Thanksgiving or penitential processions became a part of worship after 313. Pilgrimages, at first to Palestine, and later to the tombs of notable saints, became customary. Constantine's mother, Helena, visited Palestine about 326 and was supposed to have found the true Cross.

Government aid and freedom of worship under Constantine led to extensive building of churches. The Christians borrowed the basilica type of architecture which the Romans had developed for public buildings devoted to business or pleasure. The basilica was a long rectangular cruciform building with a portico at the west end for the unbaptized, a nave for the baptized and a chancel at the east end where the choir, the priests, and, if it were a cathedral church, the bishop officiated during the service. This chancel was usually separated from the nave by a screen of ironwork.

The earliest singing in the Church had been conducted by a leader to whom the people gave response in song. Antiphonal singing, in which two separated choirs sing alternately, developed at Antioch. Ambrose introduced the practice of antiphonal singing at Milan from whence it spread through the Western Church.

This also was an era of great preachers. Ambrose in the West and Chrysostom in the East were the leading preachers. Thus far these preachers wore no special vestments. Special vestments for the priests were to come as the people gave up the Roman type of dress while the clergy retained it in the church services.

The importance of this era is that during it there arose a

special sacerdotal hierarchy under a dominant Roman bishop, the tendency to increase the number of sacraments and to make them the main avenues of grace, and the movement to elaborate the liturgy. These things helped to lay the foundation for the medieval Roman Catholic Church.

BIBLIOGRAPHY

The student will find useful discussions of some of the topics of this chapter in Oscar Hardman's *History of Christian Worship* (London: Hodder & Stoughton, Ltd., 1937).

MEDIEVAL CHURCH HISTORY, 590–1517

Chapter XVI

THE FIRST MEDIEVAL POPE

The consecration of Gregory I as the bishop of Rome constitutes a watershed that divides the ancient period of church history from that of the medieval period of church history. One should always remember, however, that periodization in history is an artificial mechanism to organize the God-guided order of history into manageable segments. Some begin medieval church history in 313 with the grant of freedom of religion. Others begin at the Council of Nicaea in 325. Others prefer 378 because the battle of Adrianople resulted in the migration of the Visigoths into the Empire. Still others think that the ancient period of church history ended with the fall of the last Roman emperor in 476. The year 590 is chosen for this work because Gregory I ushered in a new era of power for the Church in the West in that year. The end of the Middle Ages of the history of the Church is also debatable. It has been variously set at 1095, the beginning of the era of the Crusades; at 1453, the fall of Constantinople; and at 1648, the peace of Westphalia. The writer has chosen 1517 because the activities of Luther in that year ushered in an entirely different era, in which the emphasis was not so much on the Church as an institution as it was upon the Church constituted as a body of individual believers by a personal faith in the redemptive work of Christ.

The name Middle Ages was originated by Christopher Keller (1634–1680) in a handbook published about 1669. He thought of three divisions in the history of the West. Ancient history, which he as a man with the Renaissance viewpoint admired, ended at 325. Modern history, he thought, had its beginning in 1453 when the fall of Constantinople brought a flood of Greek scholars and manuscripts to the West. He characterized the years between these two dates as the Middle Ages because of their apparent sterility and the absence of the classical influence.

Since that time historians have used the term Middle Ages as a convenient designation for that era. However, only the first five centuries of the era, from about 500 to 1000, may be designated as the Dark Ages, and even in that period Western Europe was not totally lacking in culture because the monasteries made intellectual contributions. The men of the Renaissance thought that this era was a chasm separating the brilliant classical and modern periods of humanism. To them, this period could be only an age of darkness. But modern historians of the period have been able to show that the Medieval Era was one of slow growth in which the Church in the West fulfilled useful cultural and religious functions by bridging the gap between the ancient city-state and the modern nation-state.

If the men of the Renaissance thought of the years between 500 and 1000 as the Dark Ages, the Roman Catholic Church has been in disagreement with them. To that church this era is the Golden Age of human history. It was preceded by classical paganism and followed by the disintegrating forces of Protestantism, which created the chaos of the modern religious scene — according to the Roman Catholic thinkers. Protestant historians have violently disagreed and have often considered the Middle Ages as the valley of shadow in which the pure Church of the ancient era of church history was corrupted. The modern era of church history, which began with Luther, was to them one of reformation in which the Church regained the ideals of the New Testament. All of these views must be tempered by the fact that the Middle Ages were not static but dynamic. The classical culture of the past, chastened by Christianity, was given to the Teutonic tribes by the Church. Development under divine direction was continuous even in the Middle Ages.

The medieval history of the Church took place in a wider arena than did that of the ancient Church. After the Teutonic tribes were won to Christianity, the Baltic basin became as important as the Mediterranean basin.

The modern era is deeply indebted to the Middle Ages. In the Middle Ages men attempted to set up a Christian civilization in which the past was integrated with the present in a meaningful synthesis. The modern era thus far lacks such a synthesis for life, and, as a result, modern man is struggling against confusion and the prospect not only of intellectual, moral and spiritual, but also of material chaos.

With this in mind the importance of Gregory I becomes obvious. He stood, as Augustine did in his day, at the divide between the two worlds of classicism and medieval Christianity and became the symbol of the new medieval world in which culture was institutionalized within the church dominated by the bishop of Rome.

Gregory (540–604), often called the Great, was born in the troublous times when the Eastern Empire under Justinian was seeking to regain the section of the Western Empire that had been lost to the Teutonic tribesmen. Pillaging bands, disease and famine were often the order of the day.

Born into one of the old, noble and wealthy families of Rome, Gregory was given a legal education to fit him for government service. He studied Latin literature extensively but knew no Hebrew or Greek. He was familiar with the writings of Ambrose, Jerome and Augustine but knew little of the classical literature or philosophy of Greece. In 573 he was made prefect of Rome, a position of importance and honor. Shortly thereafter he gave up the fortune that he had inherited from his father — his mother Silvia entered a convent after the death of his father — and used the proceeds to build seven monasteries in Italy, the most important of which was set up in his father's palace. Here he became a monk. Between 579 and 585 he was an ambassador representing the Roman bishop at Constantinople. Upon his return to Rome he was made abbot of St. Andrew's monastery, which he had founded after his father's death. If Augustine became a monk for intellectual purposes, it is fair to say that Gregory took monkish vows because he thought asceticism was a way to glorify God. When Pope Pelagius died of the plague in 590, Gregory was chosen to take his place.

This man, whose epitaph was "God's Consul," was one of the noblest of the leaders of the Roman church. His renunciation of great wealth impressed the people of his day. He was a man of humility who thought of himself as the "servant of the servants of God." He was a zealous missionary and was instrumental in winning the English to Christianity. His legal training, tact and common sense made him one of the ablest administrators the Roman Church had during the Middle Ages. But, like many men of his age, he was unduly superstitious and credulous. His *Dialogues* (593) display his unbounded credulity in what seemed to be miraculous to the medieval mind.[1] Moreover, though he had some training in sacred learning, his scholarship was marred by a lack of knowledge of the original languages of the Bible. During the seven years when he was ambassador in Constantinople, he did not even learn Greek.

Gregory's greatest work was to expand the power of the Roman bishop. Though he disclaimed the title of pope, he exercised all the power and prerogatives of the later popes. This he did to assert the spiritual supremacy of the bishop of Rome. He exercised episcopal care over the churches of Gaul, Spain, Britain, Africa and Italy. He appointed bishops and sent the pallium, the scarf of office, to those whose appointments he had made or ratified.

When John the Faster, the patriarch of Constantinople, claimed the title of "ecumenical" or universal bishop, Gregory immediately gave battle. He was willing to accept a coordinate status for the patriarchs of the Church, which would put them on a level as heads of the great sections of the Church, but he was not willing to let anyone have the title of universal bishop. But neither the patriarch nor the Eastern emperor would give in, and Gregory had to bide his time. When in 602 revolution brought a new emperor, Phocas, to the throne in Constantinople, Gregory sought to be on friendly terms with him, although this vulgar upstart had murdered the wife and family of the former emperor. In return, Phocas sided with Gregory against the patriarch and acknowledged the bishop of Rome as the "head of all the churches." Gregory did not, however, accept the name "universal pope" which the patriarch of Alexandria wanted to give to him. He preferred to be called the "servant of the servants of God." But while he disclaimed the title of supreme head of the Church, he would let no one else lay claim to the title and exercised the papal power in fact. No bishop or metropolitan in the West dared to go against his will, and he permitted no one elsewhere in the world of that day to assert universal supremacy over the Church.

Gregory's deep interest in missionary work is shown by the fine story that Bede tells in his history. According to the story, when Gregory was told that the fair-haired, blue-eyed boys up for sale as slaves in Rome were Angles, he said that they

---

[1] Jonathan Scott, Albert Hyma, Arthur H. Noyes, *Readings in Medieval History* (New York: Appleton-Century-Crofts, Inc., 1933), pp. 84-92. This is a good account of Gregory's life and times.

were not "Angles" but "Angels." When told that they were from Deiri (Yorkshire), he decided that they must be delivered from the wrath (*de ira*) of God by missionary work.[2] He therefore commissioned the monk Augustine, who must not be confused with Augustine of Hippo, to go to Britain and give the message of the Gospel to the British. Augustine landed in England in 597 and soon won the king of Kent to Christianity. But the Roman missionaries quickly ran into competition from the Celtic church, which was slowly evangelizing to the south. In 664 the Roman faith finally won. Thus Gregory may be considered as the instrument in bringing the English under the sway of the Church of Rome. He made careful plans for the development of the English church.[3]

Gregory made the bishopric of Rome one of the wealthiest in the Church of his day by his excellent work as an administrator. The papal possessions in Italy and nearby areas had never before yielded such a golden harvest as they did under Gregory's careful administrative policies. With this money he was able to act as the protector of the peace in the West. When the Arian Lombard king threatened Rome on one occasion during Gregory's pontificate, Gregory was able to raise troops and force the Lombard ruler to make peace.

He was also the organizer of the Gregorian chant which came to have a more important place in the Roman Catholic Church than that developed by Ambrose. This chant involved the use of a stately and solemn monotone in that part of worship which was chanted.

Gregory was a good preacher, too, with a real message for the time of crisis in which he lived. His sermons were practical and stressed humility and piety, but they were often marred by an excessive use of allegory, a common fault of preaching in his day.[4]

More outstanding than his sermons are his other literary works. In the *Moralia*, a commentary on the Book of Job, he emphasizes moral interpretation and resorts to allegorizing in order to derive his ethical formulas. He pictures Job as a type of Christ, his wife as a type of the carnal nature, the seven sons as types

[2] The Venerable Bede, *History of the Church of England* (New York: G. P. Putnam's Sons, 2 vols., 1930) Book II, Ch. II.

[3] Henry Bettenson, *Documents of the Christian Church* (New York: Oxford University Press, 1949), pp. 215-218.

[4] James H. Robinson, *Readings in Modern European History* (Boston: Ginn & Co., 2 vols., 1904), Vol. I, pp. 78-80.

of the clergy, and the three daughters as types of the faithful laity. He wrote other commentaries, but none of them are as extensive as his work on the Book of Job. He also wrote a work known as the *Book of Pastoral Rule* which concerns pastoral theology. He emphasizes the prerequisites for the ministry, the virtues a pastor needs and the need for introspection. The work made a great appeal to the monks of his day because of its ascetic nature.[5] There are also over eight hundred of his letters extant.

Gregory was also an outstanding theologian. He is ranked with Jerome, Ambrose and Augustine as one of the four great doctors of the Western Church. He laid the groundwork of the theology that was held by the Roman Church throughout the Middle Ages until Thomas Aquinas formulated his *Summa*. He believed that man was a sinner by birth and choice, but he softened Augustine's view by asserting that man did not inherit guilt from Adam but only sin, as a disease to which all were subject. He maintained that the will was free and that only its goodness had been lost. He believed in predestination, but he limited it to the elect. Grace was not irresistible, he believed, because it was based on both the foreknowledge of God and, to some extent, the merits of man. He upheld the idea of good works and emphasized the idea of purgatory as a place where souls would be purified prior to their entrance to heaven. He did hold to verbal inspiration of the Bible but strangely gave tradition a place of equality with the Bible. *The Canon of the Mass,* which he changed somewhat, was widely used in his day, and it revealed the growing tendency to consider the Communion as a sacrifice of Christ's body and blood each time it is performed.[6] He also emphasized good works and the invocation of the saints in order to get their aid. It may safely be said that medieval theology bore the stamp of Gregory's thought.

The pontificate of Gregory is indeed a landmark in the transition from ancient to medieval church history. Later successors built upon the foundation that he had laid as they created the sacramental hierarchal system of the institutionalized church of the Middle Ages.

[5] *Ibid.,* pp. 80-82; see also Frederic A. Ogg, *A Source Book of Medieval History* (New York: American Book Co., 1907), pp. 91-96, for other extracts from this work.
[6] F. J. Foakes Jackson, *An Introduction to the History of Christianity A.D. 590-1314* (New York: The Macmillan Co., 1928), pp. 25-27.

THE FIRST MEDIEVAL POPE

BIBLIOGRAPHY OF MEDIEVAL CHURCH HISTORY

The teacher or student who desires to pursue the study of medieval church history in more detail will find the bibliographical work by Louis J. Paetow, *A Guide to the Study of Medieval History* (New York: F. S. Crofts & Co., 1931), a useful guide to other works.

There are several fine collections of documents of importance to the student of medieval church history. These are available in most libraries:

A Source Book of Medieval History (New York: American Book Co., 1907) by Frederic A. Ogg contains many interesting documents.

Many other documents will be found in Oliver J. Thatcher and Edgar H. McNeal, *A Source Book for Medieval History* (New York: Charles Scribner's Sons, 1905).

A more recent collection of material is *Readings in Medieval History* (New York: Appleton-Century-Crofts, 1933) by Jonathan F. Scott, Albert Hyma and Arthur H. Noyes.

Documents specifically dealing with church history will be found in Volume III of B. J. Kidd, *Documents Illustrative of the History of the Church* (London: Society for Promoting Christian Knowledge, 3 vols., 1920-1941).

The writer has found *An Introduction to the History of Christianity, A.D. 590-1314* (New York: The Macmillan Co., 1928) by Frederic J. Foakes Jackson a more detailed and very interesting history of the period.

A History of the Medieval Church 590-1500 (London: Methuen & Co., Ltd., 7th ed., 1951) by Margaret Deanesly provides much additional material for the period.

The recent work on medieval missions, *Light in the Dark Ages* (Wheaton: VanKampen Press, 1950) by V. Raymond Edman gives a good account of missionary work in this era.

Kenneth S. Latourette's *A History of the Expansion of Christianity.* Volume II, *The Thousand Years of Uncertainty* (New York: Harper & Brothers, 1938) is an even more detailed history of medieval missions.

Chapter XVII

CHRISTIAN EXPANSION AND RETRENCHMENT

The Middle Ages is often thought to be a period in which society was static and in which people moved around very little. A casual study of the movement of people during the Middle Ages will show that there has never been an era in the history of Europe when there were greater mass migrations. The movement of the Mongol Huns and the Germanic Goths and Teutons into the Roman Empire after 375 has already been noticed. After 590 Christianity faced new dynamic movements of people. During the seventh and later centuries the Church in the East had to face the threat of Mohammedanism. Mohammedanism was also a matter of concern to the Western Church until it was turned back at Tours in 732. The renewed movement of peoples out of the Scandinavian Peninsula after the eighth century also threatened the Western Church with destruction.

In addition to meeting the challenge of these migrants, the Western Church had also to take on the task of evangelizing the Teutonic tribes within the bounds of the old Empire. Those who had accepted an Arian form of Christianity and who had settled in Spain and Italy presented a further challenge to Christianity. This task of winning the pagans and the heterodox Arians and the challenge of the rival religion of Mohammedanism taxed the growing resources of the Church to the limit. Between 590 and 800 the Western Church made great gains in the Northern and Western areas of Europe, but Eastern Christianity, which had become static, did little more than to hold its own against the Mohammedans who, at times, knocked against the gates of Constantinople.

The work of missions was put on a professional basis during this period. Bands of monks went out to proclaim the Gospel to the groups to whom the highest authority in the Church, the pope, had sent them.

[186]

MOHAMMEDAN EXPANSION 622-900

Indian Ocean

Aral Sea

Caspian Sea

Persian Gulf

•BAGDAD

•MEDINA   •MECCA

Red Sea

Black Sea

CONSTANTINOPLE

•CAIRO

Mediterranean Sea

TOURS 732

CORDOVA

Atlantic Ocean

BY 632   BY 750
BY 900
EASTERN EMPIRE

I. The Rise and Impact of Islam

The Mohammedans, energized by the dynamic of a new-found faith, the hope of plunder in the name of religion, and a zeal to convert the unbelievers to their faith, rapidly expanded from Arabia into North Africa, Asia, and even Europe by way of Spain. Founded by a personal leader, their religion was the latest of the three great monotheistic religions of the world. It, too, claimed to be a universal religion for all peoples. The Mohammedans finally wiped out the Church in North Africa and weakened the Church in other areas of Africa. They eventually brought about the downfall of the Eastern Empire in 1453 and put the Eastern Church under Moslem political control.

Islam had its origins in the Arabian Peninsula, a piece of land relatively isolated from the surrounding world by water or trackless desert except on the northwestern border. The area is inhospitable, and man is forced to struggle in the midst of barren rocks, sand and hot sun to maintain his existence. Faced by the power of nature, in such an area man is inclined to recognize a supreme being greater than himself.

At the time of the rise of Mohammedanism Semitic Bedouin tribesmen wandered from oasis to oasis with their camels, flocks and herds, doing only what trading was necessary with the townsmen of Mecca and Medina. Tribal warfare was frequent except during the periods of truce each year when the tribes went to worship the black stone in the Kaaba at Mecca.

One of these tribesmen was Mohammed (570–632), a member of the Koreish tribe, who made his living as a camel driver. Going with his uncle on one trip to Syria and Palestine, he came into contact with Christianity and Judaism. He then married a rich widow named Khadijah and gained the wealth whereby he could be free to devote his time to religious meditation. In 610 he felt divinely called to proclaim monotheism and in the course of three years won twelve converts, mostly among his own kinsmen. Stirring up opposition with his preaching against idolatry, he was forced to flee in 622 to Medina from Mecca. This flight, known as the Hegira, became the first year of the Mohammedan calendar. By 630 the movement had grown so much that Mohammed was able to capture Mecca. Two years later, at the time of his death, his followers were ready to expand outside of the Arabian Peninsula.

The greatest gains of this new dynamic faith took place between 632 and 732. Syria and Palestine were won in the third decade of the seventh century, and in 637 the Mosque of Omar was erected in Jerusalem. Egypt was won in the next decade, and Persia fell under Mohammedan control in 652. The crescent-shaped expansion to the West and the East threatened Christianity with a great pincers, but expansion at the Eastern end of the crescent was stopped by the brave defense of the Eastern Empire under Leo the Isaurian in 717 and 718. Mohammedan expansion on the Western wing of the crescent was halted by the defeat of the Moslems by the armies of Charles Martel at Tours in 732. But the Church had already undergone great losses as the conquered people were faced with the choice of the sword, tribute or Islam. Moslems were not always intolerant, for they often permitted people in tribute-paying areas to practice their faith. By 750 the era of conquest came to an end, and the Mohammedans, influenced by Greek culture, set out to build a splendid Arabic civilization centered in Bagdad. The peak of culture came under Haroun-Al-Raschid (786–809) the ruler of the Eastern section of Mohammedan territory.

The main source of the Mohammedan religion is the Koran. This work, two-thirds the length of the New Testament, is arranged in 114 chapters. The longest chapter comes at the beginning of the book, and the chapters become successively shorter until the last chapter consists of only three verses. It is repetitious and unorganized.

Belief in one God known as Allah is the central theme of Islam. Allah made his will known through many prophets, including Biblical characters such as Abraham, Moses and Christ, but Mohammed was the latest and greatest of these prophets. The religion is fatalistic with its idea of passive submission to the will of Allah. After judgment men will enjoy a rather sensual Paradise or face the terrors of hell. The good Mohammedan prays five times daily, facing towards Mecca. He also recites his creed daily. Fasting and almsgiving are important, and the holiest Mohammedans are those who, at least once during their life, make a pilgrimage to Mecca.

Islam has had a marked cultural and religious significance for Western Europe. It assimilated and passed on to Western Europe through Arabic Spain the Greek philosophy of Aristotle. The medieval scholastics attempted to integrate Greek scientific thought with Christian theology by use of the deductive method

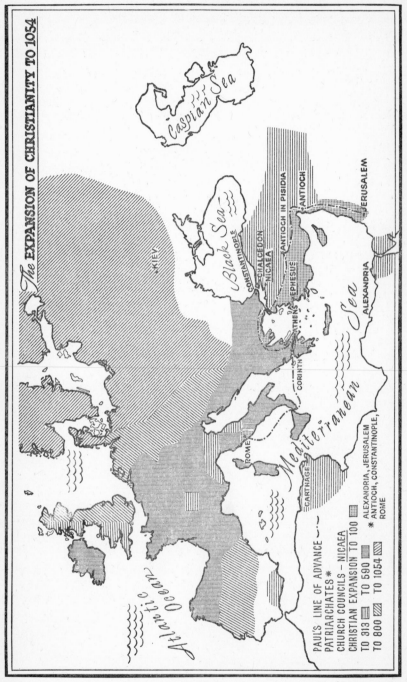

The EXPANSION of CHRISTIANITY TO 1054

PAUL'S LINE OF ADVANCE ------
PATRIARCHATES ✳
CHURCH COUNCILS — NICAEA
CHRISTIAN EXPANSION TO 100
TO 313   TO 590
TO 800   TO 1054

ALEXANDRIA, JERUSALEM
ANTIOCH, CONSTANTINOPLE,
ROME

✳ ALEXANDRIA, JERUSALEM
ANTIOCH, CONSTANTINOPLE,
ROME

of Aristotle, which they had come to know through Averroes' translation of Aristotle's writings. So great was this influence in Europe during the twelfth century that Haskins has called the period the "Twelfth Century Renaissance."[1]

Both the Eastern and Western sections of the Church were weakened by losses of people and territory to Islam, but the losses of the Eastern Church were greater than those of the West. The strong North African church disappeared, and the Holy Land was lost to Christianity. The Eastern Church was able to do little more than to hold back the Moslem hordes from sweeping past Constantinople. Consequently, missionary activity, which was carried on mainly by the Western Church, centered in Northwestern Europe. The Eastern Church also had to deal with the problem of whether images as well as pictures could be used in the church. This controversy, known as the iconoclastic controversy, came about partly because the Moslems were challenging the Christians as idolaters for having pictures and images in the church.

This weakening of the Church in the East was balanced by the stronger position of the bishop of Rome. Great rival metropolitan leaders of the church in Alexandria and Antioch were under Islamic domination and were unable any longer to speak for the Church at large. The pope was not slow to make the most of this opportunity to strengthen his own position. Islam stubbornly resisted the efforts of the papacy and Crusaders to regain the Holy Land and since that time has strongly resisted every attempt of Christian missionaries to propagate Christianity among Moslems.

II. Missionary Activity in the West

A. In the British Isles.

The Irish church, which had been planted by Patrick, was the brightest spot culturally in Northern Europe between 590 and 800. It had sent Columbanus to the Burgundians and Columba to the Scots. Irish Monks had engaged in the work of preserving, copying and beautifully illuminating manuscripts at a time when learning on the Continent was in eclipse. Not until the beginning of the eighth century did the Irish church accept Roman control. The eighth and ninth century invasions of the Vikings so weakened it that in the tenth century it fell into decay.

[1] Charles H. Haskins, *The Renaissance of the Twelfth Century* (Cambridge: Harvard University Press, 1939).

The Irish church was also indirectly responsible for the evangelization of Northern England because it was under influences from Columba's monastery on the Island of Iona that Aidan carried the message of the Gospel to the Northumbrians of the northeast coast of England. Oswald, an Anglo-Saxon ruler, had spent some time in exile among the Irish and Scotch Christians and had seen the attractiveness of the life of these Celtic Christians. Oppressed by the spiritual darkness of the Anglo-Saxons, who had driven the Celts and their Christianity out of England in the fifth century after the withdrawal of the Roman armies, he called upon the Scotch church for missionaries.

Aidan was consecrated as bishop to the people of Northumbria in 634 and set up his headquarters on the Island of Lindisfarne, known also as Holy Island. He built a monastery there which became a center of evangelism. He enjoyed the full cooperation of Oswald, who often acted as his interpreter when he made his journeys on foot among Oswald's people. Aidan gave considerable attention to education in order that the Church in Northumbria might have an able leadership. When he died in 651, Celtic Christianity had been firmly established in Northern England.

Some years before the beginning of Celtic missionary activities in the north, the Roman Church had begun missionary activity among the Anglo-Saxons of Southern England. Gregory, who was the bishop of Rome, had seen some young Anglo-Saxons for sale in the Roman slave market and decided that their people must be won for Roman Christianity. He appointed Augustine, the prior of St. Andrew's monastery in Rome, as the leader of a band of monks from that monastery. They were ordered to proceed to Southern England and to win the Anglo-Saxons to the Christian faith. Augustine and his band of monks landed in the Island of Thanet off the Kentish coast in the spring of 597. Bertha, the Gallic wife of Ethelbert, the king of Kent, had been converted before she became Ethelbert's wife, and she influenced her husband in favor of the missionaries. After the first interview between Augustine and Ethelbert, which was held in the open air where Ethelbert thought Augustine's magic might not affect him, the king gave Augustine permission to preach the Gospel.[2] Ethelbert soon submitted himself for

2 Frederic A. Ogg, *A Source Book of Medieval History* (New York: American Book Co., 1907), pp. 72-77.

baptism, and large numbers of his people followed him in the acceptance of Christianity.

The Christianity planted in the north by the Celtic Christians from Scotland soon came into contact with the Roman Catholic Christianity expanding northward from the south of England. The two forms of Christianity differed on many matters. The Celtic Christians did not acknowledge the authority of the pope. They also followed the custom of the Eastern Church in computing the date of Easter and did not always have it on the same day of the week each year as the Roman Church did. Celtic monks might marry; Roman monks could not. Celtic monks had a different type of tonsure or hair cut. These differences caused such confusion and rivalry between the two forms of Christianity that Oswy, who had united most of Anglo-Saxon England under himself, called a meeting at Whitby in 664 to decide which form of Christianity his people would follow. Roman Christianity won the day because Oswy, according to Bede, preferred the religion which claimed to have the keys to heaven.[3] Theodore was then sent to England to organize English Christians under the Roman banner and to set up dioceses and archbishoprics, which, in many cases, still exist in the Anglican Church.

English Christianity was soon noted for its scholarship because Theodore started schools. The schools of Jarrow and York were outstanding. When, about 800, Charlemagne wanted someone to help him to develop an educational system in his domain, he got Alcuin from the school at York to do the task. Bede was another outstanding scholar, spending most of his life at Jarrow. His history of England, written from the ecclesiastical viewpoint, is one of the best sources of information concerning English life and history before 731.

The Church in England also sent missionaries to the Continent of Europe who were instrumental in winning their Teutonic kinsmen to Roman Christianity. Because the English had a filial loyalty to the Roman see that persisted until the time of the Reformation, the Church in England became a bolster to the papacy.

B. Germany.

Boniface (680–755), also known as Winfrid, brought the Teutonic tribes, who occupied most of the area of modern Germany,

---

[3] B. J. Kidd, *Documents Illustrative of the History of the Church* (London: Society for Promoting Christian Knowledge, 3 vols., 1920-1941), Vol. III, pp. 54-58.

under the influence of the Gospel. At the same time he made sure that they would become loyal subjects of the pope. After he became a learned and devout priest with considerable business ability, he decided to consecrate his life to missionary activity. He went to Rome in 718 and got authority from the pope to preach the Gospel in Germany. According to one account, he cut down an oak at Geismar, which was sacred to one of the German gods, and made a chapel from the timber. Quickly he won Hesse to Roman Christianity. He next turned his attention to Thuringia and planted the Gospel there. In 732 he was elevated to the rank of archbishop by Pope Gregory III. During this part of his missionary career he began to use devoted women as missionaries. These women were among the first in a long line of women who have served Christ bravely and well throughout the history of the Church in the missionary fields of the world. Boniface next turned to Bavaria, and he established the Church there upon such strong foundations that even at the present Bavaria is the stronghold of the Roman Catholic system in Germany.

Such sweeping conquest, amounting at times to mass conversions and baptism of whole tribes and nations, raised the problem of baptism without a personal experience of Christianity. This has been a perennial problem of missionary effort wherever the conversion of an influential leader has resulted in such wholesale acceptance of Christianity that there has not been help enough to see that the converts have had a genuine experience of salvation.

C. The Low Countries.

Wilfrid, an English churchman who was shipwrecked on the coast of Friesland in 678, preached the Gospel to the people of that area during the winter of that year. But, after the death of the king who had been friendly to him, the people lapsed into paganism until the coming of Willibrord from England. Willibrord succeeded in planting Christianity on sounder foundations and won Friesland to allegiance to the papacy.

D. Italy.

Between 568 and 675 the Lombards, who had been converted to Arian Christianity, got control of Southern Italy and offered opposition to the papacy within its own land. Gregory I was able to prevent trouble during his pontificate through his influence upon the Bavarian princess Theudelinda, who had been successively the wife of two Lombard kings. The visit of the Irish monk Columbanus about 610 was instrumental in bringing many Lombards to a renunciation of their Arian faith. By 675 the Lombard rulers and most of their people had accepted the orthodox faith of Rome.

E. Spain.

The Arian Visigoths of Spain offered another challenge to the Roman Church. In 579 the son of the king was married to a woman of the Roman faith and his son Recared announced at the Synod of Toledo in 589 that he had renounced Arianism in favor of orthodox Christianity. Many of his nobles and Arian bishops followed suit. But the conquest was never complete, and dissension between the orthodox and the Arians of Spain made the area an easy prey for the Mohammedans who overran Spain in the eighth century.

By 800 the authority of the papacy was firmly established in the British Isles and in much of the area of modern Germany. The threat to the papacy from Arianism in Italy and Spain was nullified. But in the Eastern Church little missionary work was done except for the conversion of the Bulgarians and Moravians by Cyril and Methodius about the middle of the ninth century. The Moravians later came under papal jurisdiction. Most of the energies of the Eastern Church were thrown into the struggle to prevent the Mohammedans from capturing Constantinople.

BIBLIOGRAPHY

Charles Robinson's detailed work, *The Conversion of Europe* (London: Longmans, Green & Co., 1917) is a useful work to provide more background for missions than is possible within the scope of this text.

Chapter XVIII

THE REVIVAL OF IMPERIALISM IN THE WEST

The popes found themselves subject to pressures that threatened the increasingly strong claims to power which they made after 590. The emperors in Constantinople, who believed that the Church should be subordinated to the ruler of the state, were steadily encroaching upon what the bishop of Rome thought were his prerogatives and possessions. The Lombards, who held to the Arian form of Christianity, knocked upon the gates of Rome more than once during this period. These difficulties forced the pope to look around for a powerful ally who would support his claims to spiritual power and to temporal possessions in Italy. The Frankish rulers seemed to be the most promising allies, and with them the popes made an alliance which was to influence both ecclesiastical and political affairs during the Middle Ages. The new political empire in the West, to which the pope gave his assent in 800, revived the imperial idea of the Roman Empire, but the rulers of this new empire were to be Teutons rather than Romans. The glory of reviving the Roman Empire went to the Frankish rulers.

I. THE MEROVINGIAN DYNASTY

The importance of the conquest and civilization of Gaul by Caesar in the middle of the first century before Christ now became apparent because it was to the Franks in this territory that the pope turned for aid. These Franks had come to France from their homelands along the eastern bank of the Rhine River and had conquered Gaul, but at the same time they had accepted the Roman culture of their victims.

Clovis was the first leader to unify the Franks and to complete the conquest of the territories of what would be the major part of modern France. He married a Burgundian princess, Clotilda, and linked the Burgundian territories won by this marriage with others won in battle. The union of all the Frankish tribesmen from the Rhine under his leadership was a great contribution to stability in the area. Clovis accepted Christianity, partly through the influence of his wife, and partly because of what appeared to be providential aid given to him in battle. His acceptance of Christianity in 496 makes that year significant in the history of Western Europe, because the Franks, whom he had united, and their rulers were to become the bulwark of the papacy against its temporal foes and to give to the papacy the territories that it held as temporal possessions for over a millennium.

As is so often the case, Clovis' sons did not have the ability of their father, and control of the affairs of state passed into the hands of an official, known as the mayor of the palace, who held the reins of government, while the weak successors of Clovis enjoyed life in the palace. These mayors of the palace made up what is known as the Carolingian dynasty which was to reach its zenith of power under Charlemagne.

II. The Carolingian Rulers

Pepin of Heristal was the first of these mayors of the palace to reunite the divided possessions of Clovis, and from 687 to 714 he controlled the Franks for the degenerate descendants of Clovis. He made the office of mayor of the palace a hereditary position to be filled by his descendants.

Charles Martel (the Hammerer), an illegitimate son of Pepin, took over the duties of mayor of the palace after 714. His abilities as a warrior were badly needed because the Mohammedans, who had overrun Spain, were now threatening to take over all of Western Europe. Charles defeated them decisively at the battle of Tours in 732 and obligated the Roman Church to him because he had apparently saved Western Europe for orthodox Christianity. He supported the work of Boniface in evangelizing the tribes beyond the Rhine, knowing that if they were won to Christianity, he would not have difficulty with them on the western bank of the Rhine.

Charles' successor as mayor of the palace was his son Pepin, known as Pepin the Short or Pepin the Great, who ruled jointly with his brother from 741 until 747, when the brother withdrew to a monastery. Pepin was the first real Carolingian king because he took the title of king (751) as well as exercising the authority of mayor of the palace. The occasion for this extension of his authority was a request from Pope Zacharias for aid against the Arian Lombards who were threatening the authority of the papacy in Italy. Pepin was consecrated, possibly by Boniface, as the king of the Franks. Childeric III, the last of the Merovingians, was deposed and sent to spend the rest of his life in a monastery. The mayor of the palace now became the king of the Franks, with papal blessing. Pepin redeemed his promise to aid the pope by expeditions against the Lombards in 754 and 756. He granted land in central Italy from Rome to Ravenna to the pope in 754. This grant, known as the Donation of Pepin, had special significance for the people of Rome because 754 B.C. was the traditional date for the founding of the city of Rome. This allotment was the foundation for the Papal States which the pope held uninterruptedly in Italy until the union of the Italian people in 1870. It is little wonder that the reigning pope, Stephen II, crowned Pepin for the second time as the "King of the Franks and Patrician of the Romans" in 754.

For some centuries an account had been developing concerning the supposedly miraculous healing and conversion of Constantine by the bishop of Rome. The grateful Constantine was supposed to have made liberal grants of rights and territories to the bishop. These stories were combined in a document known as the *Donation of Constantine* and given wide circulation during the Middle Ages. The document was used by the papacy in the Middle Ages to buttress its claims to temporal possessions and to power in both the temporal and spiritual realms.[1] The authoritative formulation seems to have been made about the middle of the eighth century so that it was in circulation at the time Pepin made his grant of land in Italy to the papacy.

In the document Constantine greeted Sylvester and the bishops of the Church and went on to relate that he had been healed from leprosy and baptized by Sylvester. In return, he declared that the church at Rome was to have precedence over all other churches and that its bishop was the supreme bishop in the Church. He gave territories throughout his empire, the Lateran Palace, and the clothing and insignia of the imperial rank to

[1] Henry Bettenson, *Documents of the Christian Church* (New York: Oxford University Press, 1947), pp. 137-142. These pages give the text of the document. Valla's refutation of the *Donation of Constantine* is available in *The Treatise of Lorenzo Valla on the Donation of Constantine*, trans. Christopher B. Coleman (New Haven: Yale University Press, 1922).

Sylvester. Constantine then withdrew to Constantinople so that he would not interfere with the imperial rights of the pope.

Though the facts just described were in the document, they were not historically correct. No other record of any such facts exists. Moreover, Lorenzo Valla, early in the fifteen century, showed in his critique, the first document of real historical criticism, that the *Donation* was a forgery made some centuries after the events it purported to describe. Few spurious documents have exercised so potent an influence upon history as this one did.

The next ruler over the Franks was Charlemagne, son of Pepin the Short. Charlemagne (742-814) came to the throne in 768 and in 800 he became emperor in the West when the pope crowned him *Imperator Romanorum* (Emperor of the Romans). His influence was felt in every area of human endeavor in Western Europe.

Much information about Charlemagne is derived from Einhard, sometimes incorrectly known as Eginhard, writer of a biographic sketch of Charlemagne.[2] Charlemagne was about seven feet in height and had a proportionately large body. His bright face and long white hair, coupled with such height, gave him an air of dignity. He delighted in hunting, riding and swimming but also had a real interest in culture and this interest led him to combine the pleasure of the table with listening to music or having someone read to him. He was also devoted to religion. However, his religion did not carry over into his domestic life because he kept concubines as well as his legal spouse in his palace.

Charlemagne was also a man of war. He engaged in about fifty campaigns during the course of his reign in an attempt to end anarchy within his kingdom and to expand its borders into Italy, where he completed the defeat of the Lombards, and into Germany, where he conquered the Saxons. He was able to double his father's possessions until he held all of Italy as far south as Rome, most of the area of modern Germany, and all of the area of modern France. So much land in Western Europe had not been under one jurisdiction since the time of the Roman Empire. Because this kingdom was held together by the genius of Charlemagne, it did not last long after his death in 814.

[2] J. F. Scott, A Hyma and A. H. Noyes, *Readings in Medieval History* (New York: Appleton-Century-Crofts, 1933), pp. 149-166.

Charlemagne developed an able bureaucracy and a good system of imperial government to administer his large empire. The empire was divided into different areas, each of which comprised several counties, under a duke. The Emperor sent men known as *missi dominici* to the courts of these dukes at unexpected times to inspect their accounts, to announce new capitularies or laws, and to check upon how well they were keeping order.

He was also friendly to the Church. He thought that the Church might be compared to the soul and the state to the body of man. Church and state had their respective spheres of responsibility. While on a visit to Rome to finish the work of defeating the Lombards in 774, he reconfirmed the donation of lands that Pepin had made to the pope in 754. He believed, however, that the ruler of the Church should not dispute the decision of the ruler of the state and that bishops should also be subordinated to the head of the state.

When Pope Leo III was set upon by a faction in Rome, and nearly killed, he left Rome for the court of Charlemagne. Charlemagne went back to Rome with him, and at a council the Pope was cleared of the charges against him. At a holy mass in the cathedral on Christmas day in 800, while Charlemagne knelt before the altar, the Pope put the crown upon Charlemagne's head and declared that he was the emperor of the Romans. Thus was the Roman Empire revived in the West, and new Rome, led by a Teuton, took the place of the old Roman Empire.

The human dream of unity of men seemed again to be realized, for Charlemagne had the largest territory under his control that any man held since the fall of the Empire. The universal spiritual empire of the papacy over men's souls now had its counterpart in the revived Roman Empire which Charlemagne had over the bodies of men.

The kingdom of God was thought to have two arms: the spiritual, presided over by the pope, was to have responsibility for men's souls; the temporal was to have responsibility for the physical well-being of man. The pope and the emperor were to give each other mutual support. Of course, such a view was bound to bring conflict between the rulers of the Church and the new Teutonic Roman Empire. Was the emperor given power from God over men, and did the pope exercise delegated power from the emperor over men's souls, or did God give supreme authority to the Church, and did the pope delegate authority over men's bodies to the emperor, or did they hold coordinate positions in which God gave to each one directly supremacy within his respective sphere? The answer to this problem occupied the energies of popes and emperor during the Middle Ages until the popes finally succeeded in bringing the emperor under their control.

After the death of Charlemagne his empire declined under his weak son and warring grandsons until the grandsons divided it among themselves in the Treaty of Verdun in 843 after a long period of war. The imperial idea was again revived by a German prince named Otto, in 962; and from 962 until 1806 the Holy Roman Empire was an honored institution in Europe in spite of Voltaire's jibe that it was neither holy, Roman nor an empire.

Charlemagne was deeply devoted to cultural progress, and his imperial reign from 800 to 814 was a period of cultural development which has since become known as the "Carolingian Renaissance." Not since the work of Boethius and Cassiodorus during the reign of Theodoric, the Ostrogothic ruler of the land of Italy in the sixth century, had there been such cultural progress. In order to effect his cultural renaissance, Charlemagne turned to the scholars of the Church in England and persuaded the great scholar Alcuin (735–804) to come to his court from York and to assume the leadership of his palace school at Aachen where the children of the royal family and leading nobles might be educated. Alcuin had the assistance of Paul the Deacon, Einhard and other able scholars in this work.

The palace school of Charlemagne was an integral link in the chain of men and schools responsible for passing on to the medieval university the basic outlines of its curriculum, the trivium and the quadrivium that had been derived from Roman higher education by Martianus Capella in the fifth century. The cultural activities of Charlemagne were an important step in the process by which the German people assimilated classical and Christian learning. Charlemagne himself delighted to listen to the reading of great books from the past and, according to his biographer Einhard, particularly liked Augustine's works, especially the *City of God*. He also insisted that the abbots set up monastery schools so the interpreters of Scripture might be learned men who would understand and rightly interpret the Bible.[3]

Considerable emphasis should be given to the significance of Charlemagne in medieval history. His coronation marked the reconciliation and union of the population of the old Roman Empire with its Teutonic conqueror. It ended the dream of the Eastern emperor to regain for the Eastern segment of the Roman Empire the areas lost to the barbarians in the West in the fifth century. Because the pope had crowned Charlemagne, his position was enhanced as one to whom rulers owed their crowns, and the emperor was bound to aid him when he was in difficulty. Charlemagne's coronation marked the peak of Frankish power which began with Clovis' decision to become a Christian.

III. The Church and Empire in the East

Charlemagne was also interested in the Eastern Empire and Church and even made attempts to unite the East and West into one empire that would embrace most of the territories of the old Roman Empire. One must not forget that the Eastern emperors held back the Mohammedan hordes from sweeping over Europe until the West could recover from the confusion and chaos created by the fall of the Empire and the influx of the barbarians.

The East was particularly troubled by the iconoclastic controversy of the eighth and ninth centuries. Leo III in decrees of 726 and 730 had banned the use of images in the Church and ordered their destruction. Charlemagne made a statement in defense of the use of images about the time Irene became the empress of the Eastern Empire. He even offered to marry Irene in order to reunite the areas of the old Roman Empire under one crown with the capital in the West. But Irene refused his advances, and the division of the Empire, first started when Constantine moved the capital to Constantinople from Rome in 330, continued.

The Eastern Church, except for the work of John of Damascus, remained static in the development of theology from the period of theological controversy in the fourth to the sixth centuries until the modern era. John (ca. 700–754) formulated theological ideas into what became the Eastern equivalent of the *Summa* of Thomas Aquinas. His *Fountain of Knowledge* in three books

---

[3] O. J. Thatcher and E. H. McNeal, *A Source Book for Medieval History* (New York: Charles Scribner's Sons, 1905), pp. 55-56, 51-52.

became the authority for theologians in the Eastern Church as the work of Thomas Aquinas became the authority in the Western Church. The third book, *of the Orthodox faith,* is a summation of the theology developed by the Fathers and Councils from the fourth century up to his own day, and it became the standard expression of orthodoxy in the Eastern part of the Empire. Perhaps the fact that the church at Constantinople was subordinated to the authority of the emperor accounted for the static position of Eastern Christianity after the middle of the eighth century. In the East the Church was virtually a department of the state; whereas in the West the pope had been able to gain freedom from temporal control and was even able at a later date to control the temporal power.

By the end of the era between 590 and 800 some of the confusion attendant upon the fall of the Roman Empire in the West had been cleared. The Eastern section of the Empire continued under the rule of the emperor at Constantinople. The Frankish kingdom of Clovis grew into the Christian empire under Charlemagne and united the now Christian Teutons and the inhabitants of the old Empire in the West. The southern shore of the Mediterranean, formerly territory held by the Roman Empire, was lost to Mohammedanism by Rome and Constantinople, but further Mohammedan expansion was stopped in the East and West by 732. The old territories of Rome were now divided into three areas, and church history of the era between 800 and 1054 is mainly concerned with the struggle between the pope and the ruler of the Frankish Empire.

EBB AND FLOW IN RELATIONSHIPS BETWEEN CHURCH AND STATE,
800–1054

Chapter XIX

THE EMERGENCE OF THE HOLY ROMAN EMPIRE

The history of the Church in this era involves discussion of the complex web of relationships that existed between the Church and the imperial states in the East and the West. It was the period when the first great schism in the Church occurred. The Western and Eastern sections of the Church separated to go their respective ways as the Roman Catholic Church in the West and the Greek Orthodox Church in the East. And the gloom of the Dark Ages was being slowly dispelled by a reivival of learning that began under Charlemagne.

I. THE DECLINE OF THE CAROLINGIAN EMPIRE
A. *The Weak Successors of Charlemagne.*

The brilliant imperial structure established by the coronation of Charlemagne by Leo III on Christmas Day of the year 800 did not long survive its great founder. Because the Empire had been dependent upon his personal genius, his death was the signal for the beginning of its dissolution. Neither his son nor grandson had the energy and ability that he had, and the splendid Frankish Empire broke up rapidly.

B. *Teutonic Principle of Inheritance.*

An even more important factor in the decline of the Frankish phase of the Holy Roman Empire was the fragmentation introduced into the imperial structure by the fatal Teutonic principle that prescribed the division of the lands of the father among his sons. This principle was put into operation even during the life time of Louis the Pious, Charlemagne's immediate successor. The concept of an indivisible empire, held by the Romans, was foreign to the Teutonic mind. Furthermore, even if Louis had held this concept, he lacked the personal genius of his father Charlemagne to work it out. He was unable to control the strong aristocracy, and his indulgent nature weakened his control of his turbulent family.

Shortly after he took over the imperial throne, Louis announced his plans for the division of his empire among his sons. When another son, Charles the Bald, was born to him and to his second wife Judith in 823, he had to change his plans so as to include Charles among his heirs in the event of his death.

When he died in 840, after a troubled reign that had begun in 814, the quarrels of his sons made the decline of the great Carolingian Empire inevitable. His son Louis inherited the eastern section; Charles the Bald inherited the western section; and the long central section, stretching from the North Sea to the Adriatic Sea, and the imperial title of emperor went to Lothair. Lothair wished to extend his control over the whole area of his father's empire, but his two brothers, Charles the Bald and Louis the German, united against him. The latter two met at Strasbourg in 842 and took an oath in the vernaculars of their respective peoples to be loyal to each other until they had defeated Lothair. This meeting had significance for the history of modern France and Germany because Louis, whose possessions included most of the area of modern Germany, and Charles, whose possession included most of the area of modern France, each recognized the common tongue of his subjects by taking his oath in it.[1]

This alliance was too strong for Lothair, and in 843 the three brothers agreed to the treaty of Verdun.[2] The area of modern France was granted to Charles the Bald, and the area of modern Germany was to belong to Louis. Lothair was given the title of emperor and a strip between the two kingdoms that was a thousand miles long and over a hundred miles wide. This event marked the birth of the modern states of France and Germany, and rivalry between them for possession of the area between the two kingdoms has continued until modern times and has been a source of trouble in the affairs of Western Europe. By the Treaty of Mersen in 870 the rulers of the eastern and western Frankish kingdoms divided the central area between their two kingdoms and confined the descendants of Lothair to Italy.

C. The Rise of Feudalism.

Fragmentation of the great empire that Charlemagne had built up was also hastened by the rise of feudalism. Feudalism in one form or another always arises when a central government

[1] F. A. Ogg, *A Source Book of Medieval History* (New York: American Book Co., 1907), pp. 152-154.
[2] *Ibid.*, pp. 154-156.

becomes weak and can no longer exercise effective authority over the areas under its control. The decline of city life and trade after the fall of the Roman Empire forced people back to the land to make a living. These and other chaotic conditions of the ninth century encouraged the rise of the feudalistic way of life in Western Europe.

Society was divided horizontally rather than vertically in the Middle Ages so that there was little social mobility. A person usually lived his life in the social rank in which his father had lived. Society was divided after the rise of feudalism into a group of protectors, the feudal knights, who had the privilege of land ownership in return for their services; into a group of producers, the serfs on the manors which became the economic foundation of feudalism; and into a group of pray-ers, the priestly class of the universal Church. The individual was subordinated to the corporate or group interest, and every man had his master in such a hierarchal society.

Feudalism may be defined as a system of political organization based upon possession of land. The local lord gave good government in the immediate area where he owned the land. Until nation-states could emerge in England, France and Spain in the late Middle Ages, this was the only way in which justice and order could be maintained during the period of weak centralized authority after the decline of the Roman Empire, the failure of the Merovingian kingdom and the breakup of Charlemagne's Empire.

Feudalism was also an economic system that provided a living for all classes of society after the breakdown of international trade, another result of the fall of the Roman Empire. Both the lord and serf got their living from the soil, and each manor was self-sufficient except for a few items such as salt, millstones, or iron bars for the smith to work into tools. The manor, an area that could support an armed knight, was the land unit in the feudal system. Some feudal lords might own several manors. Thus the manor was the basic economic unit that made the feudal system possible.

Land tenure was the link that tied the manorial and feudal systems together. The knight, the lowest link in the feudal pyramid, was dependent for his living upon the serfs who worked the land for him. In return he gave to them protection.

Feudalism also involved personal relationships of loyalty between the vassal and the lord, such as the obligation of forty days of military service each year, the provision of food, and prayers, if the vassal were a churchman. Ideally, society was pyramidal with each vassal having a lord until the lord at the top of the pyramid, the king, was a vassal of God. Only in England under William the Conqueror in the eleventh century was the feudal pyramid realized. In what is now modern France and Germany, the tie between the feudal vassal and the ruler was weak.

This somewhat lengthy discussion of feudalism has been made necessary by the importance of feudalism as the political and economic system that gave law and order in the era of decentralization and chaos that followed the dissolution of Carolingian Empire and the invasion of Western Europe and England by the Vikings in the ninth and tenth centuries.

The influence of feudalism upon the Church in this period is even more important. About one third of the land of Western Europe was held by the Church during the late Middle Ages. Because the gifts of land by pious or repentant men, seeking to atone for a life of sin, remained in the hands of the Roman Church as a corporate body from generation to generation, that Church as a great landowner could not help but be influenced by the feudal system. These gifts were held in feudal tenure by abbots and bishops. The clergy as servants of God could not render military service to their feudal lord, and therefore they either had to give part of their lands to vassal knights who could render military service for them or devise other services. This feudalization of church land tended to secularize the Church and to distract its attention from spiritual to mundane interests. The ecclesiastical vassal faced the problem of divided allegiance. Should his primary allegiance be to the temporal lord, to whom he owed feudal dues, or to the pope, the spiritual overlord, from whom his spiritual authority came? This division of allegiance hindered the development of the sound spiritual life essential to the success of the Church.

Since the younger sons of the nobles could gain land and prestige through service in the Church, great nobles often interferred with elections to get an abbey or bishopric for their relatives. Many of these men were worldly and little interested in the spiritual matters that went with the ecclesiastical position.

The investiture controversy, the dispute as to whether the

feudal lord or the pope should grant an ecclesiastical feudal vassal the symbols of his authority, embittered relationships between the Church and state during the eleventh and twelfth centuries. The ring, staff and pallium were the symbols of spiritual authority, and the sword and scepter were the symbols of feudal authority. At times both the feudal lord and the pope claimed the right to give all of these symbols. Such controversy led to a loss of spiritual life on the part of the leaders of the Church, the neglect of their spiritual duties and the secularization of their interests as they gave more attention to control of their land and local feudal squabbles than they did to the affairs of the Church. The Church in the West had to fight feudalization while that in the East unsuccessfully fought imperial control.

The secularization of the Church, because of its involvement in the feudal system, must be balanced against the attempts of the Church to mitigate the evils of feudal warfare. Early in the eleventh century the Church was able to get the feudal lords to accept the Peace of God and the Truce of God. The Peace of God was an agreement to ban private quarrels, to attack no unarmed persons, to permit no robbery or violence, and to pillage no sacred place. This agreement was needed because the feudal lord felt no obligation not to fight his feudal neighbor. The Truce of God bound the feudal class not to fight from sunset on Wednesday to sunrise on Monday of each week and not to fight on the day of church festivals. This left less than one hundred days in the year open to feudal fighting. It also provided that churches, cemeteries, monasteries and convents should be sanctuaries where refugees could find a safe asylum in time of trouble. Women, peasants and clergy were not to be harmed. These agreements[3] did much to lessen the brutalities of feudal warfare in the Middle Ages.

D. Viking and Hungarian Invasions.

While feudalism was both effect and cause in the decline of the Carolingian Empire, the Viking and Hungarian invasions were definite factors in its rapid dissolution. These Vikings or Northmen who came from what is now modern Sweden, Denmark and Norway were a problem in Western Europe from the late eighth century until the tenth century. Any town or monastery along the coast or on the shores of a navigable river

[3] O. J. Thatcher and E. H. McNeal, *A Source Book for Medieval History* (New York: Charles Scribner's Sons, 1905), pp. 412-418.

could expect a visit from these bold sea rovers. Many of them finally settled in England and, after much fighting, merged with their kinsmen, the Anglo-Saxons, who had come to England earlier. In the process the fine Christian culture that had been built up in Ireland and England during the Dark Ages was destroyed or set back. Other Vikings settled in Normandy, from whence they came to conquer England under the leadership of William the Conqueror in 1066. Some trekked south across Eastern Europe and laid the foundations of the Russian state. Others settled in Sicily and Southern Italy, where for a time they presented a threat to the temporal power of the papacy.

II. The Importance of the Carolingian Empire

Preoccupation with the reasons for and the decline of the Carolingian Empire must not blind us to its importance in Western European history. The French and German states emerged from its ruins. Although the German state with its later claims to universal empire as the legitimate successor to the Roman and Carolingian Empires never succeeded in working out a centralized nation state until nineteenth century nationalism welded the Germans into one nation-state, it became the successor to the imperial Frankish state in the tenth century. Instead of aiding the pope as the Frankish emperors had done, it fought with the papacy for supremacy until its ruling line was defeated by Innocent III.

The ideal of a revived Roman Empire was never given up after the fall of Charlemagne's empire. The German emperors of the tenth century took over from the west Frankish state the tradition of empire, and the empire founded by Otto I, later known as the Holy Roman Empire, lasted from 962 until 1806 under the leadership of German emperors.

The Carolingian Empire also created the problem of whether the Church or the state was the representative of Deity upon earth. The issue of whether God had delegated sovereignty to the pope or emperor so that one derived his authority from the other was a heritage of Charlemagne's empire. That issue embittered relationships between Church and state for some centuries during the Middle Ages.

The beginning of the pope's claim to be a temporal ruler dated from the grant of lands in Italy to the pope by Pepin, the ancestor of Charlemagne, in 754. The pope as a temporal as well as a spiritual ruler made claims upon national rulers during the Middle Ages which they would not admit were justified. The impetus given to culture by Charlemagne must be counted as one of the great results of his empire. His reign was a bright light illuminating by contrast the cultural darkness of the Dark Ages elsewhere in Western Europe. One cannot but be impressed with the significance of Charlemagne and his empire for the subsequent history of the Church and state in Western Europe.

III. THE TENTH CENTURY REVIVAL OF EMPIRE

Even though the empire created by Charlemagne disappeared, the ideal of a universal political empire, which Western Europe had inherited from Rome, remained. It was not to be realized again by the Franks but was to be realized in the eastern section of Charlemagne's empire, which had gone to Louis the German in 843. Some consideration must be given to the rise, growth and significance of this new claimant to the power of imperial Rome in the West.

Unification in Germany has always been more difficult than unification in France. The physical geography of France provides her with the natural boundaries of the Mediterranean Sea, the Atlantic, the Pyrenees Mountains and the Alps. Only on the Rhine does she face frustration because she has never been able to make it a natural boundary for the French state. Geography works against German unity because rivers in Germany flow north to the North or Baltic Seas, and in the southern part of the country they flow east. North Germany is mostly plain while South Germany is mountainous. This makes for different interests among the people. Moreover, the traditional tribal divisions, coupled with later feudal states, led to decentralization of authority. Even after Germany was made one in name under the emperors of the Holy Roman Empire, the interest of the emperor in the affairs of the Church across the Alps was not shared by his people. But in spite of these problems the eastern part of Charlemagne's old empire became the center of the imperial power that had once been wielded in the West by the Franks.

The tribal dukes of Germany, faced with the need of unity for defense against the Northmen and the Slavic Hungarians, selected Henry the Fowler, the duke of Saxony, as their ruler in 919. He drove back the Northmen and was able to defeat the Hungarian invaders.

Henry was succeeded as king of the Germans by his son Otto. Otto made the dukes his vassals and took over supervision of the affairs of the Church by naming bishops and abbots of his choosing to take care of ecclesiastical interests in Germany. If he had been willing to confine his efforts to Germany, he might have built up a powerful centralized monarchy similar to that which later English, French and Spanish kings were to create. But he became interested in affairs across the Alps, and for centuries problems of the Church and state in Italy became a drain upon German resources. He went to Italy to aid the pope against a powerful ruler who had risen to threaten the papal power in Italy, and Pope John XII crowned him as Emperor of the Holy Roman Empire in 962. Once again there was a Roman emperor to claim jurisdiction over the people of Europe as Charlemagne and the Roman emperors had done earlier. All of Central Europe from the North Sea to the Adriatic was now united under the German Roman Empire, which was to last until Napoleon brought about its dissolution in 1806.

During the next two centuries the Roman see had weak incumbents, and the German emperors often crossed the Alps to bring order out of chaos and to extend their own interests in Italy. For example, Otto III in 996 entered Rome and, after putting down a faction of Roman nobles, forced the election of his own cousin Bruno as Pope Gregory V. This constant interference by the German rulers in the affairs of the papacy in Italy led to a struggle between the emperor and the pope until Innocent III humiliated and defeated the emperor and ended German interference in Italy.

Chapter XX

REVIVAL AND SCHISM IN THE CHURCH

Although the Western Church was under the shadow of Otto's Holy Roman Empire during the latter part of the period between 800 and 1054, it experienced an inner revival that gave it the strength to cope with imperial interference. The Eastern Church during this era became conscious of such differences between itself and the Western Church that the period ended with a schism that resulted in the creation of the Greek Orthodox Church in the East.

I. REVIVAL IN THE WEST

Although the revival in the Western Church was not always a revival of spirit, there was a renewal of strength that helped it in its struggle with the state, represented by the German Holy Roman Empire. Several things contributed to a renewal of the ecclesiastical power of the pope.

A. *Documents Supporting the Papacy.*

The Donation of Constantine (see Chapter XVIII, page 198) became the legal ground for the possession of land by the pope. The greatest grant of land, which this document was used to justify, was given by Pepin in 754. Some think that about the middle of the ninth century, Pope Nicholas I who was pope from 858 to 867, first made use of a collection of the decrees of the various pontiffs of Rome. This collection is variously known as the Decretals, the False Decretals, or the Pseudo-Isidorian Decretals. The remarkable document included the Donation of Constantine, the real and some forged decrees or decretals of the popes of Rome from the time of Clement of Rome, and some of the canons of the great councils of the Church. The collection was associated with the name of Isidore of Seville, head of the Spanish church during the first part of the seventh century. One cannot be dogmatic about the authorship of the Decretals, but it is certain that from the middle of the ninth century they played an important part in the claims of the Roman bishop to supremacy within the Church.

The Donation of Constantine, which was first used in the eighth century, was used to buttress the claims of the popes to land in Italy, but the Decretals were used to support the power of the pope within the Church. The Decretals asserted the supremacy of the pope over all ecclesiastical leaders of the Church and gave any bishop the right to appeal directly to the pope over the head of his archbishop. The right of the Church to be free from secular control was also claimed. Although it is not likely that any pope created the forgery, many popes made use of the collection to support their claims to power within the Church.

B. *The Conversion of Scandinavia.*

The power of the Roman bishop was strengthened in this era by the acceptance of the Gospel by the people of Scandinavia. Ansgar (801–865), a native of Flanders, deserves much of the credit for this gain. When the Danish king Harold asked for a missionary in 826, Ansgar felt that he should answer the call and devoted the remaining thirty-six years of his life to missionary activity in Northern Europe. Denmark was not finally won to Christianity until the eleventh century, in the days of Canute. Christianity was permanently established in Norway about 1000, and about the same time it was made the state religion in Sweden and Iceland. The work, begun by Ansgar,[1] bore fruit that strengthened the power of Rome in Northern Europe.

C. *The Doctrine of the Mass.*

The controversy regarding the nature of Christ's presence in the Communion agitated the Western Church early in the eighth century. Any acceptance of the idea of the Lord's Supper as a sacrifice by the priest was a gain for the power of the papacy because the pope headed the hierarchy of clergymen who alone had the power to perform this miracle of the Mass. About 831, Paschasius Radbertus, a monk in the monastery of Corbie near the city of Amiens, began to teach that by a divine miracle the substance of the bread and the wine was actually changed into the body and blood of Christ. Although he did not call this change transubstantiation, his teaching amounted to the same thing. He set forth these views in a book entitled *Of the Body*

[1] C. Robinson, *The Conversion of Europe* (London: Longmans, Green & Co., 1917), pp. 437-484.

and Blood of the Lord.[2] Such a view was bound to strengthen the power of the priest and his superior in the hierarchy, the pope, even though the Roman Church did not officially accept the doctrine of transubstantiation until 1215.

D. Monastic Reform.

The monastic reforms carried out by the Cluniac monasteries in the tenth and eleventh centuries made a great contribution to the supremacy of the papacy. By 529 both the solitary and communal types of monasticism had emerged. From then until 910 leaders of monasticism were busy with systematization of their work. By the tenth century the monasteries had become wealthy and corrupt and were badly in need of reform. The earlier ideal of service had been replaced by the ideal of individual salvation coupled with an easy life in a wealthy monastery. The reform movement originating at Cluny was the first of several successive reform movements in Roman monasticism.

The monastery at Cluny came about this way. In 910, Duke William of Aquitaine, "for the good" of his soul, gave a charter to Berno, who had already made a record as abbot of another monastery, to found a new monastery at Cluny in Eastern France.[3] The charter provided that the monastery was to be free from all secular or episcopal control and that it was to exercise self-government under the protection of the pope. Berno, abbot from 910 to 927, and Odo, abbot from 927 to 942, were both men of ability and character, and they did their work so well that many monasteries of the Benedictine order, including the monastery of Monte Cassino, were reorganized along the same lines as the one at Cluny.

Under the older system of monasticism each monastery had its own abbot and was independent of other monasteries of the same order. The abbot of Cluny, however, appointed the abbots of new monasteries founded by himself or others and made these abbots subject to himself. This innovation created an order that was centralized under one head, the abbot of Cluny, who worked in close harmony with the papacy. By the middle of the tenth century nearly seventy monasteries were under the leadership of the abbot of Cluny.

The Cluniac leaders called for reform in clerical life. They

[2] B. J. Kidd, *Documents Illustrative of the History of the Church* (London: Society for Promoting Christian Knowledge, 3 vols., 1920-1941), Vol. III, p. 82-84.
[3] F. A. Ogg, *A Source Book of Medieval History* (New York: American Book Co., 1907), pp. 247-249.

condemned simony — the practice of buying and selling church offices for money, and nepotism — the practice of showing favoritism to relatives in appointments to office. Celibacy was another plank in their platform. Clergymen were neither to marry nor keep concubines, in order that their whole attention would be given to the affairs of the Church. These monks also insisted that the Church should be free from temporal or secular control by king, emperor or duke. This program was put into effect by a series of reforming popes with the aid of the Cluniac monasteries. A new emphasis was also laid upon the ascetic life.

The reforming enthusiasm of the Cluniac movement made itself felt in many other areas. The men of Cluny created good monastic schools, and these schools helped to make Latin the common tongue of the Middle Ages. The movement that resulted in the Crusades being launched against the Mohammedans in the Holy Land owed much to monks from Cluniac monasteries. Cluniac monasteries on the frontiers of civilization became centers of missionary effort.

E. Capable Leaders.

Although many of the popes in the era between 800 and 1054 were corrupt or incompetent, there were several able leaders who helped to consolidate the strength of the papacy. Nicholas I, who was pope from 858 to 867, was one of the ablest of these men. He insisted both in writing and in practice upon the supremacy of the pope within the Church, as one who was responsible for the spiritual welfare of the faithful, and upon the supremacy of the pope over temporal rulers when it came to a matter of morals or religion. The Pseudo-Isidorian Decretals were often mentioned by him as a justification for this claim.[4]

Nicholas I successfully exerted his power over both bishops and the temporal ruler in the case of Lothair II of Lorraine. Lothair had married Teutberga mainly for political reasons. Becoming enamored with Waldrada, he put his legal wife aside. He got a divorce from Teutberga by calling a synod in which the bishops granted him a divorce. Appeal was made to Nicholas by both parties, but, in the meantime, Lothair had married Waldrada. Determined to bring the bishops who had acted so hastily under control and to discipline Lothair for immorality, Nicholas forced Lothair to set aside Waldrada and to restore Teutberga to her place as his rightful wife.

Nicholas also was successful in upholding the right of a bishop

4 Kidd, *op cit.*, Vol. III, pp. 92.

to appeal directly to the pope. When Hincmar, archbishop of Rheims, removed Rothad, bishop of Soissons, from his position, Nicholas reversed Hincmar's decision and forced him to restore Rothad to his bishopric.

Nicholas even tried to assert his authority over the patriarch and the Eastern emperor at Constantinople. The Emperor Michael, who had been corrupted by his uncle Bardas, deposed the Patriarch Ignatius when he refused to administer the sacrament to Bardas, and he appointed the learned Photius in his place. Ignatius asked Nicholas for aid. Nicholas declared Photius deposed, but an Eastern synod under the leadership of Photius accused the Western Church of heresy for adding to the creed the statement that the Holy Spirit proceeds from the Son as well as from the Father.[5] Ill-will between the two sections of the Church was augmented, and Nicholas, though successful in asserting his supremacy over temporal and ecclesiastical rulers in the West, was unsuccessful in the East.

Between the pontificates of Nicholas I and Leo IX there were few good leaders upon the papal throne. This was not for lack of popes because over forty popes occupied the episcopal throne in Rome during that period. A particularly bad scandal developed in the middle of the eleventh century. Benedict IX, an unworthy pope, was driven from Rome, and Sylvester III placed on the papal throne. Benedict returned to Rome and sold the papal throne for a large sum of money in 1045 to a man who became Gregory VI. During the course of events, however, Benedict refused to lay down the papacy. There were now three popes each claiming to be the rightful pope. Henry III, Emperor of the Holy Roman Empire, then called a synod at Sutri in 1046. Benedict and Sylvester were deposed, and Gregory was forced to resign in favor of Clement II. Clement soon died, and his successor, another one of Henry's appointees, was also short-lived. Henry appointed his cousin Bruno as Pope Leo IX later.

With the coming of Leo IX, the long era of poor popes between Nicholas I and Leo IX came to an end because Leo and his successors were strong men who were interested in reform along the lines of the Cluniac platform. The synod of Sutri thus marked the lowest ebb in the power of the papacy in the medieval period. Under Leo IX and Nicholas II, guided by the able hand of Hildebrand, who was to become Gregory VII, the election of the

5 *Ibid.*, Vol. III, pp. 86-91.

pope was taken out of the hands of the Roman populace and put under the control of the church leaders in the College of Cardinals in 1059. From that time until the papacy reached a peak of power under Innocent III there was steady advance in the influence of the papacy in European affairs.

The Church in the East, harassed by the fight to restrain the Mohammedans from overrunning the Eastern Empire, weakened by the control of its affairs by the emperor of that empire, and frustrated by the theological stagnation that set in after the great work of John of Damascus, was not in a position to offer much opposition to the rise in temporal as well as spiritual power of the Roman bishop. The growing antagonism between the two sections of the Church, which rose out of historic roots, led to a break in 1054. With the break two great divisions of the Christian religion appeared, and they have had few official contacts with each other since that time.

II. The Origin of the Greek Orthodox Church

The Church in the East was never able to be as independent as that in the West because it was under the eye of the emperor, and because it had to cope with the Greco-Roman tradition of culture which was preserved in the East during the time the West was going through the cultural chaos of the Dark Ages. After the fall of the Roman Empire, the Church in the West faced no great political rival on the imperial throne and grew stronger as it faced the problems associated with the cultural chaos that surrounded the fall of the Empire.

A. The Causes for Separation.

When Constantine moved his capital to Constantinople in 330, he paved the way for political and, finally, ecclesiastical separation of the Church into the East and the West. Theodosius put the administration of the Eastern and Western areas of the Empire under separate heads in 395. With the fall of the Roman Empire in the West in the late fifth century this division was completely realized. The Church in the East was under the jurisdiction of the emperor, but the pope in Rome was too far away to be brought under his control. In the absence of effective political control in the West, the pope became a temporal as well as spiritual leader in times of crisis. This gave to the two churches an entirely different outlook concerning temporal power.

The intellectual outlook of the West also differed from that of the East. The Latin West was more inclined to consider practical matters of polity and had little trouble formulating orthodox dogma. The Greek mind of the East was more interested in solving theological problems along philosophical lines. Most of the theological controversies between 325 and 451 arose in the East, but the same problems caused little difficulty in most cases in the West.

About the middle of the second century, the problem of when to celebrate Easter arose to mar relations between the two sections of the Church (see Chapter VIII, page 112). Differences of opinion regarding this question always made amicable relations between the two groups difficult.

Another difference between the two Churches concerned celibacy. Marriage of all parish clergy below the rank of bishop was permitted in the East, but in the West the clergy were not allowed to marry. Disputes even arose on some occasions over the wearing of beards. The priest in the West could shave his face, but the clergyman in the East had to wear a beard. Though these and similar matters may seem trivial now, they were of great importance at that time to both sections of the Church.

The two Churches also differed upon theological matters. In 867 Photius, the patriarch in the East, charged Nicholas I and the Church in the West with heresy because the West had the *filioque* clause in its form of the Nicene Creed. In the West theologians held that the Holy Spirit proceeded from the Son as well as from the Father. The East would not accept this idea.

Thus a series of controversies, beginning with the Easter controversy of the second century, embittered relations between the East and West. With each dispute the hostility increased. The iconoclastic controversy in the Eastern Church in the eighth and ninth centuries caused many hard feelings. In 726, Leo III, as Emperor of the East, forbad any kneeling before pictures or images, and in 730 he ordered all except the cross removed from the churches and destroyed so that the Mohammedans might have no chance to accuse the Christians of idolatry. This attempt at lay revival in the Eastern Church ran into the vested opposition of the parish and monastic clergy. In the West the pope and even the Emperor Charlemagne took a stand in favor of the use of visible symbols of divine reality. This interference by the West in the affairs of the Church in the East increased

THE SCHISM OF 1054

PAGANS LANDS

MOHAMMEDAN LANDS

Black Sea
CONSTANTINOPLE

Mediterranean Sea

ROME

Atlantic Ocean

MOHAMMEDAN LANDS

MOHAMMEDAN LANDS

ROMAN CATHOLIC
GREEK ORTHODOX
RELIGIOUS DIVISION ++++++

the antagonism between the two areas. The Church in the West continued to use pictures and statues in worship; the Church in the East, however, finally eliminated statues but kept icons, usually pictures of Christ which were to be accorded reverence but not the worship that belongs to God alone.

The people of the East particularly resented the attempt by Pope Nicholas I in the middle of the ninth century to interfere with the appointment of the patriarch of the Church in the East, even though it may have been justified on moral grounds (see page 219). Though Nicholas was not successful, his interference, in what many in the East felt was a matter for the East alone, intensified the bad feeling between the two Churches.

B. *The Schism of 1054.*

In 1053 all of these differences and bitter feelings focused around what was apparently a minor matter. Michael Cerularius, patriarch of Constantinople from 1043 to 1048, condemned the Church in the West for the use of unleavened bread in the Eucharist. Such use had been a growing practice in the West since the ninth century. Pope Leo IX sent Cardinal Humbert and two other legates to the East to end the dispute. The differences of opinion widened as the discussions went on. On July 16, 1054, the Roman legates finally put a decree of excommunication of the patriarch and his followers on the high altar of the cathedral church of Saint Sophia.[6] The patriarch was not to be outdone and thereupon he excommunicated the pope of Rome and his followers. The first great schism in Christianity broke the unity of the Church. From this time the Roman Catholic Church and the Greek Orthodox Church went their separate ways.

C. *The Consequences of Schism.*

Any ecumenical movement was plainly an impossibility after the bitter events that separated the Church in the East and the Church in the West. The modern ecumenical movement aimed at the reunion of the churches of Christendom has had no support from the Roman Catholic Church and little from the Greek Orthodox Church. The movement has been primarily a Protestant movement. Neither of the two churches desires any ecumenical church except on its own terms, although the Church of the East has been willing to confer with Protestant churches concerning reunion.

[6] *Ibid.,* Vol. III, pp. 115-117.

Separation shut the Church in the East off from many of the vitalizing influences that strengthened the Church in the West. The rise of towns, nations and the middle class, the cultural movements of the Renaissance and the Reformation passed by the Church in the East, but the Roman Catholic Church in the West was subjected to their influence and made stronger, either by assimilation of helpful features or by reaction against what appeared to Rome to be harmful.

The Church in the East did, however, engage in some missionary work in this era. The Bulgarians were won to Christianity by the efforts of Methodius shortly after the middle of the ninth century, and they adopted the faith of Constantinople. Though Cyril and Methodius won the Moravians to Christianity, the Moravians finally came under Roman jurisdiction instead of that of Constantinople. The patriarch had more success with missionary work in Russia. A princess named Olga accepted Christianity in 955 and was able to influence her grandson Vladimir so that he accepted Christianity in 988. This event marked the beginning of the triumph of Eastern Christianity in Russia. Russia along with much of Eastern and Central Europe followed the patriarch of Constantinople.[7]

The shock of Mohammedanism in the seventh century and the loss of people and land to the Moslems, coupled with the two centuries of unrest concerning the use of images, left Christianity in the East to become stagnant. Little change in ritual, polity or theology has appeared in that Church until the present time. Consequently it has not had the influence upon the world that Christianity in the West has had, although in the ancient period of church history it had led in the formulation of theology.

BIBLIOGRAPHY

The Greek and Eastern Churches (New York: Charles Scribner's Sons, 1908) by Walter F. Adeney is still a useful survey for more detail concerning the history of the Church in the East.

[7] See Robinson, *op. cit.*, Ch. XIX, for an interesting account of the winning of Russia to Christianity.

THE SUPREMACY OF THE PAPACY, 1054–1305

Chapter XXI

THE ZENITH OF PAPAL POWER

The papacy has never exercised such temporal power as that which it was able to exercise between 1054 and 1305. Hildebrand was able to humble the Emperor of the Holy Roman Empire; Innocent III was powerful enough to force rulers of rising nation-states to do his will; and the papacy dominated the early part of the great war against the infidels in the Holy Land. The rise of universities and Scholasticism strengthened the intellectual foundations of papal power. Monastic reform added to papal power by giving to the pope many zealous monks who were his obedient servants. It is doubtful whether the papacy has ever exercised such absolute power over all phases of life as it did in medieval Europe during this era.

I. GREGORY VII ASSERTS PAPAL SUPREMACY

A. *The Power Behind the Papal Throne.*

The pontificates of Gregory VII and Innocent III easily dominate the history of the medieval papacy. Both men were unwilling to accept the idea that God had given the pope and the temporal ruler coordinate sovereignty over the souls and bodies of men. The pope would not accept the idea that he derived his control over men's souls from the temporal ruler to whom God had given sovereignty, and the ruler would not willingly consent to the idea that he exercised sovereignty over men's bodies by a gracious grant of power from the pope. No subsequent pope has ever been able to enforce this last claim as successfully as these two popes did. Hildebrand (ca. 1020–1085) laid the foundations upon which Innocent was able, at a much later date, to build in making claims to supreme power.

Hildebrand's career readily divides itself into two periods. He was the power behind the papal throne for over twenty years before he became pope in 1073, and from 1073 until his death

[227]

in 1085 he exercised the powers that he had obtained for the popes while he was a humble supporter of the papacy. He was able to influence the formulation of papal policy under five popes before he finally became pope.

This small ungainly man with a weak voice, who was probably the son of a carpenter, had all the zeal of the best of the reformers of the Cluniac monasteries, with whose program of reform he sympathized. He also opposed simony, clerical marriage and lay investiture.

Leo IX gave Hildebrand his chance to become the power behind the papal throne by his selection of him and other good men from outside Rome to fill important positions in the papal curia. About the beginning of the fourth century certain churches in Rome and its environs had been designated as exclusive sites for baptisms. Pastors of these churches became known as cardinal priests. The divisions of Rome into districts for works of charity had been made somewhat earlier and the priests of these areas were known as cardinal deacons. By the ninth century bishops near Rome were known as cardinal bishops. These men were the nucleus of what was to become the College of Cardinals. Hildebrand was placed in charge of finances of the Roman see and thus became a cardinal archdeacon.

Hildebrand exercised still greater power during the rule of Nicholas II (1058–1061), when he was able to have ecclesiastical legislation passed that took the power of electing the pope out of the hands of the populace of the Roman bishopric. The bishops of Rome had been elected from the earliest time by popular vote, although the emperors of the Holy Roman Empire had often interferred in elections, and in the days of Hildebrand the aristocracy of Rome had come to exercise corrupt control over the elections. At the Lateran Council of 1059, Nicholas, advised by Hildebrand, had the method of electing popes changed so that lay aristocratic or imperial influence might be eliminated. When a pope died, the cardinal bishops would meet to consider his successor. They would then consult the cardinal priest and cardinal deacons. Only then were the people of the Roman bishopric to be permitted to vote on the nominee of the cardinals. For all practical purposes, this put the election of the pope under the control of the College of Cardinals. A clergyman from anywhere in the Roman Catholic Church might be selected as pope, and, in case of unrest, the election might be held outside of Rome. The new pope was to take office immediately after his election. This change in electoral procedure placed the choice of the pope within the power of the clergy and eliminated lay control.[1] The significance of this legislation for the rise of papal power must not be overlooked.

B. *Pope Gregory VII.*

Hildebrand was unanimously elected as Pope Gregory VII in 1073 as a result of the people shouting, "Let Hildebrand be bishop." He was now in a position to work directly for his ideal of a theocracy in which temporal as well as spiritual power would be exercised by the pope as the vice-regent of God. He wanted no civil power to dominate the Roman Church; instead, the Church was to control the civil power. For this reason, he dedicated himself to the abolition of lay investiture, the practice by which clerical leaders received the symbols of their office from their feudal lord, who was usually a layman. He was also interested in the abolition of simony and the enforcement of clerical celibacy as the best way to reform the Roman Church.

This ideal of papal supremacy within the Roman Church and over temporal rulers is clearly developed in the *Dictatus Papae,* a document that was found *among* the letters of Hildebrand after his death. Even if Cardinal Deusdedit, who is often credited with its authorship, wrote it, the document clearly expresses Gregory's ideal for the papacy. It made the most sweeping claims for papal supremacy that have thus far been noticed. It averred that the Roman Church owed its foundation to "God alone"; that its pontiff was "alone to be called universal"; that he had full power over all bishops; that only his feet should be kissed by "all princes"; that he could "depose Emperors"; and that he might absolve subjects of evil temporal rulers "from their allegiance." The peak of papal pretension to supremacy was reached in the twenty-second article of the *Dictatus* with the statement that there had never been error in the Roman Church and that, according to the Bible, it would never err.[2] Gregory was fully prepared to enforce these claims to temporal as well as spiritual supremacy. He asserted that countries such

[1] Henry Bettenson, *Documents of the Christian Church* (New York: Oxford University Press, 1947), pp. 142-143.
[2] B. J. Kidd, *Documents Illustrative of the History of the Church* (London: Society for Promoting Christian Knowledge, 3 vols., 1920-1941), Vol. III, pp. 129-130.

as England, Hungary, Russia, Spain and others had been put under the control of St. Peter and his successors.

While Gregory warred successfully against clerical marriages and simony, the claims of the *Dictatus* indicated that his greatest problem would be to bring temporal rulers under his control. The major struggle of his pontificate, the struggle over the question of lay investiture, was a heritage from his predecessor, Alexander II. The important archbishopric of Milan was vacant, and the Emperor of the Holy Roman Empire, Henry IV, selected a man named Godfrey to fill the office. The electoral body of the archbishopric, however, chose a man named Atto. Alexander II recognized Atto, and, just before he died, he excommunicated Godfrey. His successor, Hildebrand, gladly took up the struggle with Henry. In 1075 a Lateran synod forbad any high clergyman to receive investiture to a church office from a layman.

Henry was also ready for the struggle with the spiritual power of the papacy, but he had not been schooled to discipline himself. This flaw led him to take unwise courses of action in the struggle with the pope, and he soon faced the rebellious feudal lords of Saxony who resented his attempts to create a centralized state in Germany. After making a temporary peace with the Saxon nobles, Henry, five of whose councilors had been excommunicated by Gregory in 1075 for simony, called a council in January 1076 at Worms. The council rejected papal authority.[3] Gregory met this bitter denunciation and rejection of his authority by deposing Henry and releasing all his subjects from allegiance to him.[4] This was as bold a step as any pope had ever taken in a dispute with the temporal power, but Henry's weakness at home gave Gregory hopes of success.

In the fall of 1076, Henry's Saxon and other enemies declared that if he did not get release from Gregory's sentence of excommunication against him, they would depose him. They also invited Gregory to a synod that was to meet at Augsburg in the winter. Faced with the danger of losing his throne and humiliation within his own realm if Gregory came to Augsburg, Henry capitulated and, with his wife and his baby son, crossed the Alps in the winter of 1077 to meet Gregory at Canossa. It was a difficult journey; and when Henry reached Canossa,

[3] Bettenson, *op. cit.*, pp. 143-146; F. A. Ogg, *Source Book of Medieval History* (New York: American Book Co, 1907), pp. 270-272.
[4] Bettenson, *op. cit.*, pp. 146-147.

Gregory let him stand barefoot in the snow outside the gates of the palace on three successive days before he would admit him to his presence. He then released him from his sentence of excommunication.

Though the greatest ruler in Christendom was thus humiliated by the pope, Henry gained much by his submission, for he had kept Gregory from coming to a meeting at Augsburg and had defeated his German foes. The struggle continued throughout the remainder of Gregory's pontificate. Gregory later excommunicated and deposed Henry a second time; but, with Germany supporting him, Henry invaded Italy and selected Wibert as pope. After Henry was crowned by Wibert, he left Italy. Gregory then asked the Normans of Southern Italy to help him. They did but pillaged around Rome, and Gregory was forced to flee to Salerno. There this great pope died in exile because, according to him, he "loved righteousness, and hated iniquity."

The warfare over lay investiture continued until a compromise agreement was made in the Concordat of Worms between Emperor Henry V and Pope Calixtus II in 1122. The ring and staff, symbols of spiritual power, were to be given to church officials by the pope or his agent, and the church official was to take an oath of loyalty to the temporal ruler who happened to be his feudal overlord. The Roman Catholic Church had the better of the king in spite of the compromise reached[5] because it had at least asserted equality with the state and had freed itself of imperial control in Italy. In addition, by his enforcement of clerical celibacy after the ban on clerical marriage in 1074, Gregory had prevented the clergy from degenerating into a hereditary caste and had created a class of men loyal to their spiritual superior, the pope. Though he died in exile, Gregory had done his work, and later popes built upon the foundations that he had laid.

II. Papal Supremacy under Innocent III

Elected as pope in 1198, Innocent III (1161–1216) brought the medieval papacy to the zenith of its power. He was the son of a Roman noble and was given a fine education in theology at Paris and in law at Bologna. His personal humility and piety were balanced by vigor, common sense and a strong sense of the moral force that the papacy had.

[5] *Ibid.*, pp. 156-157.

Innocent was a strong believer in the right of the pope to supreme authority on earth. He believed that kings and princes derived their authority from him and that he could therefore excommunicate, depose them, or lay an interdict, which forbad the clergy to perform any but the most essential services of the church, upon their state. He believed that God had given the successor of St. Peter the task of ruling the whole world as well as the Church. The pope stood above man and below God. The state should be related to the Church as the moon is to the sun. The moon shines by the reflected light of the sun; the state was to bask in the glory of the papacy and derive its power from the pope.[6] It is little wonder that, with this view of his authority and all the power and prestige of the papacy under his control, Innocent was able to bring the rulers of the rising nation states of England and France under his control and to defeat the emperor of the Holy Roman Empire.

The position of the papacy had been further strengthened by the publication of an authoritative edition of the canon law of the Roman church in 1148 by Gratian, a teacher monk at Bologna. This edition, known as the *Decretum,* provided a complete statement of canon law that could be used in all the courts of the Roman church. It must be remembered that Roman law, which was the foundation upon which canon law was built, supported the idea of centralization of authority in one individual. The pope made full use of this law to buttress his authority.

A. *Temporal Vs. Spiritual Rulers.*

Innocent III quickly took up the challenge of the rulers of the rising nation-states of France and England and of the Holy Roman Empire after his accession to the chair of Peter. He used his power first against Philip Augustus of France in order that he might demonstrate that not even a king could flout the moral law of God concerning marriage. Philip had married Ingeborg of Denmark after the death of his first wife in 1193. When his bride came to France, he took a dislike to her and claimed that he had been bewitched. He forced the French bishops to annul the marriage and took Agnes de Meran into his home as his wife. Ingeborg appealed to the pope for redress. Innocent thereupon ordered Philip to put away Agnes and to restore Ingeborg to her place as his lawful wife. When Philip refused

6 *Ibid.,* pp. 157-158.

to do so, Innocent placed France under an interdict in 1200. The interdict, which affected everyone in the nation, closed all churches, except for the baptism of infants; forbad the granting of extreme unction to the dying, and the celebration of the mass, except for those who were sick or dying; and forbad burial in the consecrated ground. The priest could only preach in the open air.[7] The uproar that the interdict created all over France forced Philip to submit to the pope, and with bad grace he sent Agnes away and brought Ingeborg back into the palace as his wife. Ingeborg's life was still not too happy, but Innocent, by the use of spiritual weapons, had forced the ruler of one of the great new nation-states to obey the moral law.

Between 1205 and 1213 Innocent was able to defeat the brutal John of England in a contest over the election of an archbishop to the vacant archbishopric of Canterbury. Both the archbishop, elected by the clergy of the archbishopric, and the nominee forced upon them by John were set aside by Innocent when the question of his confirmation of the appointment arose. He appointed Stephen Langton instead. John refused to accept Langton. Innocent then excommunicated John and placed an interdict upon England in 1208.[8] John was forced to humble himself because the English were opposed to him, and Philip of France, at the invitation of the pope, was only too happy to have an excuse to invade England. John acknowledged in 1213 that he held his kingdom as the feudal vassal of the pope and agreed to pay a thousand marks annually to the pope. This payment was not finally repudiated until the time of the English Reformation.

Having successfully humiliated the rulers of the two most important emerging national states, Innocent III decided that it was time to deal with the problem of the ruler of the Holy Roman Empire. In 1202 he asserted the right of the pope to approve or disapprove the emperor elected by the German electors of the Empire.[9] The Compromise of Worms had created what was an uneasy armistice between emperor and pope, and the Italian people were anxious to cooperate with the pope to end imperial interference by the emperor in Italy. Henry VI, emperor between 1190 and 1197, had married a Norman princess named Constance. Through his marriage to her, he laid claim

[7] Ogg, *op. cit.*, pp. 382-383.
[8] Bettenson, *op. cit.*, pp. 229-233.
[9] *Ibid.*, pp. 158-159.

[233]

to Sicily as part of his dominion. This gave him control of lands to the north and south of the Papal States. His son, Frederick, was made King of Sicily, and Innocent was made his guardian after Constance's death. When Otto IV forgot the promises that he had made to Innocent at the time of his coronation as Holy Roman Emperor, Innocent supported the claims of Frederick to the imperial throne and was able to secure his election to that office as Emperor Frederick II in 1212. Innocent then called in the armies of Philip II of France and defeated Otto.

Thus, by clever political maneuvering, Innocent had dictated the imperial succession. But, while his reign marked the peak of medieval papal power, the great pope had unwittingly created a terrible problem for his successors. Twice, in the case of John of England and Otto of the Empire, Innocent had asked the king of France to help him win his struggle. By so doing he had destroyed the power of the Holy Roman Empire and left his successors without a balance against the powerful French state. Before this time the pope could play the French king and the emperor against each other. One does not wonder that later Boniface VIII suffered humiliation at the hands of the rulers of the powerful nation-states of England and France.

B. *Innocent III as a Crusader.*

The Fourth Crusade, to recover Palestine from the Moslems by capturing Egypt as a base for later actions, was instigated by Innocent and several French priests. It was largely a French crusade under papal direction. When boats were needed to transport the Crusaders to their objective, the Doge of Venice agreed to supply transports and supplies in return for a large sum of money. The Crusaders came to Venice but without enough money. Thereupon the Venetians asked their aid to regain Zara, which had once belonged to Venice, from the Christian king of Hungary. After the sack of Zara, the Crusaders sailed to Constantinople instead of Alexandria and, after a siege, captured the city in 1204. A Latin kingdom, which lasted until 1261, was set up at Constantinople. Although Innocent had not officially sanctioned the diversion of the crusading Christians against their fellow Christians in Zara and Constantinople, he accepted the results because it brought the Eastern Empire under his control and because Constantinople could serve as a base for the Fifth Crusade that he was planning against the Mohammedans. The Eastern Empire as well as the rulers of the West now were under his control.[10] He stood forth as the leading figure in medieval Europe.

Innocent also sponsored a crusade under the leadership of Simon de Montfort against the Albigenses of Southern France in 1208. The Albigenses were members of a heretical sect known as the Cathari. They accepted a dualistic system of theology and asceticism similar to that of earlier Gnostics and Manicheans. Because they claimed this system was based upon the Bible, the Roman church later forbad the people to possess the Bible. The crusade got under way in 1209 and virtually exterminated the Cathari in Southern France after many bloody battles. This crusade was strongly supported by both the Dominican and Franciscan orders. Heretics as well as temporal rulers must bow to the supreme head of the Roman church.

C. *The Fourth Lateran Council of 1215.*

Having abolished heresy by force, Innocent attempted to make a positive statement of truth. In order to do this, he called a general council in Rome. This council, known as the Fourth Lateran Council, made an annual confession to a priest by all the laymen mandatory. The declaration of the dogma of transubstantiation, which all members of the Roman church had to accept as authentic doctrine from this time on, was more important. It was the teaching that the substance of the bread and wine became the actual body and blood of Christ after the words of consecration by the priest. The accidents or outward form of the elements still appeared to the senses as bread and wine, but a metaphysical change had taken place in the substances so that the bread and wine became respectively the body and blood of Christ. Thus the priest performed a sacrifice each time he held a mass. Small wonder that medieval men feared the clergy, who had power to give or withhold the life-giving sacraments.

III. DECLINE OF PAPAL POWER UNDER BONIFACE VIII

The pontificate of Innocent III marked the peak of papal power in Europe. Sordid stories of nepotism, simony, drunkenness and neglect of their people by the priests antagonized many in the century following Innocent's death in 1216. Rulers of such rising nation-states as England and France were more inclined to dispute with the papacy because they had a national army and

10 See Kidd, *op. cit.,* Vol. III, pp. 150-153 for relevant documents.

a wealthy middle class to back them. The humiliation of the Holy Roman Empire by Innocent III left the pope with little support against the French ruler.

If the pontificate of Innocent III was the zenith of papal power in the Middle Ages, that of Boniface VIII between 1294 and 1303 may be said to be the nadir of papal power. On more than one occasion Boniface suffered humiliation from the temporal power. The greatest struggle took place between Boniface and Philip the Fair of France. To help pay the costs of a war between their two countries Philip of France and Edward I of England taxed the clergy. In 1296 Boniface issued the bull *Clericis Laicos*[11] which forbad the priest to pay taxes to a temporal ruler under pain of excommunication from the Roman church. Edward met the challenge by outlawing the clergy and by having Parliament pass an act forbidding them to pay any attention to the pope's claims to temporal power in England. Philip met the challenge by forbidding the export of money from France to Italy and thus deprived the papacy of its French revenues.

The struggle between Philip and Boniface was renewed in 1301 when Philip arrested a papal legate for treason against the king. When the pope ordered Philip to release him and to come to Rome to explain his conduct, Philip called the French legislative body, the Estates General, which upheld Philip's resistance to the demands of Boniface. Boniface then issued the papal bull known as *Unam Sanctum.* He claimed that "neither salvation nor remissions of sins" could be found outside the Roman Church, that the pope as head of the Roman Church had spiritual and temporal authority over all and that submission to the pope was "necessary to salvation."[12] Boniface could not, however, back up his claims with armies, and Philip temporarily made Boniface a prisoner to prevent his proclamation of excommunication of the king.

Clement V became pope after the death of Boniface but he was neither so able nor so resolute as Boniface. He came under Philip's domination and cancelled all the papal acts that were displeasing to Philip. He even transferred the papal court to Avignon, where he and his court were under direct pressure from the king whose territories were all around them. This was Canossa in reverse with a vengeance. The removal of the papal

11 Bettenson, *op. cit.,* pp. 159-161.
12 *Ibid.,* pp. 161-163.

seat from Rome in 1309 was the beginning of the era known as the Babylonian Captivity of the papacy. Until 1377 the papacy was the creature of the French monarchs and lost the tremendous moral and temporal power it had had in Europe during the pontificate of Innocent III.

BIBLIOGRAPHY

The bibliography cited at the end of Chapter XVI is also useful for the period from 1054 to 1305.

Much insight into the activities of Gregory VII can be gained by a reading of *The Correspondence of Pope Gregory VII* (New York: Columbia University Press, 1932) edited by Ephraim Emerton.

The little work by William R. W. Stephens, *Hildebrand and His Times* (New York: Anson D. F. Randolph & Co., ca. 1888), is a useful summary of the imperial papal conflict with the Empire, with an emphasis upon Hildebrand's work.

Although Joseph Clayton's *Pope Innocent III and His Times* (Milwaukee: The Bruce Publishing Co., 1941) is written from the Roman Catholic viewpoint, it is an interesting biography of that great medieval pope.

Chapter XXII

CRUSADERS AND REFORMERS

Christianity in Western Europe was marked by bursts of crusading and reforming zeal during the twelfth and thirteenth centuries. Expeditions of Christian knights fought for religious ends instead of private gain or political ends. Between 1100 and 1300 crusades against Moslems in Europe and Asia and heretics in Europe were carried on, for the most part under the aegis of the Roman Church. The Cistercian, the Dominican and the Franciscan orders appeared as reform movements to rejuvenate medieval monasticism. Spiritual zeal spurred laymen to engage in the Albigensian and Waldensian movements. The energy expended in the building of the great Gothic cathedrals of Europe was also a testimony to the spiritual zeal of the era.

I. THE CROSS VS. THE CRESCENT, 1095–1291

Christians had carried on crusades against the Moors in Spain and the Moslems in Sicily for sometime before the Crusades to the Holy Land. This Western wing of the crusading movement was aimed at expelling the Moslems from territory that they held in Western Europe. The Crusades to Palestine, which were the Eastern and great wing of this crusading movement against the Moslems, had for their aim the recapture of Palestine from the more brutal Seljuk Turks. The whole movement may be characterized as a holy war against the enemies of the Cross by the spiritual forces of Western Christendom. Already in 1074 Gregory VII had called for a crusade against the Moslems in Palestine who were harassing the Eastern Empire and who were persecuting pilgrims,[1] but the struggle with Henry IV over lay investiture kept him from being the pope who started the Crusades.

[1] O. J. Thatcher and E. H. McNeal, *A Source Book for Medieval History* (New York: Charles Scribner's Sons, 1905), pp. 512-513.

A. *Causes of the Crusades.*

One should always remember that, although the Crusaders had economic or political interests, the primary motive of the Crusades was religious. The Seljuk Turks, who had replaced the Arabs, were much more fanatical and brutal than those whom they had replaced, and European pilgrims were subjected to persecution when they landed in Palestine. Moreover, Alexius, the emperor at Constantinople had asked the aid of Western European Christians against these Moslem Asiatic invaders who were threatening the security of his kingdom. This religious motivation gave the Crusades the nature of a mass pilgrimage to Palestine. The movement of people was comparable in its scope to the barbarian migrations into the Roman Empire shortly before its fall. It has been estimated that nearly a million people took part in the activities associated with the First Crusade. The movement was also an attempt to solve the perennial problem of who should control the Near East, a problem that has always been a matter of concern to Europe.

Economic considerations led many to take the Cross. Famine was a common phenomenon in Western Europe in the century preceding the Crusades. The Venetians were interested in the stimulation of the trickle of trade with the Near East, and the Normans were apparently as much interested in plunder or setting up feudal fiefs as they were in rescuing the Holy Places from the Moslems.

The love of military adventure, which was sanctified by the Roman Church, also drew many of the feudal nobles and knights into the armies of the Crusades. Others took the Cross to escape from domestic boredom or the punishment for crimes.

B. *The Crusades.*

The direct cause of the First Crusade was the preaching of a crusade against the Moslems by Urban II at a synod at Clermont in November, 1095. He urged the Crusade as an answer to Alexius' appeal for aid in the previous year, but in Urban's mind the grander concept of the rescue of the Holy Places from Moslem hands took priority over aid to the Eastern Empire.[2] The assembled crowd, mostly Frenchmen, replied with an enthusiastic *Deus vult* (God wills it) to the proposal of Urban, who was a Frenchman.

The enthusiasm was so great that masses of peasants, aroused

[2] *Ibid.*, pp. 513-521.

by the preaching of Peter the Hermit and Walter the Penniless, started to march through Germany, Hungary and the Balkans to Palestine. Because they were unorganized and undisciplined, the Emperor at Constantinople was glad to let those still alive cross the Straits to Asia Minor, where they were either massacred by the Turks or taken prisoners and sold as slaves.

This unorganized lay crusade of French peasants was only a prelude to the organized effort of the First Crusade led by nobles from France, Belgium and Norman Italy. The various armies and their leaders arrived at Constantinople by the spring of 1097. The Crusaders took Nicaea after a short siege and by fall found themselves before Antioch, which they captured in the spring of 1098. Finally, in June, 1099, they captured Jerusalem. These Crusaders, who had been feudal lords back in Europe, succumbed to the temptation to set up feudal fiefs in areas that they had captured, and many of the castles in the Near East date from this period. Jerusalem and the surrounding country was finally organized into the Kingdom of Jerusalem under Baldwin, the brother of the godly Godfrey of Bouillon, who had been the moral leader of the Crusade. In this fashion the objectives of the First Crusade were achieved. The pressure against Constantinople by the Moslems was relaxed, and Jerusalem was again in the hands of Christian rulers. The Knights Templars and Hospitallers were organized to provide protection and aid to pilgrims and to fight the Moslems.

The occasion for the Second Crusade was the Moslem threat to the northeastern flank of the Kingdom of Jerusalem after the Moslems had captured the feudal fief of Edessa. In 1147 the saintly mystic, Bernard of Clairvaux, preached the Second Crusade. The King of France and the Emperor of the Holy Roman Empire led the crusade, but it proved to be a failure. This failure was followed by the recapture of Jerusalem by Saladin, the Moslem leader, in 1187.

The Third Crusade (1189–1192), known as the King's Crusade, was under the leadership of Philip Augustus of France, Richard of England and the Emperor Frederick. Frederick was accidently drowned on the way to Palestine, and Philip Augustus after a quarrel with Richard went home. Richard went on fighting. Although he was unsuccessful in recapturing Jerusalem, he did get Saladin to agree to give pilgrims access to Jerusalem.

Forced to be content with this Richard made his way home to England.

Innocent III, who was anxious to retrieve the failure of the Third Crusade, ardently preached the need of a crusade, the Fourth, to capture Egypt as a base for operations against Palestine.[3] An important result of this Crusade was that the Greek Church and the Eastern Empire were again made subject to the pope after a century and a half of religious independence. This crusade helped to weaken the Eastern Empire and to deepen the hatred between Latin and Greek Christians (see Chapter XXI, page 234).

Frederick II, the leader of the Fifth Crusade, was successful in negotiating a treaty in 1229 that brought Jerusalem, Bethlehem, Nazareth and a corridor to the sea under control of the Christians, but the Moslems kept the Mosque of Omar. Jerusalem was once again temporarily under a Christian king. But, in spite of several later crusades, the territories captured by the Crusaders fell once more into the hands of the Saracens, who had succeeded the Seljuk Turks as overlords in Palestine.

The Children's Crusade of 1212 was the saddest incident in the history of the Crusades. Children of France and Germany, led by two boys named Stephen and Nicholas, marched across Southern Europe to Italy, supposing that the purity of their lives would bring them success in a venture in which their more sinful parents had failed. Many perished on the way, and the rest were sold into slavery in Egypt.

C. *Consequences of the Crusades.*

The Crusades had important political and social results in Western Europe. Feudalism was weakened because many knights and nobles who went as Crusaders never returned and because many sold their lands to peasants or wealthy middle class townsmen to raise money for the Crusades. Cities controlled by feudal lords often were able to buy charters providing them with self-government. Kings were able to centralize their control with the aid of the middle class which favored a strong centralized nation-state under a monarch in order to provide the conditions of security and order so essential to business.

Some of the religious results were that the papacy enhanced its prestige during the Crusades, but the channeling of the energies of nations into the Crusades led to a rise of national

[3] *Ibid.*, pp. 537-544.

feeling that eventually weakened the papal power. The creation of the Latin Kingdom of Constantinople deepened the religious antagonism between the East and West and weakened the Eastern kingdom so that its eventual fall in 1453 was assured. The emergence of the military orders gave the pope additional bands of loyal monks.

Economic results were equally important. The Italian cities, led by Venice, started trade with the Near East as soon as possible after the successful First Crusade. The trade in luxury products from the Near East, such as silks, spices and perfumes, laid the economic foundations for the patronage of art in Renaissance Italy. People who returned from the Crusades wanted to buy the luxuries that they had seen in the Near East.

Although the Crusades failed to accomplish the permanent freedom of Jerusalem from Moslem control, they did bring many benefits to Western Europe and helped to dissipate its cultural provincialism. Arabic learning, science and literature were brought to Western Europe and were studied by the Scholastics, who tried to synthesize this learning with Christian revelation.

II. MONASTIC REFORM

Many new monastic organizations emerged in the twelfth century as an expression of the same spiritual zeal that displayed itself in the Crusades and that was also manifested in the great wave of cathedral building. The reforming zeal of the Cluniac movement of the tenth century disappeared as the order became wealthy, but new reforming groups, such as the Cistercians, arose to do in the twelfth century what Cluny had done in the tenth century. The orders of Dominicans and Franciscans came into being to meet the problem of winning Moslems and heretics to the faith by persuasion, through education, or by missionary effort. The spiritual zeal of the Crusaders resulted in the founding of lay military orders. All of these orders willingly subjected themselves to the papacy, and the vow of obedience included obedience to the pope as well as to the abbot or the head of the order. The movement also satisfied the medieval desire for the ascetic life and provided those interested in learning with an opportunity to engage in scholarly studies.

Attempts were made to reform the Benedictine order during the eleventh century by a renewed emphasis on earlier asceticism of that movement which had expressed itself in work and prayer. The decentralization of the older order, which gave autonomy to the local abbot, was replaced by centralization of authority. The Carthusian monasteries, which were organized by Bruno in 1086, followed this pattern.

The order of Augustinian canons began as an attempt to bring the canons, secular clergymen of a cathedral who aided the bishop in his work, under the rules of the regular clergy. The Rule of St. Augustine was adopted, and common dress and community of goods and residence were adopted about 1119.

A. The Cistercian Order.

The Cistercian order, founded in 1098, was the leading order to bring the idea of reform to the fore in the monasteries of medieval Europe. The order was founded at Citeaux in France by a Benedictine monk named Robert who wanted to correct the lack of discipline in contemporary monasticism. The Cistercian monks differed from those of Cluny by their greater emphasis upon ascetic self-denial, the simplicity of the architecture of their buildings, and centralized organization. The abbots of the daughter monasteries met with the abbot of Citeaux in a yearly assembly to consider the problems of the group. Though the abbot of Citeaux exercised authority over the sister houses, he did not exercise the supreme power of the abbot of Cluny but acted rather in the relation of a feudal lord to a vassal. While the Cluniacs were mainly aristocratic in background, the Cistercians attracted more from the peasant class. The Cistercians also gave more attention to agriculture than to scholastic pursuits. Their reforming program made such an appeal that the order included thirty houses by 1130, and from that point it grew rapidly. It brought a fresh spirit of zeal to a decadent monasticism.

Much of the fame of the organization was a result of the efforts of Bernard (1091–1153) of the monastery at Clairvaux. He was of noble birth and owed much to his godly mother Aletta. He took over the decaying Benedictine monastery at Clairvaux in 1115 at the age of twenty-two and, with the aid of thirty companions and his five brothers, he was able to make it one of the most famous centers of the Cistercian order.[4]

[4] F. A. Ogg, *A Source Book of Medieval History* (New York: American Book Co., 1907), pp. 251-260.

Though he was humble and inclined to a mystical life, Bernard could be practical and courageous. In the heyday of his rule at Clairvaux, the pope as well as the rulers were glad to listen to his counsel. His preaching, which emphasized the suffering of pilgrims to Palestine and the profanation of the Holy Places, was largely responsible for the Second Crusade. His great ability in homiletics and his delight in mysticism are revealed in his *Homilies on the Song of Solomon.* His mystical tendencies produced such great hymns as "O Sacred Head" and "Jesus the Very Thought of Thee." Not deficient in theology, when Abelard's conceptualist views seemed to be subverting the foundation of theology, he came forth as the champion of the orthodox position. His intellectual, mystical, oratorical and practical abilities made him the spiritual leader and second founder of the Cistercian movement, as well as a power in the affairs of the Church and state in medieval Europe.

B. *The Military Orders.*

The Crusades gave rise to a military type of monasticism which combined the art of war with the monastic life. The order of the Knights Hospitallers was founded early in the twelfth century to defend pilgrims and to care for the ill. In the early period of its history, it was the medieval equivalent to the modern Red Cross. The monks took the threefold monastic vow but did not give up the profession of arms. In fact, the order later became a strictly military organization to defend the Holy Land from the infidels. The Knights Templars, whose name was derived from their headquarters near the temple in Jerusalem, were organized into an order about 1118. The order was recognized officially in 1128 and brought under the Cistercian rule for the monastic life in 1130. It was primarily pledged to defend the Holy Land from the onslaughts of the Moslems. The order was dissolved early in the fourteenth century because it was dabbling too much in European politics. Subject only to the papacy and dedicated to the advance of its interests, these two organizations formed a standing army of monk-knights.

C. *The Friars.*

The friars represented still another type of twelfth century reforming monasticism. They took vows of poverty, chastity and obedience as did the monks; but instead of living in monastic communities to pray and labor apart from the secular world, they went among the people of the cities to help them and to preach to them in the vernacular. The monasteries had property, and the monks supported themselves by work, but the friars were supported by the alms and gifts that the people gave them. They were more directly under the leadership of the pope than had been the case with orders before the twelfth century. In addition to the more important Franciscan and Dominican Friars, the Carmelite and Austin Friars were organized in this period.

The Franciscan order was founded by Francis of Assisi (1182–1226), the pleasure-loving son of a rich merchant. He was converted during an illness and left his father's home to consecrate himself to poverty and the service of God. Gathering several young men of like interest around himself,[5] he drew up a rule to govern their lives. This rule involved poverty, chastity and obedience, but obedience to the papacy was emphasized.[6] The organization was approved by Innocent III in 1210. The Franciscan order became so popular that in 1212 the pope permitted a girl of eighteen named Clare to organize a companion order for women known as the Poor Clares. Still later, the tertiaries or third order was founded for those laymen and laywomen who lived by the rules of the order but could not leave their secular life because of family or business ties.

The name "friar," derived from the Latin word for brother, *frater*, was synonymous not only with spiritual development but also service to the Roman Church. The Franciscans have always been in the van of the missionary effort of the Roman church. During his lifetime Francis preached in Spain and Egypt. Others also went to the Near East, and even to the Far East. John de Monte Corvino reached Peking before 1300.[7] When Spain and France opened up the lands of the Western Hemisphere, most of the missionary work was done by the Franciscans. The ruins of the eighteenth century Franciscan missions along the King's Road in California testify to their activity.

As the order grew, it became more centralized under a general

---

[5] See pp. 307-397 of *Little Flowers of St. Francis* (New York: E. P. Dutton & Co., 1910) for a medieval account of Francis' life, and pp. 1-180 for the devotional work, *Little Flowers*, in which his deeds and words are recorded.

[6] H. Bettenson, *Documents of the Christian Church* (New York: Oxford University Press, 1917), pp. 181-187.

[7] B. J. Kidd, *Documents Illustrative of the History of the Church* (London: Society for Promoting Christian Knowledge, 3 vols., 1920-1941), Vol. III, pp. 160-163.

appointed by the pope. The order also had many scholars, such as Roger Bacon, Bonaventura, Duns Scotus and William of Occam. Bacon became a pioneer in scientific experiment, and the ideas of Occam concerning the nature of reality had an influence on the spiritual development of Luther and strengthened the experimental approach to life during the Renaissance.

The Dominicans were also mendicants, that is, members of a religious order who lived by alms. Where the Franciscans were great missionaries, winning men by example and emotional appeal, the Dominicans were great scholars who tried to win men from heresy by intellectual persuasion. The appeal of the Dominicans was to man's head; that of the Franciscans to his heart.

Dominic (1170–1221), a Spanish priest of noble birth, on a visit to Southern France, pitied the Albigensian heretics of that area and developed the idea of fighting heresy with the weapons of austerity of life, simplicity and argument. For this reason the Dominican "Hounds of the Lord" emphasized education. The Dominican order was approved by the pope in 1216, and a highly centralized organization was developed. The separate groups were each under a prior who, in turn, was subject to a prior in charge of a province. Over the general convocation of the order was placed a master-general who was responsible to the pope.

Thomas Aquinas and his teacher, Albertus Magnus, were the outstanding scholars of the order. The present system of theology of the Roman Catholic Church was developed by Aquinas. The Dominicans also engaged in missionary activity. It was the Dominican order that was given the task of running the machinery of the Inquisition after it was organized. Several of the leading mystics, such as Meister Eckhart and John Tauler, were Dominican friars, and Savonarola, the famous Florentine reformer, belonged to this order.

The friars strengthened religion among the people of the parishes by their unselfish service. Their good deeds and preaching in the vernacular were practical manifestations of the church that the people readily understood. In fact, preaching was restored to its proper place in the Roman Church by the friars. Directly responsible to the pope, they tended to strengthen the power of the papacy over local bishops and lay rulers. Both orders provided many fine missionaries to all parts of the world.

Franciscan hospitals ministered to the physical as well as to the spiritual needs of the people. Nearly ten thousand died while ministering to the people during the Black Death of 1348 and 1349. Above all, they made tremendous contributions to the field of learning, particularly in the realm of theology, where the name of Thomas Aquinas stands out as the best scholar of the mendicant movement.

The activities of the Dominicans in operating the Inquisition for the popes is another and blacker side to the picture. By the middle of the fourteenth century the mendicant movement formed corporations to hold wealth, and the spiritual zeal of the first generation of friars disappeared.

III. Lay Reforming Movements

Unity was the keynote of medieval society; and this unity was achieved by the universal institutions of the Holy Roman Empire, by the hierarchal Roman Church and allegiance to it, and by the spiritual standardization of the sacraments and the creeds; but underneath this unity there were always rumblings of dissent. These rumblings were to become at the time of the Reformation a volcanic explosion that would tear asunder the fabric of medieval religion. Unlike the monks and friars, who sought to bring about internal reform, the Cathari or Albigenses, the Waldenses and other sects, such as the Petrobrusians, arose as an external revolt to purify religion in the late twelfth century. The frequency of corruption in the life and practice of the papal hierarchy and the secular activities of the papacy made many react against the lack of spiritual power that they often saw in their parish churches. More information concerning these medieval sects has been preserved by their enemies than by their friends, and therefore accurate information about them is scarce. Both the Albigenses and the Waldenses sought to return to the purer form of religion that they saw in the New Testament.

A. *The Albigenses.*

The Cathari, or Albigenses, so-called because they were most numerous around Albi in Southern France, used the New Testament as a basis for their ideas, but the heretical ideas that they formulated resembled the dualistic and ascetic ideas of the Gnostic and Manichean movements in the early Church. The Albigenses believed that there was an absolute dualism between

Christ, the good son of God who made the souls of men, and Satan, the bad son who was given a material body after he was cast out of heaven. Following his expulsion, Satan made the visible world. Consequently matter is evil, and therefore the Cathari (literally, the pure) were opposed to reproduction of the race, to the sacraments, particularly the mass with its emphasis on the physical presence of Christ in the elements, the doctrines of hell and purgatory and a physical resurrection. Salvation involved repentance, the rite of *consolamentum* — performed by the laying of hands and the Gospel of John on the head of the candidate — and an ascetic avoidance of marriage, oaths, war, milk, meat, cheese, or eggs. The elite, called the *perfecti,* had forgiveness of sins and an assurance of restoration to the kingdom of God. Because flesh cannot inherit heaven, the believers who lacked this rite of *consolamentum* had to receive it before death. The Albigenses, by making the New Testament the authoritative expression of their faith, offered a challenge to the Roman church, which claimed authority, through the line of popes, from Christ Himself. Persecution and the Albigensian crusade led by Simon De Montfort and sponsored by Innocent III in 1208 were the answers of the medieval Roman church to this affront to its authority.

B. The Waldenses.

Much more like the Protestant and Puritan movements was the Waldensian movement, which emerged during the last quarter of the twelfth century. About 1176 Peter Waldo, a rich merchant of Lyons, read a translation of the New Testament and was so impressed with the claims of Christ that he gave up all his property except enough to feed his family. He then organized a band known as the "Poor in Spirit." Waldo and his followers wished to preach as laymen, but they were forbidden to do so by the pope. In 1184 they were excommunicated for their refusal to stop preaching. As is so often the case, a minority desiring reform was forced out of the organized church by a loveless majority who lost the values that such a zealous group might have supplied.

The Waldensians believed that every man should have the Bible in his own tongue and that it should be the final authority for faith and life. Following the example of Christ, they went out by twos, dressed in simple clothes, to preach to the poor in the vernacular. They accepted the standard ecumenical confessions, the Lord's Supper and Baptism, and lay ordination to preach and minister the sacraments. Their society had its own clergy, with bishops, priests and deacons. Waldo was the head up to the time of his death in 1187. Others, known as friends, were secret associates of the Waldensian groups, but they were permitted to remain within the Roman church. The Waldensians anticipated in many respects the ideas of the Protestants of the Reformation. They still exist as an earnest band of believers in Northern Italy, but they suffer periodic persecution by the Roman church.

The response of the Roman church to this affront to its authority, especially by the Cathari, was varied. The Dominican friars by preaching made every effort to win the Cathari back to the faith. Another answer was the crusade that practically exterminated this sect in Southern France. Still another answer was given at the Synod of Toulouse in 1229. This synod forbade laymen the use of vernacular translations of the Bible. In this way invidious comparisons between the New Testament Church and the Roman Catholic Church might be avoided. Still another answer was the development of the Inquisition, a secret ecclesiastical court that used torture and withheld the names of accusers in its judgment of heretics and turned them over to the state for punishment in the form of loss of property or burning at the stake. At first the Inquisition was in episcopal hands; but, as the number of heretics increased, the papacy assumed control, and in 1233 Gregory IX commissioned the Dominicans to operate the organization.

These procedures for dealing with heresy brutalized the clergy and laymen engaged in dealing with the heretics. Fear of punishment for thought other than that prescribed by the Roman Church brought intellectual stagnation. Persecution, however, often brought more people to an acceptance of heretical doctrine. The unwillingness of the Roman Catholic Church to meet the need for the spiritual reform desired by the sects tended toward an ossification that made the Reformation inevitable.

The twelfth and thirteenth centuries were marked by movements of internal and external reform. The Cistercian movement, symbolized in the person of Bernard of Clairvaux, and the mendicant movements were attempts to purify the Roman Church by a renewal of spiritual zeal. Laymen who attempted to reinstate the Bible as authority found themselves balked in their attempts and therefore set up movements outside the Roman Church in order to practice the Christianity that they saw in the Bible. Though the zeal of monk, friar and crusader was associated with an institution rather than a divine Person, the period was one of spiritual enthusiasm which the Roman Church might have put to a more constructive use than she did.

BIBLIOGRAPHY

Numerous volumes of source materials of the period have been edited and are available in most good libraries.

The little volume by Ernest Barker entitled *The Crusades* (London: Oxford University Press, 1923) is an excellent manual with a fine bibliography.

The Crusades, Iron Men and Saints (New York: Doubleday, Doran & Co., 1930) by Harold Lamb is a popular account of the Crusades that expresses the spirit of the Crusades.

Bernard of Clairvaux (New York: Charles Scribner's Sons, 1893) by Richard S. Storrs is a good biography of the outstanding monk of the period.

Chapter XXIII

MEDIEVAL LEARNING AND WORSHIP

The Scholastic intellectual movement developed between 1050 and 1350 and paralleled the development of the mendicant and heretical movements of the same period. It found a home at first in the cathedral and monastic schools and later, with the rise of universities in the thirteenth century, it dominated the curriculum of European universities. After 1050 the Scholastics replaced the Fathers of the Church as the main guardians of the truth, and "Doctor" became as great a term of honor as "Father" had been earlier in the history of the Church.

I. SCHOLASTICISM

A. Definition of Scholasticism.

The terms "Scholasticism" and "Scholastic" came through the Latin from the Greek word *schole,* which signified a place where learning went on. "Scholastic" was applied to teachers in Charlemagne's court or palace school and was applied to the medieval scholars who used philosophy in the study of religion. These scholars sought to prove existing truth by rational processes rather than to seek new truth. Scholasticism may be defined as the attempt to rationalize theology in order to buttress faith by reason. Theology was to be treated from a philosophical point of view rather than from a Biblical viewpoint. The data of revelation were to be organized systematically by the use of Aristotelian deductive logic and was to be harmonized with the newly rediscovered philosophy of Aristotle. The Scholastics faced a similar problem to that which the Church faced in the nineteenth century when the new discoveries of science had to be harmonized with religion. They had to reconcile the natural philosophy of Aristotle, gained by rational processes, with the revealed theology of the Bible, accepted by faith.

B. Causes for the Rise of Scholasticism.

The major cause for the rise of Scholasticism was the emergence in Europe of the philosophy of Aristotle. Except for some translations of parts of Aristotle's philosophy made in the fifth century by monks, led by Boethius, little was known of his philosophy until translations from Jewish or Arabic sources began to appear in Western Europe in the twelfth century. The translations of Aristotle by Averroes, the great Arabic philosopher, were introduced into the West through Spain. About the same time translations by Moses Maimonides, the famous Jewish rabbi and philosopher, were appearing in Paris. Men like Alexander of Hales welcomed this philosophy and attempted to relate it to theology.

Still another cause for the expansion of the Scholastic movement was the interest of the new mendicant orders in the use of philosophy in the study of revelation. Thomas Aquinas, the greatest Scholastic of all, and Albertus Magnus, his teacher, were Dominicans, and William of Occam and Bonaventura were Franciscans.

The expansion of the university movement, which began in the twelfth century, provided a home for the new intellectual movement, and the universities rapidly centered their curriculum around the study of theology by the aid of logic and reason. The University of Paris in the time of Abelard became the leading center of Scholasticism.

C. Content of Scholasticism.

The student of church history must always remember that the Scholastics were not so much seeking truth as they were trying rationally to organize a body of accepted truth, so that truth, whether it came by faith from revelation or by reason from philosophy, might be a harmonious whole. The medieval mind sought intellectual as well as political and ecclesiastical unity. The appearance of Aristotelian philosophy in the twelfth century forced men to take up this great task. For the Scholastics the data or content of their study was fixed, authoritatively and absolutely. The content of their study was the Bible, the creeds of the ecumenical councils, and the writings of the Fathers of the Church. The question that they wished to settle involved whether or not the Faith was reasonable.

D. Methodology of Scholasticism.

Scholastic methodology was as much subjected to the authority of Aristotle's dialectic or logic as the content was to the authoritative theology of the Roman Catholic Church. Both content and method were fixed. The modern scientist follows the empirical method of inductive logic and only enunciates a general truth on the basis of facts after he has observed and experimented for a long time. Aristotle's dialectic or logic is deductive rather than inductive and emphasizes the syllogism as the instrument of deductive logic. The deductive thinker starts with a general truth or law which he does not prove but which he takes for granted. He relates this general law to a particular fact and from the relationship between the general law and the particular fact derives a conclusion which in turn becomes a new general law or truth to be related to new facts. This method was taken by the Scholastics from Aristotle's *Organon*, which contains his elaboration of the method. The general truths of theology were to be related to the particular facts of theology so that conclusions could be derived from which a harmonious system of rational dogma might be developed. Passages from the Bible, the Fathers, the canons of the councils and papal decretals were concatenated in logical order.

E. The Framework of Scholasticism.

Both in content and method, then, the Scholastic consented to the authority both of the Church and Aristotle. The philosophic framework into which most of the Scholastics may be fitted was based upon Greek philosophy and depended upon whether a Scholastic followed the general position of Plato or of Aristotle with respect to the problem of the nature of universals or ultimate reality.

Plato had insisted, as did also his master Socrates and Aristotle, that universals have a real objective existence somewhere in the universe. In contrast to Aristotle, he insisted that these universals or Ideas exist apart from particular things. For example, he believed that there are universals of truth, beauty and goodness which exist apart from individual acts of truth, beauty and goodness by men. This view was summed up in the Latin phrase, *universalia ante rem,* that is, universals exist before created things. A good deed, for example, is simply a shadow or reflection of the reality of goodness that exists objectively apart from that deed. Plato thus insisted that men must look beyond this life for ultimate reality. Anselm was the leading Scholastic to apply this view to theology. His view is known as realism, which in less temperate realists, often became pantheism — everything merged into the universal.

Aristotle held a more moderate view of the nature of reality. He insisted that universals have an objective existence, but that they do not exist apart from individual things but rather in them. This view was summed up in the Middle Ages by the phrase, *universalia in re.* The medieval Scholastic who accepted Aristotle's framework was known as a moderate realist. Abelard, who was opposed by Anselm and Bernard of Clairvaux, and Thomas Aquinas may be classed as moderate realists.

The medieval Scholastics known as nominalists were opposed both to the realists and the moderate realists. Roscellinus and, later, William of Occam were outstanding examples of nominalistic thinking. Their view was expressed in the phrase, *universalia post rem.* General truths or ideas have no objective existence outside of the mind; rather, they are merely subjective ideas developed by the mind as a result of the observation of particular things. Universals are only class names. Justice is simply the composite idea that man derives from a consideration of justice in action. The nominalists gave much attention to individuals; whereas the realists and moderate realists were more concerned with the group and the institution. The nominalists were the medieval forerunners of the empiricists of the seventeenth and eighteenth centuries and the positivists and pragmatists of our day. The nominalists did not deny revelation; rather, they asserted that it must be believed merely on authority apart from reason, for much that was stated by the Church to be authoritative could not be demonstrated by reason.

This intellectual speculative movement of the medieval Roman Church concerned itself with the problem of unity in man's intellectual life so that his spiritual and rational knowledge could be harmonized to give him certainty both in the realm of faith and of reason. The conflict between nominalism and realism was the great problem that the Scholastics faced in the early period of Scholasticism between 1050 and 1150. In this era the realism championed by Anselm and Bernard was victorious. During the period of High Scholasticism, between 1150 and 1300, the moderate realism championed by Aquinas won out over nominalism. But in the years after 1350, nominalism gained ground in the thinking of theological leaders of the Church.

F. Great Scholastic Thinkers.

Perhaps Scholasticism will become more meaningful with a consideration of the life and works of some of the leading Scholastics. There were many minor Scholastics, but attention will be centered on the leaders in order that the true genius of the movement may be emphasized.

1. Anselm (1033–1109), who was born in Northern Italy, received his education in the Abbey of Bec. Elected as prior of the abbey, he held that position until he became archbishop of Canterbury in 1093. He fought against the practice of lay investiture, which was practiced by the English kings, but his enduring fame rests upon his intellectual activities in the realm of theology.

Anselm's idea of the relationship of reason and faith was summed up in the statement, *Credo ut intelligam* (I believe in order that I may know). Faith must be primary and must be a foundation for knowledge. This was essentially the position that Augustine had held some centuries before. Anselm applied reason to the verification of faith in two great works. The *Monologium* is really an inductive argument from effect to cause for the existence of God. This argument, known as the cosmological argument, may be stated as follows. Man has many goods which he enjoys in life. These goods are simply reflections of the one supreme Good through whom all exist. Because infinite regress is unthinkable, the cause of all must be the One whom we call God. Anselm's *Proslogium* is a deductive argument for the existence of God. This argument, known as the ontological argument, is based upon the doctrine of correspondence. Anselm wrote that every one has an idea of a supreme being in his consciousness. This idea must correspond to a reality that has an objective existence, for otherwise a still greater being could be conceived. Because no greater idea than that of God as the supreme being can be conceived, God must exist in reality.[1]

Though these and other intellectual arguments for the existence of God do not conclusively demonstrate His existence, they have a cumulative value in showing an intelligent man that nothing is really explicable if God's existence is rejected.

Anselm also developed a theory of the Atonement in his work *Cur Deus Homo* (Why God Became Man). Man, he wrote,

[1] H. Bettenson, *Documents of the Christian Church* (New York: Oxford University Press, 1947), pp. 195-196.

owed absolute obedience to God. This obedience had been withheld by natural man since the sin of Adam, and man was in debt to a God who demanded payment of the debt or satisfaction by punishment. The God-man, Christ, paid the debt that man could not pay by His death on the Cross. Thus man was freed from that obligation. Anselm's view of the atonement was commercial, but his view dominated orthodox thinking until the time of Thomas Aquinas in the thirteenth century, and it ended the patristic view of the Atonement as a ransom paid to Satan.

2. A native of Brittany, Abelard (1079–1142) early became famous for his intellectual ability. He was vain and critical of others to such an extent that he often alienated his friends. In 1115 he became a canon of Notre Dame, and his lectures on theology at the University of Paris became so famous that he had five thousand students in his classes at times. He fell in love with one of his private pupils, Heloise, the niece of a fellow canon named Fulbert. When their love affair and subsequent marriage became known, Fulbert took a brutal revenge by having some ruffians emasculate Abelard. Abelard then persuaded Heloise to go into a convent. His theological views opposed successfully by Bernard of Clairvaux, the defeated Abelard was forced to retire to a friendly monastery until his death.[2]

His theological position was that of moderate realism. He believed that reality existed here and now in individuals and things rather than above and beyond this life. In contrast to Augustine and Anselm, he held to the idea of *intelligo ut credam* (I know in order that I may believe). Emphasizing the position of reason in the development of truth, he constantly appealed to it from authority. He believed that doubt would lead to inquiry and inquiry to truth. He thought that the death of Christ was not to satisfy God but to impress man with the love of God, so that man would be morally influenced to surrender his life to God. This view of the Atonement is known as the moral influence theory of the Atonement.

Abelard's outstanding work is the book *Sic et Non*. This book consists of 158 propositions arranged to show the views of the Fathers pro and con with regard to certain ideas. Thus Abe-

---

[2] See J. F. Scott, A. Hyma and A. H. Noyes, *Readings in Medieval History* (New York: Appleton-Century-Crofts, 1933), pp. 334-348 for autobiographical data concerning Abelard's life, and *The Love Letters of Abelard and Heloise* (London: J. M. Dent & Sons, 1908) by Pierre Abailard for the letters exchanged between Abelard and Heloise.

lard was able to point out the contradictions that existed among the Fathers.[3] He did not reject the stated theology of the Roman Catholic Church, but his methods made many feel that he was overemphasizing reason and was, therefore, a danger to the truth.

3. Textbooks, such as Gratians' *Decretum,* a text on canon law, had an important place in the life of the medieval scholar. Peter Lombard (ca. 1100–ca. 1160), a brilliant theological teacher of the University of Paris, wrote what became the theological text-book of the Middle Ages. This was his *Four Books of Sentences,* known usually as *Sentences.* Book I concerns God as the object of man's happiness; Book II with how man might attain this happiness; Book III with the doctrine of Christ; and Book IV with such things as the sacraments and eschatology. Lombard emphasizes the seven sacraments that were finally accepted as authoritative at the Council of Florence in 1439.

4. Albert Magnus (ca. 1206–1280), known as the "Universal Doctor" because of the tremendous scope of his knowledge, taught at the University of Paris, but his greatest work was done at Cologne in his homeland. His chief works, compendiums of theology and of creation, treat respectively theological and natural science in an effort to reconcile science and religion. This reconciliation was to be finally accomplished for that era by Albert's pupil, Thomas Aquinas.

5. Thomas Aquinas (ca. 1225–1274), known as the "Angelic Doctor," was of noble birth, his mother being the sister of Frederick Barbarossa. Educated at Monte Cassino and at the University of Naples, he became a Dominican monk against the wishes of his parents and devoted himself to study. He was a large, shambling, taciturn, somewhat absent-minded man. When his classmates at Cologne teased him about being a "silent ox," the teacher Albertus remarked that one day the lowing of this ox would fill the world.

The prodigious learning of Thomas was applied to the problem of integrating the new (for that day) natural philosophy of Aristotle with the revealed theology of the Bible as interpreted by the Roman Church. In so doing he took the position of moderate realism and became the leading Scholastic thinker to uphold that position. He believed that in the realm of natural philosophy, comparable to modern science, man by

3 Scott, Hyma, Noyes, *op. cit.,* pp. 348-357.

the use of reason and the logic of Aristotle could gain such truths as those of God's existence and of immortality. Beyond this realm, concerning such ideas as the Incarnation and the Trinity, man could only get truth through faith in God's revelation in the Bible as interpreted by the Fathers and councils. Thomas endeavored to synthesize the two areas of faith and reason into a totality of truth in his great work called *Summa Theologiae*.[4] Because both are from God, there can be no essential contradiction between them, according to Aquinas.

The *Summa Theologiae* consists of three thousand articles grouped under six hundred questions in three major sections. It was intended to be a systematic exposition of the whole of theology. It has become, rather, the classic exposition of the system of theology held by the Roman Catholic Church. Neo-Thomistic scholars today study Thomas' great intellectual cathedral with as much interest as medieval scholars did. The first part, which discusses the existence and nature of God, emphasizes God's being. The Trinity and the work of the Trinity in creation are also discussed. The second section discusses man's "advance toward God." Thomas takes note of the nature of morality and the virtues and points out that man's will is bent by sin, although it is not completely determined to evil. Here he breaks with Augustine who believed that the human will is helpless to help man move toward God. The third section concerns Christ as our Way to God and stresses Christ's incarnation, life, death and resurrection. It concludes with a discussion of the sacraments as channels of grace. Thomas shared with other medieval men belief in a hierarchy of truth and order. His view was later expressed poetically by Dante in his *Divine Comedy*.

Aquinas rationalizes the idea of indulgences, created to free one from the satisfaction normally necessary in the sacrament of penance, by his emphasis upon the availability of the extra merits of Christ and the saints. These merits can be drawn upon by the Church for the penitent. His moderate realism leads him to emphasize the Church as a corporate institution at the expense of the freedom of the individual. There is also the danger that his postulate of the two realms of knowledge, natural philosophy and Biblical revelation interpreted by the

[4] Anton C. Pegis, ed., *Basic Writings of Saint Thomas Aquinas* (New York: Random House, 1945).

Church, may lead to a belief in double truth and the separation of knowledge into two realms.

6. The Franciscans soon began to criticize the work of the great Aquinas, who was a member of the rival Dominican order. This criticism led to the development of a nominalistic position that became dominant during the fourteenth century, a time of decline for Scholasticism. Although John Duns Scotus laid more emphasis on the individual than on the institution, he was not a nominalist. It was William of Occam (ca. 1300–ca. 1349) who developed full-fledged nominalism. Occam insisted that theological dogmas were not rationally demonstrable and that they must be accepted on the authority of the Church. This view denied Aquinas' synthesis of the realms of reason and revelation. Occam also denied the existence of objective universals and held that the universals are only mental concepts that men develop in their minds. The individual was much more important than the institution, according to him. Occam's undermining of the authority of the Church as a rationally derived institution aroused Luther's interest in his work. From Occam's day until some time before the Reformation, nominalism became the main philosophical system.

7. Roger Bacon (1214–1294) belonged to the same tradition as Occam but devoted his time to scientific experiments. In so doing, he laid the foundation for experimental science, the method of which Francis Bacon was to develop in the seventeenth century. Bacon spent about ten thousand dollars on scientific experiment in twenty years. This approach to truth through the realm of nature by experiment was in full accord with the nominalistic position.

G. *Results of Scholasticism.*

There is no doubt but what realism and moderate realism buttressed the sacramental and hierarchal system of the Roman Church by an emphasis on universals that led to the subordination of the individual to the corporate group or institution. Aquinas' emphasis upon the sacraments as the channels of grace strengthened the hold of the Roman Catholic Church upon the individual, for there could be no salvation apart from the sacraments dispensed by the hierarchy.

Aquinas' view that reason precedes revelation as a means of knowledge but is completed by revelation led to a danger that truth known by these two methods might become separated into two spheres, the secular and sacred. The actual divorce is apparent in the thinking of many people who believe that there is a realm of scientific truth and another of theological truth instead of seeing that the two are simply parts of a greater whole that is unified in God as the Creator.

Nominalism created a new interest in man since, according to it, the individual was more important than the institution. This interest sponsored much of the materialism of the Renaissance as people began to think of man as autonomous, and it led to an exaltation of the experimental method as the main avenue to truth. Others who followed the nominalistic views moved in the direction of mysticism as a way whereby the individual could come directly into the presence of God.

Above all, in the *Summa* of Aquinas Scholasticism furnished the medieval and modern Roman Catholic Church with an authoritative, integrated synthesis that harmonized philosophy and religion. The Neo-Thomists seek today in a restudy of the work of Aquinas to furnish an integration of science and religion for the modern Roman Catholic. One cannot dismiss the Scholastics as hair-splitting dialecticians any more than one can condemn modern scientists as grubbers for facts who have no sense of integration or morality in the use of their facts.

II. The Rise of Universities

The university as a center for teaching and research developed about 1200. By 1400 there were over seventy-five European universities. In these schools Scholastic studies formed a large part of the curriculum. Most of the great universities of modern Europe had their beginnings in this period. Teaching on the higher level had gone on before the development of the universities, but after their rise most of higher education, which had centered in monastic and cathedral schools, was given in university classrooms.

A. Reasons for the Rise.

Several reasons account for the rapid rise of universities around 1200. Martianus Capella about 425 adapted the Roman quadrivium and trivium to the use of religion. Grammar, rhetoric and logic made up the trivium; geometry, arithmetic, astronomy and music were included in the quadrivium. The trivium was useful for training the clergy in public speaking so that they could fulfill their preaching function effectively; the quadrivium was useful in the establishment of the dates of the sacred festivals of the Church. These studies were used in Charlemagne's palace school and were based on the model of monastery schools for learning between 550 and 1100. Other centers for higher learning sprang up in connection with the cathedral church of the bishop or archbishop. The University of Paris developed from the cathedral school connected with Notre Dame cathedral.

A second reason for the rise of universities was the presence of a great teacher in a school. In the eleventh century, Irnerius developed a reputation as a great scholar of Roman law, and students flocked to Bologna to hear him. Soon there was a thriving university at Bologna. Abelard's fame as a teacher contributed greatly to the development of the University of Paris.

Other universities came into being as a result of student revolts or migrations. Because the English and French kings were quarreling shortly after the middle of the twelfth century, English students, who felt that they were mistreated at the University of Paris, revolted against conditions there and moved to Oxford in England. From this revolt grew the great University of Oxford. Cambridge grew out of a student revolt and exodus from Oxford to Cambridge.

B. Organization of the Universities.

Medieval university organization differed considerably from that of modern times. The *universitas,* from which our word for university is derived, was a guild or corporation of students or teachers set up for purposes of common protection while the group went on with its work. The words *studium generale* were used to describe this group in its educational function. The universities of Southern Europe followed the practice of Bologna, where the corporation was made up of students who organized for mutual protection against abuses from the towns where they were located or from failure on the part of their teachers. From a king or other overlord of the area the university received a charter that set forth its rights, privileges and responsibilities. Bologna was noted for the study of law, but Salerno gained its fame as a university of advanced medical teaching and research. The universities of Northern Europe were organized on the model of Paris. Here the guild, which received the charter, was made up of teachers.

The university usually had four faculties. The arts was the general course for all. Theology, law and medicine were more advanced studies. The student in the general curriculum of the arts studied the trivium which led to the bachelor's degree. Further study of the quadrivium gave him a master's degree, which was essential if he desired to become a teacher. Continued study in other faculties might give him a doctorate in law, theology or medicine.

Students in the medieval university began their studies as early as their fourteenth birthday, although they were usually between sixteen and eighteen when they entered the university. They had the privileges of clergymen. Examinations were oral, comprehensive and public; and during the course of an examination the student had to defend a thesis against teachers or students. Instruction was in Latin. Because there were only textbooks for the teachers, the student had to do a good deal of memorizing. A good memory and the use of logic were as important then as reading and research now are in the modern university.

Most of the paraphanalia of modern university life comes from medieval times. The nomenclature of many degrees, examinations, gowns, hoods and basic elements of the curriculum were created in medieval times. The teaching of successive generations of students and the advancement of learning by research are functions that the modern university has inherited from its medieval ancestor. Above all, the university in medieval times kept alive and developed the study of theology. The great Scholastics were also the greatest university teachers. Universities served the interests of the Church in medieval times by preparing men for service in it instead of preparing them for service in the fields of science and industry as the modern university does. Scholasticism and the universities were closely associated in the service of the Church. They poured a steady stream of personnel trained in arts, law and theology into its hierarchy.

III. Medieval Life and Worship

Medieval university towers, representative of Scholasticism, had their counterpart in the spires of the Gothic cathedral which has often been described as a "Bible in stone." The great medieval cathedrals, emphasizing vertical lines, often took about a century to build. They expressed the spiritual nature of the age as much as the skyscraper expresses the materialistic spirit of the twentieth century. Many of these great churches were raised in Northern and Western Europe between 1150 and 1550. Gothic architecture like Scholasticism was at its peak during the thirteenth century.

Although the earth-bound Renaissance architect thought of medieval architecture as barbaric and, therefore, Gothic, later ages have not sustained his viewpoint. Gothic buildings have certain characteristics that show the skill of the medieval builders. On going into a Gothic cathedral one notices the cross-shaped floor plan of the building expressive of the central symbol of the Christian Church. The use of the pointed arch instead of the rounded Roman arch is instantly noticeable and leads the eye and aspirations upward from this earth. Flying buttresses — long ribs attached to the roof and to separate pillars — or buttresses built into the walls of the cathedral convey the weight of the roof to the earth so that the upper walls can be thin and windows can be put in to admit light, so badly needed in the gloomy days of Northern European winters. Usually there are three doors at the west end of the church. All ornamentation, whether stained glass windows or statues, is subordinated to the design of the whole building. A statue, seen on the ground, might seem grotesquely out of proportion, but the same statue in its niche above the doors blends into the design of the building harmoniously. Colors are used by the worker in stained glass to illustrate stories as clearly as possible.

The best examples of the medieval Gothic cathedral were built within a hundred mile radius of Paris. The cathedral of Notre Dame is noted for its beautiful facade. Both the cathedrals at Chartres and Notre Dame have outstanding rose windows above the main entrance that show the skilful use of colored glass by the medieval artisan.

The significance of the Gothic cathedral is much more important than its characteristics. The cathedral represented the supernaturalistic spirit of the age clearly by its dominating position in the town and by its symbolic expression of Biblical truth. The social solidarity of medieval man was expressed by the fact that the great cathedrals were built as community enterprises extending over decades, with all ranks and classes taking part in the work. The cathedral also had a real educational value because in stained glass window and statue the illiterate peasant might see for himself the truth of the Bible. Often a center for social and many other activities of the town, the cathedral was, above all, a place where the soul might come into contact with God in the act of worship.

All of the ceremonies important to the religious life of the individual occurred in the cathedral, if he were fortunate enough to live in a cathedral town. He was baptized, confirmed and married in the church. He was buried from the church in the cemetery within the grounds of the church. But the most important part of worship, be the building a cathedral or a simple church, was the mass. After the Fourth Lateran Council of 1215, it was a part of Roman Catholic dogma to believe that the priest's words of consecration changed the bread and the wine into the actual body and blood of Christ. Christ was sacrificed afresh by the priest for the benefit of the believers. It did not matter that the cup was withheld from the believer after the twelfth century, for the body and blood were, according to Roman dogma, in each element. The practice of elevating the elements by the priest became a custom in the thirteenth century in order that the faithful might worship Christ in the mass.

The development of polyphonic music, which consisted of many parts and hence was better sung by trained choirs, ended the practice of congregational singing in unison. Music became elaborate and colorful as a proper accompaniment to the sacred mysteries of the mass.

One cannot overlook the real and positive contributions of the Roman Church between 590 and 1305, despite the many evidences of failure in personal and institutional practices. It gave Greco-Roman culture and the Christian religion to the barbaric Germans who took over the Roman Empire. It provided the only real culture and scholarship, which kept learning alive through the work of such scholars as Bede, Alcuin, Einhard and others. The moral tone of society was improved by the mitigation of the evils of slavery, the elevation of the position of women and the softening of the horrors of feudal war. The Roman Church sponsored what relief and charitable work was done in the Middle Ages. It provided an intellectual unity for life in the theological system that the Scholastics developed and impressed upon men their solidarity as members of the human race, despite the decentralizing tendencies of feudalism. God used the Roman Church to further His own ends in spite of its failure at so many points when it is compared with the true Church, depicted in the New Testament.

BIBLIOGRAPHY

University Records and Life in the Middle Ages (New York: Columbia University Press, 1944) by Lynn Thorndike contains a fine collection of documents relating to the universities of medieval Europe. Matters such as the curriculum, fees, charters, rules and student life are illustrated from contemporary documents.

A helpful discussion of Scholasticism is given by Neve and Heick in their *A History of Christian Thought* (Philadelphia: The Muhlenberg Press, 2 vols., 1946), Vol. I, pp. 188-203.

Art Through the Ages (New York: Harcourt, Brace & Co., rev. ed., 1936) by Helen Gardner has a useful section on Gothic architecture, pp. 303-334.

MEDIEVAL SUNSET AND MODERN SUNRISE, 1305–1517

Chapter XXIV

ATTEMPTS AT INTERNAL REFORM

Many people mistakenly think that the return to the Scriptures began with such leaders of the Reformation as Calvin and Luther. On the contrary, there were attempts before the Reformation to halt the decline in papal prestige and power by reforms of various kinds. The problem of a corrupt, extravagant papacy that resided in France instead of in Rome, and the schism that resulted from the attempts to get the pope to return to Rome, provided the impetus which led mystics and reformers, such as Wycliffe, Huss and Savonarola, and the reform councils of the fourteenth century to seek ways to bring about a revival of spiritual life within the Roman Catholic Church.

I. THE PAPACY IN DECLINE, 1309–1439

A. Immorality of the Clergy.

Between the above dates the Roman Church sank to a new low in the estimation of the laity. The hierarchal organization, with its demand for celibacy and absolute obedience to the pope, and the feudalization of the Roman Church led to a decline in clerical morale and morals. Celibacy was opposed both to the natural instincts of man and to the Biblical statements in favor of the married state for man. Many priests took concubines or indulged in illicit love affairs with the female members of their congregations. Some had the problem of caring for children that were born to these unions and gave more attention to that problem than they did to their clerical duties. Others, especially during the Renaissance, enjoyed luxurious living. Feudalism was still a problem because the dual allegiance to the pope and the feudal lord created a division of interest in many cases. The cleric often gave more attention to his secular responsibilities than he did to his spiritual responsibilities.

[269]

B. *The Babylonian Captivity and the Great Schism.*

The papacy itself lost the respect of the laity of the various areas under its control. The Babylonian Captivity and the Great Schism, which must not be confused with the Schism of 1054, were the events responsible for the papacy's loss of prestige. The zenith of papal power was reached in the pontificate of Innocent III, but the papacy slid rapidly from that dizzy eminence of power after Boniface VIII was unsuccessful in his attempts to subjugate the rulers of England and France at the beginning of the fourteenth century.

Clement V, a Frenchman chosen as pope by the cardinals in 1305, was a weak man of doubtful morality. Soon falling under the influence of the French king, he moved the papacy from Rome to Avignon in Southern France in 1309. In the eyes of the people of Europe this put the pope under French control even though Avignon was not technically French territory. Except for a brief period between 1367 and 1370 the papal residence was maintained at Avignon until 1377 and was dominated by strong French kings. The godly mystic, St. Catherine of Siena, strongly pressed Gregory XI to return to Rome to restore order there and to regain prestige for the papacy as an independent international authority. In 1377 he returned and ended the Babylonian Captivity.

When Gregory XI died in the next year, the cardinals, even though dominated by a French majority, were forced by the people of Rome, who did not want to lose the papacy again, to elect the man who became Urban VI. Urban's lack of consideration of the cardinals soon won him their enmity, and they elected Clement VII as pope. Clement dutifully removed the capital to Avignon for the second time. Both men, elected by the same body of cardinals, claimed to be the legitimate pope and the true successor to St. Peter. This forced the people of Europe to decide to which pope they would give their allegiance. Northern Italy, most of Germany, Scandinavia and England followed the Roman pope; France, Spain, Scotland and Southern Italy gave allegiance to the pope at Avignon. This schism continued until it was resolved early in the next century by the reforming councils (see page 278). The Captivity and the Great Schism strengthened the rising clamor for reform within the Roman Church.

C. *Papal Taxation.*

Papal taxation to support two papal courts became an onerous burden to the people of Europe. Papal income was made up of income from the papal estates; tithes, which the faithful paid; annates, which was the payment of the first year's salary by a church official to the pope; the right of purveyance, by which churchmen and their constituents had to pay the pope's traveling expenses while he was in their area; the right of spoil, by which the personal property of the upper clergy went to the pope upon their death; Peter's Pence, which was paid annually by the laity in many lands; and the income from vacant offices as well as numerous fees.[1] The now powerful rulers of national states and the strong middle class that supported them resented the drain of wealth from the national treasury to the papal treasury. This was especially true of the rulers of England and France. During the long period of the Captivity in the fourteenth century the English hated to pay money which they thought would only go to England's enemy France because the pope's residence was in territory dominated by the French king.

D. *The Rise of Nation-States.*

A political factor that played an important part in the decline of papal influence in Europe was the rise of national states opposed to the idea of universal sovereignty inherent in the concepts of the Holy Roman Empire and the Roman Catholic Church. King and middle class cooperated: the king with his national army gave security so that the middle class could carry on business safely; and the middle class in return gave money so that the king could run the state. The resulting strong, centralized nation-state was strong enough to defy the pope's dicta.

All the reasons discussed thus far created a clamor for internal reform of the papacy in the fourteenth and fifteenth centuries. Leaders soon came to the fore. The mystical, Biblical and conciliar reformers were the successors of the monastic reformers of the twelfth and thirteenth centuries.

II. The Mystics

The recurrence of mysticism in eras when the Church lapses into formalism testifies to the desire of the human heart to have

[1] William E Lunt, *Papal Revenues in the Middle Ages* (New York: Columbia University Press, 1934), Vol. I, pp. 57-136.

direct contact with God in the act of worship instead of passively participating in the coldly formal acts of worship performed by the clergyman. The mystic desires direct contact with God by immediate intuition or contemplation. If the emphasis is on the union of the essence of the mystic with the essence of deity in the experience of ecstasy, which is the crown of mystical experience, then mysticism is philosophical. If the emphasis is on an emotional union with deity by intuition, then mysticism is psychological. The main objective in either case is immediate apprehension of God in an extra-rational fashion as the mystic waits before Him in a passive receptive mood. Both types were to be found in the mysticism of the fourteenth century.

A. *Causes for the Rise of Mysticism.*

Scholasticism contributed to the rise of mysticism because it emphasized reason at the expense of man's emotional nature. Mysticism was a reaction against this rationalistic tendency. Movements emphasizing the subjective aspect of man's relation to God usually come as a reaction to movements that emphasize the intellectual aspect. In a similar manner, Pietism was to follow the period of cold orthodoxy in the Lutheranism of the seventeenth century. Scholastic nominalism led to an emphasis upon the individual as the source of reality and upon experience as the way in which to gain knowledge. In this way, one wing of nominalistic Scholastics turned to mysticism as a way to gain knowledge of God, while other nominalists were emphasizing materialism and experiment.

The movement was also one of protest and reaction against the troubled times and a decadent and corrupt church. Social and political upheaval in the fourteenth century was a common experience. The Black Death in 1348 and 1349 took away by painful death about one-third of the population of Europe. The Peasants' Revolt of 1381 in England was an evidence of social unrest associated with the ideas of Wycliffe. The Babylonian Captivity and the Great Schism made people question their spiritual leadership.

B. *Outstanding Mystics.*

The mystics of this era fall into two major groups, the Latin and the Teutonic mystics. The Latin mystics, having a more emotional outlook upon life than the Teutons, emphasized mysticism as a personal emotional experience of Christ. Such an

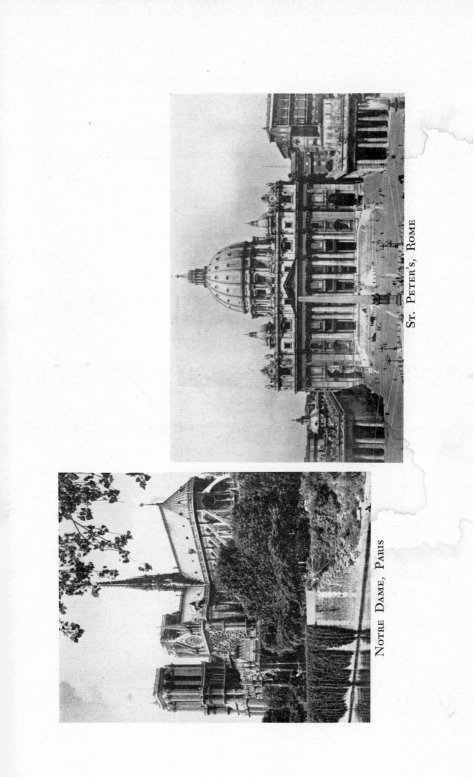

ST. PETER'S, ROME

NOTRE DAME, PARIS

John Wycliffe

Christianity Through the Centuries

A New Church History

By EARLE E. CAIRNS, M.A., Ph.D.

Head of History Department, Wheaton College,
Wheaton, Illinois

Church History textbooks come and go — it is only those which have something new to offer that live on. Dr. Cairns has written not only a tremendously readable text, vast in its scope, but one which is destined to long life — because it has something no other church history text ever had!

SOME UNIQUE FEATURES OF THIS TEXT ARE:

It is both conservative and interdenominational.

It is widespread in its scope, fitting Christianity into the political, economical, social, intellectual and aesthetic backgrounds of secular history.

It is illustrated with class-tested diagrams, graphs and maps at pertinent points in the text.

It pictures the outstanding events and key figures of church history.

A complete section is devoted to the often neglected period of church history since 1914.

ENTHUSIASTIC COMMENTS

". . . one of the most valuable and most interesting books on the subject . . . useful for Bible institutes, Bible colleges and theological seminaries . . . very valuable for the ordinary layman or for the individual pastor who wants to refresh his mind with regard to the tremendous contribution which the history of the Christian church is making to our own lives." *Dr. Peder Stiansen,* Dean, Northern Baptist Theological Seminary.

". . . a scholarly approach to the study of church history, readable and clear in its presentation of the facts." Professor *Morris E. Nelson,* Moody Bible Institute.

Another ZONDERVAN BOOK ★★

emphasis had been true of Bernard of Clairvaux in the twelfth century. He had emphasized a oneness of will and affection with God rather than any oneness of essence. Most of the Teutonic mystics stressed a more philosophical approach to God, which in the case of Meister Eckhart led to a species of pantheism.

St. Catherine of Siena (1347–1380) represented Latin mysticism at its best. She firmly believed that God spoke to her in visions, but she always seemed to use these visions to good practical ends. It was she who fearlessly denounced clerical evils, and who, in the name of God, was able to persuade Gregory XI to return to Rome from Avignon in 1377. Her courage[2] led her to oppose sin even in the papacy.

The mystical movement in Germany centered in the Dominican order. Meister Eckhart (ca. 1260–ca. 1327) was the Dominican who is usually credited with the founding of German mysticism. Before going to Cologne to preach he studied at the University of Paris. Believing that only the divine was real, he taught that the aim of the Christian should be the union of the spirit with God by a fusion of the human essence with the divine essence during an ecstatic experience. He differentiated between the *Gottheit,* which to him signified God in the absolute sense as the philosophical unity back of the universe, and *Gott,* who was the personal Creator and Ruler of the world. His aim was unity with the *Gottheit* back of all creation. He is reputed to have said, "God must become I, and I God." Eckhart's beliefs came so close to Neoplatonism that charges of pantheism were brought against him by the Inquisition, and his views were condemned as pantheistic in a papal bull issued after his death. Though his views were somewhat pantheistic, it must be said that Eckhart also emphasized the need for Christian service as the fruit of mystical union with God.[3]

A group of Dominicans known as the Friends of God carried on the tradition of Eckhart's teaching. John Tauler (1282–1361), more evangelical than his master, emphasized an inward experience of God as being much more vital to the soul's welfare than external ceremonies were. He was associated with the

---

[2] B. J. Kidd, *Documents Illustrative of the History of the Church* (London: Society for Promoting Christian Knowledge, 3 vols., 1920-1941), Vol. III, pp. 190-191.

[3] Raymond B. Blakney, *Meister Eckhart* (New York: Harper & Brothers, 1941). This book gives several of Eckhart's writings.

Friends of God who made their headquarters in the Rhine valley. Heinrich Suso (1295–1366) was the poet of the group and expressed mystical ideas similar to those of Eckhart in poetical form. A banker named Rulman Merswin (1307–1382) was the good angel who provided a religious house where members of the group could take up residence. The little mystical volume entitled *Theologica Germanica* (*German Theology*) is usually associated with this group. Luther found this book a help in his struggle for salvation and had it issued in a German edition in 1516. It has, however, the same undertone of pantheism as is found in the writings of Meister Eckhart.

The movement in the Netherlands known as the Brethren of the Common Life, which had its main center at Deventer, was a much more practical and, certainly, less pantheistic expression of mysticism than the Friends of God movement. John of Ruysbroeck (1294–1381), who had come under the influence of Eckhart's writings, and who knew some of the Friends of God, influenced the mystical movement in Holland. He helped Gerhard Groote (1340–1384) to emphasize the New Testament in the development of the mystic experience, and Groote became the leader of the Brethren of the Common Life. Groote inspired his disciple Florentius Radewijns to open a house for the Brethren of the Common Life at Deventer. The order consisted of laymen who lived under a rule and devoted their lives to teaching and other practical service rather than to the passive experience of God that had been emphasized by Meister Eckhart. The group built another center at Windesheim in 1387 where those who were interested in a more ascetic way of life could repair. Both groups emphasized the education of young people and built up large and excellent schools. Other houses of the group were founded all over the Netherlands.[4]

The *Imitation of Christ* has contributed more than anything else to the lasting reputation of the Brethren of the Common Life. This book is associated with the name of Thomas a Kempis (1380–1471) or, as he was known then, Thomas Hemerken of Kempen. Educated in Deventer under the kindly eye of Radewijns, he entered the Augustinian monastery near Zwolle, underwent ordination, and later became the head of the monastery. He was either the writer or the editor and compiler of the *Imi-*

---

[4] Albert Hyma's *The Christian Renaissance* (New York: The Century Co., 1924) is a scholarly discussion of the Brethren of the Common Life.

tation of Christ.[5] This work reflects the more practical emphasis of the Brethren. It does not stop with mere negative renunciation of the world but asserts the need of a positive love for Christ and service for him in humble practical ways.

C. *Consequences of the Rise of Mysticism.*

The mystical movement developed as a reaction against formal and mechanical sacerdotal ritual and dry Scholasticism in the Church of the day. It reflected the perennial tendency toward the subjective aspect of Christianity which always occurs when too much emphasis is laid upon outward acts in Christian worship. In that sense mysticism may be thought of as anticipating the more personal approach to religion that was such an outstanding characteristic of the Reformation.

Tendencies to substitute a subjective inner authority for the Bible and to minimize doctrine were some of the dangers in such a movement. In its excesses, as in the case of Meister Eckhart, there was danger of it being so passivist that its adherents became introspective and anti-social. In Eckhart's case it also led philosophically to a kind of pantheism that identified God with His creation and creatures.

II. Forerunners of the Reformation

The mystics had attempted to personalize religion, but reformers such as Wycliffe, Huss and Savonarola were more interested in an attempt to return to the ideal of the Church presented in the New Testament. Wycliffe and Huss were able to capitalize on nationalistic anti-papal sentiment during the period of the Babylonian Captivity when the pope was resident in Avignon.

A. *John Wycliffe* (*ca.* 1320–1384).

The English people resented sending money to a pope in Avignon who was under pressure from England's enemy, the French king. This natural nationalistic feeling was augmented by royal and middle class resentment over the money lost to the English treasury and to the service of the English state by papal taxation. The Statue of Provisors of 1351 banned appointment by the pope of clergymen to offices in the Roman Church in England. The Statute of Praemunire of 1353 forbad the practice of taking cases concerning clergymen out of English

[5] *Ibid.,* Ch. V contains an able discussion of the authorship of the *Imitation.*

courts for trial in the papal court in Rome. Payment of the annual tribute of one thousand marks, which had been begun by John, also was stopped by Parliament in this period. It was in this era of nationalistic reaction against ecclesiasticism that Wycliffe appeared on the scene. Aided by the powerful John of Gaunt, Wycliffe was able to defy the pope.

Wycliffe studied and taught at Oxford for the greater part of his life. Until 1378 he was a reformer who wanted to reform the Roman Church by the elimination of immoral clergymen and by stripping her of property which he felt was a root of corruption. In a work entitled *On Civil Dominion* (1376) he asserted a moral basis for ecclesiastical leadership. God gave the use and possession of property, but not the ownership, to church leaders as a trust to be used for His glory. Failure on the part of ecclesiastics to fulfill their proper functions was a sufficient reason for the civil authority to take the property from them and to give it to someone else who would serve God acceptably. This view suited the nobles who were waiting to seize the property of the Roman Church. They and John of Gaunt championed Wycliffe so that the Church of Rome did not dare to touch him.

Wycliffe was not satisfied with this more negative approach and after 1378 began to oppose the dogma of the Roman Church with revolutionary ideas. He attacked the authority of the pope in 1382 by insisting in writing that Christ and not the pope was the head of the Church. He asserted that the Bible instead of the Church was the sole authority for the believer and that the Roman Church should model itself after the pattern of the New Testament Church. To support these beliefs, Wycliffe made the Bible available to the people in their own tongue. By 1382 he had made the first complete manuscript translation into English of the New Testament. Nicholas of Hereford completed the translation of the Old Testament into English in 1384. Thus, for the first time, Englishmen were able to read the whole Bible in their own tongue. Wycliffe went still further in 1382 by opposing the dogma of transubstantiation. Whereas the Roman Church believed that the substance or essence of the elements changed while the outward form remained the same, Wycliffe argued that the substance of the elements was indestructible.[6] If adopted, Wycliffe's view would mean that

[6] Kidd, *op. cit.*, Vol. III, pp. 201-202.

the priest could no longer withhold salvation from one by with-holding the body and blood of Christ in the Communion.

Wycliffe's views[7] were condemned in London in 1382, and he was forced to retire to his rectory at Lutterworth. He had made provision for the continued dissemination of his ideas, however, by the founding of a group of lay preachers, the Lollards, who preached his ideas all over England[8] until the Roman Church, by forcing the statute *De Haeretico Comburendo* through Parliament in 1401, made the death penalty the punishment for preaching Lollard ideas.

Wycliffe's accomplishments were influential in paving the way for subsequent reformation in England. He gave the English their first Bible in the vernacular and created the Lollard group to proclaim evangelical ideas all over England among the common people. His teachings of equality in the Church were applied to economic life by the peasants, so that they rose in the Peasants Revolt of 1381. Bohemian students studying in England carried his ideas to Bohemia where they became the foundation for the teachings of John Huss.[9]

B. *John Huss* (*ca.* 1369–1415).

When Richard II of England married Anne of Bohemia, students from that land came to England to study. When they returned to Bohemia, they carried Wycliffe's ideas back with them. John Huss, who had studied in the University of Prague, and who became its rector in about 1402, read and adopted the ideas of Wycliffe. His preaching of these ideas coincided with a rise of Bohemian national feeling against the control of Bohemia by the Holy Roman Empire. Huss proposed to reform the Roman Church in Bohemia along lines similar to those proclaimed by Wycliffe. His views exposed him to papal enmity, and he was ordered to go to the Council of Constance under a safe-conduct from the emperor. But the safe-conduct was not honored. Both his and Wycliffe's views were condemned there. After Huss refused to recant, he was burned at the stake by order of the Council.

Persecutors may destroy men's bodies, but they cannot de-

[7] H. Bettenson, *Documents of the Christian Church* (New York: Oxford University Press, 1947), pp. 246-248.

[8] *Ibid.*, pp. 248-254.

[9] George M. Trevelyan, *England in the Age of Wycliffe* (London: Longmans, Green & Co., 1920). *John Wycliffe* (Oxford: Clarendon Press, 1926), a two-volume work by Herbert B. Workman, is an interesting account of Wycliffe's life and work.

stroy ideas, and the ideas of Huss[10] were spread by his followers. His more radical followers, known as the Taborites, rejected all in the faith and practice of the Roman Church that could not be found in Scripture. The Utraquists took the position that only that which the Bible actually forbade should be eliminated. Some of the Taborite group formed what was known as the *Unitas Fratrum* (United Brethren) or Bohemian Brethren about the middle of the fifteenth century. It was from this group that the Moravian Church, which still exists, developed.

Even though the Roman Church took his life, it could not destroy the influence of John Huss. The Moravian Church became at a later date one of the most missionary-minded churches in the history of the Christian Church. John Amos Comenius, the progressive evangelical educator, was one of the Brethren. Huss may be said to have indirectly influenced Wesley because it was the Moravians who helped to lead Wesley to the light in London. The teachings and example of Huss were an inspiration to Luther as he faced similar problems in Germany in his day.

C. Savonarola (1452–1498).

Wycliffe and Huss were branded as heretics who made the Bible the first standard of authority, but Savonarola was more interested in reform within the church at Florence. Becoming a Dominican monk in 1474, he was assigned to Florence some years later. He tried to reform both state and church in the city, but his preaching against the evil life of the pope resulted in his death by hanging. He never took the more advanced position that Wycliffe and Huss held, but he did demand reform in the Roman Church. All three of these men anticipated the spirit and work of the Reformers to such an extent that Wycliffe, as the outstanding exponent of reformation measures, has often been called the "Morning Star of the Reformation."

III. The Reforming Councils, 1409–1449

Leaders of the councils of the fourteenth century sought reform by making church leadership represent the laity. Councils made up of representatives of the people of the Roman Church were to eliminate corrupt church leaders. The councils did not emphasize the Scriptures to the extent that Huss and Wycliffe did, nor did they seek reform by the subjective religious expression favored by the mystics.

[10] Kidd, *op. cit.*, Vol. III, p. 213.

The need of reform within the Roman Church became clear with the development of the Great Schism in 1378. In that year, Urban VI and Clement VII each claimed to be the legitimate successor to St. Peter. Since the countries of Europe had to choose whom they would follow, Europe became split ecclesiastically as well as politically. France and Spain backed Clement VII of Avignon, and England and some other countries backed Urban VI of Rome. Both had been chosen by the College of Cardinals. Who was to decide their claims? Leading theologians of the University of Paris proposed that a council of the Roman Catholic Church should decide the matter. They used the precedent of the ecumenical councils of the fourth, fifth and sixth centuries. A council, representative of all the church, seemed to be the best solution because neither pope would abdicate nor accept the decision of arbitrators.[11]

Justification for a council's deposing a pope was not wanting. Dante in his *Of Monarchy*, written about 1311, had insisted that the Church was not independent of the state; the state as well as the Church was an arm of God. Both were given by God. The emperor was to secure man's happiness here; the pope to lead men to heaven. Neither was to seek supremacy over the other, but it was conceivable that the emperor might promote reform if the Church failed.

Most important of all the rationalizations of conciliar reform were set forth in a book, *Defensor Pacis* (1324), by Marsilius of Padua (ca. 1290–ca. 1343) and John of Jandum. Marsilius had been for a time the rector of the University of Paris. The book destroyed the idea of an absolute hierarchy in either the Church or state. Marsilius believed that the people in the state and Christians in the Church were the repository of sovereignty and that they could through representative bodies elect the emperor and the pope. The Church in a general council guided by the New Testament alone could proclaim dogma and appoint its officials. The church council and not the pope was thus the highest authority in the Church, and it should act for the good of the whole body of Christians.[12] If Marsilius' views had been victorious, the Roman Catholic Church would have been transformed into a constitutional monarchy led by a pope appointed by a council, and the absolute papacy of the medi-

11 F. A. Ogg, *A Source Book of Medieval History* (New York: American Book Co., 1907), pp. 391-392.
12 Thatcher and McNeal, *Source Book*, pp. 317-323.

eval church would have disappeared. But this view was not to triumph permanently, although the councils did some good in other areas.

The council was called to end the schism in the leadership of the Roman Church, to reform that church from within, and to put down heresy. It might also put into practice a theory of government along the lines laid down by Marsilius.

A. *The Council of Pisa.*

When the Council of Pisa met in July and August of 1409, Benedict XIII was safely in control of Avignon and Gregory XII held the papal chair in Rome. The Council, which was called by the cardinals, at once stated that the cardinals had the authority to call it and that it was competent even to call the popes to account for the Great Schism.[13] It deposed both Benedict XIII and Gregory XII and appointed the man who became Alexander V as the rightful pope.[14] But the other two popes refused to recognize the decision of the Council and excommunicated its members. Now there were three popes instead of two. Alexander V was succeeded by John XXIII when the former died in 1410.

B. *The Council of Constance.*

The Council of Constance was then called by Sigismund, the Emperor of the Holy Roman Empire, and John XXIII. This Council, which sat from 1414 to 1418, was thus called because of the precedent set by Constantine when he called the Council of Nicaea in 325. Nearly five hundred high officials of the hierarchy met. In order to frustrate John's attempt to control the Council through the use of a majority vote, which would have permitted his Italian followers to dominate the decisions of the Council, the members of the Council agreed to vote as national groups of clergymen. Each national group was allotted one vote, and a unanimous vote of the five nations represented was necessary for binding action by the Council. The Council declared its legality and its right to supreme authority in the Roman Church.[15] This decree of the Council, which substituted conciliar control of the Church of Rome for papal absolutism, was given the title *Sacrosanct*.

Presently Gregory XII abdicated, and after much negotiation

13 *Ibid.*, pp. 327-328.
14 Kidd, *op. cit.*, Vol. III, pp. 208-209.
15 O. J. Thatcher and E. H. McNeal, *A Source Book for Medieval History* (New York: Charles Scribner's Sons, 1905), pp. 328-329 cf. 329-330.

both Benedict XIII and John XXIII were deposed. Martin V was then elected by the Council as the new pope. The Council thus took the power of electing a pope from the College of Cardinals. The Council also dealt with the problem of heresy by condemning the ideas of Wycliffe and by burning Huss at the stake. It then went on to discuss the problem of reform, schism and heresy. A decree of the Council, called *Frequens,* provided for the meeting of general councils at stated times in the future as a technique to keep order in the Roman Church. One was to be held five years after the close of the Council of Constance; a second after another seven years; and thereafter councils were to convene once every decade to deal with problems of schism, heresy and reform.[16]

C. *The Councils of Basel, Ferrara and Florence.*

The unrest in Bohemia after the martyrdom of Huss and the need of continued reform brought about the Council of Basel in 1431. It dragged on until 1449, but the strength of the reforming movement was matched by a resurgence of papal power. Eugene IV, the pope at that time, was deposed by the Council in 1438, the same year in which the rival council, which he had called, met at Ferrara. Because of the plague, the rival council was moved to Florence. The Council of Florence made an unsuccessful attempt to reunite the Greek and Roman Catholic churches. It was this Council that declared the seven sacraments to be accepted by the Roman Church. The Council of Basel acknowledged defeat by dissolving itself in 1449.

Thus the attempt to create a constitutional monarchy in the Roman Church came to an end, and the papacy reverted to the system of papal despotism that it had followed for so many centuries. Pius II in a papal bull entitled *Execrabilis* issued in 1459 condemned any appeals to future general councils.[17] But the French clergy concurred with the French ruler in the proclamation of the Pragmatic Sanction of Bourges in 1438, which made the French church autonomous of the pope, but which in turn put it under the power of the state.[18]

Although the reforming councils had failed in the attempt to set up a constitutional monarchy in the Roman Church, they had saved it from the disorder of the Great Schism. The lack of·success in securing effective reform destroyed the last chance

16 *Ibid.,* pp. 331-332.
17 *Ibid.,* pp. 332.
18 Ogg, *op. cit.,* pp. 395-397.

of reform of the Roman Catholic Church from within by mystics, reformers, or councils. From this time the Protestant Reformation became inevitable.

BIBLIOGRAPHY

Citations have been made in the chapter of appropriate documents in the various collections of sources that are available to most teachers and students.

The work by Charles Lucas, *The Renaissance and the Reformation* (New York: Harper & Brothers, 1934), is still one of the most helpful surveys of the era between 1305 and 1517 concerning such matters as the reforming councils, the rise of nations and the Renaissance. The bibliography will be found helpful for information on the mass of literature available concerning the subjects discussed in this unit.

Chapter XXV

THE PAPACY FACES EXTERNAL OPPOSITION

The work of the mystics, reformers and the reforming councils was an earnest attempt from different angles to bring about internal reform that would make religion more personal, the Scriptures the source of authority and the Roman Church more democratic in its organization. The defeat of these movements or their absorption by the Roman Church ended all attempts at internal reform. At the same time external forces were creating opposition to the papal system. These forces were the humanistic spirit of the Renaissance, nationalism and an expanding geographical world which was a result of exploration in the Far East and in the Western Hemisphere. These forces strengthened the movement that was eventually to break forth as the Protestant Reformation and to bring to an end the dominance of the papacy.

I. THE RENAISSANCE

The Renaissance, which took place in the important countries of Europe between 1350 and 1650, marks the transition from the medieval to the modern world. The name, which is derived from the Latin words for birth and back, expresses the idea of a rebirth of culture. The name was first used about 1850 as a term descriptive of this era. In a narrower sense, the Renaissance has been linked with the fourteenth century in Italy, during which time men's minds were stimulated to literary and artistic production by the rediscovery of the treasures of the classical past. The classical spirit is apparent in the works of men like Petrarch and Boccacio. This classical Humanism south of the Alps was to be matched by the religious Humanism of Reuchlin, Colet, Erasmus and others north of the Alps in the early sixteenth century. The Northern Humanists went back to the Bible in the original, but the Southern Humanists emphasized the study of the classical literature and languages of Greece and Rome.

In a broader sense the Renaissance may be defined as that era of cultural reorientation in which men substituted a modern secular individualistic view of life for the medieval religious corporate approach to life. Attention was focused upon the streets of Rome and Athens instead of upon the streets of the New Jerusalem. The medieval theocentric conception of the world, in which God was the measure of all things, gave way to an anthropocentric view of life, in which man became the measure of all things. Emphasis was placed upon the glory of man instead of upon the glory of God. Urban middle class society became more important than the old rural agrarian society of the feudal era. In this connection it must be remembered that the Renaissance was confined largely to a small upper class in society, and that their ideas and way of living trickled down slowly to the lower segments of the social order. Commerce became more important than agriculture as the way to make a living. A humanistic, optimistic and experimental approach to the things of this life became common. Although the age clung to religion, it was only as a mere formality upon the holy days of the Church, and the tendency was to forget the claims of God upon the individual in daily life.

Several things contributed to the rise of this view of life. The Italian cities, where the movement first appeared, had become wealthy through serving as the middlemen in the rich commerce between Western Europe and the Near East. The wealth provided leisure for study and enabled merchants to act as patrons to scholars and artists. The new middle class with money to spend was interested in that which would make life more pleasant and comfortable. Centralized government provided security and order. The advent of printing with movable type about 1456 in Germany made it possible to spread information quickly during the latter part of the Renaissance. Nominalism, with its interest in the individual and in experimentation as a way to truth, had stimulated tendencies which were to flower in the Renaissance.

A. *The Italian Renaissance.*

The Renaissance appeared first in Italy during the fourteenth century because the classical tradition was stronger there than elsewhere. Italians were surrounded with the material remains of their past greatness, and the Italian spirit was sympathetic with an emphasis upon the finer cultural values of this present life. Moreover, in Italy there were wealthy men who could give financial aid to artists so that they could be free to create. The great merchant, Lorenzo de' Medici, gave commissions to scholars and artists in order to create beautiful surroundings for himself. Popes of the Renaissance era became interested in literature and the arts to such an extent that these interests took precedence over their spiritual functions. The fall of Constantinople in 1453 caused many Greek scholars to bring themselves and thousands of valuable Greek manuscripts to Italy in order to escape destruction by the Mohammedans.

Certain characteristics seem to be typical of the era. The men of the early Renaissance in Italy were interested in the classical or humanistic culture of Greece and Rome. This interest in classical literature replaced an interest in theology. When Manuel Chrysoloras came to Florence in 1393 as an ambassador to get aid for Constantinople against the Turkish threat, he remained there over three years teaching the Greek language to interested Florentines. Petrarch, the earliest of the Italian Humanists, sought diligently to discover Greek and Roman manuscripts which he might study. These men found a new world as they studied these manuscripts, a world in which men were interested in the enjoyment of life here and now. The joys of this life appealed to these Italian scholars, and religion, which pertained to eternity, faded into the background.

Renaissance scholars and artists tended to be individualistic in their outlook. Cellini, who has left an interesting account of his life in his *Autobiography*, was intensely individualistic in his enjoyment of life and gave primary consideration to his own desires. This attitude on the part of artists and scholars led to a secularization of society that was in strong contrast to the otherworldliness of medieval society. Something of this amoral secularization becomes apparent in Machiavelli's book, *The Prince*. Machiavelli advised the ruler of a state to subordinate absolute standards of conduct to expediency. If a lie or deceit would strengthen his position or his state, then he should not hesitate to use it.

The student is also impressed with the versatility of men of the Renaissance. Michaelangelo could decorate the ceiling of the Sistine Chapel with magnificent paintings. He also became the able architect who supervised the completion of St. Peter's in Rome and crowned the building with its lovely dome. Leonardo da Vinci could paint the beautiful *Last Supper* or the *Mona Lisa* and could leave sketches of machine guns and submarines that are remarkable in their similarity to such modern machines.

The men of the Renaissance were lovers of beauty in nature or in man. In fact, they made a cult of beauty. Paintings of the era indicate increasing interest in the careful study of human anatomy so that pictures would be accurate. This love of beauty is to be seen in the skillful presentation of colorful rich fabrics in the pictures drawn by Titian, the great portrait painter of Venice. These pictures are in contrast to the emaciated, distorted figures and paintings of the Gothic era.

Interest in and enjoyment of this life was given precedence over consideration of a future life. The dogmas of the Church were accepted and the rites of worship were practiced, but there was a divorce between man's religious life and his daily life. This worldly spirit even affected the popes of the Renaissance era. There were few heretics or atheists in the Latin countries, but spirituality took second place to formal religion.

A brief consideration of the activities of the leading Renaissance popes between 1447 and 1521 will show how the papacy capitulated to the secular and humanistic spirit of the age. Nicholas V (1447–1455) was a Humanist who had risen through the ranks in the church until he became pope. His interest in the classical world made him seek to repair the buildings, bridges, aqueducts and the great churches of Rome. His interest in the classical past was clearly shown in his giving up his own library to form the nucleus of the Vatican Library, which was to be a treasure trove for future scholars. His secretary was Lorenzo Valla, who, about 1440, after he had left the papal employ, wrote a treatise in which he exposed the Donation of Constantine as a forgery by his use of literary and historical criticism. He was thus the first to develop the rudiments of historical criticism. The fact that Lorenzo got into no trouble because of this daring act was a testimony to the indifference of the papacy to religion.

Julius II (1503–1513) spent much time in the political endeavor of unifying the Papal States of Italy. He was also a patron of artists. He commissioned Michaelangelo to decorate the ceiling of the Sistine Chapel which Sixtus IV (1471–1484) had built.

Leo X (1513–1521), who was pope when Luther took his stand against indulgences, was a member of the Medici family of Florence. He sanctioned the sale of indulgences to raise money for the building of the present St. Peter's cathedral in Rome. He was also a patron of the arts and letters. With such popes it is little wonder that Luther was scandalized at the formalism and lack of real spirituality when he made his famous visit to Rome.

B. The Teutonic Renaissance.

Renaissance scholars north of the Alps had in common with their brethren south of the Alps a love for sources from the past, an emphasis on human beings as individual entities with a right to develop their own personalities, and an interest in the powers of the human mind to interpret the data that the senses brought to it. However, they were not so much interested in the classical past as they were in the Christian past. They studied the Biblical documents in the original tongues as much as or more than they studied the writings of Plato or Aristotle. Their emphasis was upon the Jewish-Christian heritage rather than upon the Hellenic heritage of Western Europe. They were essentially Christian Humanists who applied the techniques and methods of Humanism to the study of the Scriptures. They were more interested in man as a human being with a soul than they were in him as a rational creature. Their Humanism was ethical and religious; whereas that of their Latin brethren to the south of the Alps was aesthetic and secular.

Though what has been said of the Italian Humanists was true of the majority, there was a small group in Florence, led by Pico della Mirandola (1463–1494), which had fallen under the influence of Savonarola. Pico wished to integrate the Bible with Greek philosophy, particularly that of Plato. In his effort to achieve this aim he began a study of the Bible from the literary viewpoint of the Humanists. Financial aid from the de' Medici family made possible a Platonic Academy in Florence where Christian Humanists might pursue their studies. John Colet from England, Jacques Lefevre from France and Reuchlin from Germany all spent some time at the Academy.

Although Lefevre (1450–1536) used a literal and spiritual interpretation of the Bible in writing his philological work on the Psalms, he did emphasize the study of the text of the Bible. About 1512 he published Paul's Epistles and a commentary upon them in Latin. His work helped to pave the way for the rise of the Huguenots when the influence of the Reformation reached France.

John Colet (ca. 1467–1519) was one of a group in England who were known as the Oxford Reformers. After his visit to Italy, Colet began in lectures to develop the literal meaning of the Pauline Epistles. This was an innovation because former theologians had been more interested in allegory than they were in what the writer of the Scriptures was trying to say to his or a later day. The work of the Oxford Reformers was a contributing factor in the coming of the Reformation in England.

Reuchlin and Erasmus were, however, the most influential of the Humanists because the influence of their work was felt all over Europe. John Reuchlin (1455–1522) had studied under Pico in Italy and had developed a taste for Hebrew language, literature and theology. The fruit of his scientific study of the Old Testament was a combined Hebrew grammar and dictionary which he called *On the Elements of Hebrew*. This work helped others to become familiar with the tongue of the Old Testament so that they could study that book in the original language. It is a matter of interest that Reuchlin gave advice concerning the education of Melanchthon, Luther's right-hand man and the first theologian of the Reformation.

Desiderius Erasmus (ca. 1466–1536) was even more influential than Reuchlin. He had received part of his early education in the school of the Brethren of the Common Life in Deventer and later studied at many of the universities of Europe and England. He became a universal scholar who was at home in cultured circles in any land. His scholarly spirit inclined him to reform rather than revolution, and his negative opposition to the abuses of the Roman Catholic Church was expressed in his books, *Praise of Folly* (ca. 1510) and *Familiar Colloquies* (1518).[1] In these books Erasmus attempted by clever satire to point out the evils in the life of the priestly and monastic hierarchy. The positive aspect of his work was the Greek New Testament which was published in 1516 by the publisher Froeben of Basle, who was desirous of getting the fame and market

1 J. F. Scott, A. Hyma, and A. H. Noyes, *Readings in Medieval History* (New York: Appleton-Century-Crofts, 1933), pp. 624–636.

ULRICH ZWINGLI

MENNO SIMONS

DESIDERIUS ERASMUS

Martin Luther

that would accompany the publication of the first printed and published Greek New Testament. The Spanish scholar Ximenes had had a Greek New Testament printed in 1514, but he could not sell it until the pope approved. In order to reach the market before him Froeben urged Erasmus on. Erasmus used four Greek manuscripts, which were available at Basel; but, when he found that the last few verses of Revelation were missing in all of them, he translated the Latin back into what he thought the Greek should be. The influence of the book was tremendous, for scholars were now in a position to make accurate comparison between the Church that they saw in the New Testament and the Church of their day. The comparison was decidedly unfavorable to the latter.

At first Erasmus sympathized with Luther but later he opposed him because he did not desire the break with the Roman Catholic Church that Luther was forced to make. Moreover, his theology differed greatly from that which Luther held. In his book *Free Will* (1524) he emphasized the reform of abuses rather than an attack upon doctrine and upheld the freedom of the human will, which Luther said was completely bound as far as salvation was concerned.

Both in Northern and Southern Europe the Renaissance had abiding results. The study of the classical pagan past led to a secular approach to life in which religion was reduced to a formal affair or ignored until one came to the hour of death. The ideal of the person as an independent human being with the right to develop as his tastes led him took precedence over the medieval ideal of one who was to be saved by taking his humble place in the corporate hierarchal society of the Roman Catholic Church. The impetus given to the use of the vernacular by the scholars and poets of fourteenth and fifteenth century Europe was helpful later in bringing to the people the Bible and the services of the Church in their mother tongue. The return to sources of culture from the past and the scientific study of them made possible a far more accurate knowledge of the Bible than had been the case before this time. In the political realm the amoral note struck in Machiavelli's work, *The Prince*, led to the ignoring of moral principles in the conduct of the foreign affairs of the city-states of Italy and the rising nation-states of Northern Europe. One who seeks a balanced view of the impact of the Renaissance can call it neither a tragedy nor an unmixed blessing but will have to consider it a mixture of blessing and bane to the people of Europe.

In addition to the development of man's interest in himself as an individual with a mind and a spirit, the Renaissance resulted in the development of a wider knowledge of man's physical universe. Man became interested in his environment as well as in himself, and scientific and geographical studies led to a new world of science and to an increased knowledge of how large man's world actually is. The beginning of geographical exploration was again the work of the Latin. Prince Henry of Portugal sent out explorers from his land until Vasco da Gama discovered the way to India around the southern tip of Africa. Columbus made the Western Hemisphere known to the world, and his work was speedily supplemented by that of French and English explorers, all of whom were seeking a shorter route to the wealth of the Far East. Copernicus and Galileo also made men conscious of the immensity of the universe about them, and the invention of the telescope and its increasingly effective use substantiated their earlier theories.

II. THE RISE OF NATION-STATES AND THE MIDDLE CLASS

The classical world had been dominated by the ideal of the city-state as the largest political unit into which men might organize themselves. Even the Roman Empire was simply an expansion of the city-state of Rome. Any man who became a citizen became a citizen of Rome no matter where he resided. The Middle Ages was dominated by the concept of political as well as spiritual unity, and, in theory, all men were to be united in a new Rome, the Holy Roman Empire. In practice, however, feudalism with all its decentralization gave security and order in chaotic periods. The revival of towns prior to the Renaissance created strong city-states in Italy. But the future in Europe was with the nation-state as a form of political organization. England, France and Spain were pioneers in the development of such nation-states. The development in England was along the lines of a constitutional monarchy in which sovereignty was shared by the monarch and parliament. The bodies representing the people in France and Spain never became as powerful as Parliament in England, and France and Spain developed as centralized nation-states in which the ruler was absolute.

A. *The Rise of the English Nation-state.*

The English Parliament grew out of the feudal assembly, known as the *curia regis,* that was introduced into England during the reign of William the Conqueror after his successful invasion of England in 1066. This assembly of the feudal lords served as a high court, an advisory body to the king, and as a money-granting body when the king asked for more than the standard feudal grants. Its powers were strengthened by the signing of the Magna Charta by John in 1215. John agreed not to levy new taxes without the consent of the *curia regis* and to permit the barons to rise against him if he violated the charter. Justice was to be administered fairly, and men were given the right to be tried before a jury of their equals. Although this document benefited only the feudal class at the time, it did introduce the principles that the ruler was limited by the law and that taxes could only be levied by consent of the people. In 1295 Edward I called the Model Parliament in which representatives of the counties and the cities were present as well as the feudal lords and great churchmen. The two former groups developed the House of Commons, and the last two groups eventually formed the House of Lords. During the fourteenth century the king's need of money led to the development of the law-making powers of Parliament since the members of Parliament would not grant the king desired revenues unless he would sign their bills which then became law.

The representative Parliament, to which the king's ministers were responsible, was only one of the foundations of English constitutional monarchy. In the reign of Henry II the common law, which protects the liberties of the individual better than Roman law does, and the jury system were developed. The individual thus had protection against the arbitrary acts of the ruler.

The Hundred Years War with France (1337–1453) served to create English national pride as the English archers with their long bows found that the arrows could defeat the French mounted knight, and the final loss of territories held by the English ruler in France tended to draw the upper and lower classes together into national unity. The War of the Roses in the third quarter of the fifteenth century led to the wiping out of the old feudal nobility and made possible an alliance between the king and the middle class in the state. The middle class in return for order and security willingly granted money and authority to the rulers. The freedom of the fifteenth century Parliament gave way to the veiled despotism of the Tudors, who ran the state along Machiavellian lines during the sixteenth century. They did, however, keep Parliament to secure popular backing for their acts.

B. The Rise of the French Nation-state.

The French nation-state faced great obstacles in its development. English rulers held much territory in France, and the great feudal nobles were not controlled by the French king, who only held a small area of land around Paris. France had no racial or geographic unity because of the diverse racial elements in the population and the geographic composition of the country, which stimulated provincialism. In spite of these problems, the Capetian line of rulers in Paris, beginning with Hugh Capet in 987, was able to unify France. The Estates General, the French Parliament, never became as powerful as the English Parliament, and the ruler was consequently more absolute in his control of the state. Able rulers and hatred of the common enemy England during the Hundred Years War did much to unify France. This war also gave the French their national heroine, Joan of Arc.

C. The Rise of the Spanish Nation-state.

The development of the Spanish nation-state was given a religious aspect by the struggle to free the Iberian Peninsula of the Mohammedan invaders. The crusade, known as the *Reconquista*, was at its height during the eleventh century. The Roman Catholic faith and nationalism became partners in Spain, and the absolutism of the Roman Church was paralleled by the political absolutism of the ruler.

The rise of the nation-state provided opposition to the Roman Catholic Church, particularly in France and England, where rulers and the powerful middle class resented the flow of money from the state treasury or from their own pockets into the papal treasury. The noble class resented the control of so much land by the Church of Rome. The kings were not pleased with the divided sovereignty that caused their subjects to give allegiance to the pope as well as to themselves. Church courts, in which alone clergymen might be tried, were an affront to the royal system of courts, and appeals to the papal courts were particularly obnoxious. It will be remembered that about 1300 the powerful rulers of England and France successfully defeated the efforts of Boniface VIII to control the clergy of their states and that France in the Pragmatic Sanction of Bourges in 1438 insisted that the Roman Church in France must be controlled by the French ruler. England in two statutes, in 1351 and 1353 respectively, forbade the pope to fill vacancies in church offices in England without elections by the local clergy and the consent of the king, and banned appeals from courts in England to the papal court. This tendency to resent ecclesiastical interference in affairs of state was an external force that fostered the work of the Reformers when they appeared on the scene.

It should be noted that the rulers of Europe could never have successfully fought the papacy if it had not been for the backing of the wealthy middle class that was created by commerce arising from the rebirth of towns and revival of trade after 1200. The middle-class merchants of the city and the wealthy middle-class landowners backed the rulers in their opposition to the papal control of their lands.

III. THE GREEK ORTHODOX CHURCH, 1305–1517

While dynamic external forces of opposition and reform were building up in Western Europe forces that would shatter the unity of the medieval Roman Catholic Church, the Eastern Church remained static in its theological outlook and expanded very little. In fact, the importance of Constantinople as a religious center declined after its fall to the Turks in 1453, and the Russian patriarchs became increasingly important in the leadership of the Greek Orthodox Church.

Two changes took place in Russia that deeply affected the future development of its Christianity. Between 1227, when Mongol invaders first came into Russia, and 1380, when they finally lost control of the state, Russia was under the control of Mongol Tartar invaders. Although this invasion put Russia back culturally, it worked to the advantage of the Russian Church because the invasion cut the Russian Church off from Constantinople and forced it to fall back upon its own native leadership. Russian nationalism and religion were unified as the Russians strove to maintain their religion and culture in spite of their conquerors. People turned to religion for solace as well as for leadership in their time of crisis.

In 1305 the metropolitan archbishop of the Orthodox Church

in Russia moved his headquarters from Kiev, which was near Constantinople, to Moscow. Here he could be more independent of Constantinople, but at the same time he was more subject to secular control by the rulers of the Russian state. After 1453 the Russian metropolitan became independent of the patriarch at Constantinople because that city and the leader of the Orthodox Church were under the control of the Turks. Shortly after the fall of Constantinople the Russian bishops elected the metropolitan as the "Metropolitan of Moscow and all Russia." Free to develop along independent lines, although its theology and liturgy were not changed appreciably, the Russian Orthodox Church became a national church and, later, even became closely identified with the state.

Between 1305 and 1517 forces promoting change were at work both in the Church in the East and the Church in the West. In the East, the changes were to be primarily along the lines of ecclesiastical leadership and organization, but in the West, the Reformation brought about fundamental changes that not only created the national Protestant churches, but which also brought reformation within the Roman Catholic Church so that it could meet the challenge of Protestantism.

BIBLIOGRAPHY

The Renaissance and Reformation (New York: Harper & Brothers, 1934) by Charles Lucas is one of the most helpful general treatments of the Northern and Southern Renaissance and also gives attention to the rise of nation-states and the middle class as important influences during the Reformation.

The little volume by Wallace Ferguson, *The Renaissance* (New York: Henry Holt & Co., 1940), in the Berkshire Series in European history, is a helpful survey of the Renaissance.

Preserved Smith's *Erasmus* (New York: Harper & Brothers, 1923) is a scholarly and interesting account of the life and work of Erasmus.

More source material may be found in J. A. Froude's *Life and Letters of Erasmus* (New York: Charles Scribner's Sons, 1912).

The student should be given opportunity to read the satirical *Praise of Folly* in order to capture the critical spirit of the Christian Humanists.

The Greek and Eastern Church (New York: Charles Scribner's Sons, 1908) by Walter F. Adeney will provide sufficient information concerning the Church in the East in this period.

MODERN CHURCH HISTORY, 1517 AND AFTER

Chapter XXVI

THE BACKGROUND OF REFORMATION

The unwillingness of the medieval Roman Catholic Church to accept reforms suggested by sincere reformers such as the mystics, Wycliffe and Huss, the leaders of the reforming councils and the Humanists; the emergence of nation-states, which opposed the papal claim to have universal power; and the rise of a middle class, which disliked the drain of wealth to Rome— all these combined to make the Reformation a certainty. Its gaze fixed upon the pagan classical past, oblivious of the dynamic forces that were creating a new society, Italian society, of which the papacy was a part, adopted a corrupt, sensual and immoral, although cultured, way of life.

I. THE EMERGENCE OF AN EXPANDING DYNAMIC WORLD

By 1500 the foundations of the old medieval society were breaking up, and a new society with a larger geographic horizon and with changing political, economic, intellectual and religious patterns was slowly coming into being. The changes were so great as to be revolutionary, both in their scope and in their effects upon the social order.

A. *Geographical Change.*

The *geographic* knowledge of the medieval man underwent remarkable changes between 1492 and 1600. The civilization of the ancient world has been characterized as potamic because it was linked with the river systems of the ancient world. That of the Middle Ages has been called thalassic because it developed about seas — the Mediterranean and the Baltic. By 1517 the discoveries of Columbus and other explorers ushered in an era of oceanic civilization, in which the oceans of the world became the highways of the world. By the time Luther had translated the New Testament into German — 1522, Magellan's ship had completed a voyage around the world. Southeastern and southwestern water routes to the riches of the Far East had become possibilities. The Roman Catholic countries of Portugal, France and Spain were leaders in this voyaging, but the Protestant nations of England and Holland were soon to overtake them in geographical exploration and settlement. Two rich new continents in the Western Hemisphere were opened up for exploitation by the Old World. Spain and Portugal had a monopoly in South and Central America, but the greater part of North America, after a struggle between France and England, became a new home for Anglo-Saxons. It seems providential that the Western Hemisphere was not opened up for settlement until the time of the Protestant Reformation so that Protestants might also play an important part in the work of discovering, exploiting and settling the New World.

B. *Political Change.*

Perspectives were also changing in the *political* realm. The medieval concept of a universal state was giving way to the new concept of the nation-state. Since the end of medieval times states have been organized on a national basis. These centralized nation-states with powerful rulers, ably served by army and civil service, were nationalistic and opposed to domination by a universal state or a universal religious ruler. Some of them were consequently anxious to support the Reformation in order that national churches might be more directly under their control. The theoretical political unity of the medieval world was replaced by nation-states, each of which was insistent upon its independence and sovereignty. The practical feudal decentralization of the medieval world was replaced by a Europe made up of centralized nation-states. Because each state was independent, the new principle of balance of power as a guide in international relations became prominent in the religious wars of the sixteenth and early seventeenth centuries.

C. *Economic Change.*

Startling *economic* changes were also taking place just before the Reformation. During the Middle Ages the economy of the countries of Europe was agricultural, and land was the basis of wealth. By 1500 the revival of towns, the opening of new markets and the discovery of sources of raw materials in colonies in the newly discovered lands ushered in an age of commerce in which the middle-class merchant replaced the medieval feudal noble as a leader in society. Not until the advent of the Industrial Revolution about 1750 was this commercial pattern of economic life appreciably changed. Trade became international rather than interurban. An economy in which money became important emerged. The rising capitalistic middle class resented the drain of their wealth to the international church under the leadership of the pope in Rome, and in Northern Europe it threw its influence behind the Reformation.

D. *Social Change.*

The horizontal *social* organization of medieval society, in which one remained in the class into which one was born, was replaced by a society organized along vertical lines. One might rise from a lower class in society to a higher class. In medieval times, if one were the son of a serf, there was little chance to be anything but a serf, except for service in the church. By 1500 men were rising, by dint of industry, to higher social rank. Serfdom was fast disappearing, and a new middle class which had been missing in medieval society appeared in which the free farmer, the country gentry and the merchant class of the town were most prominent. This strong middle class generally supported the changes made by the Reformation in Northern Europe.

E. *Intellectual Change.*

The *intellectual* changes wrought by the Renaissance both north and south of the Alps created an intellectual outlook that favored the development of Protestantism. The desire to return to sources of the past led the Christian Humanists of the north to a study of the Bible in the original tongues of the Scriptures. Thus the difference between the Church of the New Testament and the medieval Roman Catholic Church became clear to them, and the difference was to the disadvantage of the medieval papal ecclesiastical organization. Renaissance emphasis upon the individual was a helpful factor in the development of the Protestant insistence that salvation was a personal matter to be settled by the individual in immediate relationship with his God without a priest standing by as a human mediator. The critical spirit of the Renaissance was used by the Reformers to justify observation of the hierarchy and sacraments of the medieval Roman Church and a critical comparison of them with the Scriptures. Though the Renaissance in Italy proceeded along Humanistic and pagan lines, the tendencies that it fostered were taken over in Northern Europe by the Christian Humanists and the Reformers and used by them to justify individual study of the Bible in the original as the source document of the Christian faith.

F. Religious Change.

Medieval *religious* uniformity gave way in the early sixteenth century to religious diversity. The seamless garment of the international and universal Roman Catholic Church was rent again, as it had been before in 1054, by schisms that resulted in the founding of national Protestant churches. Such churches were generally under the control of the rulers of the nation-states, particularly the Anglican and Lutheran churches. Not until after 1648 were denominations and freedom of religion to emerge. The authority of the Roman Church was replaced by the authority of the Bible, which the individual was to be allowed to read freely. The individual believer could now be his own priest and conduct his own religious life in fellowship with God after he had accepted His Son as His Saviour by faith alone.

Within the generation between Columbus' discovery of America (1492) and Luther's posting of the ninety-five theses upon the door of the church in Wittenberg (1517), the startling changes that have been described took place or had their beginnings. The static patterns of medieval civilization were replaced by the dynamic patterns of modern society. The changes in the religious realm were by no means the least remarkable changes in the civilization of Western Europe. The Christian is compelled to bow in reverence as he traces the hand of God in the affairs of men in this era.

II. NAME AND DEFINITION OF THE REFORMATION

Both the name and definition given to the Reformation are somewhat conditioned by the outlook of the historian. The Roman Catholic historian will never look upon it as other than a revolt by Protestants against the universal Church. The Protestant historian considers it as a reformation that brought religious life back to the pattern of the New Testament. The secular historian thinks of it as a revolutionary movement.

If one considers the Reformation solely from the viewpoint of *polity* or church government, it may be considered as a revolt from the authority of the Church of Rome and its head, the pope. In thus conceding that the Reformation had a revolutionary character, it does not necessarily follow that the true Church was confined to Rome. The Reformers and many others who preceded them had tried unsuccessfully to bring reform to the medieval Roman Catholic Church from within its fold, but they were forced out of the older organization because of their ideas of reform.

The more familiar term "Protestant Reformation" has become hallowed by age; and because the Reformation was an attempt to return to the early purity of the Christianity of the New Testament, it is wise to continue to use the term to describe the religious movement between 1517 and 1563. The Reformers were anxious to develop a theology that was in complete accord with the New Testament and believed that this could never be a reality as long as the Church instead of the Bible was made the final authority.

Many Protestants forget that the Protestant movement called forth, partly as a reaction to check Protestant gains, a movement of reform within the Roman Catholic Church that prevented the Reformation from making many new gains after it had once got under way. This reform movement that developed in the Roman Catholic Church between 1545 and 1645 is known as the Counter Reformation.

For the most part, the Reformation was confined to Western Europe and to Teutonic peoples. Neither the Eastern Church nor the Latin peoples accepted the Reformation. In those areas the medieval ideals of unity and uniformity still held sway, but in Northern and Western Europe the Teutonic peoples moved from religious unity and uniformity to the diversity of Protestantism.

The definition of the term "Reformation" is no easy task. If one considers the Reformation simply as the creator of national churches it would be a religious movement between 1517 and 1648. Because only Holland was won to Protestantism after the Council of Trent, it would seem wise to limit the most important part of the Reformation to the years between 1517 and 1563. The Reformation is here defined as that movement of religious reform that resulted in the creation of the national Protestant churches between 1517 and 1563. Consequently, the Counter Reformation may be defined as a movement of religious reform within the Roman Catholic Church between 1545 and 1563 that stabilized and strengthened that church after its heavy losses to Protestantism.

III. The Genesis of the Reformation

A. *Interpretations of the Reformation.*

The interpretation that historians give to history has influenced their consideration of the causes of the Reformation. Emphasis upon one or another factor in history is made depending upon what school of historical interpretation is followed.

The Protestant historian interprets the Reformation largely as a religious movement that sought to recover the purity of the primitive Christianity that is depicted in the New Testament. This interpretation tends to ignore the economic, political and intellectual factors that helped to promote the Reformation. According to this interpretation, Providence is the primary factor that takes precedence over all other factors.

Roman Catholic historians interpret the Reformation as a heresy inspired by Martin Luther from base motives, such as his desire to marry. Protestantism is looked upon as a heretical schism that destroyed the theological and ecclesiastical unity of the medieval Roman Church. It is true that, viewed from the Romanist viewpoint, Luther was a heretic and became a schismatic, but from such a viewpoint historians usually fail to see how far the medieval church had departed from the ideal of the New Testament. The Counter Reformation was in itself an admission that all was not well in the medieval church.

Secular historians give more attention to secondary factors in their interpretation of the Reformation. Voltaire illustrates the rationalistic interpretation of the movement quite well. To him the Reformation was little more than the consequences of a monastic squabble in Saxony, and the religious Reformation in England was an outcome of the love affairs of Henry VIII. It is true that the Augustinian order of monks clashed with the Dominicans on the issue of indulgences and that the love of Henry VIII for Anne Boleyn made the early stage of the Reformation in England a matter of politics, but this type of interpretation ignores many other important factors, such as the essentially religious Reformation in England in the reign of Edward VI, the son of Henry VIII.

Other historians, who accept the Marxian concept of economic determinism, cannot interpret the Reformation in any other than economic terms. The Reformation is looked upon as the result of the attempt of the Roman papacy to exploit Germany economically for the material benefit of the papacy.

Political historians see the Reformation as a result of nation-states opposing an international church. To them the Reformation is simply a political event caused by the rise of nationalism.

Although there are elements of truth in all of these interpretations, the student will notice that they emphasize, for the most part, secondary causes and, often, only one particular secondary cause. The causes of the Reformation were not simple and single but were complex and multiple. The Reformation was both derivative and determinative in its causation. Many causes had their roots in the centuries preceding the Reformation, when Rome had opposed any internal reform and had ignored the rising tide of external opposition that was to cause her so much trouble. The creative personalities of such leaders in the Reformation as Luther, Calvin and others were determinative of the direction which the Reformation took. The leaders of the Protestant Reformation usually came from the middle class, but those of the Counter Reformation were aristocratic. For these reasons, the interpretation of the Reformation in this work is synthetic. Providence is given primary consideration, but secondary political, economic, moral and intellectual factors are not ignored.[1]

B. *Causes of the Reformation.*

The *political* factor may be considered as one of the important *indirect* causes for the coming of the Reformation. The new centralized nation-states of Northwestern Europe were opposed to the concept of a universal church that claimed jurisdiction over the national state and its powerful ruler. The ideal of such a universal church clashed with the rising national consciousness of the middle class in these new states.

This basic political problem was complicated by particular questions. It will be noticed that the nations which accepted Protestantism during the Reformation were located outside the orbit of the old Roman Empire and that the powerful middle classes in them had a different cultural outlook from that of the Latin nations. Some even think of the Reformation as a revolt of northern Teutonic nations against the Latin nations with their Mediterranean culture and with their concept of international organization which were their heritage from the old Roman Empire. Rulers of these nation-states resented the jurisdiction of the pope within their territory. This jurisdiction

---

[1] See Preserved Smith, *The Age of the Reformation* (New York: Henry Holt & Co., 1920), Ch. XIV, for an account of the interpretation of the Reformation.

was often temporal as well as spiritual because the Roman Church owned great amounts of land all over Europe. Church ownership of land created a division of sovereignty within the state which such despotic rulers as the English Tudors resented. Appointments to important positions in the Roman Church were made by a foreigner, the pope. Clerics were not subject to trial in civil courts but were tried in church courts rather than royal courts. Appeals could be carried from these courts to the papal court. The national ruler and his civil service were opposed to the international religious hierarchy of the Roman Church. Henry VIII broke with the Church of Rome over the issue of whether the royal divorce was an international matter for the pope to decide or a national matter which the national clergy could settle.

The recent attention given to *economics* as a motivating factor in human affairs cannot be dismissed casually by the Christian historian even though he does not accept the materialistic interpretation of Marx or the economic determinists. The land possessed by the Roman Church in Western Europe was regarded with greedy eyes by the national rulers, nobles and middle class of the new nation-states. The rulers resented the loss of the money that went to the papal treasury in Rome. Moreover, the clergy were exempt from the taxes of national states. The papal attempt to get more money out of Germany in the sixteenth century was bitterly resented by the rising middle class of such states as Saxony. This drainage of money from the state to Rome was complicated by inflation and the rising cost of living. Inflation had grown out of the great sums of money that Spain gathered by the exploitation of her possessions and subjects in the new world. This money Spain had poured into the economic blood stream of Europe. It was the abuse of the indulgence system as a tool to get wealth from Germany for the papacy that angered Luther.

The *intellectual* factor in the Reformation was that men with awakened minds and a secular outlook became critical of the religious life of their day as represented in the Roman Catholic Church. As the middle class grew in numbers, it became individualistic in outlook and began to revolt against the corporate concept of medieval society which put the individual under authority. This tendency to individualism was reinforced by the rise of absolutist nation-states in which the interests of the international Roman Catholic Church took second place to those of the nation and of the ruler and his loyal supporters of the middle class business group. Renaissance Humanism, especially in Italy, created a secular spirit similar to that which had characterized classical Greece. Even the popes of the Renaissance adopted the intellectual and secular approach to life. This spirit and approach grew out of the desire of scholars to go back to the sources of man's intellectual past. A comparison of the corporate hierarchal society of the day with the intellectual freedom and secularism of Greek society and with the principle of freedom for the individual seen in Scriptural sources made men skeptical of the claims of the Church of Rome and its leaders. Men began to have wider intellectual horizons and began to be interested in secular rather than religious life.

The *moral* factor of the Reformation was closely allied to the intellectual. The Humanistic scholars, who had the New Testament in Greek, clearly saw the discrepancies between the Church about which they read in the New Testament and the Roman Catholic Church of their day. Corruption had spread through both head and members of the hierarchy of the Roman Church. Self-seeking clerics bought and sold offices freely. Too many enjoyed sinecures, positions in which they received the salary but did none of the work usually associated with the office. Some held several offices at once, as did Albert of Mainz, whose agent Tetzel, Luther so strenuously opposed in Saxony. Justice was bought and sold in the church courts. One could for a payment of money get a dispensation that would permit one to marry a close relative, even though the canon law forbade it. Many priests lived in open sin or kept concubines. The people of the dioceses were neglected by the bishops, who often failed to engage in the episcopal visitation necessary to supervise the clergy under them and to see that the clergy did not neglect their flocks. Many parish clergy consequently neglected preaching and visitation, being content to say the mass which they proclaimed as a magic rite that would bring grace to one. People became tired of the ceaseless cry for money from the head of an institution which did not seem to be rendering that service to communities that one would associate with the Church.[2]

Changes taking place in the social structure accelerated the disillusionment of medieval men with the Roman Church. The

2 *Ibid.,* pp. 20-25.

rise of towns and a prosperous middle class within the towns created a new spirit of individualism. The new money economy freed men from dependence upon the soil as the main way by which they could make a living. Middle class burghers were not as tractable as their feudal forerunners had been, and even the artisans of the cities and the agricultural workers were beginning to realize that all was not well with a social order in which they were oppressed by those above them in society. Social discontent and the demand for reform was a definite *social* factor in the coming of the Reformation.

Behind the failure of the Roman Church to meet the real needs of the people was the *theological* or *philosophical* factor of the Reformation. Some have so overemphasized this element that they can see the Reformation only in terms of a struggle between the theology of Thomas Aquinas and that of Augustine. It is true that the medieval church adopted the philosophy of Thomas Aquinas. It emphasized his teaching that man's will was not totally corrupted. By faith and the use of the means of grace in the sacraments dispensed by the hierachy, man could achieve salvation. Augustine believed that man's will was so totally depraved that he could do nothing toward his salvation. God would extend the grace to man to energize his will so that he could by faith take the salvation which Christ proffered to him. However, any careful study of the writings of the Reformers will indicate that they went to Augustine from the Bible to seek the aid of his powerful authority, but they did not arrive at the doctrine of justification by faith by studying the writings of Augustine. It was the Scriptures that brought home that profound truth to them. The theological cause of the Reformation was the desire of the Reformers to go back to the classic source of the Christian faith, the Bible, in order to meet the claims of Thomistic theology that salvation was a matter of grace obtained through the sacraments dispensed by the hierarchy.

Usually discontent becomes so great when men face adverse conditions that their dissatisfaction will express itself through some great *leader* who expresses their ideas for them. The refusal of the medieval Roman Catholic Church to accept reform, indeed, the impossibility that it would reform itself, opened the way for the providential coming of a leader who would embody the desire for reform of abuses and who would be used to bring about revolutionary changes. Such was the function of Martin Luther in whom the spirit of Reformation, with its insistence upon the right of the individual to go directly to God through the Christ revealed in the Scriptures, was embodied.

Glaring abuse of the indulgence system in Germany was the *direct* cause for the coming of the Reformation in that country. Archbishop Albert, a prince of the House of Hohenzollern, who was already in control of two provinces of the Roman Church, cast covetous eyes upon the vacant archbishopric of Mainz. Because Albert had been only twenty-three, and because canon law also forbade one man to hold more than one office, he had had to pay about $25,000 to Pope Leo X for the dispensations necessary before he could fill the two offices. Fortunately for him, his desire for the archbishopric of Mainz and that of Pope Leo X for money to build the present St. Peter's cathedral in Rome coincided. Albert was to be permitted to become Archbishop of Mainz if he would pay the pope about $250,000 in addition to the regular fees — more than $250,000 — for taking over such an office. Because this sum was in the realm of high finance, the papacy suggested that Albert might borrow the money from the wealthy Fugger banking family in Augsburg. A papal bull, authorizing the sale of indulgences in certain German states, was granted as security that Albert would repay his loan to the Fuggers. Leo got over $100,000 as a cash payment and the remainder of the approximately $500,000 was to be paid as money was raised by the sale of indulgences.

Indulgences were associated with the sacrament of penance. After one had repented of sin and had confessed sin, one was assured of absolution by the priest, provided satisfaction was made. It was thought that the guilt of sin and eternal punishment for sin were forgiven by God but that there was a temporal satisfaction that the repentant sinner must fulfill either in this life or in purgatory. This satisfaction might be a pilgrimage to a shrine, a payment of a sum to a church, or some meritorious deed. The indulgence was a document that could be bought for a sum of money and that would free one from the temporal penalty of sin. It was believed that Christ and the saints had achieved so much merit during their earthly lives that the excess merit was laid up in a heavenly treasury of merit upon which the pope could draw on behalf of the living faithful.[3] This dogma was formulated by Alexander of Hales in the thirteenth century. A later papal bull extended this privilege to souls in purgatory, provided their living relatives purchased indulgences for them.

It was this system for raising money that was so unblushingly abused in the papal bull issued to Albert. Albert's main agent was a Dominican monk named Tetzel, who was paid over one thousand dollars a month and his expenses to sell these indulgences. With him and other sellers of indulgences went an agent of the Fuggers to see that half of the money paid for each indulgence was turned over to the bank to discharge the loan that had been granted to Albert. Tetzel used high pressure sales methods to step up sales and promised remission of temporal punishment for the gravest of sins if the sinner would only buy an indulgence.[4] The amount charged was determined by the sinner's wealth and social position. Indulgences were given free to the destitute, but a king might pay more than three hundred dollars for his indulgence. It was Luther's famous protest in the ninety-five theses against the abuse of indulgences that precipitated the train of events which resulted in the Reformation in Germany. From Germany the Reformation spread all over Northern and Western Europe.

The Reformation was not an isolated event but was closely related to the Renaissance and other movements that brought about the birth of the modern era in the sixteenth century. Its relationship to the Renaissance and to the Catholic Counter Reformation can be more clearly seen by reference to a simple diagram.

The Protestant churches that came out of this upheaval differed in the extent to which they departed from the medieval Church, but all of them accepted the Bible as the final authority. Luther retained many things in the ritual that were not prohibited in the Bible. The Anglican Church departed little further from the ritual and practice of the medieval Church than the Lutherans did, but it must be understood that both the Anglicans and Lutherans completely disavowed the hierarchal sacramental system of the Roman Church. The Reformed and Presbyterian churches, which followed Calvin in France,

3 H. Bettenson, *Documents of the Christian Church* (New York: Oxford University Press, 1947), pp. 259-260.
4 *Ibid.*, pp. 260-263.

Holland, Scotland, Switzerland and Hungary, disavowed all practices that could not be proved to be in accordance with the New Testament. The Anabaptists made the most radical break of all the Reformation groups and sought to create a church patterned after the primitive New Testament churches. Only those peoples who were of Teutonic extraction in Northern and Western Europe accepted the Reformation; Latin nations generally remained true to the pope. The Reformation ushered

THE BIRTH OF THE MODERN ERA, 1350-1650

RENAISSANCE
(*Intellectual*)

REFORMATION
(*Spiritual*)

LATIN
South of the Alps
Classical sources

TEUTONIC
North of the Alps
Biblical sources

TEUTONIC
Protestant
Reformation,
1517 - 1563
Middle class and
from below

LATIN
Counter
Reformation,
1545 - 1563
Aristocratic and
from above

in startling changes by which the one universal Roman Catholic Church was replaced in Western Europe by national churches. These churches took the Bible as the final authority and believed that man needed no human mediator between himself and God to obtain the salvation that had been purchased for him by Christ on the Cross.

BIBLIOGRAPHY FOR MODERN CHURCH HISTORY

Several one-volume histories that cover the modern period of church history are available: J. W. C. Wand's *A History of the Modern Church* (New York: Thomas Y. Crowell Co., 1929) is a useful survey of the entire field of modern church history.

The work by Samuel Cheetham entitled *A History of the Christian Church Since the Reformation* (London: The Macmillan Co., 1907) can be consulted with profit.

Religion Since the Reformation (Oxford: Clarendon Press, 1924) by Leighton Pullan is a useful series of lectures on modern church history. It begins with the Counter Reformation, but it has no treatment of the Protestant Reformation.

Raymond P. Stearns has included many useful documents relevant to modern church history in his *Pageant of Europe* (New York: Harcourt, Brace & Co., 1947).

There are several good histories of the Reformation. The student can consult *The Renaissance and the Reformation* (New York: Harper & Brothers, 1934) by Charles Lucas for an interesting and authentic history of the Reformation in the various countries.

The older volume by Edward M. Hulme entitled *Renaissance and Reformation* (New York: The Century Co., 1915) will repay study.

Albert Hyma's *Renaissance to Reformation* (Grand Rapids: Wm. B. Eerdmans Publishing Co., 1951) brings together the mature observations of a Christian historian on the Renaissance and Reformation.

Although Preserved Smith's *The Age of the Reformation* (New York: Henry Holt & Co., 1920) is at times unsympathetic with the Reformers, it contains a wealth of valuable material based upon an intensive study of the sources. It also has a good bibliography.

The Reformation (New York: Charles Scribner's Sons, 1873) by George Fisher is an older but able treatment of the Reformation by an outstanding church historian.

A History of the Reformation (New York: Charles Scribner's Sons, 2 vols., 1906-1907) by Thomas Lindsay has a wealth of useful detail.

Williston Walker's *The Reformation* (New York: Charles Scribner's Sons, 1900) is a good factual one-volume survey of the field.

Roland Bainton's *The Reformation of the Sixteenth Century* (Boston: The Beacon Press, 1952) contains illuminating insights and has a good bibliography of the Reformation.

Students can also consult with profit the relevant volumes of Philip Schaff's multi-volume *History of the Christian Church*. Schaff's great history has been republished recently by the William B. Eerdmans Publishing Co. in Grand Rapids, Michigan.

Schaff's *Creeds of Christendom* (New York: Charles Scribner's Sons, 3 vols., 6th ed., 1890) gives the origin of the Protestant creeds and confessions (Vol. I) and presents the creeds in the original language or translation (Vol. III).

Volume I of *A History of Christian Thought* (Philadelphia: The Muhlenberg Press, 1946) by J. L. Neve and O. W. Heick has several fine chapters (pp 217-335) on the theology of the reformers.

Other source materials of the Reformation are available to the student who reads Latin and French in Beresford J Kidd's *Documents Illustrative of the Continental Reformation* (Oxford: Clarendon Press, 1911).

The important documents of the English Reformation are given in the compilation entitled *Documents Illustrative of English Church History* (London: The Macmillan Co., 1921) by Henry Gee and William J. Hardy.

Harry Emerson Fosdick has also compiled an excellent collection of documents of the ideas of the Reformers in the book, *Great Voices of the Reformation* (New York: Random House, 1952).

Most of the books cited in the bibliography above have sections or chapters which deal with the causes of the Reformation. The student should read them with care so that he will not confuse the indirect and direct causes.

Chapter XXVII

LUTHER AND THE GERMAN REFORMATION

Not enough emphasis has been given to the Reformation as a religious movement that took place, for the most part, among people of Germanic stock in Northern and Western Europe. Most of the nations that adopted the principles of the Reformation had never been a part of the old Roman Empire or its border territories. The Latin nations of Southern Europe did not accept the Reformation; rather they remained true to the Roman Catholic system.

Perhaps the rationalistic and critical spirit of the Renaissance took such hold upon the people of Southern Europe that they were not concerned with matters of the spirit. It is likely that they were satisfied with a religion that was external and formal and that left them free to devote their lives to the enjoyment of material things. Even the Renaissance popes gave more time to cultural pursuits than they did to their religious functions. Whatever the ultimate reasons may be, the Protestant Reformation found no congenial home south of the Alps, but its principles were welcomed by the people of Teutonic descent.

Several reasons may account for this phenomenon. The German Humanists with their negative satirical criticism of the Roman Church in such books as *In Praise of Folly* and with their presentation of a more positive Christianity, which they saw in the Greek Testament, were widely read by the cultivated classes of Northern Europe. Such reading created a spirit of discontent with the papal system and a desire to have reform in religion.

Another reason may be that the mystical tradition of religion was more strongly entrenched in Teutonic lands than in Italy or Spain. The student will remember that most of the important mystics were German or Dutch. The pious burgher read his *Imitation of Christ* and endeavored to make his religion

[311]

practical. They were not at this time quite so sophisticated in their culture as the Southern Europeans.

Because Germany had no powerful national ruler to protect her interests, it was easier for the papacy to get money from Germany. The opening up of new mines created new wealth in Germany, and this wealth the papacy wanted to tap. The Roman Church also owned much land in Germany. The German middle classes were also subjected to financial abuses by

the hierarchy. Nationalism and resentment against the drain of wealth from Germany combined to create an atmosphere that would be favorable to whatever movement might lead a revolt against Rome.

The man and the hour met in sixteenth century Germany. Germany had her Luther in whom all of the forces of opposition to Rome could be concentrated in a declaration of spiritual independence. Up to 1517 Luther went through a formative period. At the end of this period he was critical of the indulgence system; between 1518 and 1521 he was forced to break with the church; 1522 to 1530 was a period of organization; and from 1531 to the peace of Augsburg in 1555, Lutheranism, led by Luther and, after his death, by his friend Melanchthon, faced an era of conflict with Romanism and the consolidation of its gains.

I. Luther's Formative Years to 1517

Martin Luther was born on November 10, 1483, in the little town of Eisleben. His father, who was of free peasant stock, had migrated from the ancestral home some distance from Eisleben. He gained wealth from the copper mines of that area in which he had an interest and became a man of considerable wealth. Although he owned shares in six mines and two smelters by 1511, times were still difficult for the family when Luther was born. Luther was raised under the strict discipline of those times. He told of being whipped by his mother until the blood came because he had stolen a nut. One morning in the Latin school at Mansfeld he was whipped fifteen times because he faltered in declining a Latin noun. His peasant parents, particularly his pious but superstitious mother, inculcated many of the superstitions of their class in him. Some of these terrors haunted him as he struggled so long in seeking salvation for his soul. His love of hard work, his strong will and his practical conservatism were present in him from the beginning.

After a short period in a school of the Brethren of the Common Life in Magdeburg, Luther was sent to school in Eisenach between 1498 and 1501. He was given food and lodging by kindly friends, such as Ursula Cotta. Here he received the advanced instruction in Latin that was essential if he were to go on to the university. In 1501 at the University of Erfurt he began to study the philosophy of Aristotle under the influence of teachers who followed the nominalistic ideas of William of Occam. William had taught that revelation was the only guide in the realm of faith; reason was the guide to truth in philosophy. Thus Luther's philosophical studies at Erfurt made him aware of the need of divine intervention if man were to know spiritual truth and to be saved. In 1502 he received the bachelor of arts degree, and in 1505 he was granted the degree of master of arts.

His father wished him to study law, but Luther became frightened during a severe thunderstorm on the road near Erfurt and promised Saint Anne that he would become a monk if he were spared. Perhaps his growing concern about his soul was brought to a focus by this experience in July of 1505, an experience that his father dryly suggested might be "a trick of the devil." About three weeks later he entered a monastery of the Augustinian order at Erfurt. Here, in 1507, he was ordained and celebrated his first mass.

During the winter of 1508 he taught theology one semester at the new university that had been founded in Wittenberg by Frederick, the Elector of Saxony, in 1502. His studies at Erfurt were also mainly theological. These studies only made his soul struggle more intense, but he found some help in the admonitions of the godly Staupitz, the vicar-general of his order, who urged him to trust God and to study the Bible.

During the winter of 1510 and 1511 he was sent to Rome on business for his order. There he saw something of the corruption and luxury of the Roman Church and came to realize the need of reform. He spent much time visiting churches and viewing the numerous relics that were in Rome. He was shocked by the levity of the Italian priests who could say several masses while he said one.

In 1511 Luther was transferred to Wittenberg. During the next year he became a professor of Bible and received his doctor of theology degree. He held the position of professor of theology until his death. At this time he was also given the office in the tower where he came to a realization of justification by faith. It was in this university that he and a loyal band of fellow professors and students accepted the faith that was to spread all over Germany.

Luther now began to lecture in the vernacular on the books of the Bible, and in order to do so intelligently he began to study the original languages of the Bible. He found that he could not even trust Augustine fully, and he gradually developed the idea that only in the Bible could true authority be found. From 1513 to 1515 he lectured on the Psalms, in 1515 to 1517 on Romans, and, later, on Galatians and Hebrews. Between 1513 and 1517, while preparing these lectures, he found the peace of soul that he had not been able to find in rites, acts of asceticism, or in the famous *German Theology* of the mystics. A reading of Romans 1:17 convinced him that only faith in Christ could make one just before God. From that time on justification by faith and *sola scriptura,* the idea that the Scriptures are the only authority for sinful men in seeking salvation, became the main points in his theological system. Staupitz, the visit to Rome, the writings of the mystics, and the writings of the

Fathers had been formative influences in his life, but it was his study of the Bible that led him to trust in Christ alone for his salvation.

In 1517 Tetzel, the wily agent of the Archbishop Albert, began his sale of indulgences at Juterbok near Wittenberg. Luther, and those who followed him in his new found faith, resented the exploitation of the people by this nefarious system, and he decided to make public protest. Tetzel claimed that repentance was not necessary for the buyer of an indulgence and that the indulgence gave complete forgiveness of all sin. On October 31, 1517 Luther posted his ninety-five theses on the door of the Castle Church in Wittenberg. In them he condemned the abuses of the indulgence system and challenged all comers to debate on the matter. A reading of the ninety-five theses[1] will reveal that Luther was merely criticizing abuses of the indulgence system in order to reform it. However, during the years between 1518 and 1521 he was forced to accept the idea of separation from the Roman system as the only way to get a reform that would involve a return to the ideal of the Church revealed in the Scriptures. The translation into German and the printing of the theses spread Luther's ideas rapidly.

II. THE BREAK WITH ROME, 1518–1521

After the publication of the theses, Tetzel endeavored to use all of the power of the Dominican order to silence Luther, who found support in the Augustinian order. It was this conflict in the early years of the Reformation that has given rise to the foolish charge of the rationalist that the Reformation was only "a squabble of monks." Luther was ordered to debate the problem before members of his order at Heidelberg in 1518, but little came of the debate except a widening of the circle of those who accepted Luther's ideas.

A valuable ally, who later supplemented Luther's bold courage with his gentle reasonableness, came to Wittenberg as professor of Greek in 1518. At the age of twenty-one Philip Melanchthon (1497–1560) was already well trained in the classical languages and Hebrew. While Luther became the great prophetic voice of the Reformation, Melanchthon became its theologian. He and others of the Wittenberg faculty loyally supported Luther's views.[2]

[1] H. Bettenson, *Documents of the Christian Church* (New York: Oxford University Press, 1947), pp. 263-271.

[2] Ernest G. Schwiebert, "The Reformation from a New Perspective," *Church History*, 17:3-31 (March, 1948).

By the fall of 1518 Luther was insisting that his only authority in the coming dispute would be neither the pope nor the Church but the Bible. He would have fallen before the Dominicans had it not been for the aid of Frederick the Elector of Saxony, who was one of those who elected the emperor of the Holy Roman Empire. When Luther was summoned to appear before the Diet of Augsburg in 1518, Frederick promised that he would give his powerful support to this brave reformer. The pope did not seem to realize the extent of popular support for Luther in Germany. At the Diet Luther met Cardinal Cajetan, who demanded that he retract his views, but Luther refused to do this until he became convinced of their falsity by Scripture. Early in 1519 Luther promised the papal nuncio, Karl Von Miltitz, that he would not proclaim his views if his opponents also kept silence.

Later Luther appealed for a general council to deal with the problem. In July, 1519, he debated with John Eck at Leipzig. The clever Eck was able to force Luther into an admission of the fallibility of a general council and his unwillingness to accept the decisions of the pope without question.

In 1520 Luther decided to carry the issue to the German people by the publication of three pamphlets. The *Address to the German Nobility*[3] was aimed at the *hierarchy*. Rome claimed that spiritual authority was superior to temporal authority; that the pope alone could interpret the Scriptures; and that no one but the pope could call a council. After stating the arguments for these claims, Luther proceeded to demolish them from Scripture. He stated that princes should reform the Church when necessary; that the pope should not interfere in civil affairs; and that all believers had the right to choose their own ministers. In October he published his *Babylonian Captivity*.[4] In this pamphlet he widened his attack by challenging the *sacramental system* of Rome. The first document had been an historical attack on the hierarchy, but this pamphlet attacked the center of the Roman system — the sacraments as a means of grace when dispensed by the priesthood. Luther emphasized the sure validity of only the Lord's Supper and Baptism. Henry VIII won from the pope the title "Defender of the Faith" for himself and future English royalty by his attempt to answer this attack of Luther upon the sacramental system. The third

[3] Bettenson, *op. cit.*, pp. 272-279.
[4] *Ibid.*, pp. 279-282.

pamphlet, *On the Freedom of the Christian Man,* really attacked the *theology* of the Roman Church by its assertion of the priesthood of all believers as a result of their personal faith in Christ. The issues were clearer than ever now that Luther had attacked the hierarchy, sacraments and theology of the Roman Church and was appealing for national reform.

In June, 1520, Leo X issued the bull *Exsurge Domine* which eventually resulted in the excommunication of Luther. Luther's books were also burned at Cologne. Not to be outdone, Luther promptly burned Leo's bull publicly. Charles V, the new emperor, now issued a summons for an imperial diet at Worms in the spring of 1521, at which Luther was to appear to answer for his views. Luther went to Worms with the assurance of protection by Frederick and other German princes. He again refused to recant unless he could be convinced of fault by "the testimony of the Scriptures" or by reason. He said that he would take his stand on this alone and appealed to God for help.[5] His friends kidnapped him on the road back to Wittenberg and took him to Wartburg Castle where he remained until 1522. After his departure from Worms the Diet issued an edict that ordered any subject of the Emperor to seize Luther and to turn him over to the authorities. The reading of his writings was also banned.

III. Years of Separation, 1522–1530

During the trying year of May, 1521 to March, 1522 Melanchthon was not idle. His little work on the theology of the Reformers of Wittenberg, *Loci Communes,*[6] came out in 1521. This little work in Latin was the first theological treatise of the Reformation and went through numerous editions during the lifetime of its author. It established Melanchthon as the theologian of the Lutheran movement.

Melanchthon rejected the authority of the Roman Church, the Fathers, the canon law, and the Scholastics. He put the Bible above these as the final authority for Christians. His little book grew out of studies of Paul's Epistle to the Romans. In it, Melanchthon attempts to deal with the "most common topics of theological science" in a methodical fashion in order that he might "incite people to the Scriptures." He pictures

5 *Ibid.,* pp. 282-285
6 Philip Melanchthon, *Loci Communes Rerum Theologicarum,* trans. by Charles L. Hill (Boston: Meador Publishing Co., 1944).

man bound by sin and unable to help himself. The law, he writes, cannot help because its main function is to reveal sin. God must initiate the work of the salvation that the individual receives by faith in Christ. Luther, who recognized that he was bold and violent where Melanchthon was irenic and gentle, fully approved of this work as the theological expression of his ideas. He characterized it as "immortal."

But Luther had not been idle either during his enforced residence at Wartburg Castle between May of 1521 and March of 1522. Making use of Erasmus' edition of the Greek Testament, he completed his German translation of the New Testament in less than a year. When it was published, it not only gave the German people the Bible in their own tongue, but it set the standard form of the German language. The whole Bible was translated from the Hebrew into German by 1534. He also wrote *On Monastic Vows*, in which he urged monks and nuns to repudiate their wrongful vows, to leave the cloister and to marry.

Luther was indeed a national hero and held in high regard by prince, peasant, Humanist and knight alike, but his policies in the subsequent years alienated some of those who had followed him so readily at first. While he was at the Wartburg, Nicholas Storch and Mark Stubner, who were known as the Zwickau prophets, appeared at Wittenberg and began preaching ideas similar to some of the Anabaptists. They taught that the kingdom of God would soon appear on earth and that their followers would have special revelations. Even the usually stable Carlstadt was influenced by them. At the risk of his life Luther returned to Wittenberg in 1522. After eight days of fiery sermons, in which he stressed the authority of the Bible and the need for gradual change in the Church, he defeated the Zwickau prophets. The radical wing of the Reformation, however, felt from this time that it could not count upon help from Luther, and in 1535 Luther broke openly with Anabaptist movement.

He also lost the support of the Humanists, such as Erasmus, by 1525. Erasmus had supported Luther's demands for reform at first but recoiled when he saw that Luther's views would lead to a break with Rome. He also disagreed with Luther's view that man's will was so bound that the initiative in salvation must come from God. Erasmus emphasized the freedom of the human will in his book, *The Freedom of the Will,* which he published in 1524 as an answer to Luther's denial of the freedom of the will.

The peasants also became hostile to Luther in 1525 when he opposed the Peasant's Revolt. The peasants had heard him denounce the authority of the Church and assert the authority of the Scripture and the right of the individual to come directly to God for salvation, and they applied these arguments to their social and economic problems. Feudalism had caused much oppression of the peasants, and in their "Twelve Articles"[7] of 1523 they demanded the reform of feudal abuses that could be demonstrated as abuses on the authority of Scripture. When Luther realized that this revolutionary social movement might endanger the Reformation and might subvert the foundations of orderly government even in Protestant provinces, he urged the princes in violent language in his pamphlet, *Against the Robbing and Murdering Horde,* to put down disorder. The authorities needed no urging to use severe measures and slaughtered about one hundred thousand peasants. Southern German peasants remained in the Roman Catholic Church partly because of this apparent betrayal of them by Luther.

Others felt that Luther's repudiation of monastic vows by his marriage to the escaped nun, Katherine Van Bora, in 1525, was an abrupt break with the past that was not justified. Luther, however, always felt that he had done the right thing and derived much joy from his homelife. His six children as well as numerous students graced his table to such an extent at times that his "Katie" was hard pressed to provide the necessary food.

It also was unfortunate that Luther could not see his way clear to join forces with Zwingli, who was leading the Reformation in the northern cantons of Switzerland. Luther and Zwingli met in the fall of 1529, in what was known as the Marburg Colloquy, at the Marburg Castle of Philip of Hesse. They found themselves in agreement on fourteen out of fifteen propositions but could not agree concerning the Communion. Zwingli contended that it was a memorial of Christ's death, but Luther argued that there was a real physical presence of Christ in the Communion although the substance of bread and wine did not change. Just as iron remains iron but becomes cherry red when

7 Beresford J. Kidd, *Documents Illustrative of the Continental Reformation* (Oxford: Clarendon Press, 1911), pp. 174-179.

it is heated, so he contended that the substance of the bread and wine do not change but that around and under the symbols there is a real physical presence of Christ. This view became known as consubstantiation.

Events in Germany forced Luther into a position where he had to develop church organization and liturgy suitable for his followers. At the Diet of Speier in 1526 the princely followers of Luther were able to get the Diet to agree that, until a general council met, the ruler of each state should be free to follow what he felt was the correct faith. The principle of *cuius regio eius religio,* the principle that the ruler should choose the religion of his state, was adopted for the time being. Perhaps the fact that Emperor Charles the V was fighting to prevent his French foe, Francis I, from gaining control of Italy during the 1520's and the absence of many Catholic German princes at the Diet may account for this decision and the later rapid growth of the Lutheran movement.

A second Diet at Speier in 1529 cancelled the decision of the previous Diet and declared that the Roman Catholic faith was the only legal faith. The princely followers of Luther read a *Protestation.* From then on they were known as Protestants by their opponents. Such was the honored derivation of the word "Protestant."

In 1530 the Diet of Augsburg was held. Melanchthon with Luther's approval had drawn up the *Augsburg Confession,* which was presented at the Diet.[8] It became the official creed of the Lutheran Church. It was the first of several creeds that made the period between 1517 and 1648 as great a period of Protestant creedal development as the period between 325 and 451 had been for the development of the ecumenical creeds of the Church, such as the Nicene Creed. Only seven of the twenty-nine articles were negative repudiation of religious abuses; the remaining articles were a positive statement of the Lutheran faith.

Luther had also drawn up the *Small Catechism* in 1529[9] as a concise statement of the Ten Commandments, the Apostles' Creed, the Lord's Prayer and other matters of theology and liturgy. The Lutheran movement then made rapid progress

[8] P. Schaff, *Creeds of Christendom* (New York: Charles Scribner's Sons, 3 vols., 6th ed., 1890), Vol. III, pp. 1-73; Bettenson, *op. cit.,* pp. 297-300.

[9] Schaff, *op. cit.,* Vol. III, pp. 74-92; Bettenson, *op. cit.,* pp. 286-297.

in Northern Germany despite armed opposition from the Emperor and the Catholic princes.

IV. The Era of German Religious Wars and Church Organization, 1531–1555

The Protestant princes decided to organize for mutual defense and formed the Schmalkaldic League early in 1531. They agreed to defend their faith by force of arms if necessary. But the Emperor was kept busy with wars against the Turks and the French between 1532 and 1542, and the Protestant League did not have to fight. Thus Lutheranism was able to make great gains in Northern Germany. In 1535 a Lutheran order of ordination was adopted. This meant an ecclesiastical break with the Roman hierarchy.

Luther's last years were troubled by the bigamy that Philip of Hesse, one of his supporters, committed when he married Margaret von der Saale in 1540 without the formality of divorcing his first wife. Luther temporized at this point by consenting to the marriage and by urging that the second marriage be kept secret. In 1546 he died, leaving the Lutheran movement to the leadership of Melanchthon.

Finally the Emperor was ready for war with the German Protestants, and the Schmalkaldic wars occupied the stage of German history between 1546 and 1552. Fighting was finally ended by the Peace of Augsburg in 1555. The agreement put Lutheranism on a basis of legal equality with Roman Catholicism in Germany. The prince was to determine the religion in his territory, but any dissenters were to be given the right to emigrate. If a Catholic leader turned Protestant, he must give up his position. This agreement safeguarded the Roman Catholic control of the areas in Southern Germany that were predominantly Roman Catholic.

It will be noticed that the Peace of Augsburg made the prince a power in the religious affairs of the Church. As early as 1539 a Consistorium was appointed by the Elector Frederick in Wittenberg to serve as a court in cases involving discipline and divorce. During the next decade the Consistorium became a governing body to govern the affairs of the Church under the supervision of the prince. Superintendents, who had been used as early as 1526, were sent out to supervise the affairs of the local church. Luther believed in order and wrote that, while the state had no right to interfere with the individual in the matter of salvation, the state was given the sword by God to maintain order so that the godly might live their lives in peace. The ruler of the state was responsible to God for the manner in which he ruled the state. Luther was, however, opposed to revolution to overthrow an arbitrary and oppressive government on the grounds that time or external enemies would correct the condition.[10]

Luther was indeed one of the titanic figures of the Church because of his influence upon later times as well as upon his own era. The national Lutheran churches of Germany and the Scandinavian countries were a result of his work. To these churches he gave the *Large* and *Small Catechisms; Postils,* which were sermonic aids for the minister; a system of church government, which he, to a large extent, developed; the German Bible, which helped to standardize the German language; and beautiful and stately hymns, such as "Away in the Manger" and "A Mighty Fortress," which were to be sung in the vernacular by the whole congregation. He set up a system of universal elementary education in Germany in order that the people might be taught to read the Bible in the vernacular. He urged this duty upon the governing bodies of German cities in a letter to them in 1524, and in 1530 he wrote concerning the duty of parents to send their children to school. Universal compulsory elementary education had its early beginnings in his efforts. He was also interested in secondary schools and university education. He restored preaching to its rightful place in the Church and thus recreated a medium of spiritual instruction that had been so widely used in the Early Church. Above all, he awakened his day to the fact that culture was not merely a matter of reason but of regeneration by faith in Christ. He did not repudiate the individualism of the Renaissance but made it a spiritual matter as the individual was brought into saving relationship with God by faith in Jesus Christ. In the place of an authoritative church he put an authoritative Bible as the infallible rule of faith and practice that each believer-priest should use for guidance in matters of faith and morals. Luther did not repudiate the necessity of a corporate relationship of the individual and others in the Church; on the contrary, he was insistent upon the importance of communion with other members of the Body of Christ.

[10] Hugh Thomson Kerr, Jr., *A Compend of Luther's Theology* (Philadelphia: The Westminster Press, 1943), pp. 213-232.

V. LUTHERANISM, 1555–1580

From the Peace of Augsburg until the publication of the *Book of Concord* in 1580 the peace of the Lutheran churches was marred by doctrinal controversy. Most of the issues were similar to the points on which Melanchthon and Luther had had differences of opinion. One dispute concerned the place of the Law in preaching. Luther had urged the preaching of the Law as a means of revealing to men how sinful they were. Others urged that only the Gospel should be preached because it was the Gospel that brought salvation. The Majoristic controversy grew out of George Major's contention that good works were an important part of our salvation even though one was saved by faith alone. Those Lutherans who were close followers of Luther argued that this was really a return to the Roman doctrine of salvation by faith and works. Arguments also developed over the Lord's Supper, and over whether or not the human will was able to cooperate with the divine grace in salvation.[11]

Because these disputes created political as well as religious disunity, the princes of Germany decided that the problems must be settled if the Lutheran movement were not to go to pieces. A document known as the Formula of Concord was completed by 1577 and published in 1580.[12] Most of the Lutherans of Germany accepted this expression of their theology. Lutheran theologians also took up the task of creating a complete statement of the Lutheran theology that would differentiate it from Roman Catholic theology. This was done by the preparation of the *Book of Concord* in 1580. The *Book* contained the three great universal creeds of the Early Church and the various Lutheran formulas that had been drawn up between 1529 and 1580.

These disputes made the Lutherans very conscious of the importance of doctrine and brought about a viewpoint that emphasized correctness of doctrine. This emphasis led to a cold orthodoxy that ignored the more subjective spiritual aspects of Christianity. The Pietistic movement, which emphasized Bible study, prayer and the daily practical application of Christian truth, arose in the seventeenth century as a reaction to this strong intellectual emphasis.

11 P. Schaff, *op. cit.*, Vol. I, pp. 258-307.
12 *Ibid.*, Vol. III, pp. 93-180.

VI. Lutheranism in Scandinavia

Church reform in Denmark began in the reign of a nephew
of Frederick of Saxony, Christian II (1513–1523), who had
strong humanistic sympathies and who was anxious to free the
crown from the control that a council of nobles and the clergy
were able to exert over it. He wanted to create a state church
that would be under royal control. His successor, Frederick I
(1523–1533), was favorably disposed to the Lutheran faith and
permitted Hans Tausen (1494–1561) to do in Denmark what
Luther had done in Germany. Tausen was helped greatly by
the publication of a Danish translation of the New Testament
in 1523. Frederick came out openly in favor of the Reformation
in 1526 and made Tausen the royal Chaplain. He was loyally
supported by the common people who were disgusted with the
corruption of the higher clergy and the indulgence traffic. By
1530 a Lutheran confession of faith was available. Frederick's
successor, Christian III, had the Diet of 1536 abolish the Roman
religion and confiscate all Roman Church property. This property was then divided between the king and the nobles. From
that time on Lutheranism was the state religion of Denmark.

Because Norway was dominated by Denmark until 1814, it
had to accept the religious changes that came in Denmark.
Lutheranism was introduced into Norway during the reign of
Frederick I and became the state religion during the reign of
Christian III.

A clergyman by the name of Einarsson, who had come under
the influence of the Lutheranism of the University of Wittenberg during his stay in Germany, preached Lutheran doctrines
in Iceland upon his return in 1533. When he became bishop
in 1540, he introduced Lutheranism into his bishopric. The
publication of the New Testament in Icelandic in the same
year promoted the cause of Protestantism. By 1554 Lutheranism became the official religion of Iceland.

Sweden became independent of Denmark by the revolution
of 1521 during the reign of Christian II, and her new reforming ruler, Gustavus Vasa, also favored the Reformation as a
tool whereby he could confiscate the wealth of the Roman
Church. Olavus Petri (1493–1552), after three years study in
Wittenberg, did the work in Sweden that Luther had done in
Germany and laid the popular base for reform. Petri's work

enabled the ruler to bring Sweden into the Lutheran fold. A Swedish translation of the New Testament in 1526 made it possible for the reading public to compare the teaching of their clergy with the Bible so that they could see that the Lutheran doctrines of Petri were nearer to the Scriptures. Lutheranism was made the religion of the state at the Diet of Westeras, held in 1527, and was accepted gradually by the people. During Gustavus Vasa's long reign from 1523 to 1560 the Reformation was thoroughly established in the country.

The Reformation spread from Sweden to Finland because Finland was controlled by Sweden. Michael Agricola was its apostle in that country. After 1528 the Lutheran faith became that of the Finnish people and their leaders.

Lutheranism was also influential in other countries. Lutheran ideas laid the groundwork for the Reformation in Scotland under John Knox. Lutherans also spread their teachings in England. Even though these countries finally adopted other forms of the Reformation, Lutheranism was a factor in the transition from Catholicism to Protestantism. Lutheranism was temporarily triumphant in Poland, but divisions among those favorable to the Lutheran faith and internal struggle enabled the Roman Church to regain Poland for Catholicism. It was in Germany and the Scandinavian lands that Lutheranism made the greatest and most permanent gains. The authority of the Bible, which the Lutheran leaders translated into the vernacular of their countries, and justification by faith became the watchwords of those lands in the sixteenth century. Luther did an even greater work than he could ever have imagined when he first opposed Tetzel's traffic in indulgences in 1517.

BIBLIOGRAPHY

Written from the Lutheran point of view, *A History of the Christian Church* (New York: Thomas Nelson & Sons, 1942) by Lars Qualben has excellent chapters on the Lutheran Reformation in Germany and elsewhere.

A biography that should become the classic biography of Luther's life is *Luther and His Times* by Ernest G. Schwiebert (St. Louis: Concordia Publishing House, 1950). It is the result of exhaustive study of the sources and shows the influence of the University of Wittenberg upon the Reformation in Germany.

Here I Stand (Nashville: Abingdon Cokesbury Press, 1950) by Roland Bainton is a popular and interesting account of the Reformer's life.

Preserved Smith's *The Life and Letters of Martin Luther* (New York: Houghton Mifflin, 1911) allows one to see Luther through his letters and work. It has a helpful chronology of Luther's life.

The older biography by Arthur C. McGiffert, *Martin Luther, The Man and His Work* (London: T. Fisher Unwins, 1911), is interestingly written and has many fine pictures of places of importance in Luther's life.

Hugh Thomson Kerr, Jr., *A Compend of Luther's Theology* (Philadelphia: The Westminster Press, 1943) is a helpful compilation of Luther's theological views that the average student would not otherwise get.

The little source book by Albert Hyma entitled *Luther's Theological Development from Erfurt to Augsburg* (New York: F. S. Crofts & Co., 1928) gives insight from the sources into the development of Luther's theological ideas until 1530.

The various editions of Luther's *Table Talks* are an excellent source from which to obtain a knowledge of Luther's personality. The revised edition by William Hazlett is useful to the student.

Chapter XXVIII

THE REFORMATION IN SWITZERLAND

Switzerland was the freest land in Europe at the time of the Reformation although it was nominally a part of the Holy Roman Empire. As early as 1291 the three forest cantons of Schwyz, Uri and Unterwalden had entered into a federal union that left each canton free to develop as a self-governing republic. By the time of the Swiss Reformation there were thirteen cantons in the confederacy. The sturdy democratic Swiss were in demand throughout Europe as mercenary soldiers. They provided the armies that the pope engaged to protect his interests by force of arms.

The Swiss cities were also centers of culture, and Humanism was able to establish itself in the city cantons. Basel had a famous university. It was here that the great Erasmus had edited his printed Greek New Testament. Because of these developments the Swiss Reformation had as one of its major sources, Humanism.

The government of each canton was in complete charge of local affairs, and for that reason the individual canton was free to accept the form of religion that it would follow. Hence, the Reformation in Switzerland was accomplished by the legal action of democratically elected local government.

Three types of Reformation theology developed in Swiss territories. The German-speaking cantons of the northern part of the country followed Zwingli's view of the Reformation. Those in the south, led by Geneva, followed the views of Calvin. In addition, the radicals of the Reformation, known as Anabaptists, developed as an extreme wing among those who at first worked with Zwingli. From Zurich the Anabaptist movement spread throughout Switzerland, Germany and Holland, where, under Menno Simons, it had a steady development.

I. THE ZWINGLIAN REFORMATION IN THE GERMAN CANTONS
OF NORTHERN SWITZERLAND

Huldreich Zwingli (1484–1531) was also of the first generation of the Reformers. In him the forces of discontent with
Rome crystallized into a Reformation Church. His father was
a farmer and the chief magistrate of Wildhaus. The family
had a good income which made it possible for Zwingli to have
a good education for the priesthood. He attended the University
of Vienna and in 1502 went to the University of Basel where
he received his bachelor of arts degree in 1504 and his master
of arts degree in 1506. His teachers' emphasis upon Humanism
appealed to him. Erasmus became his idol; the humanities
were his chief desire; but theology had little interest for him.

Between graduation in 1506 and the year 1516 Zwingli served
the pope well as a parish priest, chaplain and an ardent Swiss
patriot. His first parish was at Glarus. At this time his Humanistic sympathies caused him to interpret the Pauline Gospel
by the philosopher Plato and Christ's Sermon on the Mount
so that he emphasized the ethical aspects of Christianity. Study
of Erasmus' teaching led him away from scholastic theology
to the study of the Bible. His patriotic tendencies led him to
oppose mercenary service by Swiss young men, except for the
pope. To get his support, the pope gave him a generous annual
pension. In 1512, 1513 and 1515 he went with the mercenaries
from Glarus to serve as their chaplain.

Between 1516 and 1518 he served as pastor at Einsiedeln, a
center for pilgrims. There he began to oppose some of the
abuses of the Roman system of indulgences and of the black
image of the Virgin Mary by ridiculing them in the fashion of
Erasmus. When Erasmus' Greek Testament came out in 1516,
he copied the letters of Paul from a borrowed copy so that he
might have his own copy. He was a Biblical Humanist when
he left Einsiedeln. Called to be a pastor at Zurich, he began
his work there early in 1519. It was at this time that he took
a definite stand against the enlisting of the Swiss as mercenaries
in foreign service, because of the corrupting influences that he
saw the men encounter in such service, and Zurich stopped the
practice in 1521.

An attack of the plague in 1519 and contact with Lutheran
ideas led him into an experience of conversion. Zwingli first
raised the issue of Reformation when he declared that tithes

paid by the faithful were not of divine authority and that their payment was a voluntary matter. This struck a blow at the financial basis of the Roman system. It seemed odd that the Reformer should have entered into a secret marriage with a widow, Anna Reinhard, in 1522. Not until 1524 did he publicly legitimize their union by marrying her openly.

When citizens broke with the idea of the lenten fast and cited Zwingli's assertion of the sole authority of the Bible to excuse themselves, and when changes were made that modified the Roman system of worship, the authorities decided to hold a public debate in which Zwingli would meet all comers. The elected authorities would then decide what faith the city and canton should adopt. Thus the Reformation in the northern Swiss cantons was put into effect by governmental action after debate. Before the debate Zwingli prepared the *Sixty-seven Articles* which emphasized salvation by faith, the authority of the Bible, the headship of Christ in the Church and the right of clerical marriage. They also condemned unscriptural Roman practices.[1] The town council decided that Zwingli had won, and the ideas of the Reformer were rapidly given legal status. Fees for baptisms and burials were eliminated. Monks and nuns were allowed to marry. Images and relics were banned, and in 1525 the Reformation was completed in Zurich by the abolition of the mass. Zwingli's belief that the ultimate authority resided in the Christian community, which exercised its authority through an elected civil government acting on the authority of the Bible, had borne fruit in the Zurich Reformation in which the Church and state were linked in a theocratic manner as body and soul were in men.

Bern was won over to the side of the Reformation by a debate similar to that in Zurich. Zwingli took part in the debate on the basis of his *Ten Theses*,[2] and, as a result, the city council ordered the acceptance of the principles of the Reformation in 1528. By 1529 the mass was also abolished in Basel through the influence of Zwingli's warm friend, Oecolampadius.

From 1522 on Zwingli was hampered by followers who became known as the Anabaptists because they insisted on the rebaptism of converts. In 1525 the city council forbade their meetings and banished them from the city. Later many were

[1] Samuel M. Jackson, *Huldreich Zwingli* (New York: G. E. Putnam's Sons, 1901), pp. 183-185.

[2] Schaff, *op. cit.*, Vol. I, pp. 365-366.

executed by order of the authorities by drowning, a horrible parody upon their practice of re-baptism.

Zwingli also lost the support of Luther at the Marburg Colloquy in 1529 when the two men could not come to an agreement over the presence of Christ in the Communion. Zwinglianism thus developed separately from Lutheranism.

The acceptance of the Zwinglian principles by several cantons made some kind of religious organization necessary, and in 1527 a synod of the Swiss evangelical churches was formed. About the same time the Bible was translated into the vernacular for the people. Up to this time the pope had not interfered because of his need of Swiss mercenaries, but the older rural cantons, faithful to the pope, decided to stop the march away from Rome. They organized a Christian Union of Catholic Cantons, and open war broke out between Protestant and Roman Catholic cantons in 1529. The two groups made a peace at Cappel by which the majority of citizens in each canton were to decide the form of religion and by which Protestants were to be tolerated in the papal cantons. When Zwingli tried to win Geneva to his cause, war broke out again in 1531. Zwingli took the field as a chaplain with his soldiers and was killed in the fighting. As a result of the fighting each canton was given full control over its internal affairs, and Zurich gave up its alliance with the Christian Civic League of Reformed Cantons. There was little change in the religious situation after this time in German Switzerland. Heinrich Bullinger became the able and conciliatory successor of Zwingli. Later the Zwinglian forces were merged with the Calvinistic forces in the Reformed churches of Switzerland.

Zwingli was the most Humanistic of the Reformers. He believed that such Greeks as Socrates and Plato and the Romans: Cato, Seneca and the Scipios would be in heaven. But apart from this he upheld the absolute authority of the Bible and would permit nothing in religion that could not be proved by the Scriptures. He accepted unconditional predestination to salvation but believed that only those who heard and rejected the Gospel in unbelief were predestinated to condemnation. He believed that faith was the essential element in the sacraments, that the Lord's Supper was a "commemoration" rather than a "repetition" of the Atonement, and that the believer partook of Christ by faith. He thought of original sin as a moral disease, but he did not think of it as guilt. Infants consequently could be saved by Christ without baptism.

Such were the views of the man who laid the foundation of the Reformed faith in German Switzerland. Though Calvin became the hero of the Reformed faith, the Church should not forget the part that the cultured, democratic and sincere Zwingli played in liberating Switzerland from the chains of the papacy. He was more liberal than Luther but as courageous as that great Reformer.

II. THE ANABAPTIST MOVEMENT

Treatment of the Anabaptists in a chapter devoted to the rise of the Reformed faith in Switzerland is justified by the fact that the Anabaptist movement was at first closely linked with the Zwinglian movement in Northern Switzerland. From there it spread to Moravia, Holland and other lands. It was the spiritual and lineal ancestor both of the modern Mennonite and Baptist churches throughout the world.

A. *The Anabaptists in Switzerland.*

Anabaptists appeared first in Switzerland because of the freedom which existed in that land. Neither feudalism nor the papacy had been able to gain a hold upon this land of courageous mercenary soldiers. Zwingli's insistence upon the Bible as the basis for the teaching of the preachers encouraged the rise of the Anabaptist concepts based upon the Bible.

Conrad Grebel (ca. 1490–1526) may be regarded as the founder of the Swiss Anabaptist movement. He was born of an influential patrician family and received a good education at the universities of Vienna and Paris. After his conversion in 1520 he worked closely with Zwingli until he broke with him in 1525. Zwingli's early view that infant baptism had no Biblical warrant had appealed to him. In 1525 the Zurich council ordered Grebel and Felix Manz, another well-educated Anabaptist leader, to desist holding meetings for Bible study. At the same time, because insistence upon adult baptism would deprive many of the franchise, Zwingli gave up his earlier insistence upon the lack of a Scriptural basis for infant baptism. The more radical Anabaptists were also endangering his plans for enlisting the slow-moving conservative authorities on the side of reform. At first Zwingli was willing to use his technique of debate to persuade them to give up their views, but, when this failed, the council adopted stronger measures, such as fines and exile. In 1526 the council decided to punish the advocacy of Anabaptist views by drowning. The movement was practically nonexistent in Zurich by 1535 because of this treatment, and the lowly Christians fled to other lands.

B. *The Anabaptists in Germany.*

The radical fringe of the Anabaptist movement helped to discredit the many sound believers in the ranks of the Anabaptists in Germany. The Zwickau prophets, who caused Luther trouble in 1522 in Wittenberg, were often, though perhaps mistakenly, associated with the movement to its discredit. The Munster rebellion of 1535, led by some radical, chiliastic Anabaptists, served to alienate Luther and his followers from these people.

Balthasar Hubmaier (1481–1528), one of the early German Anabaptists, had an excellent education and received a doctor of theology degree from the University of Ingolstadt where he studied under Luther's opponent, John Eck. His pastorate at Waldshut, near the Swiss border, gave him contact with the Swiss radicals whose ideas he adopted. He and three hundred followers were baptized by affusion in 1525, and he had to flee to Zurich to escape the Austrian authorities. From here he was banished to Moravia where he assumed leadership of those who fled from the Zwinglian persecution and of the thousands of Moravian converts to Anabaptist views. He was burned at the stake by order of the Emperor in 1528, and his wife was drowned in the Danube by the Roman Catholic authorities. Throughout his career as an Anabaptist leader, he insisted upon the separation of the Church and state, the authority of the Bible and the baptism of believers.[3]

The Anabaptists in Germany faced extinction by the fanatical excesses of their own number as well as by persecution from the state. Bernhard Rothmann, one of the canons of the cathedral of Munster, began an effort to win Munster to the evangelical faith. In 1532 the council allowed Lutheran ministers to man the pulpits, but the Emperor ordered the bishop of Munster to drive out Rothmann and his followers, who were becoming increasingly radical — adopting Anabaptist ideas of socialism and proposing to sell property to aid the poor. At this point Melchior Hoffman, who had arrived in Strasbourg to await the coming of the millennium in 1533, was superseded

[3] Henry C. Vedder, *Balthasar Hubmaier* (New York: G. P. Putnam's Sons, 1905), pp. 69-71; 130-136.

as leader of the chiliastic Strasbourg Anabaptists by the lean blackbearded Jan Matthyszoon. Matthyszoon proclaimed himself to be Enoch and sent emissaries to Munster in 1534. Later he decided that Munster and not Strasbourg was to be the New Jerusalem and moved there with his wife, the beautiful former nun Divara. When he was killed in fighting, John of Leyden succeeded him and married Divara and sixteen additional wives. Polygamy was decreed because of the large surplus of unmarried women in Munster and the practice of some Old Testament patriarchs. Community of goods and a fanatical anticipation of the coming of the heavenly kingdom led to disorder. The bishop of the area, aided by a large fighting force and by treachery in the Anabaptist ranks, recaptured the city, and the Anabaptist leaders were executed. Anabaptist denial of the ideas of Luther and Zwingli, as well as the fanatical Munster incident, brought condemnation and persecution down upon the movement from both Protestants[4] and Roman Catholics.

C. *The Anabaptists in the Netherlands.*

The wreckage of the Anabaptist movement by the Munster chiliasts was averted by the sane leadership of Menno Simons (ca. 1496–ca. 1561) in the Netherlands. Simons had embraced Anabaptist views and had given up his priesthood in the Roman Church in 1536. He assumed leadership of the "brethren," the name that the Anabaptists of the Netherlands adopted in order to get rid of the stigma attached to the name "Anabaptist." After his death the "brethren" were known as Mennonites. They were finally granted freedom of religion in 1676.

Because there were so many different Anabaptist groups with slightly different variations in belief, which grew out of the insistence upon the believer's right to interpret the Bible as a literal and final authority, it is difficult to give an organized statement of Anabaptist beliefs. However, there were some doctrines that all Anabaptists and Mennonites held in common. They insisted upon the authority of the Bible as a final and infallible rule for faith and practice. Many of them gave it a literal interpretation. They believed that the pure Church was to be an association of the regenerated rather than a state church with some unsaved in it. They also practiced the baptism of believers, at first by affusion or pouring, and later by immersion. Their opposition to infant baptism as unscriptural and their in-

---

[4] Schaff, *op. cit.*, Vol. III, pp. 13, 17, 173, 291, 306, 433.

sistence on rebaptism gave them the name of Anabaptists. Most of them insisted upon the complete separation of the Church and state and would have nothing to do with state churches. Because of this some were inclined to pacifism and objected to the taking of oaths in court and to serving as magistrates. Some were millenarian in their view of the future, and, partly because of that, practiced community of goods. Some, following Casper Schwenkfeld (1489–1561) were inclined to mysticism and believed in an inner spiritual voice that would guide them.

The Anabaptists appealed particularly to the workers and the peasants who were not reached by the other Reformers. This fact, coupled with a frequent tendency to literal interpretation of the Bible by ignorant men, often led to mystical or chiliastic excesses. The hard times of the sixteenth century led many of the lower class to accept the consolation that they found in the views of the Anabaptists. The Anabaptists were not "Bolsheviks of the Reformation" nor were all of them "left wing" fanatical visionaries. They were simple Bible-believing people, some of whom were led astray by ignorant leaders, who interpreted the Bible literally to their own advantage. Neither the Mennonites nor the Baptists should be ashamed to count them among their spiritual ancestors.

III. The Calvinistic Reformation in Geneva

The millions today who accept the Reformed faith as their doctrinal basis testify to the importance of the system of theology that John Calvin (1509–1564) developed. The term "Calvinism" usually designates the system of theology authored by Calvin. The phrase "Reformed faith" has reference to the system of theology developed upon the basis of Calvin's system. "Presbyterianism" is the word used to express the system of church government which Calvin developed. Geneva was the center where Calvin fully worked out his ideas. Calvin may be ranked as the leader of the second generation of Reformers.

A. *Luther and Calvin.*

Calvin was an interesting contrast to Luther. Luther had been born of peasant stock; but Calvin's father was a notary. This made Calvin a member of the professional class. Luther had studied philosophy and theology during his university career; but Calvin had a Humanistic and legal training. Because of this he was more the organizer of Protestantism; whereas Luther was its prophetic voice. Luther was physically strong; but Calvin fought illness during the period of his work in Geneva. Luther loved his home and family; but Calvin was essentially the lonely student. Luther, who lived in monarchial Germany, looked for aristocratic and princely support; Calvin, in republican Switzerland, was interested in the development of representative government in the Church.

Luther and Calvin differed theologically as well as personally. Luther emphasized preaching; but Calvin was interested in the development of a formal system of theology. Both accepted the authority of the Bible; but Luther's main emphasis was upon justification by faith whereas Calvin stressed the sovereignty of God. Luther held to consubstantiation as the proper explanation of the Lord's Supper; but Calvin rejected the physical presence of Christ in favor of the spiritual presence of Christ by faith in the hearts of the participants. Luther only rejected what the Scriptures would not approve; but Calvin refused everything of the past that could not be proved by the Scriptures. Luther believed in predestination of the elect but said little about election to condemnation. Calvin held to a double election to salvation and to condemnation based on the will of God, and he rejected any idea of merit on the part of the elect or foreknowledge on the part of God, in the sense that God elected to salvation those whom He foreknew would believe.

B. Calvin's Life to 1536.

Calvin's life can be readily divided into two major periods. Until 1536 he was a wandering student; from 1536 until his death in 1564, except for a short period of exile to Strasbourg between 1538 and 1541, he was the leading citizen of Geneva. He was born at Noyon in Picardy in Northeastern France, where his father was a respected citizen who was able to have the income from a church benefice set aside for his son's education when Calvin was only six. Two other better livings made it possible for Calvin to have the best preparation available before he went to the university. He studied for a time at the University of Paris, where he met the Humanist, Guillaume Cop. After he finished his Humanistic studies, his father sent him to the university at Orleans to study law. Here he was introduced to Protestant ideas by his cousin Pierre Olivetan. He transferred to the University of Bourges in 1529. His successful completion of an able commentary on Seneca's *De Clementia* in 1532 marked the peak of Humanistic influence upon his life. Some-time between the completion of the commentary and the end of 1533 Calvin was converted and adopted the ideas of the Reformation. He gave up the income from the benefices. Forced to leave France in 1534 after he had collaborated with Nicholas Cop, the rector of the University of Paris, in an address that was tinged with Humanistic and Reformation ideology, he went to Basel.

In Basel he completed his greatest work, *The Institutes of the Christian Religion,* in the spring of 1536 at the age of twenty-six. The little work was addressed to Francis I of France in an attempt to defend the Protestants of France, who were suffering for their faith, and to urge Francis to accept the ideas of the Reformation. The first edition was thus an apologetic in which Calvin developed his understanding of the Christian faith. The influence of Luther's *Catechism* can be discerned in the order of this first edition. Calvin first discussed the Ten Commandments; then, on the basis of the Apostles' Creed, the Faith; next, prayer on the basis of the Lord's Prayer; the two Sacraments; the evils of the Roman view of the Lord's Supper; and finally Christian liberty of the citizen, which he also related to political liberty. The work went through several editions until the final edition of 1559. This final edition consists of four books and eighty chapters and is a large text on theology.[5]

C. Calvin's Theology.

At the risk of oversimplification one can summarize the essence of Calvin's theology by the use of a simple mnemonic device that has been often used by students. The first letters of the main words of Calvin's theology spell the world "tulip." The coordinating idea of his theology is the complete sovereignty of God. Calvin had the majestic conception of God that is so characteristic of some of the Old Testament prophets. He believed in the total depravity of all men. Man has through Adam inherited the guilt of Adam's sin and can do nothing for his own salvation because his will is totally corrupted. Calvin next taught that salvation is a matter of unconditional election apart from human merit or divine foreknowledge. Election is based on the sovereign will of God and is a dual predestination of some to salvation and others to condemnation. Calvin

[5] See Wilhelm Pauck's article, Calvin's *Institutes of the Christian Religion* in *Church History*, 15:17-27 (March, 1946) for an able discussion of the history of this great work.

also believed that the work of Christ on the cross is limited to those elected to salvation. This belief is his doctrine of a limited atonement. The doctrine of irresistible grace is an inevitable corollary to this. The elect will be saved apart from their own desire as the Holy Spirit irresistibly draws them to Christ. Perseverance of the saints is the final point of importance in his system. Those elect who are irresistibly saved by the work of the Holy Spirit will never be finally lost.[6] Although Calvin's theology has an emphasis similar to that of Augustine, Calvin owes his system to his study of the Scriptures rather than to Augustine. Like other Reformers he went from the Bible to Augustine to seek the support of that prince of the Fathers rather than going from Augustine to the Bible and the doctrines of the Reformation.

D. Calvin's Life after 1536.

While Calvin was thus engaged, the Reformation advanced into the French cantons of Switzerland. Guillaume Farel (1489–1565), a red-headed, hot-tempered, strong-voiced, prophetic individual, established the Reformation in Geneva. Born into a middle class French family and educated in French universities, soon after 1521 he accepted Luther's idea of justification by faith. Protected by Bern, he helped spread Reformed ideas. In 1532 he began work in Geneva. In 1535 he won a dispute with those opposed to the Reformation, and the General Assembly of Citizens formally adopted the ideas of the Reformers in 1536. Farel realized that he needed someone with more organizing ability to help him to establish the Reformation in Geneva. Calvin stopped one night in 1536 in Geneva on his way to Paris. Farel went to him and urged him to help him. When Calvin demurred because he loved the life of a student and writer of theology, Farel told him that the curse of God would be on him if he did not stay. Stricken by fear, as Calvin later confessed, he decided to remain. He and Farel cooperated until they were exiled in 1538.

In 1537 Calvin and Farel succeeded in getting an ordinance passed which decreed that the Lord's Supper was to be celebrated at stated times, a children's catechism was to be prepared, congregational singing was to be adopted, and those

---

[6] *A Compend of the Institutes of the Christian Religion by John Calvin*, Hugh Thomson Kerr, Jr. (Philadelphia: Presbyterian Board of Christian Education, 1939). This is an excellent condensation of Calvin's *Institutes* which only omits the mass of Biblical references and the references to the Fathers, among whom Augustine is the most quoted.

under severe discipline could be excommunicated. The two introduced a catechism, and a short confession of faith, but a dispute over their withholding the Lord's Supper from some led to their exile in 1538.

Between 1538 and 1541 Calvin ministered to French religious refugees in Strasbourg and lectured on theology. In 1540 he married Idelette de Bure the widow of an Anabaptist pastor. Their only son died in infancy, and in 1549 Idelette herself died.

In 1541 the reforming forces again gained control in Geneva and Calvin was invited back there. That same year he had the *Ecclesiastical Ordinances* promulgated. This outlined the activities of the four classes of office bearers in the Church. It provided for an association of pastors to administer discipline, a group of teachers to teach doctrine, a group of deacons to administer the work of charity and, most important of all, the consistory, composed of six ministers and twelve elders, to supervise the theology and morals of the community and to punish when necessary the wayward members of the Church by excommunication. In order to set up an effective system Calvin used the state to inflict more severe penalties.

Such penalties proved to be much too severe, fifty-eight being executed and seventy-six exiled by 1546. Servetus, who questioned the doctrine of the Trinity, was executed in 1553. While one cannot justify these procedures, one can understand that people of those days believed that one must follow the religion of the state and that disobedience could well be punished by death. This belief was held by both Protestants and Roman Catholics. Some of Calvin's regulations also would today be considered as an unwarranted interference with the private life of the individual.

In 1564 Calvin died, worn out because of his weak body and arduous labors for the sake of the Gospel. Theodore Beza took over his work of leadership in Geneva.

E. Calvin's Contributions.

Calvin's greatest contribution to the Reformed faith was his *Institutes*, which has been accepted as the authoritative expression of the Reformed theology. In this work, he laid the foundation for the Reformed emphasis upon the importance of doctrine and the centrality of God in Christian theology.

He was also a voluminous letter-writer to the many who

wrote to him for advice from all over Europe and the British Isles. His letters and other writings fill fifty-seven volumes of the *Corpus Reformatorum.*

Calvin also encouraged education. He set up in Geneva a three-level system of education at the top of which was the Academy, now known as the University of Geneva, which was founded in 1559. His emphasis on education affected America later as the Calvinistic Puritans created colleges in the new world.

Geneva under his leadership became an inspiration and model to those of the Reformed faith elsewhere, and it provided a refuge for those who were oppressed for their Reformed faith. John Knox for a time sought refuge in Geneva and fell under the spell of Calvin's able preaching. Calvin's many commentaries on the books of the Bible have been studied by those who have adopted his ideas since his death. The government of the Genevan church became the model for Reformed churches.

Calvin also influenced the growth of democracy because he accepted the respresentative principle in government of the Church and state. He believed that both the Church and state were created by God for the good of men and that they should work together amicably in the furthering of Christianity. His emphasis on a divine call to a vocation and his stress on thrift and industry stimulated capitalism.

Some have thought that Calvinistic theology cuts the nerve of evangelism and missionary effort. However, any study of the history of the propagation of the Gospel will show that those who have professed the Reformed faith have had an important part in the great revivals of the past and the modern missionary movement. The influence of this emaciated, temperate scholar and able preacher, who was never ordained, upon the spiritual development of modern society has been out of proportion to his frail physique. Only the grace of God operative in his life is an adequate explanation of the work that he accomplished and that has gone on since his death. He was indeed an international reformer.

BIBLIOGRAPHY

In addition to the general works cited at the end of Chapter XXVI, many fine biographies of the men discussed in this chapter are available.

Conrad Grebel (Goshen: Mennonite Historical Society, 1950) by Harold S. Bender is a useful biography of that leader.

Samuel M. Jackson's *Huldreich Zwingli* (New York: G. P. Putnam's Sons, 1901) has excellent maps, several helpful appendices and documents of importance.

CHRISTIANITY THROUGH THE CENTURIES

Oskar Farner's condensation of his larger work on Zwingli, *Zwingli the Reformer* (London: Lutterworth Press, 1952), translated by D. G. Sear, gives up-to-date opinion concerning Zwingli and his work.

Balthasar Hubmaier (New York: G. P. Putnam's Sons, 1905) by Henry C. Vedder is an interesting account of the life of one of the early leaders of the Anabaptists.

Robert N. Hunt in his *Calvin* (London: Geoffrey Bles Ltd., 1933) writes a useful account of the important events in Calvin's life, his character and personality.

Arthur Dakin has given a useful summary of Calvin's system in his *Calvinism* (Philadelphia: The Westminster Press, 1946).

Schaff wrote an excellent appreciation of Calvin's life and work in his *Creeds of Christendom* (New York: Charles Scribner's Sons, 3 vols., 6th ed., 1890), Vol. I, pp. 423-466.

Chapter XXIX

THE REFORMED FAITH OUTSIDE SWITZERLAND

While Lutheranism made gains among the Scandinavians, Calvinism won adherents during the sixteenth century in other European countries. It gained many adherents in the Rhine valley in Germany, in Hungary, in France, in the Netherlands, in Scotland, in Northern Ireland and, for a brief time, in Poland.

I. THE REFORMED FAITH IN FRANCE

Francis I, who ruled France between 1515 and 1547, engaged in an almost constant struggle with the Spanish ruler over Italy. French interference in Italian affairs brought about the rise of Biblical Humanism because Frenchmen studied in Italy and developed an enthusiasm for sources of knowledge from the past. Jacques Lefevre (1455–1537) was one such Frenchman. Studying under the Humanists of Italy who were interested in studying the Bible in the original, Lefevre in 1523 completed a translation of the Bible into French from the Vulgate and the Greek texts. Even Margaret, the sister of the ruler, became a member of the group around him that included Farel, Bude, the classicist, and Vatable, an able Hebraist. Meaux became the center of the teaching of these Humanists, who wished to reform the Roman Church from within so that it would more nearly correspond to the Scriptures.

Lutheran influence, chiefly through the import of Luther's writings, became another factor in the rise of the Reformation in France. The upper middle-class merchants of the town and the workers in town and country were dissatisfied with the monopoly of social and political position that the nobles and the clergy held, and they were opposed to the corruption of the Roman Church. The ideas of the Biblical Humanists of Meaux and the teachings of Luther made an appeal to them as a way by which reform could come.

[341]

Francis, alarmed at the rise of Protestant ideas, decided to use force to stop the continued spread of heretical ideas. In 1525 the group at Meaux was scattered, and many fled from France. The Sorbonne had also condemned Luther's writings as early as 1521, but it could not prevent the spread of Protestant ideas.

The movement in France lacked effective leadership, but those who adopted the principles of the Reformation emphasized the authority of the Bible for faith and morals and the doctrine of justification by faith. Lefevre's Bible, which was based largely upon the Vulgate, was distasteful to many, and Olivetan, who had influenced Calvin at Orleans, made a new translation which was ready for use by 1535.

Though the strength of the French Reformation at first was drawn from the ideas of the Biblical Humanists and Luther, the conversion of John Calvin provided a writer who was able to popularize the Reformation faith, and in 1532 the Waldenses of Southern France adopted Calvinism. It was persecution of French Protestants that caused Calvin to issue his first edition of the *Institutes* in 1536 as an apologetic to defend the French Christians as loyal subjects and to suggest that persecution stop. He was as much the leader of the French Protestants as he was of those in Geneva. Over one hundred and fifty pastors, trained in Geneva, were sent to France between 1555 and 1556. Despite the wave of severe persecution that begun in 1538, unorganized Protestants of different theological shades of opinion were consolidated into an organized, self-conscious group by 1559 with aid from Geneva. Early in the reign of Henry II (1547–1559), about one-sixth of the French population was Protestant, according to one estimate. The great French admiral Coligny became a Protestant. In 1559 the first national synod, which marked the first evidence of national organization, was held in Paris. The synod adopted the Gallican Confession of Faith,[1] the first draft of which had been prepared by Calvin. The Confession was essentially a summary of his theology. After 1560 the Protestants became known as Huguenots. The origin of the name is uncertain, but it became the badge of honor of French Calvinistic Protestants.

The Huguenots became so powerful and so well organized that they formed a kingdom within a kingdom. Realization of

[1] P. Schaff, *Creeds of Christendom* (New York: Charles Scribner's Sons, 3 vols., 6th ed., 1890) Vol. III, pp. 356-382.

this situation by the government brought a transition from the government's policy of steady, fierce, bloody persecution between 1538 and 1559 to a policy of religious war to restore France to the bosom of Rome. Between 1559 and 1598 there were eight fierce wars and massacres. The terrible massacre of St. Bartholomew was begun in 1572 by the murder of the godly Coligny. Over two thousand were killed on the nights of August 23 and 24 in Paris, and in all between ten thousand and twenty thousand were massacred and their property seized by the Roman Catholics. The Roman Catholics had been inspired to this bloody deed by Catherine de' Medici who had a strong influence over the king, Charles IX.

In 1593 Henry of Navarre, the leader of the Huguenots, became a Roman Catholic and ruled as Henry IV. He issued the Edict of Nantes in 1598[2] which granted freedom of religion to the Huguenots so that they formed a tolerated state within the body politic of France. They were allowed to keep garrisons in several of the two hundred towns in their hands. This charter of liberty protected Protestantism in France until the charter was revoked in 1685 by Louis XIV, who desired to have one state, one ruler and one faith. Then the Huguenots were forced to flee from France to England, Prussia, Holland, South Africa and the Carolinas in North America. Because they were skilled artisans and professional men of the middle class, the loss of the Huguenots was a serious economic blow to France. This loss helped to bring her defeat by England in the struggle for colonies in the eighteenth century. Since that time Reformed Protestantism has not had too much influence in France, and Protestants have been a small minority within the population.

II. The Reformed Faith in Germany

When Luther lost the support of the peasant class of the Rhine valley by his uncompromising opposition to the Peasant's Revolt, many peasants became Anabaptists. With the coming of Calvinism, those who were better off turned to Calvinism. Earlier, in 1530, three cities of the Rhine area and Strasbourg presented their Tetrapolitan Confession to the Diet of Augsburg.

Calvinism also made gains in the Palatinate, whose ruler, the Elector Frederick III, was sympathetic toward Calvinistic theology and Presbyterian church government. After a public

[2] H. Bettenson, *Documents of the Christian Church* (New York: Oxford University Press, 1947), pp. 304-306.

disputation in 1560, Frederick decided in favor of Calvinism. Ursinus and Olevianus were given the task of drawing up a catechism for the use of the Church. They prepared the Heidelberg Catechism, which was officially adopted in 1562[3] and published in 1563. It became the official creed of the German Reformed Churches. When the Reformed faith was finally established after a short Lutheran interlude, the University of Heidelberg became a center of Calvinism.

III. The Reformed Faith in Hungary

Few realize that between two and three million people in Hungary profess the Reformed faith. Because the Magyars disliked the German, Lutheranism did not receive a kindly reception. But after 1550 as Hungarians, who had studied at Geneva and Strasbourg, returned home to spread Protestant ideas and after the translation of the Bible into the Magyar tongue by Kasper Karoli, the people of Hungary eagerly adopted Protestantism. By the end of the sixteenth century a large part of the people and the nobility had adopted the Reformed faith. Peter Melius was largely responsible for this turn of events. By 1570 the Hungarian Confession, which had been prepared in 1558, was widely circulated. Because the Socinian or anti-Trinitarians were making such progress, the Confession was preceded by a statement of the Biblical arguments against Unitarianism.

After 1572 severe persecution became the lot of the Magyar Reformed Church for about two centuries. The Jesuits also made strong efforts to win the Magyars back to the Roman system. In spite of this persecution, the Protestants remained firm and were granted toleration in 1781 and freedom of religion by 1848. *Unitarian movement.*

Socinius-founder of

IV. The Reformed Faith in Scotland

From about 1300, when Edward I tried unsuccessfully to bring Scotland under the English crown, Scotland made common cause with England's great enemy France. England could always count upon a flank attack from the Scotch in the north whenever she went to war with France. It was not until the Reformation, which brought both countries into the Protestant fold, that relations became better. The common fight between episcopacy and presbyterianism during the first half of the

---

[3] Schaff, *op. cit.*, Vol. III, pp. 307-355.

seventeenth century helped to heal the old breach between the two states after both were brought under one ruler in 1603.

Politics were dominated by religion during the Scottish Reformation; but in England religion had been secondary to political considerations. The barons and good burghers of the middle class in Scotland united under John Knox against the crown to bring about reform; in England, the Reformation had been created from above by law of the ruler. It is little wonder that the Reformation in Scotland was more radical than that in England. In no other area, except Geneva, was the influence of Calvinism so strong.

Lack of a strong ruler in Scotland had created many local areas under the leadership of strong clan chieftains. Small wonder that in this anarchic situation morals and religion deteriorated. Concubinage, drunkenness, simony, greed for wealth coupled with disregard for the people characterized the leaders of the Roman Church in Scotland. This condition of the Roman Church constituted the negative cause of the Reformation.

One positive cause of the Scottish Reformation was the Lutheran teaching of Patrick Hamilton, who had studied at Marburg and Wittenberg. Hamilton's emphasis upon justification by faith and his assertion that the pope was antichrist so aroused the authorities that he was burned in 1528. George Wishart also began teaching Protestant doctrine and was burned for his faith in 1546. He exerted considerable influence upon the spiritual development of John Knox. Copies of Tyndale's New Testament, brought to Scotland by Scotch merchants, also had their effect in the promotion of Protestant ideas.

The Scotch were also alienated from the royal family when Mary Stuart was sent to France for her education and when she married the young heir to the French throne. Scotchmen were worried lest Scotland should become a part of French dominions because of this marriage. They were also antagonized by the lax morality of the Frenchmen in Scotland. Failure of the Roman Church and the spread of the theology of the Reformation created an atmosphere favorable to the coming of the Scottish Reformation.

In the meantime, the man who was to establish the Reformation in Scotland was being prepared for his task. John Knox (1505–1572) was a courageous, sometimes harsh, man who feared no one except God. He was educated at the University of Glasgow and ordained to the priesthood in 1530. He became a follower of Wishart and preached to the Protestant soldiers in the garrison of St. Andrews until the French captured him. For nineteen months he served as a galley slave in a French warship until he was released through an exchange of prisoners. Edward VI of England offered him the bishopric of Rochester, but Knox refused it. Knox then became a royal chaplain. When Mary Tudor ascended the English throne, he fled to Europe where he ministered to religious exiles at Frankfort. He was much influenced by Calvin. To him Calvin was "that notable servant of God."

A number of Scottish nobles, who were disgusted with French influence in Scotland and the "idolatry" of the "Congregation of Satan" (their name for the Church of Rome), met in Edinburgh in December, 1557. These lords made a covenant to use their lives and possessions to establish "the Word of God" in Scotland. At this juncture Knox returned to Scotland as a fiery prophet of Calvinistic thought. When Mary Stuart and her husband became rulers of France and French soldiers were brought into Scotland, the Scotch appealed to Elizabeth, the new queen of England, for aid. Elizabeth, a skillful diplomat, hesitated to assist a people in revolt against their sovereign. Further, she disliked Knox because in 1556 he had published a tract against the Scottish lady-regent and Mary Tudor entitled *First Blast Against the Monstrous Regiment of Women* in which he argued that it was contrary to nature, God and His Word to have a woman ruler because it would mean "the subversion of good order, of all justice and equity." However, because French troops in Scotland were a threat to English security, she sent money and a fleet in 1560. The Treaty of Edinburgh in 1560 provided that only a harmless token force of one hundred and twenty French troops could stay in Scotland, that Frenchmen could not hold public office in Scotland, and that Francis II, Mary Stuart's husband, was not to engage in war against England. This ended French control of Scotland and left the Lords of the Congregation, as the Scottish nobility interested in reform were called, free to promote the cause of religious reformation.

The Scottish Parliament met in 1560 and, led by Knox, proceeded to the work of Reformation. It ended the rule of the pope over the Scottish Church; declared the mass to be illegal;

and repealed all statutes against heretics. It accepted the Confession of Faith that the "Six Johns," Knox and five other men with the first name of John, drew up in less than a week.[4] The Confession was definitely Calvinistic in tone and remained the major Scottish confession until the adoption of the Westminster *(Presb)* Confession in 1647. Later the first *Book of Discipline* and the *Book of Common Order* were drawn up. The Scottish Church was also organized into presbyteries, synods and a national assembly, with the system of representative government of the church by elders that had been used in Geneva. It was formally established in 1567. Thus was the Reformation accomplished bloodlessly by the decree of the Scottish legislature, but Knox and his friends still faced severe tests before it was firmly established.

Mary Stuart, whose husband, the French ruler, had died, landed in Scotland in 1561 during these changes. She was a beautiful and clever woman who was devoted to Catholicism. The dour, outspoken Knox had many tempestuous interviews with her, but he would not yield in any way despite her tears and blandishments. Mary's domestic problems led to her final defeat. In 1565 she married her cousin, the handsome but vain and jealous Darnley, who murdered her Italian secretary in her presence because he thought Mary was in love with him. A son, who became James VI of Scotland and James I of England, was born to them, but after the murder Mary had no use for Darnley and fell in love with Lord Bothwell. Darnley was blown up in a cottage in Edinburgh where he was staying. Mary immediately married Bothwell, and it was assumed that he had murdered Darnley. This so enraged the Scottish Parliament that it forced her to abdicate. She escaped to England and appealed to Elizabeth for protection in 1569. Elizabeth put her in protective custody until plots to put Mary on the English throne threatened Elizabeth with assassination. Elizabeth then reluctantly agreed to Mary's execution in 1587.

John Knox passed to his reward in 1572 but left the Presbyterian Church in Scotland on a firm footing. The middle class was firmly in political control, and the Presbyterian system of church government and Calvinistic theology were willingly adopted by the Scotch people. The French threat through Scotland to English security was forever ended, and the religious barrier to political union between England and Scotland was

[4] *Ibid.*, Vol. III, pp. 436-479.

removed so that the two lands were united under the same ruler in 1603 and became one kingdom with one Parliament in 1707. Indirectly, the Scottish Reformation affected America because many Scottish Presbyterians migrated to Northern Ireland early in the sixteenth century, and, from there, thousands migrated to America in the first half of the eighteenth century. Thus Presbyterianism in America is a lineal descendant of Scottish Presbyterianism.

In 1572 an attempt was made to establish episcopalian church government in Scotland. The battle against prelacy now took the place of the war against popery. Andrew Melville, the principal of Glasgow University, led the battle to restore the Presbyterian system of church government, and in 1581 presbyteries were again set up on an experimental basis. In 1592, despite strong opposition from King James VI, Melville's cause was triumphant, and Presbyterianism was made the established form of religion in Scotland. The Stuarts unsuccessfully tried to re-establish the episcopal system between 1603 and 1640.

V. The Reformed Faith in Ireland

Although the English were able to unite Wales and, finally, Scotland with England, they were never able to win the native Irish to unification except for brief periods and only then by force. This was the result of the hatred of the conquered race for the conquering race, Ireland's economic bondage to England and the failure to win Ireland for Protestantism.

When the Irish revolted against England during the Reformation, Parliament in 1557 by law confiscated the land of the defeated rebels and granted two-thirds to English settlers. This inaugurated the policy of colonization that was to result in a divided Ireland in modern times. Plots between the Spanish and rebellious Irish leaders led to the revolt from 1598 to 1603 which marred the end of Elizabeth's reign. When James I ascended the English throne, he decided to colonize Northern Ireland with Protestants. Most of the Protestants were Scottish Presbyterians and they came to form the bulk of the population in the northern counties. Ulster became a Presbyterian county, and Belfast became the Presbyterian city. These Scotch-Irish Presbyterians were the ancestors of those now living in Northern Ireland. When England placed economic disabilities upon them around 1700, thousands migrated to North America. By 1750 they had planted Presbyterianism in America, particularly around what is now Pittsburgh. This colonization of Ireland by the Scottish Presbyterians was also the reason why the northern part of Ireland is united with England and Scotland under one crown today while the southern part is a free republic. Southern Ireland did not accept the Reformation but remained loyal to the pope.

VI. The Reformed Faith in Holland

The revolt of the seven northern provinces of the Netherlands against the pope must not be disassociated from the political revolt of the Netherlands against Spanish domination. In this struggle England gave aid during the reign of Elizabeth in order to harass Philip II, who was supporting the Roman Church and making a claim to the throne of England through his dead wife, Mary Tudor, the former queen of England. The Dutch people finally gained their freedom and adopted the Reformed faith.

Lutheranism failed to win the loyalty of the Dutch, although it, as well as Humanism, contributed to religious revolt in Holland. However, after the Peasants' Revolt, Luther's insistence upon the authority of the prince was distasteful to the Dutch who were to revolt against their Spanish ruler. The more democratic Calvinism appealed to them as a way to escape from the corruption of the Roman system.

It must also be remembered that this was the land of Erasmus and the Brethren of the Common Life. The first Dutch New Testament was also published in 1523 so that the Dutch could compare the Roman Church in their land with the New Testament Church.

All of these forces coalesced in a political-ecclesiastical revolt against domination by the Spanish ruler and the pope. Holland was the only land gained for Protestantism after the Counter Reformation got under way.

Up to 1525 those who accepted the Reformation followed Luther, but the Anabaptists gained a strong following from that date until about 1540. From 1540 the Reformation in Holland proceeded along Calvinistic lines. By 1560 the majority of Protestants were Calvinistic, a minority were Anabaptists, led by Menno Simons, and a tiny minority followed Luther's ideas. Neither the passive obedience of Lutheranism nor the revolutionary spirit of Anabaptism had the appeal for the independent Dutch burghers that Calvinism, which insisted upon freedom from tyranny, had. Protestantism spread in spite of the organization of the Inquisition by 1524 to stamp it out in these valuable Spanish possessions.

When Philip II, an earnest and devout Roman Catholic, ascended the throne of Spain after his father, Charles V, abdicated in 1555, he determined to bring the Spanish Netherlands back to the fold of the pope. His vacillation between indulgence and savage cruelty caused the Netherlanders to rise against him. Noblemen of the Netherlands formed the Compromise of Breda in 1565 and presented a petition asking for the suspension of the Inquisition and the laws against heretics. Uprisings in Flanders, Holland and Zeeland by Protestants in 1565 brought the plundering of four hundred Roman churches and the desecration of the host, used in the mass. This profanation determined Philip to take strong measures, and these he took through the Duke of Alva whom he made the regent of the Netherlands. Alva set up a special tribunal backed by the power of ten thousand Spanish soldiers and inaugurated a reign of terror. Between 1567 and 1573 he executed about ten thousand people, and by the end of the century forty thousand had migrated to other countries. Heavy Spanish taxation also threatened to impoverish the Netherlands.

Opposition to the Spanish policy came to be centered in William of Orange, known as the Silent. The standard of revolt was raised in 1568, but William's army was no match for Alva's trained soldiers, and he had to retire to Germany. Because war on land was hopeless, the Dutch became "Beggars of the Sea." They took to the sea by 1569 and preyed upon Spanish commerce. After long sieges, Alva took the revolting cities and engaged in wholesale massacres. Attack upon one city by the Spanish was stopped by the cutting of the dikes and the flooding of the countryside with sea water. In 1576 Antwerp was looted and seven thousand were killed by the Spanish soldiery under Alva's successor. This act, known as the "Spanish fury," aroused such nationalistic spirit that Holland and Zeeland, which were definitely Calvinistic, united with the other provinces in the Pacification of Ghent in 1576 to drive out the Spanish.

Differences of race, language, ways of making a living, and, above all, religion brought about a division between the Roman Catholic Flemish (modern Belgians) in the south and the Calvinistic Dutch in the northern provinces. The seven northern provinces signed the Union of Utrecht in 1579 and in 1581 formally repudiated the sovereignty of the Spanish king. The foundations of the modern state of Holland were laid under the leadership of William of Orange. The Dutch eventually won their war for freedom, but in the process they lost their great leader William to an assassin's dagger in 1584. English aid and England's defeat of the Spanish Armada in 1588 left the Dutch relatively free from Spanish efforts at recapture, but the end of the war and the independence of the Dutch Republic were not formally recognized until the Treaty of Westphalia in 1648. Holland became a great sea power in the seventeenth century, built up a wealthy empire in the Far East and the Western hemisphere, and gave a king to England in 1689.

The Dutch did not neglect the development of church organization and theology during the struggle for national independence. At a national synod in Emden about 1570 it was decided that the church should adopt the Presbyterian system of church government. The consistory, the classis and the synod were to be the units of organization. The synod also adopted the Belgic Confession,[5] which had been prepared by Guido de Bres in 1561 and revised by Francis Junius, a Calvinistic pastor at Antwerp. It was adopted by a Dutch synod as early as 1566 but received approval by the national synod at Dort in 1574. It and the Heidelberg Catechism became the theological standards of the Reformed Church of Holland. The University of Leyden, which was formed in 1575 in gratitude for the freeing of the city from a siege, became a center for Calvinistic theological study. The Dutch Calvinists have always been sturdy defenders and exponents of Christianity.

Victorious Calvinism, however, found its first opposition in Holland in the development of Arminianism. James Arminius (1560–1609), its exponent, was educated with funds given by friends and, later, by the civic authorities of Amsterdam. He studied at Leyden and at Geneva under Beza and traveled widely in Italy. In 1603 he became professor of theology at Leyden. His attempt to modify Calvinism so that, according to him, God might not be considered the author of sin, nor man an automaton in the hands of God, brought down upon him the opposition of his colleague, Francis Gomar. Arminius asked the government to call a national synod concerning the matter, but he died before it was called. The supporters of Arminius,

5 *Ibid.*, Vol. III, pp. 383-436

among whom were such men as Hugo Grotius who wrote on international law, compiled their ideas in the *Remonstrance*[6] of 1610.

Both Arminius and Calvin taught that man, who inherited Adam's sin, is under the wrath of God. But Arminius believed that man was able to initiate his salvation after God had granted him the primary grace to enable his will to cooperate with God.[7] Calvin thought that man's will had been so corrupted by the fall that salvation was entirely a matter of divine grace. Arminius accepted election but believed that the decree to save some and damn others had "its foundation in the foreknowledge of God."[8] Thus election was conditional rather than unconditional. Calvin, on the other hand, accepted an unconditional election by a sovereign God to grace and condemnation. Arminius also believed that Christ's death was sufficient for all but that it was only efficient for believers. Calvin limited the atonement to those elected to salvation.[9] Arminius also taught that men might resist the saving grace of God;[10] whereas Calvin maintained that grace was irresistible. Arminius answered the Calvinistic insistence upon the perseverance of saints by stating that God would give the saints grace so that they need not fall but that the Scriptures seemed to teach that it was possible for man to fall away from salvation.[11] Arminius did not want to make God the author of sin[12] nor man an automaton. He thought that these modifications of Calvinism would eliminate those dangers to theology.

Not until 1618 was a synod held at Dort. It was really an international Calvinistic assembly because 28 of the 130 present were Calvinists from England, Scotland, the Palatinate, Switzerland and other countries. The 13 Arminians came before the meeting in the role of defendants.

Five Calvinistic articles opposing the *Remonstrance* of 1610 were drawn up, and the clerical followers of Arminius were deprived of their positions. Not until 1625 did persecution of Arminians cease. Arminianism had considerable influence upon

---

[6] *Ibid.*, Vol. III, pp. 545-549; H. Bettenson, *Documents of the Christian Church* (New York: Oxford University Press, 1947), pp. 376-377.

[7] James Arminius, *Works*, trans. by James Nichols and W. R. Bagnall (Buffalo: Derby, Miller & Orton, 3 vols., 1853), Vol. I, p. 329, Vol. II, pp. 472-473.

[8] *Ibid.*, Vol. I, pp. 248.

[9] *Ibid.*, Vol. I, pp. 316-317.

[10] *Ibid.*, Vol. I, p. 254, Vol. II, p. 497.

[11] *Ibid.*, Vol. I, pp. 254, 281.

[12] *Ibid.*, Vol. II, p. 490.

one wing of the Anglican Church in the seventeenth century, the Methodist movement of the eighteenth century and the Salvation Army.

BIBLIOGRAPHY

Henry Cowan's biography entitled *John Knox* (New York: G. P. Putnam's Sons, 1905) gives an excellent account of the life and work of John Knox in the Scottish Reformation.

The *History of the Reformation in Scotland* (New York: Philosophical Library, 2 vols., 1950) by John Knox himself and edited by William C. Dickinson, is an interesting first-hand account of his work.

The general works cited at the end of Chapter XXVI have useful sections on the development of the Reformed faith in the countries that have been discussed in the preceding chapter.

Chapter XXX

THE REFORMATION AND PURITANISM IN ENGLAND

The Protestant Reformation created four major types of faith. The Lutheran, Anabaptist and Reformed aspects of the Reformation have already been considered. The fourth and, for America, one of the most important, was the Anglican Reformation in England. It may be ranked with the Lutheran movement in its conservative approach to reform. Having no dominant ecclesiastical leader, such as Calvin or Luther, it was dominated by the ruler who became the head of the national church. For that reason it began as a political movement, continued as a religious movement, and concluded with the Elizabethan settlement in the middle of the sixteenth century. Its scope, direction and progress were in each case determined by the religious convictions of the ruler.

I. Reforming the Church in England

A. *Causes of the Reformation in England.*

The Lollards, who had been organized to spread the teachings of John Wycliffe, had never been stamped out. On the contrary, their teachings had circulated in the homes of the more humble people of England through a religious underground movement during the fifteenth century. Their emphasis upon the authority of the Scriptures and the need of a personal relation to Christ was revived with the emergence of the political Reformation in England in the first quarter of the sixteenth century.

One must also remember that the Tudor rulers, who ruled England between 1485 and 1603, had created a strong national state in which the ruler through the army and a bureaucracy was able to give to the rising middle class the security that was essential to business. In return, the middle class accepted restrictions on their liberty and cooperated with the ruler, who also used them in the government. The older feudal nobility had practically disappeared by 1485 because it had committed class suicide during the Wars of the Roses. King and middle class united in promoting the welfare of the land. Because of this there was a rising tide of national consciousness which gave support to the ruler in his efforts to separate the English Church from the papacy. Control of much land in England by the Roman Church; papal taxation, which took good English money to Rome; and church courts, which were rivals of the royal courts, angered both ruler and subjects. These problems caused the nation to support the ruler when he decided to break with Rome.

The intellectual factor must not be ignored. The Biblical Humanists or Oxford Reformers of Oxford University, such as John Colet, dean of St. Paul's Church, began early in the fifteenth century to study the Bible in the original tongue through the medium of Erasmus' Greek New Testament and to expound the meaning of the Bible to their people. These Humanists were extremely critical of the failure that they saw in the Roman Church and were anxious to bring about reform. William Tyndale and Miles Coverdale, who later made the Scriptures available to the English people in their own tongue, were in this same tradition of reform. Tyndale published three thousand copies of his English New Testament at Worms in 1525. This translation from Erasmus' Greek Testament was the first printed English New Testament. It was distributed in England by friendly merchants. Although Tyndale was martyred near Brussels in 1536, his work lived on and helped to stimulate religious reform in England. Miles Coverdale published the first complete printed English translation of the whole Bible in 1535. The student of the Reformation is always impressed with the way in which the fortunes of the Reformation were so closely identified with the translation of the Bible into the common tongue of the people.

Luther's writings were also circulated widely in England. Scholars at Oxford and Cambridge studied his *Babylonian Captivity* with relish because of its criticism of the abuses of the Roman Church. In 1521 Henry VIII attacked this tract in a scurrilious work called *Defence of the Seven Sacraments*. The grateful pope gave him the title of "Defender of the Faith," and this title has been used by the Protestant rulers of England since that time. Public burning of Luther's books did not stop

[355]

the spread of his ideas, and thus men, such as Tyndale and Thomas Cranmer, were attracted to Protestant ideas.

The direct cause of the coming of the Anglican Reformation was not so much the love affairs of Henry VIII as his desire to have a male heir. It seemed that he and Catherine could never have a son. In order to get a divorce from her and the right to marry Anne Boleyn, with whom he was in love, he had to bring the Roman Church in England under his control. Henry's action constituted the direct and personal cause for the beginning of the Reformation.

B. *Political Reformation under Henry VIII.*

Henry VIII, who ruled from 1509 to 1547, was a handsome, generous, strong, cultured prince, who knew theology, was a good musician, and could speak Latin, French and Spanish as well as English. He enjoyed the chase, archery and tennis, sports which helped to make him more popular with the English people than his parsimonious father Henry VII had been. His father had endeavored to relate his line to the important royal families of Europe by strategic marriages. His daughter Margaret was married to James of Scotland. (Her grandson, James VI of Scotland, became James I of England in 1603.) His son Arthur was married to a Spanish princess, Catherine of Aragon. When Arthur died, the miserly king, in order not to lose Catherine's dowry, persuaded the pope to grant a dispensation so that Catherine could be married to Arthur's younger brother, Henry. Henry and Catherine had one child. Later this child ruled as Mary Tudor.

When it became apparent that he could not have a son by this marriage, Henry became concerned because he believed that England would need a male ruler after his death in order to see the land through the period of international turbulence. He also thought that possibly God was punishing him for marrying his brother's widow, an action prohibited by both canon law and Leviticus 20:21. Falling in love with the pretty Anne Boleyn, Henry ordered his adviser Cardinal Wolsey to negotiate with Clement VII for a divorce from Catherine. Clement VII was unable to grant this request because in 1527 he was under the control of Catherine's nephew, the powerful Charles V, the ruler of Spain and the emperor of Germany. Henry accused Wolsey of high treason when he failed to get the divorce, but Wolsey died before Henry could execute him.

Thomas Cromwell now became Henry's chief minister, and the Protestant Thomas Cranmer was made archbishop of Canterbury. Because it was apparent that the pope would not grant him a divorce, Henry decided to get it through the English clergy who could be coerced into granting it by Parliament. The Tudor Parliament was representative of the people but was responsible to the king rather than to the people because the Tudors ruled as dictators, concealing the iron fist in a velvet glove. Thus the Reformation was initiated in England by the lay authority of the ruler and Parliament. The Reformation Parliament lasted from 1529 to 1536.

In 1531 Henry accused the English clergy of violating a statute prohibiting recognition of any appointee of the pope without the ruler's consent because they had accepted Wolsey as a papal legate, even though Wolsey had been Henry's trusted adviser. Henry had them accept himself as head of the church in England "as far as the law of Christ allows." He also fined them 118,000 pounds. He again fined them in 1532 and forced the clergy in Convocation, the national meeting of the Roman Church in England, to agree in the *Submission of the Clergy* that they would promulgate no papal bull in England without the ruler's consent. In this manner the clergy accepted Henry as their head,[1] and his marriage to Catherine was declared invalid in 1533.

Henry then turned to Parliament for aid. Parliament prohibited residence of the English clergy outside of the country. Another act forbade the payment of annates to the pope. Parliament banned appeals from church courts in England to the papal courts in Rome.[2] The most important step in the separation of the Church in England from the papacy was then taken in the Act of Supremacy of 1534. The Act declared that the king was "the only supreme head in earth of the Church of England."[3] This constituted the political break with Rome. Parliament in the same year passed the Act of Succession which gave the throne to the children of Henry and Anne. Subjects were to take an oath to observe the statute and to repudiate papal authority. When the courageous Thomas More refused to do so, he was executed. Henry, now head of the English Church, had married Anne in 1533.

1 H. Bettenson, *Documents of the Christian Church* (New York: Oxford University Press, 1947), pp. 308-309.
2 *Ibid.*, pp. 309-315.
3 *Ibid.*, 321-323.

Henry believed that his settlement would be final only if he could tie the middle class of England to the changes he had made by giving them an economic interest in the change. With this thought in mind, he cast covetous eyes upon the property of the Roman Church and had Cromwell gather evidence, some of it genuine, of the sins of the monks. In 1536 Parliament ordered the closing of all monasteries with less than two hundred pounds annual income. About 375 monasteries were closed, and their property taken over by the crown. In 1539 the larger ones were closed by act of Parliament. Twenty-eight abbots disappeared from the House of Lords. The king kept part of the lands and wealth for himself; the rest he gave or sold cheaply to the middle class landed gentry. These people became a new nobility and loyal supporters of the ecclesiastical changes that Henry and Parliament had made. Henry gained an income of approximately ten thousand pounds annually. Because the dispossessed monks must be cared for, the state, for the first time, began to engage in relief by grants of aid to some of the monks.

The passage of the Six Articles by Parliament in 1539 was proof that Henry had broken only the ecclesiastical tie between the Church in England and Rome. These Articles reaffirmed transubstantiation, Communion in one kind, celibacy and auricular confession.[4] In theology the Church of England remained true to Rome. Henry had made concessions to reform in 1536 by issuing the Ten Articles and by authorizing an English translation of the Bible. Hence the Great Bible was issued in 1539 as a revision of the work of Tyndale and Coverdale. It was also known as the "Chained Bible" because it was chained to its stand in many churches. When the danger of foreign attack passed, Henry again enforced the reactionary Six Articles of 1539.

In the meantime, Henry had tired of Anne Boleyn, especially because their child had been a girl, whom they named Elizabeth. In 1536 Anne was tried and beheaded on charges of adultery. Henry next married Jane Seymour, who bore the son he wanted before she died. Later Henry married Anne of Cleves, whom he divorced; Catherine Howard, whom he had executed; and Catherine Parr, who had the singular fortune to outlive him.

4 *Ibid.*, p. 331.

In his will[5] he stated that after his death his son Edward should take the throne. Edward would be followed by Mary, the daughter of Catherine of Aragon, and Mary by Elizabeth, the daughter of Anne Boleyn. When Henry finally died, the English Church was a national church with the ruler as its head, but it was Roman Catholic in doctrine. The Bible was, however, available to the people in their own tongue. Henry's son Edward was to carry out the religious phase of the Reformation that Henry had begun as an ecclesiastical movement between 1527 and 1547.

C. Religious Reformation under Edward VI.

Because Edward VI was only nine when he came to the throne, his mother's brother, the Duke of Somerset, was appointed as regent. Somerset had Protestant sympathies and believed in religious liberty. He therefore persuaded the young king to institute changes that would make the Reformation in England religious and theological as well as political and ecclesiastical. In 1547 Parliament granted the cup to the laity in the Communion service, repealed treason and heresy laws and the Romish Six Articles, legalized the marriage of priests in 1549, and ordered the dissolution of the chantries, which were endowed chapels for the saying of masses for the soul of the one who made the endowment.

Positive action was also taken by Somerset and the young ruler. Church services were to be in the common tongue rather than in Latin. An Act of Uniformity in 1549 provided for the use of a Book of Common Prayer which was the work of Cranmer. The book emphasized the use of English in the services, the reading of the Bible and the participation of the congregation in worship. The second and more Protestant edition, issued in 1552, reflected Calvinistic influences. The churches were ordered to use it by a second Act of Uniformity.[6] This Prayer Book, with slight modifications adopted in Elizabeth's reign, is the prayer book that the Anglican Church has used since that time. Cranmer also engaged in the drawing up of a creed with the advice of various theologians, such as John Knox. The resulting Forty-two Articles were made the creed of the Anglican Church by Act of Parliament in 1552.

5 Carl Stephenson and Frederick G. Marcham, *Sources of English Constitutional History* (New York: Harper & Brothers, 1937), pp. 323-324.

6 Henry Gee and William J. Hardy, compilers, *Documents Illustrative of English Church History* (London: The Macmillan Co., 1896, reprinted 1921), pp. 369-372 cf. pp. 358-366.

The Articles were somewhat Calvinistic in tone, especially in the matter of predestination and the view of the Communion. Signature of this act was followed by the young king's death.

D. *Catholic Reaction under Mary Tudor.*

Mary, who ruled from 1553 to 1558, was the daughter of Henry VIII by Catherine of Aragon. Her reign coincided with the development of the Counter Reformation in the Roman Church on the Continent and may be thought of as the English parallel to the Counter Reformation on the Continent. Advised by Cardinal Reginald Pole, Mary, who was Roman Catholic to the core, forced Parliament to restore religious practices in England to what they were at the death of her father in 1547 and to repudiate the changes that had been made under Edward. Parliament agreed to the necessary measures, but it would not restore the lands that had been taken from the Roman Church during the reign of Henry VIII. Mary married Philip II of Spain in 1554, but the marriage was unpopular with the English people, and Philip never requited Mary's love.

About one-quarter of the English clergy refused to accept these changes and lost their parishes. They were forced to flee to Geneva and to Frankfort for refuge if they were not to perish in the persecution that Mary initiated. About three hundred, mainly from the commercial areas of Southeastern England, were martyred for their faith. Chief among them were Latimer, Ridley and Cranmer. Latimer encouraged Ridley at the stake by his remark that their burning would light a candle in England that by God's grace would never be put out. Cranmer at first recanted but later recanted his recantation and, when he was burned, put the hand that had signed the recantation in the fire until it was burned. Nothing strengthened the cause of Protestantism more than the death of these brave martyrs. Their earnest conviction and courage convinced Englishmen of the truth of their opinions. Mary's great mistakes were the Spanish marriage, the restoration of the authority of the pope and this persecution. Englishmen have never favored extremes, and they reacted against Mary's extreme as some had against the extreme Protestant changes under Edward VI. The way was prepared for a compromise settlement with the accession of Elizabeth.

E. *The Elizabethan Settlement.*

When Elizabeth ascended the throne at the age of twenty-five, she faced many problems. Mary Stuart had a valid claim to the throne; Spain was ready to intervene to substantiate Philip's claim as the husband of Mary to the English throne; and England was divided between the Protestant and Roman religious views. Elizabeth could hardly be other than a Protestant because the Roman clergy would not admit the legality of her parent's marriage, but she did not want to risk open conflict with the powers supporting the pope. For that reason she favored the course that would be acceptable to most of the people of England, who favored a moderate settlement of religion that would avoid the extremes of either side.

Elizabeth had Parliament pass the Act of Supremacy in 1559[7] which made the queen "the only supreme governor of this realm" in spiritual and ecclesiastical as well as temporal matters. This title gave less offense than that of "supreme head of the church," upon which Henry VIII had insisted, because, while it gave the queen administrative authority, it implied that matters of faith and morals should be settled by the Church of England.

An Act of Uniformity[8] provided for the use of the Prayer Book of 1552 with only slight modifications. Absence from church was to be punished by a shilling fine. The Forty-two Articles were revised by the omission of articles condemnatory of the Antinomians, Anabaptists and Millenarians, and the reorganization of others until there were thirty-nine articles. The Thirty-nine Articles were accepted by Parliament in 1563 as the creed of the Anglican Church[9] to which all pastors must subscribe. This creed, with slight modifications in 1571, has been the creed of the Anglican Church since that time.

These steps, even though moderate, aroused the undying emnity of the pope, and in 1570 Pope Pius V issued a bull excommunicating Elizabeth and freeing her subjects from allegiance to her.[10] Elizabeth retaliated by an act aimed at the Jesuits who planned to recapture England for the papacy. A school had been set up at Douai on the French coast where men could be trained by the Jesuits to minister secretly to the followers of the pope in England. The pope then enlisted the

[7] Bettenson, *op. cit.*, pp. 332-333.
[8] *Ibid.*, pp. 333-339; Gee and Hardy, *op. cit.*, pp. 458-467.
[9] P. Schaff, *Creeds of Christendom* (New York: Charles Scribner's Sons, 3 vols., 6th ed., 1890), Vol. III, pp. 486-516; Gee and Hardy, *op. cit.*, pp. 477-480.
[10] Bettenson, *op cit.*, pp. 340-341.

stronghold of R. Catholicism

aid of Philip of Spain to recover England for the Roman Church. Philip was only too glad to do this because he was a loyal son of the Church of Rome and because he knew that Elizabeth was secretly aiding his rebellious Dutch subjects. In 1588 he gathered a great fleet known as the Spanish Armada and sailed against England. His fleet was ignominiously defeated by the English fleet, which consisted of smaller, more maneuverable ships manned by expert sailors. This victory established England as the champion of Protestantism in Europe and blasted the pope's last hope of regaining England for the Roman Church.

The Reformation brought the Bible to the English people in their own tongue. England became the champion of Protestantism in Europe and aided the Dutch and French Calvinistic Protestants against their Catholic rulers. A state church was adopted. Irish bitterness toward England was intensified because Ireland remained loyal to the papacy. An Irish revolt near the end of her reign taxed Elizabeth's financial genius to the limit. The sale and gift of the land, taken from the Roman Church, to the middle class created a new Tudor nobility. The abbots, who lost their monasteries, no longer met with the House of Lords. The need for an agency to take over the welfare work of the Church led to an extension of the activities of the state in this area. The Elizabethan settlement did put England on the road to greatness and empire, but the road ahead was not to be without trouble. The defeat of Spain and the pope left the English rulers free to give attention to the problem of Puritanism. From 1567 to 1660 the Puritans were a dominant force in English domestic affairs.

II. Puritans and Separatists

A. *The Puritans.*

Victory in the struggle with the papacy did not give the Queen rest because of the rising power of the Puritans, who threatened to change the episcopal state church into a Presbyterian or Congregational church. The Puritans contended that too many "rags of popery" were still in the Anglican Church, and they wanted to "purify" the Anglican Church in accordance with the Bible, which they accepted as the infallible rule of faith and life. This desire led to their being nicknamed Puritans by 1568. Up until 1570 their main objections were directed against the continued use in the liturgy of the church of ritual and vestments that seemed popish to them. They opposed the use of saints' days, clerical absolution, the sign of the Cross, godparents in baptism, kneeling for Communion, and the use of the surplice by the minister. They also deplored the loose observance of Sunday by the Anglicans. Cambridge became the university center where the Puritans had their greatest influence.

Puritanism continued to grow and won the support of many lawyers, merchants and country gentry. After the ending of the danger from the pope, Elizabeth had an act passed against the Puritans in 1593.[11] This act gave the authorities the right to imprison the Puritans for failure to attend the Anglican Church. It must be remembered that the Puritans were not dissenters, but a party in the Anglican Church which, in the case of Cartwright and his followers, wanted a Presbyterian or, as Jacob and his followers, a Congregational state church. The latter group formed the group of Puritans known as Independents. The Independents must be distinguished from the Separatists who wanted separation of the Church and state and congregational government of the Church. Both groups continued to grow in strength in spite of opposition from the ruler and to give useful criticism to the Church of England. Extreme fashions in dress, laxity in keeping Sunday and the lack of consciousness of sin were all condemned. The roots of English Nonconformist sects and New England Congregationalism were in the Puritan movement.

A few years before his death Richard Hooker (ca. 1554–1600), in order to meet the Puritan threat to the state church, wrote *Of the Laws of Ecclesiastical Polity,* a work primarily philosophical in nature. In it Hooker maintains that law, given by God and discovered by reason, is basic. Obedience to the ruler, ruling by consent of the people and according to law, is necessary because the ruler was head of both state and church. Members of the state are also members of the state church and in both areas are subject to divine law. Bishops, subordinate to the king, are to supervise the state church. Hooker opposed both the tendency of the Puritans to separate the Church and state and the papal claims to power over the state. It was little wonder that the Puritan theologians opposed his ideas because they believed that the people, under God, were the source of sovereignty in the Church.

The emergence of Thomas Cartwright (1535–1603) as pro-

11 *Ibid.,* pp. 343-344.

fessor of theology at Cambridge about 1570 shifted the emphasis in the Puritan efforts from reform of liturgy to reform in theology and church government. Insistence upon the final authority of the Scriptures led his followers to adopt a Calvinistic theology that would make the Thirty-nine Articles even more Calvinistic. In his lectures on the Book of Acts in 1570 Cartwright opposed government by bishops. The government of the church, he wrote, should be in the control of a presbytery of bishops or elders who had only spiritual functions, and each congregation should choose its own minister. This system was essentially the Calvinistic system of church government by elders who were elected by the congregation. Later Cartwright and another Cambridge man, Walter Travers, wrote a *Book of Discipline* in which they advocated the setting up of a presbytery in every diocese of the Church. He laid the foundations of the English Presbyterianism which was so influential between 1643 and 1648. Presbyterianism in modern England owes its existence to his initial work.

A number of the Puritans, who did not follow the Presbyterian pattern of Cartwright, adopted the ideas of Henry Jacob (1563–1624). Jacob may be considered to be the founder of the Independents or Puritan Congregationalists. The Independents were not so inclined to separatism as the followers of Robert Browne, who emphasized the church covenant as the link that bound Christians together. Jacob was one of the signers of the Millenary Petition to James I in 1603 which asked for a change from episcopacy in England. He was imprisoned for his view that each congregation was to be left free in the state church to choose its own pastor, determine its policies, and manage its own affairs. About 1605 Jacob migrated to Holland and became the minister of Englishmen in Middleburg. John Robinson, pastor of the Separatist congregation in Holland whose members later migrated to Plymouth, and Jacob had considerable influence upon each other. Jacob returned to England in 1616 and became the pastor of a congregation of Independents in Southwark, London from 1616 to 1622. Independent or Congregational Puritanism in England grew slowly from this humble beginning until under Oliver Cromwell it became more powerful than Presbyterianism.

In 1658 at Savoy in London, Congregationalist followers of Jacob and Separatist congregations formulated a Calvinistic

THE DEVELOPMENT OF ENGLISH PROTESTANTISM

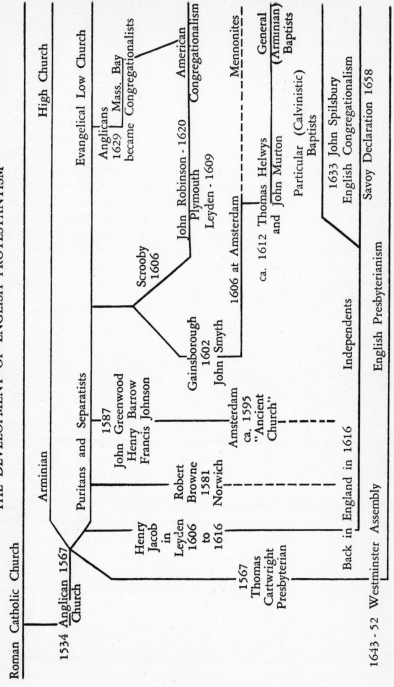

creed known as the Savoy Declaration.[12] English Congregationalism is a lineal descendant of this Puritan Congregationalism rather than that of the Separatist Congregationalism of Robert Browne, although the Brownists were possibly a part of the strong Congregationalist group at the time of Cromwell.

B. *Separatist Puritans.*

The major point of difference between the Presbyterian and Independent Puritans so far discussed and the Separatist Puritans was the idea of the church covenant by which the latter group bound themselves in loyalty to Christ and one another apart from a state church. The following diagram will give some idea of the development of the various Puritan groups.

The earliest group of Separatist Congregationalists who set up a church based on a covenant was that organized by Richard

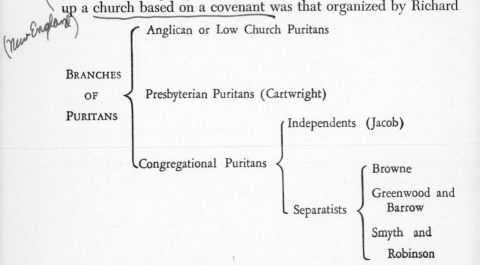

Fitz about 1570. Robert Browne (ca. 1550–1633), who graduated from Cambridge in 1572 in the stirring days of Cartwright's proclamation of Presbyterian ideas, gathered together a group under a church covenant in Norwich in 1581. From there he was forced to flee with his congregation to Holland, where he wrote three treatises elaborating the principles of Separatist Congregationalism. The most important was entitled *A Treatise of Reformation without Tarrying for Anie.* In this work Browne argued that believers were to be united to Christ and to one another by a voluntary covenant; that officers were to be chosen by the members; and that no congregation was to have authority

[12] Schaff, *op. cit.,* Vol. III, pp. 707-729.

over another. Unlike the Independent Congregationalists, the Separatists would have nothing to do with the state church. Browne returned to England in 1584 and in 1591 was ordained in the Anglican Church which he served until his death. But the advanced principles which he had developed were to live on. His congregation possibly returned to Norwich from Holland.

Browne's principles of advanced Congregationalism were somewhat modified by the congregation that appeared in London about 1587 under the leadership of John Greenwood and Henry Barrow, who were both hanged by the authorities for their views. Francis Johnson became the pastor of the flock that migrated to Holland. By 1640 several hundred of these Barrowists were in England.

A third Separatist group of Congregationalists appeared in Gainsborough and Scrooby in 1606. The Scrooby group was led by John Robinson, under whose leadership the group finally settled in Leyden, Holland in 1609. William Bradford, of later fame in Plymouth, was a member of this group. It was members of this group who finally migrated to America in 1620 in the *Mayflower*. It is interesting to note that the immigrants applied the covenant idea to political life by entering into the Mayflower Compact before landing at Plymouth. Later in 1629 the Puritan Anglicans of the Massachusetts Bay Company migrated to America and were won over to Congregationalism by Plymouth settlers. Because of persecution the Gainsborough group also migrated to Amsterdam in 1606 or 1607 under the leadership of John Smyth (ca. 1570–1612). There they came under the influence of the Mennonites. In 1608 or 1609 Smyth baptized himself, Thomas Helwys and other members of his flock by pouring. Part of his congregation became Mennonites after a long period of negotiation for inclusion in that body.

Thomas Helwys, John Murton and their followers returned to England about 1611 and organized the first English Baptist Church. This group practiced baptism by affusion and held to Arminian doctrines with which they had become familiar during the Arminian dispute in Holland. Because of this they were known as General Baptists. Thus the first English Baptist Church emerged from the Separatist Congregationalist group.

The stronger group of Calvinistic or Particular Baptists originated in a schism from Henry Jacob's congregation in London in 1633. They held to the baptism of believers by immersion and a Calvinistic theology that emphasized a limited atonement. It was this congregation, first led by John Spilsbury, that became the main influence in the English Baptist movement. The antecedents of the American Baptist movement are to be found in this group. Although Roger Williams was not a Baptist when he went to America, he had imbibed Baptist principles, and he used these as soon as opposition to his preaching developed among the Congregationalists.

C. *The Puritan Struggle with the Stuarts.*

The religious forces generated by the exiles under Mary Tudor, which exiles had become acquainted with Calvinism in Europe, and by the Geneva Bible of 1560 resulted in the Puritanism that caused Elizabeth no little difficulty. When her successor, James VI of Scotland, became James I of England in 1603, the Puritans hoped that this Calvinistic king, who liked episcopacy, would set up a Presbyterian government in the Anglican Church. To emphasize their hope they presented him with the Millenary Petition, signed by nearly a thousand Puritan ministers, upon his arrival in 1603 and asked that the Anglican Church be completely "purified" in liturgy and polity.[13] The pudgy, ricket-deformed, vain, garrulous ruler called the Hampton Court Conference in 1604. When the Puritans again demanded reform, James became angry and said that he would "harry them out of the kingdom" if they would not conform, and, as for Presbyterian polity in the state church, he said that Presbyterianism "agreeth as well with monarchy as God and the devil." Permission to make a new English translation of the Scriptures was the net result of this meeting, and a group of learned divines began work on the Bible popularly known as the Authorized or King James Version. This translation was completed in 1611 and in time replaced the Genevan Bible in the affections of the Anglo-Saxons.

The issues between James and the Puritans included more than the religious disagreement over Presbyterian or episcopal forms of government for the state church. The judicial issue concerned the struggle between the legal common law courts of England and the extra-legal court system that the Tudors had set up to give them complete control of their subjects. Another problem concerned the question as to whether monarch or Parliament was sovereign. Was the king, the divinely ap-

---

[13] Gee and Hardy, *op. cit.*, pp. 508-511.

HENRY VIII

JOHN CALVIN

JOHN KNOX

JOHN WESLEY

GEORGE FOX

PHILIP SPENER

ROGER WILLIAMS

pointed sovereign, responsible only to God, or was he appointed by the consent of the people in Parliament? The economic question involved the problem of whether the king could levy taxes or whether that was the exclusive prerogative of Parliament. Unfortunately for the Stuarts, neither James nor his three successors had any of the skill of the Tudors in hiding the iron fist in the velvet glove of a monarch apparently supported by Parliament. During Elizabeth's and James's reign the Puritans had been winning adherents to their views among the merchants of the city and the country gentry. These groups were forced into opposition to the ruler on all the points just mentioned and bided their time until they could act.

Charles I, who ruled from 1625 until he was executed in 1649, was an honorable, brave, able but weak man who believed more strongly in the marriage of divine right monarchy and episcopacy than his father did. He also insisted on a subservient Parliament and, when he could not get one, ruled without Parliament from 1629 until 1640. Many Puritans, wearied with hoping for better conditions in England, migrated to America. At least twenty thousand left England for America between 1628 and 1642.

Charles' appointment of Laud, a man of small stature and narrow mind, as the Archbishop of Canterbury created a set of conditions that in time brought his downfall. Laud was favorable to uniformity in polity and to Arminian theology, which the Calvinistic Puritans disliked, and he appointed Arminians to the best church positions.

The attempt to force a new Book of Common Prayer upon the Church of Scotland in 1637 proved to be the incident that started the struggle between the Puritans and their ruler. The Scotch rebelled against this attempt to change their liturgy, polity and faith in order to have religious uniformity in the two lands. This was the period when Jenny Geddes was supposed to have hurled the stool on which she was sitting at the head of the minister for daring to "say mass at my lug" (ear) in historic St. Giles' Church in Edinburgh. In 1638 the Scottish leaders signed a National Covenant to defend Presbyterianism and invaded England. Charles made an attempt to repel the invasion but finally had to buy them off. The Scotch marched into England a second time and remained in the north as a threat. To get money he called a Parliament in 1640, which was known as the Long Parliament because it was not replaced until 1660.

The Long Parliament, before granting any funds, imprisoned or executed Charles' advisers, abolished all the illegal courts and took control of finance in the state, but it could not reach an agreement on the subject of religion. Moderates, who wanted to retain episcopacy, were known as the Royalists or Cavaliers, and the Puritan country gentry and merchants, who desired Presbyterian or Congregational polity and doctrine, were known as Puritans or Roundheads. In 1642 the Royalists withdrew from Parliament after Charles tried unsuccessfully to arrest five members of the House of Commons for treason, and the Civil War, which was to last until 1646, began. Success in the conflict came to the Puritans of the Long Parliament because of the unexpected military skill of Oliver Cromwell. His well-trained and highly disciplined cavalry of godly Puritans, the Ironsides, became the model upon which the victorious New Model army was organized. By 1646 the king was captured by Parliament and, after his subsequent escape and a short second civil war in 1648, was executed.

Parliament, in the meantime, abolished episcopacy in 1643 and commissioned the Westminster Assembly, composed of 151 English Puritans and, to secure Scottish aid in the war, 8 Scottish Presbyterians, to advise it on the polity and creed of the national church.[14] The group held 163 daily sessions between 1643 and 1649, during which time its real work was done although it was not disbanded until 1652. The Directory of Worship along Presbyterian lines was completed in 1644 and accepted by both the Scottish and English Parliaments in 1645. The Form of Government, which advocated Presbyterian polity for the national church, was completed by 1645 and adopted by Parliament in 1648. The Calvinistic Westminster Confession of Faith, the Assembly's most important work, was completed by 1646 and adopted by the Scotch in 1647 and by the English in 1648.[15] Thus the state church of England was a Calvinistic Presbyterian church by 1648. The Longer and the Shorter Catechisms were also completed by 1648. With these things done, the real work of the Westminster Assembly of divines was completed. The constitutions of the larger American Presbyterian churches include all the above documents.

[14] Schaff, *op. cit.*, Vol. I, pp. 727-816.
[15] Schaff, *op. cit.*, Vol. III, pp. 598-673.

The Presbyterians in Parliament had not paid as much attention as they should have to the army, which had become Congregationalist in sentiment. Tired of the Presbyterian refusal to pay arrears of wages to the army and of their unwillingness to have any but a Presbyterian state church, Cromwell, an Independent or Congregationalist, ordered a Colonel Pride to "purge parliament" in 1648. The Presbyterians were driven out, leaving a "rump" of Congregationalists in charge. Cromwell, after the execution of Charles in 1649, created a commonwealth headed by himself. He dismissed the Rump Parliament in 1653, set up a Protectorate, and until 1660 ruled as dictator with the aid of the army. He was tolerant in matters of religion.

After his death the Long Parliament voted itself out of existence in 1660, and the English, tired of the strict way of life of the Puritans, recalled Charles II to become their ruler and adopted episcopacy again. A stiff code of laws, known as the Clarendon Code,[16] put positions in the state church and state in the hands of Anglicans and forbade the meetings of Puritans. About two thousand Calvinistic clergymen were driven from their churches, and Puritanism became a part of the Nonconformist tradition of England. Its most distinguished writers were Milton, whose epic poem, *Paradise Lost,* is a theological treatise in verse form and whose tract, the *Areopagitica,* defended freedom of thought, and Bunyan, whose allegory of the progress of the christian life in *Pilgrim's Progress* has brought help to many since that time. Not until James II was driven from England in the Glorious Revolution of 1689 was toleration granted to the Nonconformists of England.

III. Roman Catholic "Puritanism"

Jansenism in the Roman Catholic Church of France was the Continental counterpart of English Puritanism. Both found their main theological roots in Augustine's views. The Jansenist movement was a reaction from the Thomistic orthodoxy of the Council of Trent to a Bible-based Augustinianism that would vitalize personal life. The movement took its name from the bishop of Ypres, Cornelius Jansen (1585–1638), who had been a professor at Louvain. In 1640 his book *Augustinus,* was published posthumously. The book taught that conversion came through grace, which was irresistible and which reason could

protestant influence in R.C. Church

not make known.[17] Jansen's views were widely received among devout Frenchmen but at no place were they more strongly held than at the nunnery of Port Royal near Paris. His ideas were opposed by the Jesuits whom he accused of a semi-Pelagianism because they emphasized human effort as well as grace in salvation.

Blaise Pascal (1623–1662) supported the Jansenists. He had been a sickly but precocious child who had been trained in mathematics by his father. When his father withheld geometry books to make him study languages, the boy worked out thirty-two of Euclid's propositions without previous knowledge of them. Pascal became the leading mathematician of France. In 1654 a profound religious experience made the teachings of Jansen and the Bible, which he had accepted about five years earlier, real to him, and he threw his efforts into the defense of Jansenism and Port Royal, where his sister Jacqueline had become a nun in 1652. Faith in mystical communion with God was his major emphasis. He wrote a volume called *Provincial Letters* in 1656–1657 in which he attacked the questionable moral code of the Jesuits. His famous *Pensees* appeared after his death in 1670. In it he emphasized the corruption of man and the redemptive power of God in Christ as over against the way in which the senses and reason might deceive man.

But not even Pascal's able defense could save the cause for which he fought. Port Royal was razed in 1710 by royal order, and Louis XIV, influenced by the Jesuits, persecuted the Jansenists. The new leader, Pasquier Quesnel (1634–1719), had to flee to Holland. Clement XI, urged on by the Jesuits, condemned Quesnel's writings in a papal bull issued in 1713. In 1723 a Jansenist Catholic Church was organized in Holland. Such was the end of attempts to promote Augustinianism in the Roman Church.

BIBLIOGRAPHY

Tudor Puritanism (Chicago: The University of Chicago Press, 1939) by Marshall M. Knappen is an excellent study of the rise of Puritanism in Elizabeth's reign.

The *Rise of Puritanism* (New York: Columbia University Press, 1938) by William Haller is a helpful study of the writings of the leading Puritans.

Harry G. Plum describes the fate of Puritanism after 1660 in *Restoration Puritanism* (Chapel Hill: The University of North Carolina Press, 1943).

Andrew Pearson in his *Thomas Cartwright and Elizabethan Puritanism 1553-1603* (Cambridge, England: The University Press, 1925) authoritatively describes the rise of Presbyterian Puritanism.

[17] Bettenson, *op. cit.*, pp. 377-378.

THE REFORMATION AND PURITANISM IN ENGLAND

Champlin Burrage in his *The English Dissenters* (Cambridge, England: The University Press, 2 vols., 1912) has an excellent historical study of the various Presbyterian and Congregationalist groups that developed in Puritanism. The second volume contains important documents written by them. The writer has followed Burrage's interpretation of the relationships between the Puritans and the Separatists.

The most useful study of the Westminster Assembly is *The Westminster Assembly and Its Work* (New York: Oxford University Press, 1931) by Benjamin B. Warfield.

H. Gee and W. J. Hardy's *Documents Illustrative of English Church History* (London: The Macmillan Co., 1921) contains most of the essential documents of interest to the student of this period.

The general works on the Reformation mentioned in the bibliography at the end of Chapter XXVI have useful sections on religion in England between 1527 and 1689.

The role of Port Royal in the Jansenist movement is described in *The Story of Port Royal* (London: John Murray, 1907) by Ethel Romanes.

Emile Cailliet ably pictures the work and contributions of Pascal in the Jansenist controversy in his *Pascal* (Philadelphia: The Westminster Press, 1945).

Chapter XXXI

COUNTER REFORMATION AND EVALUATION

Protestantism seemed to be well on the way to winning all Europe north of the Alps by 1545. It was firmly planted in Germany, France, Scandinavia, Switzerland, England and Scotland. But it won only Holland after 1560 because a wave of religious energy vitalized the Church of Rome. This was the Counter Reformation or Catholic Reformation, which brought internal reform and resulted in the formulation of an official statement of doctrine. It was largely under aristocratic leadership and emphasized reform by direction from the top. It also unleashed forces that were to bring about a final struggle between Protestantism and the papacy in Germany during the Thirty Years War from 1618 to 1648.

I. THE COUNTER REFORMATION

A. *Internal Reform in the Papacy.*

Several causes prevented Protestantism from winning Italy. Italian disunity led to domination by Spain, the champion of Catholicism. Rome was also the seat of the papacy, and the papacy prevented the translation of the Bible into the vernacular.

Another powerful factor in preventing the spread of Protestantism was the Oratory of Divine Love, founded about 1517. This informal organization of important churchmen and laymen was interested in deepening spiritual life by spiritual exercises. It also supported works of charity and reform. The most important of the fifty odd members were Giovanni Pietro Caraffa (1476–1559), who became Pope Paul IV in 1555, and Gaetano di Tiene, who was a source of inspiration to the reforming popes. Caraffa was strongly attached to the medieval dogma of the Roman Church. This group of spiritually minded churchmen sponsored any movement that would contribute to a return of personal conviction in their beloved church.

Pope Paul III made the most able of these earnest men cardinals. He put such men as Caraffa, Contarini, who sympathized

[374]

with the Protestant doctrine of justification by faith, Pole, and others on a commission to report to him on a plan for religious reform. They presented a report in 1538 that pointed out that the abuses in the Roman Church were the fault of former pontiffs who had sold offices and dispensations indiscriminately.[1]

The Oratory of Divine Love also inspired the founding of new religious orders that helped to stop the spread of Protestantism. Gaetano di Tiene, aided by Caraffa, founded the Theatine order in 1524. This order bound secular priests to live under the threefold rule of poverty, chastity and obedience in a religious community, but it left them free to serve the people just as parish priests did. The preaching, teaching and social service of these priests led to a new respect for the Roman Church in Italy, and the Theatine movement spread rapidly in that country.

Both the leadership and the membership of the Theatines were aristocratic, but the Capuchin order, founded by Matteo da Bascio in 1525 as a reformed branch of the Franciscans, made an appeal to the peasants with its self-sacrificing spirit of service and its popular type of preaching. The order was easily recognizable by the pointed hood and bare feet of the monks. Their form of life and their chapels were much simpler and more austere than those of the Theatines.

The Ursuline order for women was founded by Angela Merici in 1535 to care for the sick and to educate girls. These orders and many others were organized in this period, and they have served the Roman Church well since that time. Many of them are still strong today. The most important order, to be discussed later, was the Society of Jesus. All of these orders put at the disposal of the pope loyal and obedient men and women, dedicated to the service of the Church of Rome in the attempt to save souls and in social service to benefit the people of their day.

The fact that the luxury-loving, greedy, yet cultured popes of the Renaissance were succeeded during the sixteenth century by many popes who zealously supported reform also helped to prevent the growth of Protestantism. Paul III (1534–1549) was so favorable to the cause of reform that his pontificate marks an important point in the Counter Reformation. During his rule the Jesuit order was formed, the Inquisition was set up, the

---

[1] Beresford J. Kidd, *The Counter-Reformation* (London: Society for Promoting Christian Knowledge, 1933), pp. 12-14.

Index of Books, which listed the books that Catholics were not to read, was published, and the Council of Trent was opened in 1545. He had also permitted the commission of nine to make their famous report in 1538 on abuses in the Roman Church. Cardinal Caraffa became pope Paul IV (1555–1559), and all the reforming zeal of the Oratory and the strength of this able courageous man were thrown back of the Counter Reformation. As a cardinal he had encouraged Paul III to set up the Roman Inquisition and to publish the Index in order to rid the church of heresy. As pope he made these two weapons even more powerful. He failed however to free the papacy of the political control of Spain, and he was even guilty of nepotism.

Pius IV, his successor, succeeded in eliminating nepotism and in regulating the powers of the College of Cardinals. Sixtus V was able to bring about financial reform. With renewed spiritual zeal and with these practical reforms the Church of Rome, purged in its head, was able to undertake reform in its members throughout Europe and to try to win many Protestants back to the Roman fold. By 1590 the papacy had made considerable gains because of these reforms.

B. *Weapons for Reconquest.*

Spain became the national leader in the work of the Counter Reformation because nationalism and religion had been united in the attempt to unify and consolidate the Spanish state by driving out the Moslem Moors and the Jews. After their marriage in 1469, the intensely religious Isabella of Castile and the equally religious Ferdinand of Aragon worked for a united Spain loyal to Rome. It was in Spain that the Inquisition was set up in 1480 and developed under the leadership of Thomas Torquemada into an organ to exterminate heretics. It was from Spain that the idea of the Italian Inquisition was borrowed by Paul III. It was also a Spaniard, Ignatius Loyola, who was instrumental in the founding of the Society of Jesus. Cardinal Ximenes, another Spaniard, revived the study of the Scriptures among the clergy trained at the University of Alcala, and was the first to have the Greek New Testament printed. He also led in the publication of the *Complutensian Polyglot* in 1520. This work gave the text of the Bible in the original languages as well as in the Latin of the Vulgate. Charles V and Philip II, successive rulers of Spain, the Netherlands and the Holy Roman Empire were earnest supporters of the papal system. Philip poured the treasure and blood of Spain into efforts to hold the Netherlands to the Roman Catholic faith and to regain England for the papal system. In these many respects Spain provided the dynamic that could be used to consolidate the position of the Roman Church and to regain lost territories.

The most effective weapon of positive propaganda for the Church of Rome was provided by the Jesuit order, which emphasized preaching by well-educated monks as a means to win men back from Protestantism. The founder of the order, Ignatius Loyola (ca. 1491–1556), was born into a wealthy noble Basque family. After the usual fighting, gaming and love-making antics of the son of a noble Spanish family, he became a soldier. His leg was smashed in a battle against the French in 1521, and for a long time he had to be in a hospital while his leg was improperly set, broken and reset. During this period his reading of religious literature resulted in a spiritual experience in 1522 that led him to dedicate his life to the service of God and the Church. He made a trip to the Holy Land in 1523 and returned from it to get an education. In 1528 he enrolled at the University of Paris. In 1534 he and six companions became the nucleus of an order that was given papal approval by Paul III in 1540. The little, deformed, scarred man became the general of the new order in 1541.

Earlier he had written a work called *Spiritual Exercises* to guide the recruits into a spiritual experience that would make them faithful members of the order. Much time was to be spent in meditation upon the life, work and death of Christ. This long period of spiritual exercise made his recruits faithful to God and their human leadership.[2] The members finally had to take a vow of special obedience to the pope as well as to their general. Under the general were provincials in charge of districts. Loyola's *Rules For Thinking with the Church* required absolute, blind obedience to the pope in addition to purity and chastity.[3]

The main functions of the organization were education, fighting heresy and foreign missions. The order has always had control of the most important educational institutions of the Roman Church. By way of preaching large parts of Germany were regained for the Roman Church. The order has also provided

[2] Paul Van Dyke, *Ignatius Loyola* (New York: Charles Scribner's Sons, 1926), Ch. XVIII.
[3] H. Bettenson, *Documents of the Christian Church* (New York: Oxford University Press, 1947), pp. 363-366.

some heroic missionaries. Francis Xavier (1506–1552) was an early outstanding missionary of the order. Traveling to the Far East, Xavier preached in India, the East Indies and Japan and baptized many thousands in the Roman faith. The Jesuits were able to regain the southern provinces of the Netherlands and Poland for the Church of Rome, although Lutheranism seemed to be strongly established in Poland. But in these struggles the very efficiency of the Jesuits made them soulless; their ethical relativism made them justify any means to accomplish what seemed to be good ends; and their enlistment of the rulers of state in the fight against heresy led to an undue interference in politics that later made them unpopular.

The Roman Church had two weapons of coercion to back up the propaganda of the Jesuits. These were the Inquisition and the Index. The Inquisition had originated in the struggle against the Albigenses in Southern France early in the thirteenth century. It had been established in Spain by papal license in 1480 to deal with the problem of heresy in that land. Because of Caraffa's urging, the Roman Inquisition was proclaimed by a papal bull of Paul III in 1542 as an instrument to deal with heresy anywhere. Those accused were always presumed guilty till they proved their innocence; they were never confronted with their accusers; they could be made to testify against themselves; and they could be tortured to extract a confession. If sentenced, they were punished by loss of property, or imprisonment, or burning at the stake, unless they confessed and recanted. These punishments were carried out by the secular authorities under the watchful eye of the inquisitors.

The development of printing in the middle of the fifteenth century helped the Protestants to disseminate their ideas. To counteract this, the Roman Church developed the Index, a list of books that the faithful were not permitted to read. Such a list was issued as early as 1543 under the guidance of Caraffa and approved by Paul III. As Paul IV, Caraffa issued the authoritative Roman Index of Prohibited Books in 1559. The books of Erasmus and some Protestant editions of the Bible appeared on the list. A special Congregation of the Index, created in 1571, was charged by the pope with the task of keeping the list up-to-date. The Index kept many Roman Catholics from reading Protestant literature, and the Inquisition forced many to recant their Protestant views.

C. *The Consolidation of Doctrine at the Council of Trent, 1545-1563.*

Paul III seemed to see the need for reform in the Roman Church more than any other because it was he who authorized the Jesuit order in 1540, set up the Roman Inquisition in 1542, and issued the bull of 1544 which called the Council of Trent. The Council opened December 13, 1545 and ran, with long periods when there were no sessions, until December 4, 1563. It was not permitted to state its superiority to the pope. Voting was by head and not by nations as had been the case at the Council of Constance. Italians always numbered about three-quarters of those present. Thus the papacy and the Italian hierarchy were assured of control of its actions. Paul wanted to consider the doctrine of the Church of Rome, reform of clerical abuses and the possibility of a crusade against the infidel. Although the final decrees were signed by 255 churchmen, there were never more than about 75 present at most of the 25 sessions.

The first series of sessions between 1545 and 1547 was taken up with various doctrinal questions. The Council declared that not the Bible alone but the canonical Scriptures and the Apocrypha in the Vulgate edition of Jerome and the tradition of the Church constituted the final authority for the faithful.[4] The discussion of justification by faith resulted in the decision that man was justified by faith and subsequent works rather than by faith only. The seven sacraments were reaffirmed by the Council, and decrees concerning reform of ecclesiastical abuses were formulated.

During the second series of sessions between 1551 and 1552 the dogma of transubstantiation was reaffirmed and further decisions on reform were formulated. The final series of sessions between 1562 and 1563 were occupied with detailed discussions concerning other sacraments, rules concerning marriage, decrees concerning purgatory, and various matters of reform. The control of the pope over the Council was demonstrated by its request that he confirm its work by a papal bull. Another papal bull, issued in 1564, contained a summary of the faith formulated at the Council of Trent. It was known as the Tridentine Profession of Faith. All Roman Catholic clergy and teachers must subscribe to it as well as converts to that faith

[4] *Ibid.*, p. 367.

from Protestantism. The individual so subscribing must swear "true obedience" to the pope.[5]

The real significance of the Council was the transformation of medieval Scholastic theology into an authoritative dogma binding upon all the faithful.[6] It rendered any chance of reconciliation with Protestantism impossible because the Protestants would not accept the equal authority of tradition and Scripture. It did, however, promote a higher moral standard among the clergy by needed reforms. It opened seminaries to train ministers, provided for the Roman Catechism of 1566, and adopted an authoritative version of the Bible, the Vulgate.

Armed with a system of dogma spread by faithful Jesuit educators and missionaries and backed by the power of the Inquisition, the papacy was able to stop Protestant gains, except in Holland, after 1560 and to go on and regain territories, such as Poland, where it seemed that Protestantism would triumph. The peak of conquest and reform was reached about 1600. The Counter Reformation divided Europe into peoples who adhered to the papacy and those who accepted the Protestant faith.

The Reformation and Counter Reformation in the West had little effect upon the Church in the East. Cyril Lucar (1572–1638), who became patriarch at Constantinople in 1621, was interested in the Calvinistic religious movement in the West but was opposed by his own people and by the Jesuits who did not want the Eastern Church to become Protestant. He developed a Confession of Faith in 1629 that was strongly tinged with Calvinistic views of doctrine. He also sent one of the three oldest manuscripts of the Bible, the Codex Alexandrinus, to Charles I of England in 1628. His enemies persuaded the Sultan to put him to death for supposedly instigating rebellion among the Cossacks, and a synod of Bethlehem in 1672 repudiated all the aspects of Reformation doctrine in his Confession and even claimed that he did not write it. In this humiliating fashion the attempt to make the Greek Church Protestant failed.

II. THE THIRTY YEARS WAR

Because many clerical rulers of Germany, who became Protestants, made their lands Protestant in spite of the Peace of Augs-

---

[5] *Ibid.*, pp. 374-375.

[6] See P. Schaff, *Creeds of Christendom* (New York: Charles Scribner's Sons, 3 vols., 6th ed., 1890), Vol. II, pp. 77-206 for the canons and decrees.

burg, which made it mandatory that they give up their lands if they became Protestant, both Roman Catholics and Lutherans became dissatisfied. Calvinism, which had not been recognized in the negotiations at Augsburg, had won areas in Germany, such as the Palatinate, and Calvinists desired legal recognition. The Jesuits lost no chance to interfere in political affairs in countries such as Bavaria and Bohemia in order to regain lost territories for the Roman Church. Emperor Ferdinand II and Maximilian of Bavaria had been trained to hate Protestantism by the Jesuits. Lutherans of Donauworth stoned a procession of monks in 1606. Even though the monks had agreed not to demonstrate their religion outside the monastery walls, Maximilian took their part, captured the city and garrisoned it with soldiers. Fearing the breakdown of the Augsburg agreement, the Protestant rulers organized an Evangelical Union in 1608, and in 1609 the princes supporting the pope organized a Catholic League. Thus were the lines drawn in the empire for battle between the rival faiths.

The Defenestration of Prague in 1618 provided the spark to set off the Thirty Years War. Ferdinand, who became emperor in 1619, was selected in 1617 to succeed the childless Matthias as ruler of Bohemia. In 1618 Protestants had thrown the representatives of Ferdinand out of a window of a castle in Prague into the muddy moat. When Matthias died, the Bohemians elected Frederick, ruler of the Protestant Palatinate, as ruler of Bohemia.

The resulting war went through four phases. The Bohemian period lasted from 1618 to 1624 and was fought between Ferdinand the emperor and Maximilian of Bavaria on the one side and Frederick and the Bohemians on the other. The Battle of White Hill outside Prague in 1620 led to the temporary defeat of Protestantism in Germany.

The Danish phase of the war between 1625 and 1629 was fought to protect the Northern German Protestant states from the fate of Bohemia. Christian IV of Denmark, as much to add to his own territories as to aid Protestantism, came to the aid of the German princes but was defeated by the forces of Emperor Ferdinand II, led by the able general Wallenstein. The Emperor in the Edict of Restitution of 1629 ordered that all lands of the Roman Church that had been taken by Protestants since 1552 should be surrendered, that Protestants should be expelled from areas ruled by Catholic princes, and that only Lutherans should have recognition and toleration.

Dissension among the Roman Catholic German princes over the spoil and the aid of Gustavus Adolphus of Sweden to the Protestants brought on the Swedish phase of the war between 1630 and 1634. The Swedish ruler wanted to make the Baltic a Swedish lake as well as to aid his fellow Protestants. In a battle at Lutzen in 1632 the imperial forces under Tilly, the successor of Wallenstein, were defeated by the Protestants. Sweden got the territory that she desired on the shores of the Baltic; Northern Germany was freed from domination by Roman Catholics; but Southern Germany was not reconquered by the Protestants.

The final phase of the war between 1635 and 1648 involved the interference of Roman Catholic France on the side of the Protestants because Richelieu hoped to gain land for France and to harass the Hapsburg ruler of Spain and the Holy Roman Empire.

The Peace of Westphalia ended the long bloody struggle in 1648. Holland and Switzerland were recognized as independent Protestant states. France, Sweden and the tiny state that was to become Prussia made important gains of territory, and France became the dominant power in Europe. Both Lutheranism and Calvinism became recognized religions, and Protestants were given the right to hold offices in the state. Lands that were Protestant in 1624 were permitted to remain Protestant. This brought about the end of religious persecution. The Holy Roman Empire became a mere geographical term and lost its former political significance after the Peace of Westphalia because its only unity had been religious and the Reformation and the war had shattered that.

The cost of the settlement was high. The population of Germany was cut by about a third with a loss of about ten million lives. Property had been destroyed in the numerous battles and sackings of towns and villages. It took decades before Germany recovered from the devastation of property, the loss of life and the breakdown of morals incurred in the Thirty Years War.

III. The Reformation in Retrospect

The Reformation meant the end of the control by a universal church. The corporate Roman Catholic Church was replaced

RELIGION IN EUROPE ABOUT 1648

RUSSIA

Caspian Sea

Black Sea

CONSTANTINOPLE

MOHAMMEDAN

POLAND

OTTOMAN EMPIRE

Mediterranean Sea

SWEDEN

NORWAY

DENMARK

NETHERLANDS

HOLY ROMAN EMPIRE

HUNGARY

WITTENBERG

ZURICH

SWITZER- LAND

LORRAINE

ROME

EDINBURGH

CANTERBURY

FRANCE

SPAIN

PORTUGAL

MOHAMMEDAN

Atlantic Ocean

ROMAN CATHOLIC
LUTHERAN
ANGELICAN
GREEK ORTHODOX
CALVINISTIC

by a series of national Protestant state churches in the lands where Protestantism was victorious. The Lutherans dominated the religious scene in Germany and Scandinavia. Calvinism had its adherents in Switzerland, Scotland, Holland, France and Hungary. The English had set up the Anglican state church. The radicals of the Reformation, the Anabaptists, had not set up state churches but were strong in such countries as Holland. They alone of the Reformation groups were opposed to the union of the Church and state, but they were equally opposed to domination by the pope.

Some link the Socinians, the forerunners of the modern Unitarians, with the Anabaptists. It is certain that they belonged to the radical group of the Reformation, but they were not specifically Anabaptists. Socinian ideas developed in Italy. Lelio Sozzini (Socinus) (1525–1562) of Siena was attracted to anti-Trinitarianism by the death of the anti-Trinitarian Servetus in Geneva. His nephew, Fausto Sozzini (1539–1604), moved to Poland in 1578 and remained there until his death in 1604. Socinianism developed rapidly in Poland, and Fausto gave the movement the Racovian Catechism which was published in 1605. According to Socinianism, Christ is to be worshiped as a man who obtained divinity by his superior life. His death was simply an example of the obedience that God desires from His followers. Original sin, the deity of Christ, the Trinity, and predestination are denied. The Jesuits were able to suppress it in Poland, but Socinian ideas spread to Holland and to England from whence they spread to America. The modern Unitarian Church is a lineal descendant of the Socinians of Poland, who were first called Unitarians in Transylvania about 1600.

Although great doctrinal changes were brought about by the Reformation, the student must not think that the new national churches broke completely with all that was handed down by the Church from the past. Protestants and Roman Catholics alike accepted the great ecumenical creeds, such as the Apostles' Creed, the Nicene Creed and the Athanasian Creed. They all held the doctrines of the Trinity and, except for the Socinians, the deity and resurrection of Christ, the Bible as a revelation from God, the fall of man, original sin and the need of a moral life for the Christian. The Protestants had a common area of agreement concerning salvation by faith alone, the sole author-

CHARLES DARWIN

WILLIAM CAREY

DAVID LIVINGSTONE

KARL MARX

Dwight L. Moody

Horace Bushnell

Billy Graham

Walter Rauschenbusch

Karl Barth

ity of the Scriptures as an infallible rule of faith and life and the priesthood of believers. In addition, each denomination held to its own particular viewpoint that distinguished it from other Protestants, such as baptism by immersion in the case of the Baptists, and predestination in the case of the Calvinists. This relationship can be illustrated by the following diagram of the faith of any Protestant.

The student of church history will also notice that the Reformation constituted the second great period of creedal development. The ecumenical creeds were hammered out between 325 and 451, but between 1530 and 1648 many Protestant confessions and creeds were developed that are still held by the various branches of Protestantism today. The formulation of great

THE ELEMENTS IN A PROTESTANT'S FAITH

DENOMINATIONAL
DOCTRINES

PROTESTANT
DOCTRINES

CREEDS HELD IN COMMON
BY PROTESTANT, ORTHODOX
AND ROMAN CATHOLIC CHURCHES

Protestant theological systems, such as that of Calvin in his *Institutes,* is also closely related to the development of creeds.

Protestantism was also responsible for certain great doctrinal emphases that have had a marked effect on both man's temporal and spiritual interests. The assertion that justification was by faith alone marked the resurgence of religious individualism, which had been lost during the Middle Ages because of the view that man best developed as a part of the corporate organization of the Church. Man now could have direct personal access to God. Such an assertion of the individual did not mean that the Reformers neglected the group aspect of life, for all of them, except the Anabaptists, laid great emphasis on the Church, which was to be recognized by the preaching of the Word and the sacraments. But, so far as salvation was concerned, man need not come to God by the sacraments of the Roman Catholic Church.

The doctrine of the priesthood of believers struck at the importance of the hierarchal system of mediators between God and man, just as the doctrine of justification by faith had made the sacramental system unnecessary. No mediator was needed because each believer was a spiritual priest who offered spiritual sacrifices to God.

The assertion of the final authority of the Scriptures marked a repudiation of the authority of the Church. The Bible, rather than the decrees of councils, the writings of the Fathers and the bulls of the popes was the final rule of faith and practice. Because individuals were thought to be able to interpret it for themselves by paying attention to the grammatical and historical background, the right of private interpretation was emphasized. This helped to make possible the rise of sects which differed from one another on some point of Biblical interpretation.

The Reformation helped to create a demand for universal elementary education because, if each was to interpret the Bible for himself, he must have some knowledge of reading. All of the Reformers gave considerable attention to the founding of schools on the three levels of elementary, secondary and university education.

Insistence upon the spiritual equality of men led to an insistence upon their political equality. In this way the Reformation, particularly where Calvinistic doctrines were accepted, promoted the rise of democracy in both the Church and state. Laymen were given a greater share in the government of the Church.

The Reformation also stimulated capitalism because the medieval opposition to usury was dropped by most of the Reformers. The insistence upon thrift, industry and separation from costly worldly amusements resulted in the creation of savings that could be used as capital for new economic ventures. It is not fair, however, to say that any of the Reformers were responsible for the rise of capitalism because it was in existence long before the Reformation. The modern welfare state, which assumes responsibility for the economic welfare of its citizens, also had its beginnings in the need of the state to provide for those who were dispossessed and impoverished by the confiscation of church property during the the Reformation.

The Reformation also brought a much needed revival of preaching. Men, such as Luther, excelled as preachers of the Word. Calvin spent much of his time in preaching as well as in teaching the Word.

The Reformation also had an impact upon the Roman Catholic Church through the reformation in morals and the clear statement of dogma of the Counter Reformation at Trent. The Jesuit order became the leader in Roman Catholic missionary work in Asia and the Western Hemisphere.

By 1648 the main churches of the Christian religion were in being. The period from then to the present is concerned with the fortunes of these various forms of Christianity as they faced the secularism that first began to make a marked impression upon Western Europe during the seventeenth century.

BIBLIOGRAPHY

Beresford J. Kidd has provided an excellent history of the Counter Reformation in his volume *The Counter-Reformation, 1550-1600* (London: Society for Promoting Christian Knowledge, 1933).

The Roman Catholic viewpoint on the same subject is ably presented in *The Catholic Reformation* (Milwaukee: The Bruce Publishing Co., 1949) by Pierre Janelle.

Paul Van Dyke's *Ignatius Loyola* (New York: Charles Scribner's Sons, 1926) is an able and interesting biography of the founder of the Jesuits.

Henry J. Schroeder has provided the original text and an English translation of the canons and decrees of the Council of Trent in his volume, *Canons and Decrees of the Council of Trent* (St. Louis: B. Herder Book Co., 1941).

The Thirty Years War (New Haven: Yale University Press, 1939) by Cicely V. Wedgwood is a scholarly discussion of that war.

movements in the Church have been rationalism
1. *Deism - Eng → France → U.S.*
2. *- Germany → Eng → U.S.*
3. *modern Denominationalism - Germ.*
4. *Evangelism - U.S.*
5. *Ecumenical move of 20th Cent. -*

RATIONALISM, REVIVALISM AND DENOMINATIONALISM, 1648–1789

Chapter XXXII

THE ESTABLISHMENT OF CHRISTIANITY IN
NORTH AMERICA

The Peace of Westphalia in 1648 is a dividing point between religious patterns developed in the Reformation and tendencies in church history since that time. Recurrent revivalism and various manifestations of rationalism developed concurrently. Rationalism, which gave birth to liberalism in the Church, led to a break with the Bible and the theology of the Reformation; but it has been checked in the twentieth century by the influence of the theology of Karl Barth. Denominationalism grew out of the separation of the Church and state. The rise of toleration and freedom of religion brought about the necessity of voluntary support of the Church and more democratic control over its affairs by the laity. Because people were not born into a state church, evangelism became important as a means of winning them to Christianity. Unfortunately, separation of the Church and state often meant not merely the refusal to favor one religion above another but an irreligious attitude in affairs of state. Separation has created the secular state of the twentieth century, which in some lands threatens the existence of the Church. The tendency to denominationalism has been somewhat offset in the twentieth century by tendencies toward reunion and ecumenical movements. A great Protestant missionary movement since 1792 and philanthropy to meet social needs have been definite parts of modern Christianity.

Nowhere have these characteristics of modern church history been so pronounced as in America. One cannot but be impressed with the fact that Columbus' discovery of America and the beginning of the Reformation took place within twenty-five years of each other. Nearly every one of the Protestant churches of the Reformation came to be represented in America between 1607 and 1732. Distance from Europe, the early rise of voluntarism and consequent lay control of the church, recurrent revivals, the influence of the frontier, and the relative religious radicalism of the sects who came to America have made American Christianity amazingly creative in its activities. The temperance movement, the institutional church to provide for social and cultural as well as religious needs, youth work, home missions and the ecumenical movement — all illustrate this creative aspect of American Christianity.

I. The Planting of American Christianity

The motives stimulating Anglo-Saxon colonization along the Atlantic seaboard of North America varied. Many of the colonists hoped to find the western sea route to the riches of Asia, valuable raw materials and markets for profitable trade. Others were sent because it was believed that the colonies could absorb the surplus population of the homeland. The planting of the colonies would also help to meet the military threat from Spain in the New World. But the religious motivation was extremely important in the founding of the colonies. Most of the charters mention the desire of the stockholders to convert the natives and to extend Christ's dominion.[1] In other cases, such as those of the Puritans of Plymouth and Salem, the colonists were interested in worshiping in their own way, and it must be admitted, making all who came to their colony worship in that same way. Thus the transplanting of Europeans to North America cannot be disassociated from the transplanting of their religion to the same land. The instrument used in this transplanting of people was the joint stock company, the forerunner of the modern corporation. It made possible the gathering together of the great sums of money needed to finance such undertakings.

A. *The Anglican Church in America.*

The Virginia Company, which was given a charter in 1606 to settle and to exploit land in America, sent out settlers to Jamestown in 1607. This settlement of gentry and workers was organized on a communal basis, and provision was made for the establishment of the Anglican Church. Among the settlers was Robert Hunt, a chaplain, who first gave the Lord's Supper to the colonists under the protection of an old sail while the worshipers sat on logs. John Rolfe, who married Pocohontas, laid the foundation for the early wealth of the colony by successfully growing tobacco in 1612. The colony did not prosper economi-

---

[1] Peter G. Mode, *Source Book and Bibliographical Guide for American Church History* (Menasha, Wisconsin: George Banta Publishing Co., 1921), pp. 9-10, 26.

cally until the communal experiment was ended in 1619, and land and the privilege of electing a representative governing body were granted to the colonists by the Company. Increasing numbers of Puritan Anglicans migrated to the colony. Alexander Whitaker, who had Puritan leanings, became the leading minister of the Anglican Church in Virginia between 1611 and 1617. Slavery was established with the purchase of slaves from Dutch traders in 1619 to work the tobacco plantations. In 1624 the Company was dissolved, and Virginia became a royal colony ruled for the king by a governor. The Anglican Church remained as the Established Church of the new colony. Its pastors gave indifferent service until James Blair came to Virginia as Commissary in 1689 to inspect the churches and to work out definite reforms.

The Anglican Church also finally became the Established Church of Maryland in 1702, despite the opposition of the Roman Catholics, who had been permitted to settle there by Lord Baltimore. The religious toleration which Lord Baltimore had permittted was thus ended. It was made the Established Church in New York in 1693 in spite of opposition from the Dutch, who had originally settled New York. A final act of 1765 made the Anglican Church the Established Church in North Carolina, and earlier, in 1706, it was established in South Carolina. Georgia accepted Anglican establishment in 1758. Not until the American Revolution was this pattern changed.

The founding of the Society for the Propagation of the Gospel in Foreign Parts in 1701 made possible a more consecrated and spiritual ministry in the various established churches. Before that time the established churches had often been characterized by moral and spiritual laxity. The Society sent over three hundred missionaries to the colonies.

B. *The Planting of New England Congregationalism.*

Early in the seventeenth century, the Scrooby congregation, which had migrated to friendly Leyden in Holland to escape persecution because of their Congregationalist ideas, decided to migrate to America in order to prevent the eventual incorporation of their young people into the Dutch population. A London company of merchant "adverturers" loaned them seven thousand pounds to finance the voyage. The immigrants, who had nothing to contribute but their labor, were to repay them by helping them to build up a fishing industry. In August of 1620 about one hundred colonists, known as the Pilgrims, set sail from England for America in the *Mayflower*. For some reason they landed at Plymouth in New England rather than in northern Virginia, so they had to get a new charter from the company in whose territories they were living. In order to prevent the unruly from disturbing the colony they drew up the Mayflower Compact as an instrument of government before they landed.[2] It was really an extension of the covenant idea of the Separatists to civil government, and the Compact remained their main constitution until Plymouth was incorporated with the Salem settlements into Massachusetts in 1691. The landing at Plymouth was providential, for if they had landed in Virginia, they would have been persecuted as much as they had been in England. Elder Brewster served as their religious leader, and William Bradford became their first governor. At least fifty of the colonists died during that first hard winter; but from the next spring on the fortunes of the colonists flourished, and they were soon able to pay off their debts. The church was the center of spiritual and social life in their community.

The larger number of Puritans settled in Salem and Boston after 1628. In 1626 John White, a Puritan minister of Dorchester in England, organized a company to settle a few people at Salem. About fifty of this company landed in Salem in the fall of 1628 and chose John Endicott as their governor. These people were either Puritan Congregationalists, or, possibly, Anglicans inclined to Congregationalism before they left England.[3] They were soon brought under the influence of Dr. Samuel Fuller, who came from the Separatist Plymouth colony to give them medical aid during the winter of 1628–1629 and who promoted the cause of Congregationalism so well that in 1629 the Salem colony set up the Congregational system of church government based on a covenant.

In 1629 White's organization was incorporated into the Massachusetts Bay Company. All of the stockholders of the Massachusetts Bay Company who did not want to migrate from England withdrew, and about nine hundred sailed to America with the governors of the company and the charter in order to get away from the despotic personal rule of Charles I. In 1631 the Massachusetts General Court limited the right to vote to church

---

[2] *Ibid.*, p. 49.

[3] *Ibid.*, pp. 64-65. Cf. Perry Miller, *Orthodoxy in Massachusetts 1630-1650* (Cambridge: Harvard University Press, 1933), Ch. V, especially pp. 127-131.

members; Congregationalism became the state religion; and the theocracy became a reality. The colonists rejected episcopacy but upheld the principle of uniformity of faith. Winthrop was made governor of these settlements at Salem and Boston. Over twenty thousand Puritans came to these settlements between 1628 and 1642. The ministers for the increasing number of churches were university graduates, most of whom were educated in Cambridge. They interpreted the authoritative Scriptures to the people so that they would know how to apply them in their private and civil life. Although the polity of the churches was Congregational, the theology of these Puritans was Calvinistic.

The desire to occupy adjacent fertile areas and the intolerance of theocratic rulers of the New England settlement led to what one might term the "swarming" of the Puritans. Thomas Hooker, appointed as minister of Newtone in 1633, became irked with the limitation of the franchise to church members. He and his congregation petitioned the magistrates for permission to migrate to the fertile Connecticut River valley to the west. They were permitted to leave, and by 1636 three towns were founded. In 1638 the Fundamental Orders of Connecticut were drawn up as the constitution for the new colony. This constitution was more liberal than that of the mother colony because only the governor was required to be a church member,[4] and government was based on the consent of the people expressed through their vote for the magistrates.

The founding of still another colony may be credited to John Davenport, pastor of a church in London, and one of his members, Theophilus Eaton, who sailed to America with many members of the congregation in 1636. They decided that they would not be happy in Boston and set up the colony of New Haven in the southern part of modern Connecticut. They obtained land from the Indians by treaty and in 1639 created a commonwealth, based on the Bible, in which only church members could vote. In 1664 this colony was merged with the others to form the colony of Connecticut.

Unity of theology and polity was secured after the Cambridge Synod of 1646, at which representatives of the four Puritan colonies adopted the Westminster Confession as an expression of their theology and finally drew up the *Cambridge Platform*[5]

[4] *Ibid.*, pp. 97-98.
[5] *Ibid.*, pp. 76-77.

in 1648. This Platform declared that each church was autonomous but was related to other churches for fellowship and council. Each church was created by a church covenant linking the believers to one another and to Christ, the Head of the Church. Pastors and deacons became the most important officials, and ordination was performed by neighboring ministers when a church wanted to ordain someone.

The early Puritans did not entirely ignore their pagan neighbors. John Elliott, who began work among the Indians in 1646, organized his converts into towns. He also translated and published the Old and New Testaments in the Indian tongue in 1663 and 1661 respectively.

C. Planting the American Baptist Churches.

The beginning of the Baptist churches in America was also associated with the swarming of the Puritans. Roger Williams (1603–1683), who was educated for the Anglican ministry at Cambridge, soon adopted Separatist views. His independency of mind brought him to Boston from unfriendly England in 1631. He went from there to Plymouth because he thought the Boston church had not purified itself sufficiently. For two years he ministered at Plymouth. When the church in Salem called him as pastor in 1634, the General Court, inspired by John Cotton, interfered. It ordered him out of the territory under its jurisdiction within six weeks because he upheld the Indian ownership of land, opposed a state church, and insisted that the magistrates had no power over a man's religion. Leaving his wife and children in a mortgaged home, he plunged into the forest in the depth of winter and wandered until friendly Indians gave him aid. In 1636 he purchased some land from the Indians and founded Providence.

In the next year Mrs. Anne Hutchinson fell under the ban of the authorities because she held meetings in her home where she proclaimed what she called a covenant of grace. This covenant was opposed to the covenant of works which she said all the ministers but John Cotton proclaimed. Exiled from the colony shortly before her baby was born, she was forced to walk in the depth of winter to Rhode Island, where she and her followers settled at Newport and Portsmouth. John Clarke, a physician and preacher, became a teaching elder of a church in Newport in 1638, but it is not certain that this was a Baptist church.

In 1638, or more likely in 1639, a church was founded in Providence, and all of the members were rebaptized, including Williams. There is some question whether or not this was by immersion, but at any rate, the twelve members organized the church along Baptist lines. It is considered to be the first Baptist church in America. Although there was a church in Newport in 1638, the first distinct Baptist church in Newport appeared in 1648, according to the records. Both the Newport and Providence churches still dispute for the title of the oldest Baptist church in America. Williams later withdrew from the Providence church, but he continued to serve the settlement by securing a temporary charter for Rhode Island in 1643. This charter was confirmed by the charter of 1663 granted by Charles II.[6] Williams' greatest contribution was his emphasis upon the separation of the Church and state and freedom of conscience. From his early activities in Rhode Island the great Baptist fellowship of modern times has sprung.

D. *Planting Roman Catholicism in Maryland.*

The Lords Baltimore, George Calvert and his son, Cecil Calvert, were successive proprietors of what became known as Maryland. Unlike the idealistic Roger Williams, the Calverts were interested in profits. From 1634, when the colony began, they permitted religious toleration in Maryland so that Protestants as well as Roman Catholics would settle there. The strict political control by Calvert was balanced by religious liberty until Maryland was made a royal colony in 1692. Anglicanism became the established religion in 1702 when the English government finally approved the 1692 act of the Colonial Assembly.

E. *Pennsylvania and the Quakers.*

Quakers appeared in Boston in 1656 but soon found that they were not welcomed by the New England Puritans because of their idea of separation of the Church and state and their indifference to doctrine. After 1674 New Jersey was divided into East and West Jersey, and West Jersey became a Quaker settlement. But it was Pennsylvania that became the great Quaker refuge, through the efforts of William Penn. Charles II owed sixteen thousand pounds to Penn's father and gave William Penn control of Pennsylvania in 1681 to pay the debt. Penn took a great interest in the founding of the colony and made it an asylum where oppressed of any belief might find refuge. This

[6] *Ibid.*, p. 119-120.

explains the great diversity of sects which is apparent in the study of the religious history of Pennsylvania. In 1683 great numbers of German Mennonites settled at Germantown near Philadelphia. In 1740 numbers of Moravians settled in Pennsylvania after a short residence in Georgia between 1735 and 1740. Zinzendorf himself, leader of the Moravians, visited Pennsylvania in 1741 and unsuccessfully attempted to unite the German sects. Bethlehem became a leading center for the Moravians. Although American Lutheranism had its beginnings in the Dutch colony of New Amsterdam and in the Swedish colony along the Delaware River, it had no definite organization until Henry Muhlenberg landed in America in 1742. He was able to form a Lutheran Synod in Pennsylvania in 1748. By the time of the Revolution there were about seventy-five thousand Lutherans in Pennsylvania alone. Religious diversity was the keynote of religion in Pennsylvania and the Middle colonies; whereas the Anglican Church dominated the Southern colonies, and the Congregational Church the Northern colonies.

F. *Presbyterianism in America.*

During the first half of the sixteenth century the Scotch Presbyterians, who were brought in by James I to displace the native Irish, continued to migrate to northern Ireland. Many of the Scotch-Irish migrated to the colonies after 1710 because of the economic discrimination practiced against Ireland by the trade laws of England. By 1750 about one hundred thousand had come to America. Many, after a short stay in New England, moved to New Jersey and to New York where they populated Ulster and Orange counties. More went into central and western Pennsylvania where they became influential in the Pittsburgh area, which became a leading center of American Presbyterianism. Others went south into the Shenandoah Valley of Virginia.

Francis Makemie (1658–1708), an Irishman who arrived in the colonies in 1683, became the father of American Presbyterianism. By 1706 he had organized a presbytery in Philadelphia, and in 1717 the first synodical meeting in the colonies was held. In 1729 the synod adopted the Westminster Confession as the standard of faith. The Presbyterians ranked with the Anglicans, Congregationalists and Baptists as the largest churches in the colonies.

In this manner the various churches created by the Reformation were transplanted in America during the first 150 years of the history of the colonies. Except for a while in Maryland and the Middle colonies, an established church held sway until the American Revolution. After the Revolution the separation of the Church and state made the churches of America dependent upon voluntary support for money to finance their ventures and upon evangelism to win the unchurched and children of members of the Church into the fellowship of the Church.

II. Education in the Colonies

After homes had been built, churches erected, civil government set up, and means of livelihood secured, education was one of the earliest concerns of the colonists, according to the pamphlet, *New England's First Fruits*. This interest was in the tradition of the Reformation because Calvin and Luther had emphasized the need of education so that the individual could read his Bible and so that leaders for the Church and state be trained. Both in their curricula and those of the educational institutions of early America, the Bible had first place and classical training took second place as an aid to the full knowledge of the Bible. Vocational education in the colonies was assured by the continuance of the apprenticeship system of England. By this system one was apprenticed to a master in a particular trade until one learned that trade. Elementary education was by law the concern of the government in the Northern colonies, but in the Southern the same end was secured in wealthy families by the hiring of a private tutor. A literate individual would be a better citizen and a better Christian. Secondary schools, known as Latin or grammar schools, were set up to prepare the student for university by giving him a grounding in the classical languages. Colleges were to provide scholars and civic and religious leaders.

Harvard was founded in 1636 to "advance learning" and to secure a literate ministry who could pass on the cultural and religious tradition of the current generation to that which was to succeed it.[7] The main end of life and study was to know God and His Son Christ so that He would become "the only foundation" of learning. John Harvard, after whom the college was named, willed half his estate and his library to the infant college.

William and Mary College in Williamsburg was founded in

[7] *Ibid.*, pp. 73-75. See also E. E. Cairns, "The Puritan Philosophy of Education" in *Bibliotheca Sacra*, 104:326-336 (July-September, 1947).

1693 with the idea that one of its main functions should be "the breeding of good ministers." Shortly thereafter the Puritans of Connecticut opened Yale College in 1701 to give youth a "Liberal & Religious Education" so that leaders for the churches should not be lacking. In 1726 William Tennent Sr., an Irish minister, set up a "Log College" near Philadelphia to educate his sons and other boys for the ministry. Jonathan Dickinson secured a charter in 1746 for a school to continue this effort. This school, known as the College of New Jersey, moved to Princeton, and was eventually known as Princeton University. King's College (Columbia) came into existence by royal charter in 1754. The Baptists set up Rhode Island College in 1764 as an institution that would teach religion and the sciences without regard to sectarian differences. In due course it became Brown University. Dartmouth was founded in 1770; the present Rutgers came into being in 1825; and the Quaker school, Haverford, was founded in 1833. Each group sought to set up an institution of higher learning to provide godly leaders in the Church and state.[8]

III. THE GREAT AWAKENING

Recurrent revivals have been a characteristic of American Christianity. The need to reach the unchurched as well as the need of stirring the believers seem to have motivated these spiritual awakenings. Shortly after 1700 a decline of morals and religion, caused by the influence of the frontier, a dynamic population on the move, a series of brutalizing wars and the tendency in some areas to separate the Church and state, became noticeable.

The Great Awakening had its beginning in the preaching of Theodore Frelinghuysen to his Dutch Reformed congregations in New Jersey in 1726. The revival stimulated earnest moral and spiritual life among the people. Frelinghuysen's work influenced the Presbyterian pastors, Gilbert Tennent and William Tennent, Jr., so that they became fiery evangels of revival among the Scotch-Irish of the Middle colonies. Whitefield thus found the groundwork for revival soundly laid when he came to the Middle colonies in 1739.

The revival fires that had started among the Calvinistic Dutch Reformed and Presbyterians of the Middle colonies soon spread to Congregationalist New England through the efforts

8 *Ibid.*, pp. 20-21, 109-110, 244-250, 288-290. These pages give some of the charters of these schools.

greatest thinker of America

of Jonathan Edwards (1703–1758). Edwards was a precocious student who graduated from Yale in 1720 at the age of seventeen, and became pastor at Northampton in western Massachusetts in 1727. Although he read his manuscript sermons, his earnest manner and prayer had a great effect upon his people. His 1741 sermon, "Sinners in the Hands of an Angry God," is an impressive example of his pulpit power. The revival, which began in 1734, spread throughout New England until it reached its high tide in 1740.[9] Whitefield made his appearance at this time in Boston, and his preaching there and throughout New England was attended with great success. When Edwards lost his pulpit in 1750, he served as an Indian missionary until 1758. In that year he became president of Princeton, where he died of smallpox inoculation in the same year. He upheld a Calvinistic theology and believed that, while men have a rational ability to turn to God, because of total depravity they lacked the moral ability or inclination. This ability must be imparted by divine grace. He made much of the sovereignty and love of God in his work on *Freedom of the Will*. He wrote that God's love draws men to Himself and to His service after they have become Christians.

Presbyterians from the Middle colonies carried the revival fires to the South. Samuel Davies became the leader of the revival among the Presbyterians in Virginia. The Baptist phase of revival in the South grew out of the work of Shubal Stearns and Daniel Marshall of New England. Their preaching was more emotional, and many were won to the Baptist Church in North Carolina. Revivalistic Methodism also took deep roots in the South through the efforts of lay preachers during the revival.

Whitefield unified the efforts of all these revivalistic preachers as he traveled in all the colonies in seven visits between 1739 and 1769. In all cases a preaching revival was held. Though unusual phenomena followed the preaching in many cases, it was a soberer type of revival than the Second Awakening which was to come near the end of the century. It was the American counterpart of Pietism in Europe and the Methodist revival in England.

Such a movement was bound to have unusual results. Between 30,000 and 40,000 people and 150 new churches were added to those in New England alone out of a population of

9 *Ibid.*, pp. 214-221.

300,000. Thousands more came into the churches in the Southern and Middle colonies. A higher moral tone was noticed in the homes, work and amusements of the people. Colleges, such as Princeton, King's (Columbia), Hampden-Sydney and others, became necessary to provide ministers for the many new congregations. Missionary work was spurred so that men like David Brainerd in 1743, with great personal sacrifice, engaged in missionary work among the Indians. Whitefield founded an orphanage at Bethesda, Georgia, and many other humanitarian enterprises owed their birth to the revival.

The revival also brought schism as ministers took sides concerning the attitude of the Church to the movement. New England clergymen split into the "Old Lights," led by Charles Chauncy, who opposed the revival, the itinerant evangelists and the Calvinism of many of the revivalists, and into the "New Lights," led by Edwards, who supported the revival and a slightly modified Calvinism. This schism led eventually to the development of an orthodox group and a liberal group. Out of the latter the Unitarian group, which split off New England Congregationalism, emerged early in the nineteenth century.

The revival split the Presbyterians in the Middle colonies into two groups in 1741. They were not reunited until 1758. The "Old Side," made up of the older ministers in and near Philadelphia, opposed the licensing and ordaining of untrained men to the ministry, the intrusion of the revivalists into established parishes and the critical attitude of many of the revivalists toward the work of the ministers. The "New Side" supported the revival and the licensing of untrained men who showed unusual spiritual gifts to take care of the new churches. The Dutch Reformed of New Jersey and the Baptists of the South also split for a time over what attitude the Church should take toward the revival. But it cannot be denied that the revival was a valuable influence in the life of America and helped to prepare the people spiritually to face the problems of the French and Indian Wars of 1756–1763.

IV. The Churches and the American Revolution

The American Revolution also brought many problems to the colonial churches. The Anglican Church remained loyal to the revolutionary cause in Southern colonies, such as Maryland and Virginia; in the Middle colonies its loyalty was about equally divided between the revolutionists and the English; in New England it was generally loyal to England. Because John Wesley was a Tory and supported the ruler, the Methodists were accused of disloyalty to the colonial cause. Generally, however, they took a neutral position. The Quakers, Mennonites and Moravians were at heart patriotic, but their pacifist principles kept them from any participation in the war. Congregationalists, Baptists and Presbyterians espoused the cause of revolution with ardor; and in their sermons and teachings, the ministers and educators amplified the idea of the church covenant based on the consent of the people into a political compact based on the consent of the people as necessary to the setting up of any state. The ruler cannot violate his contract or act contrary to God's laws, they reasoned, and not expect the people to revolt. John Witherspoon, the president of Princeton, led Presbyterians in support of the Revolution, and many pastors became chaplains in the army. Lutherans also supported the Revolution loyally.

The ending of the war in 1783 had important results for religion. The influence of the Church contributed to the development of a ban on any established church and of the right to a free exercise of religion in the First Amendment to the Constitution. It also brought about the separation of the Church and state in states where there had been an established church. Disestablishment took place in Maryland and New York during the Revolution, but not until 1786, through the efforts of Jefferson, did the Anglican Church lose its privileged position in Virginia. New Hampshire in 1818, Connecticut in 1819 and Massachusetts in 1833 separated the Congregationalist Church from the state.

The churches, following the analogy of the nation, which had created a national government by 1789, made constitutions and set up national organizations. The Methodists, led by Coke and Asbury, created a national church in 1784 which became known as the Methodist Episcopal Church. The Anglicans set up the Protestant Episcopal Church in 1789. The Presbyterians created a national church in 1788, and the first national General Assembly met in 1789. The Dutch Reformed created a national church in 1792, and the German Reformed emerged in 1793. New England churches were not greatly affected by the tendencies to centralization and nationalization of organization. It is fortunate that the new national churches were given fresh spiritual zeal by the Second Awakening, which began about the time the new nation adopted its constitution. The American churches had been tried by the fires of war, and they were now ready to take up their mission to the new united nation.

BIBLIOGRAPHY

The Story of Religion in America (New York: Harper & Brothers Publishers, 2d. rev. ed., 1950) by William W. Sweet is an excellent survey of church history in the United States, although it is marred in a few places by the author's liberal bias.

The shorter survey, *The History of Christianity in America* (New York: American Tract Society, 1938), by Frank G. Beardsley is a brief but useful volume.

Henry K. Rowe's *The History of Religion in the United States* (New York: The Macmillan Co., 1928), a somewhat liberal work, has many helpful interpretations.

Although *American Faith* (New York: W. W. Norton & Co., Inc., 1940) by Ernest S. Bates leans toward an economic interpretation, it is a useful survey of American church history before 1865.

The most useful work for colonial church history is *Religion in Colonial America* (New York: Charles Scribner's Sons, 1943) by William W. Sweet.

The most valuable collection of source materials for American church history is Peter G. Mode's *Source Book and Bibliographical Guide for American Church History* (Menasha, Wisconsin: George Banta Publishing Co., 1921).

There are excellent discussions by denominational experts of the European background and history in America to the present of the leading American denominations in *The American Church of the Protestant Heritage* (New York: Philosophical Library, 1953), edited by Vergilius Ferm.

The *History of American Congregationalism* (Boston: The Pilgrim Press, 1942) by Gaius G. Atkins and Frederick L. Fagley is a standard history of the American Congregational churches.

Robert G. Torbet has presented an able account of the Baptists in his *A History of the Baptists* (Philadelphia: The Judson Press, 1950).

The story of the Presbyterians is described by William T. Hanzsche in *The Presbyterians* (Philadelphia: The Westminster Press, 1934).

Several good biographies of leading religious leaders in the colonial period have been published and are available in the larger libraries.

Excellent brief biographies of the leading characters of the colonial and later periods may be found in Volume III of William W. Sweet's *Makers of Christianity* (New York: Henry Holt & Co., 1937).

A Faithful Narrative, describing the revival at Northampton, and *Thoughts* on the Great Awakening are contained in Jonathan Edwards, *Edwards on Revival* (New York: Dunning & Spalding, 1832).

William W. Sweet's little volume, *Revivalism in America* (New York: Charles Scribner's Sons, 1945), is an excellent discussion of the various revivals.

A History of American Revivals (New York: American Tract Society, 1904) by Frank G. Beardsley may still be consulted with profit.

Chapter XXXIII

THE RELIGIONS OF RATIONALISM AND REVIVALISM

The sixteenth century was marked by the rise of Protestantism and the development of its basic ideas through the efforts
of such creative leaders as Calvin and Luther. Unfortunately,
during the seventeenth century Protestantism developed merely
a system of orthodox dogma which one accepted intellectually.
This system brought about a new Scholasticism, particularly
among the Lutherans in Germany who became more interested
in dogma than in the expression of doctrine in practical life.
This cold intellectual expression of Christianity, coupled with
the severe religious wars between 1560 and 1648 and the rise
of rationalistic philosophy and empirical science, led to rationalism and formalism in religion between 1660 and 1730 in England, Europe and, later, in America. The distaste for cold orthodoxy among the rationalistic philosophers and scientists, the
rise of natural religion and the insistence upon the Church as
a group of believers covenanting together with God and one
another led to the rise of toleration and denominationalism.

During the late seventeenth and eighteenth centuries two
responses to this Protestant Scholasticism developed. The one
response was rationalism, which had its religious expression in
Deism, and the other was revivalism. The latter expressed itself in some cases in an emphasis upon what is called the
theology of the inner light and in other cases in a stress upon
the importance of the Bible and personal piety. The following
diagram will illustrate the relationships between these various
movements between 1648 and 1789.

I. RATIONALISM AND RELIGION

Modern thought has emphasized the importance of reason and
the scientific method in the discovery of truth and has refused
to be bound by traditions of the past. These ideas had their
rise in the period between the end of the Thirty Years War

and the beginning of the French Revolution. Some attention should be given to the reasons for the rise and the results of these ideas because of their impact upon religion.

SEVENTEENTH AND EIGHTEENTH CENTURY RELIGIOUS MOVEMENTS

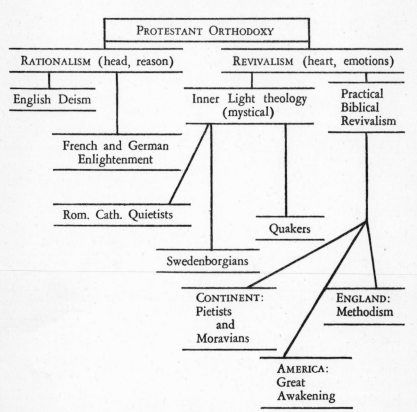

A. *The Origin of Deism.*

Several developments contributed to the rise of rationalism in the seventeenth century. The scientific horizon was greatly expanded by the work of outstanding scientists of the day. The old theory of a geocentric universe gave way to the theory of a heliocentric universe. This theory was developed by Nicholas Copernicus (1473–1543) and popularized by Galileo Galilei (1564–1642). Isaac Newton (1642–1727), while still a young man, became interested in the question of whether there were basic principles that operated throughout the universe. In 1687 he wrote *Principia Mathematica* in which he developed the idea of the law of gravitation. Gravitation provided the key to unify the phenomena of science. Until it was replaced by Darwin's concept of growth, the principle of natural law was considered to be basic, and men came to look upon the universe as a machine or mechanism that operated by inflexible natural laws. Men applied the principle of natural laws discovered by reason to many other areas of knowledge, such as political science and religion.

Europeans also became acquainted with other cultures as adventurous traders went to the far corners of the earth to carry on their business. Knowledge of non-Christian religions was brought back to Europe, and scholars began to compare this knowledge with Christianity. They found similarities in principles. This led many to wonder if there were not a basic natural religion which all men had apart from the Bible or priests. In this way men were led in their thinking toward deism, which seemed to provide a religion both natural and scientific.

The new philosophies of empiricism and rationalism also challenged tradition in the name of reason. These philosophies substituted reason and man's senses for revelation as the main avenues to knowledge. They were earth-bound in their concern for the knowing subject, man, rather than for the reality to be known, God.

Empiricism provided science with a method, a method that has been somewhat deified by Positivists and Pragmatists. Francis Bacon (1561–1626) published his *Novum Organum* in 1620. In this work he developed an inductive method of interpreting nature. This method, he thought, would replace the deductive method of Aristotle, so widely used by the Scholastics in the Middle Ages. Using the inductive method, which is also known as the scientific method, the scientist accepted nothing on the basis of authority alone. He developed a hypothesis, observed facts concerning his tentative idea, checked the facts by repeated experimentation, and only then developed a general law. In the older deductive method, men linked a general principle, accepted on authority, to a fact and drew a conclusion without testing the validity of the general principle.

The empirical philosophy of John Locke (1632–1704) reinforced Bacon's contention. In his *Essay Concerning Human*

Understanding (1690), Locke denied the existence of fixed ideas in the mind, such as time and space, and asserted that the mind of a baby is a blank. Knowledge comes to the baby as his senses present sensations to his mind, which by reflection upon the sensations creates knowledge. This tying of knowledge to sensation created a materialistic approach to life, although Locke himself was an orthodox Christian. The combination of Locke's ideas with those of Bacon led to an exaltation of the scientific method as the major way to get knowledge.

The rationalistic school of philosophers had also earlier exalted man's own ability to discover truth by reason without recourse to revelation. Theology was to be natural theology rather than revealed theology. Rene Descartes (1596–1650) developed a philosophy in which his starting point was doubt of everything except his own consciousness and his ability to think. From this self-evident fact he built up a system of thought in which various axioms could be known with mathematical certainty. He argued that there were certain innate concepts in human reason, such as time and space, which enable the mind to organize the data that the senses bring to it. Although Descartes was a dualist who believed in the existence of mental and material worlds, he believed that by reason alone could he accept the existence of God and the soul. His ideas, which were amplified by Leibnitz and Spinoza, tended to strengthen man's belief in his ability to attain knowledge by unaided reason and scientific method. Rationalistic philosophy and the scientific laws of Newton gave rise to the view that by reason and the scientific method man could discover natural laws and could live in accord with them.

Deism was a natural result of the scientific and philosophic approach to knowledge that has just been described. It arose in England during the seventeenth century and spread from there to France, Germany and America. It was a natural religion or a religion of reason. Deism (Latin *deus*, God) set forth a system of belief in a transcendent God who left His creation after He had created it to be governed by natural laws discoverable by reason. God thus became an "absentee God." The Deist insists that God is above and beyond His creation. The pantheist tends to emphasize the immanence of God in His creation; but the theist has always insisted that the transcendent God is not a part of His creation but that He is immanent in it as Providence and as a Redeemer through Christ.

B. *The Dogmas of Deism.*

One of the main dogmas of Deism — because the Deists also had their dogmas, the natural laws of religion discoverable by reason — was the belief in a transcendent God who was the First Cause of a creation marked by evidences of design. The Deists believed that God left His creation to operate under natural laws; hence there was no place for miracles, the Bible as a revelation from God, prophecy, providence, or Christ as a God-man. The Deists taught that Christ was only a moral teacher and insisted that worship belonged to God. Another dogma was the belief that "virtue and piety" was the most important worship that one could give to God. God's ethical laws are in the Bible, which is an ethical guidebook, and in the nature of man, where they can be discovered by human reason. Man must repent of wrongdoing and have his life conform to ethical laws because there is immortality for the soul and the soul faces reward and punishment after death.

Deism dominated the thinking of the upper classes in England between the presentation of the basic tenets of Deism by Herbert of Cherbury (1583–1648) in 1624 and the work of David Hume (1711–1776). Herbert's belief may be summed up in the statement that God, who exists, must be worshiped by repentance and an ethical life so that the immortal soul may enjoy eternal reward rather than punishment. Charles Blount (1654–1693) was another influential deist. John Toland (1670–1722), Lord Shaftesbury (1671–1713), and others insisted that Christianity was not mysterious but could be proved by reason. What could not be proved by reason should be repudiated. David Hume, one of the last influential deistic writers, centered his attacks upon the miracles of the Bible.

Many rose to defend orthodox Christianity. William Law (1686–1761), who wrote the fine work concerning the devotional life of the Christian entitled *A Serious Call to a Devout and Holy Life* (1728), also wrote *The Case for Reason* (1732) in which he argues that man cannot comprehend the whole of religion by rational processes because God is above reason. Joseph Butler's *Analogy of Religion* (1736) shows that the arguments the Deists used against the God of the Bible would apply to the God of nature if reason were the authority. Butler used the argument from probability to demonstrate that orthodox Christianity answered problems better than Deism. William Paley (1743–1805) used the argument from design to prove the existence of a God who revealed Himself in the Bible, Christ and miracles so that man might be led to a good life of obedience to God and of preparation for immortality.

C. The Spread of Deism.

Because the English Deists, such as Herbert and Shaftesbury, traveled in France, because Deistic books were translated and published abroad, and because Frenchmen, such as Rousseau and Voltaire, traveled in England, Deistic ideas spread to France where they found a favorable climate of opinion among the *philosophes* of the eighteenth century. Rousseau's Deism was developed in his *Emile,* and Voltaire's Deism permeated all his writings against the Church and in favor of tolerance. Denis Diderot (1713–1784) edited the *Encyclopedie,* a large rationalistic and Deistic encyclopedia of universal knowledge. The contest in France was between the Roman Catholic Church and these Deistic freethinkers. Because their Deistic ideology provided a rationalization for the French revolutionaries in 1789, the freethinkers had an important influence on the coming of that revolution which was to bring such great changes in Europe.

Such things as the writings of the Deists, Toland's visit to Hanover, and the residence of Voltaire at the court of Frederick the Great spread the religion of reason to Germany, where it found a congenial home despite the earlier work of the Pietists.

Immigration of English Deists, Deistic writings and Deistic officers of the English army in America during the war of 1756–1763 helped to spread Deism in the colonies. Franklin, Jefferson, Ethan Allen and Thomas Paine were among the leading Deists of America. Paine's *Age of Reason* (1795) helped to popularize the ideas of the Deists. In this manner America as well as England, France and Germany were exposed to the destructive influences of Deism.

D. The Results of Deism.

Deism helped to strengthen the idea of the omnipotence of the state because men, such as Rousseau, insisted that the state was of natural origin. The state originated, so the argument went, in a social compact among sovereign people who chose their rulers. The rulers were responsible to the people to such an extent that if they failed in their duties, the people had the right to revolt against them. The state, subject only to the sovereign people, is supreme in all areas of life. Deism helped to foster the idea that human reason by use of the scientific method could discover truth of universal validity. It also helped to develop the concept of man's essential goodness and perfectibility so that continued human progress toward a more perfect order upon earth could be expected. Deism was unduly optimistic because it tended to ignore human sin. Modern liberalism with its emphasis upon rationalism can look to Deism as its spiritual ancestor.

Deists also helped to create the modern system of higher criticism of the Bible. While there is a legitimate higher criticism, which investigates the historical background of the books of the Bible in a reverent manner, that which developed in the nineteenth century led to a denial of the full inspiration of the Bible.

However, some gains for Christianity, came from Deism. No one will condemn the rise of tolerance, and in this rise Deists played a leading part because they believed that religious ideas, which were rational, should be held freely. The Deists also cooperated with orthodox Christians in various humanitarian activities because they believed in the dignity of man as a rational being. The impetus to study also led to beneficial results in the field of textual criticism and exegesis. Scholars helped to develop an authoritative text of the Bible and to demonstrate that it has come down to us from the original authors in an excellent state of preservation. The application of grammar and history to a correct exegesis of the Bible was stimulated indirectly by the rationalistic movement.

II. The Religions of Revivalism

Numerous revivalistic movements on the Continent and in England and America arose concurrently with the development of rationalism and Deism. In some cases these movements were based upon an emphasis upon an "inner light" by which man could be illumined spiritually apart from the Bible. Roman Catholic Quietism and English Quakerism illustrated this tendency. Revivalism based upon the Scriptures may be illustrated by Pietism and Methodism in the Protestant church.

A. *Movements upon the Continent.*

Quietism was a mystical movement within the Roman Catholic Church during the seventeenth century. It emphasized an immediate intuitional approach to God by the passive soul opening itself to the influence of the inner light. It was a reaction against the emphasis upon the rationalization of dogma. Forerunners of the Quietists were godly Charles Borromeo (1538–1584), cardinal and archbishop of Milan, Ignatius Loyola, St. Theresa of Spain and Francis of Sales (1567–1622) of France. The latter's *Introduction to the Devout Life* (1609) could be read by Protestants today with profit. These mystics of the Counter Reformation were succeeded by the Quietists of the seventeenth century.

Michael Molinos (1640–1690) in his *Spiritual Guide* (1675) emphasized passivity of soul as the way to open oneself to the impartation of divine light from God. In such a state the human will was not even to be exercised. His ideas were adopted by Madame Guyon (1648–1717) who emphasized passive contemplation of the Divine as the method and absorption into the Divine as the goal of mystical experience. Francis Fenelon (1651–1715), the royal tutor, defended her from Bossuet's attacks, and in his work, *Christian Perfection,* gave a positive note to Quietism. The work has been an aid to the devotional life of Protestants as well as Roman Catholics.

Protestant mysticism may be illustrated by the work of the great Swedish scientist, Emanuel Swedenborg (1688–1772), who came to the conclusion that back of the physical world of nature was a corresponding spiritual world. He maintained that communication between these two worlds was possible through conversation with heavenly beings. He spiritualized the Bible to correlate it with the revelations that these heavenly visitants brought to him. By 1828 a church was organized in England, and the denomination is still in existence in several countries. His views led him and his followers into error because he gave Scripture a mystical meaning instead of accepting its real meaning.

Quite different from the inner light mysticism just discussed was the Pietist movement in Germany which arose as an evangelical corrective to the cold orthodoxy of the seventeenth century Lutheran Church. Pietism emphasized a subjective and individual return to Bible study and prayer. Biblical truth should be manifested daily in a life of piety by laymen and ministers alike. Although there were other contributing factors, the movement was primarily a result of the efforts of Philip

Spener (1635–1705), who became a Lutheran pastor in Frankfort in 1666. In 1670 he organized what he called *collegia pietatis*, meetings in a home for practical Bible study and prayer. His *Pia Desideria* (1675) emphasized these "cottage prayer meetings" as an aid to the cultivation of personal piety among Lutherans. In 1686 he went to Dresden as court preacher. From here in 1691 he went to an influential pastorate in Berlin where he remained until his death.

August Francke (1663–1727) and some friends at Leipzig University also founded a group for the study of the Bible. During a visit to Dresden Francke was influenced by Spener, who was finally able to get him a professorship in 1691 at the University of Halle, which soon became a center of Pietism. Francke organized the *Paedagogium*, a free elementary school for poor children, in 1695, and a secondary school two years later. He also set up an orphan house for orphans and was influential in the creation of the Bible Institute founded after his death in 1710, to publish and to circulate copies of the Scriptures.

Pietism brought a new stress on the study and discussion of the Bible and its application to daily practice and the cultivation of a pious life. Stress was laid upon the function of the Holy Spirit as an Illuminator of the Bible. Good works as an expression of true religion were emphasized. Fresh spiritual vigor was infused into the Lutheran Church. Halle became a center of missionary effort. Pioneer work was done in Africa and the islands of the Pacific by missionaries from Halle. The scientific study of languages and church history was stimulated in the attempt to get at the true meaning of the writers of the Bible for daily life. Indifference to doctrine on the part of Pietists led some to adopt the philosophy of idealism.

In addition to its infusion of fresh spiritual vigor into the Lutheran Church, Pietism resulted in the founding of the Moravian Church by Count von Zinzendorf (1700–1760), who studied in Francke's lower school at Halle and in Wittenberg where he read law. Von Zinzendorf emphasized a life of vital personal devotedness to Christ. In 1722 Bohemian refugees founded Hernnhut on Zinzendorf's Berthelsdorf estate, and in 1727 he became leader of their organization. The Moravian Church was recognized as a separate church by 1742. It had a threefold organization of bishop, elder and deacon by 1745. The movement had such a missionary vision that missionaries were sent to the West Indies, Greenland and Africa by the middle of the century. After a short period in Georgia, the Moravians moved to Pennsylvania where Zinzendorf during his stay in America tried to unite all German Protestants under the Moravians. Zinzendorf's passionate, poetically expressed devotion to Christ was put into theological expression by August Spangenberg, the theologian of the movement. It is interesting to note that the circle of influence was completed when Wesley was helped to a personal faith in Christ by the Moravians. Wycliffe's teachings had influenced Hus, the founder of the Bohemian Brethren, out of which the Moravian Church, which was to have such an influence upon the spiritual life of the Englishman John Wesley, emerged. It is unfortunate that the English influence on the Continent in the seventeenth and eighteenth centuries promoted Deism and rationalism.

B. *Revivalism and the Inner Light in England.*

The Quakers appeared on the English religious scene during the chaotic period of the Civil War and the Commonwealth. They set aside the doctrines of an organized Church and the Bible as the sole and final revelation of God's will in favor of the doctrine of the Inner Light by which they meant that the Holy Spirit can give immediate and direct knowledge of God apart from the Bible. They resembled the Montanists, but their mystical tendencies were fortunately balanced by moral earnestness and a strong social passion.

George Fox (1624–1691), who was born in a weaver's home and apprenticed to a shoemaker who was also a dealer in wool, started his search for spiritual truth in 1643 when he was challenged by two Puritans to a drinking bout in which the one who stopped first would have to pay the bill. In disgust he left the Church, and not until 1647 did he have a satisfactory religious experience that ended his seeking. Christianity then became a way of life to him, a mystical experience in which one could come directly to God. He began to preach, and a group of his followers, who called themselves Friends, was organized in 1648. They were also called Quakers. In 1652 Margaret Fell of Swarthmore Hall was won to Quakerism, and her home became the unofficial center of Quakerism. Fox later married her. The expansion of Quakerism was rapid as missionary zeal and persecution by the authorities caused its adherents to seek new homes outside of England. When Fox traveled in the Thirteen Colonies (1671–1673), he found many Quaker groups. In 1666 monthly meetings were established to provide order and a means of checking on the conduct of the membership.

Robert Barclay (1648–1690) became the theologian of the movement. He published his Latin *Apology for the Quakers* in 1678. His propositions give the essence of Quaker theology.[1] To him the Spirit was the sole Revelator of God and the Source of the Inner Light within man which gave him spiritual illumination. The Bible was but a secondary rule of faith, and the inspiration of the writers was placed on the same level as the inspiration of Fox or any Quaker. However, revelations to a Friend should not contradict "the Scriptures, or right and sound reason." Because of the Inner Light a professional ministry was unnecessary, and the two sacraments, being inward and spiritual, were separated from material symbols and ceremonies. Quakers were not to engage in war, and slavery was banned. Woolman, an American Quaker, was one of the earliest to speak and write in favor of the abolition of slavery. Oaths in court were banned, and human titles were not to be honored. This latter teaching got the Quakers into much trouble in class-conscious England where the upper class expected titles and doffing of hats from lower classes. By 1661 nearly thirty-two hundred Quakers suffered imprisonment, but the movement grew in spite or because of persecution. By 1660 there were about sixty thousand Quakers in England.

William Penn (1644–1718) was able to bring relief from persecution when Charles II gave him a large grant of land in America in 1681 as payment of a sixteen thousand pound debt to Penn's father. Penn organized Pennsylvania in 1682 on a basis of complete religious freedom and invited the oppressed sects of Europe, including the Quakers, to find refuge there. Both in Pennsylvania and West Jersey, Quakers become quite numerous.

The Friends have always emphasized the spread of their faith by a strong missionary program in which social service plays an important part, but in doing this they have not neglected education. The excellence of Haverford and Swarthmore Colleges, as well as many other schools, is a testimony to Quaker

---

[1] H. Bettenson, *Documents of the Christian Church* (New York: Oxford University Press, 1947), pp. 354-359; P. Schaff, *Creeds of Christendom* (New York: Charles Scribner's Sons, 3 vols., 6th ed., 1890), Vol. III, pp. 789-798.

interest in education. But the movement has not been free from dangers of schism and the cooling off of spiritual zeal. The lack of interest in doctrine and the absence of an objective historical standard, such as the Bible, has in some cases brought excessive mysticism or led in others to a vague theism in which the person of Christ is not sufficiently exalted.

The Methodist revival was the third religious awakening in England, coming after the sixteenth century Reformation and seventeenth century Puritanism. It was associated with the name of John Wesley (1703–1791), who dominated the century so far as religion was concerned. Historians readily acknowledge that Methodism ranks with the French Revolution and the Industrial Revolution as one of the great historical phenomena of the century, and some subscribe to the idea that Wesley's preaching saved England from a revolution similar to that of France.

We have already seen that the rationalistic religion of Deism was widely accepted among the upper classes. Sermons in the Established Church were often only long homilies filled with moral platitudes. The upper clergy were highly paid while the lower clergy with small incomes of twenty to fifty pounds a year could hardly be expected to be efficient. Too often they became hangers-on of the local squire and joined in his coarse sports and drinking bouts. Morals were at a low ebb, too. In the first half of the century the death rate went up as cheap gin killed many and sent others to the asylum. Gambling was rampant. Charles James Fox, a political leader, was said to have lost one hundred thousand pounds in an evening of gambling. Bull-, bear-, fox-, and cock-baiting were regular pastimes, and a series of executions by hanging on Tyburn Hill was a gala occasion for the whole family. It was indeed a "sick century."

Wesley was the fifteenth of nineteen children born to Samuel and Susannah Wesley. He was narrowly saved from death when the Wesley home burned in 1709. After this experience he often referred to himself as a "brand plucked from the burning." He entered Oxford in 1720 on a scholarship. In 1726 he was made a fellow of Lincoln College and was ordained in the Anglican Church. After two years, during which he helped his father handle a second parish adjoining Epworth, he returned to his duties as a fellow. Wesley then became the leading spirit in the "Holy Club," which included his brother Charles. The members of this club were nicknamed Methodists by the students because of their methodical Bible study and prayer habits and regular attempts at social service in jails and homes of the poor. Between 1735 and 1738 Wesley was in Georgia as chaplain in Oglethorpe's colony.[2] His ritualistic ideas, strict churchmanship, his simplicity and frankness in his relations with women created such difficulties with his parishioners that he was forced to go home in 1738. On May 24, 1738, while listening to the reading of Luther's preface to his *Commentary on Romans,* Wesley's heart was "strangely warmed," and he trusted Christ alone for salvation from sin. His brother Charles had had a similar experience two days earlier. Because of the brave conduct of Moravians in a storm at sea on the way to Georgia, the words of Spangenberg in Georgia,[3] and the efforts of Peter Bohler[4] all of which had been important influences in his conversion, Wesley paid a visit to Hernnhut to study the Moravian Church more closely.

In 1739 George Whitefield, with whom he later broke because of the former's Calvinistic theology, asked Wesley to engage in field preaching at Bristol. Thus began John Wesley's career of field preaching during the course of which he traveled about 250,000 miles on horseback in England, Scotland and Ireland, preached about 42,000 sermons, wrote over 50 books, and organized his followers. He organized a Methodist society and built a chapel in Bristol in 1739. In that same year he also bought the "Foundery" building in London which became the headquarters for his work.

The fine hymns which his brother Charles wrote were a great help in the meetings. Charles wrote over six thousand hymns, among which "Jesus Lover of My Soul" and "Hark the Herald Angels Sing" are still universal favorites. Following the path blazed by Isaac Watts (1674–1748), the Congregationalist theologian and "father of English hymnody," Charles wrote hymns

[2] In 1733 philanthropist James Oglethorpe founded Georgia as a refuge for debtors and for persecuted Protestants from Germany.

[3] When Wesley arrived in Georgia, he met the Moravian leader Spangenberg. The Moravian asked him: "Do you know Jesus Christ?" Wesley could only reply: "I know He is the Saviour of the world." To this Spangenberg replied: "True, but do you know that He has saved *you?*"

[4] Bohler was another Moravian whom Wesley met. The three main points of Bohler's teaching were a complete self-surrendering faith, an instantaneous conversion and a joy in believing.

other than rhymed passages of Scripture, which had been used up to that time.

Wesley did not want to break with the Anglican Church, and therefore he organized his converts into societies similar to Spener's *collegia pietatis*. The societies were subdivided into bands and again into classes of twelve under a lay leader who had the spiritual oversight of the class. In 1744 the first annual conference of his preachers was held in London, and in 1746 he divided England into five circuits. In 1784 he ordained two men as ministers and set apart Thomas Coke as superintendent of the Methodist Church in America. The Church set up its own national organization in America in that year. Not until after Wesley's death were the Methodists of England organized into a Methodist Church separate from the Anglican Church. The Anglican influence in the Methodist Church was demonstrated by episcopal polity and the reception of the Communion while kneeling at the altar rail.

The Methodist Church accepted an Arminian theology after Wesley's break with Whitefield, but the major doctrine that Wesley stressed was justification by faith through an instantaneous experience of conversion. He also laid great emphasis upon the doctrine of Christian perfection or perfect love. This was a belief in the possibility of absolute Christian perfection in motive in this life because the love of God so filled the heart of the believer that God's love would expel sin and promote absolute holiness of life. This progressive process was to be initiated by an act of faith. Wesley made it clear that this was not sinless nor infallible perfection but rather the possibility of sinlessness in motive in a heart that was completely suffused with the love of God. Mistakes in judgment might still result in bad moral consequences, but the possibility of achieving the ideal was there. This seems to be the teaching of his letters[5] and his book, *A Plain Account of Christian Perfection*.

Wesley insisted that the Gospel should have an impact upon society, and no one can deny the impact of the Methodist revival upon English society. There is some reason to believe that England might have had an uprising of the workers similar to that in France if they had not been won to Christ. Most of the later labor leaders got their training in speaking in the class

[5] John Telford, ed., *The Letters of the Rev. John Wesley* (London: Epworth Press, 8 vols., 1931), Vol. II, pp. 280-281; Vol. IV, p. 213; Vol. V, pp. 38, 223. P. Schaff, *op. cit.*, Vol. III, pp. 807-813.

meetings. The gin traffic was stopped, partially because of the influence of the revival. Wesley was an advocate of the abolition of slavery and a friend of the early abolitionists. His love of amateur doctoring led him to establish the first free medical dispensary in England in 1746. He had an influence upon the founder of the Sunday school movement, Robert Raikes, and upon John Howard, the leader in prison reform. By the time of his death a strong Methodist Church was in existence in the United States. About seventy thousand followers in England were organized into a national church very soon after his death. This neat, almost dapper, little, hardworking man had under God transformed the religious life of the workers of England. The Evangelical Revival within the Anglican Church, a result of the Methodist revival, was to transform the upper class of England and to help England become the great leader of nations and the keeper of world peace during the nineteenth century.

BIBLIOGRAPHY

The student will find *English Deism* (Grand Rapids: Wm. B. Eerdmans Publishing Co., 1934) by John Orr a helpful discussion of the development and expansion of English Deism.

George Fox becomes more real to the student who reads the *Journal* which he faithfully kept.

The *Beginnings of Quakerism* (London: The Macmillan Co., 1912) by William C. Braithwaite describes the rise of the Quaker movement.

Elbert Russell in *The History of Quakerism* (New York: The Macmillan Co., 1943) ably describes the worldwide expansion and contributions of the Quaker movement.

Although the liberal bias is apparent, *John Wesley* (New York: The Dial Press, 1929) by Arnold Lunn is an accurate and interesting account of Wesley's life and work.

The longer work entitled *Life and Times of John Wesley* (New York: Harper & Brothers, 3 vols., 1872) by Luke Tyerman is perhaps the best longer biography of Wesley's life.

Leslie F. Church presents a clear picture of the early Methodists in his volume, *The Early Methodist People* (New York: Philosophical Library, 1939).

Wesley's influence is depicted in a scholarly fashion in J. Wesley Bready's *England: Before and After Wesley* (New York: Harper & Brothers, 1938), which appeared in an American edition without the footnotes under the title, *This Freedom Whence* (New York: American Tract Society, rev. ed., 1943).

The Theology of John Wesley (New York: Abingdon-Cokesbury Press, 1946) by William R. Cannon is a well-documented account of Wesley's theological views.

The student should consult abbreviated or, if time permits, the complete editions of Wesley's *Journals* and *Letters* to grasp the spirit of Wesley.

Wesley's contributions are also discussed in J. Ernest Rattenbury's *Wesley's Legacy to the World* (Nashville: Cokesbury Press, 1929).

Albert D. Belden has ably presented the evangelistic and humanitarian work of George Whitefield with documentation from the sources in *George Whitefield the Awakener* (New York: The Macmillan Co., 1953).

REVIVALISM, MISSIONS AND MODERNISM, 1789–1914

Chapter XXXIV

ROMAN CATHOLIC VICTORIES AND VICISSITUDES, 1789–1914

The Roman Catholic Church suffered the loss of her temporal possessions and much of her political influence between 1789 and 1914. The ignominious fate of the papacy during the French Revolution was in marked contrast to the advances made during the period of the Counter Reformation. During the Romantic reaction after the Napoleonic wars, she regained prestige and power until 1870. From then until World War I her story is one of loss of prestige and the rise of anti-clericalism in many countries of Europe. These difficulties grew out of the problem of the relation of the national churches to the universal papal church.

I. THE PAPACY DURING THE REVOLUTIONARY ERA

Before the outbreak of the revolution in France, bad economic, political, social and legal conditions and the successful example of the English Revolution of 1689 and the American Revolution of 1776 were fused by the development of an ideology that rationalized the right of popular revolution against Louis XVI. This ideology was the result of the teachings of the *philosophes,* among whom were Rousseau, Montesquieu, Diderot and Francois M. Arouet or, as he is better known, Voltaire. While Rousseau and Montesquieu provided the political ideology for revolution, Voltaire criticized the Church of Rome and cried out for tolerance. It must be admitted that there were grounds for criticism of the Roman Catholic Church in France. It owned much land, the revenues from which went for the most part to the upper clergy. Voltaire favored a religion of reason rather than the religion of the corrupt leaders of the Roman Catholic Church in France.

The National Assembly of France in November, 1789 declared that church lands were public property and it issued bonds that were redeemable in this land. Later these bonds were circulated as money. Early in 1790 monasteries were abolished by law. In the summer of 1790 the Assembly passed the Civil Constitution of the Clergy[1] by which the number of bishops was reduced to eighty-three, a number corresponding to the number of provincial units. The bishops were to be elected by the voters who chose the civil officials, and the pope was merely to be notified of their choice. Clergymen were to be paid by the state and were to take an oath of loyalty to the state. The pope's power was reduced to that of stating the dogma of the Roman Catholic Church. Churchmen did not object too strenuously to the loss of church lands, but they thought that this new act meant secularization of the church, and they were violently opposed to it.

The Roman Catholic Church and the French state were completely separated during the Reign of Terror of 1793 and 1794 when so many were executed for counter-revolutionary activities. At this time support of the church became voluntary. The more atheistic of the leaders even tried for a time in 1793 to force a religion of reason on France, and they crowned an opera dancer of doubtful morals as the goddess of reason in Notre Dame Cathedral. Others, who would not accept this extreme, did accept the change in the calendar that made every tenth day rather than Sunday a day of rest. This calendar, which lasted from 1792 to 1804, was designed to eliminate Sundays and the numerous saints' days. Robespierre preferred a religion of Deism, which involved a belief in God and the immortality of the soul. In this short period the Roman Catholic Church faced tremendous opposition. Even the pope was captured and taken as a prisoner to France where he died.

When Napoleon took control in 1799, he realized that the majority of Frenchmen were Roman Catholic in religion, and he proposed a liaison between the Roman Catholic Church and state by the Concordat of 1801. In the Concordat Napoleon recognized the Roman Catholic religion as "the religion of the great majority of French citizens," but he did not make it the established religion. Bishops were to be named by the state and consecrated by the pope. The clergy were to be paid by the state, but the property taken from the Roman Catholic Church in 1790 was not to be returned to it. This Concordat governed the relations between the Church and state in France until 1905.

[1] John H. Stewart, *A Documentary Survey of the French Revolution* (New York: The Macmillan Co., 1951), pp. 158-159; 169-181.

But the Organic Articles of 1802 provided that papal bulls could not be published in France nor synods held without the consent of the government. The Church was thus controlled by the state.

II. PAPAL GAINS, 1815–1870

Until 1870 the papacy was able to regain lost ground in Europe. Metternich, the chancellor of Austria, favored an alliance of the rulers of Europe with the Roman Church to protect the *status quo* and to prevent national or democratic uprisings anywhere in Europe. Because of this reactionary viewpoint, he favored the papacy wherever possible. The Congress of Vienna, of which he was chairman, restored the Papal States to the pope. Metternich wrote of the importance of religion as a bulwark of society in his "Confession of Faith" (1820).

The Romantic movement also aided the papacy because it was a revolt from the rationalism and individualism of the eighteenth century. It emphasized an intuitional approach to life. Romanticists expressed themselves in poetry rather than prose; they emphasized content rather than form; they glorified the medieval past and nature; and they made their appeal to the heart of man rather than to his head. Wordsworth emphasized the presence of God in nature; Walter Scott and Hugh Walpole glorified the medieval past in their novels; Chateaubriand glorified the church in his literary works. Rousseau wrote that man was happiest in a state of nature. He expressed his belief in the fitness of the people to rule by his insistence upon their right to choose their rulers through an expression of their general will, which was to be discovered by a majority vote. His *Social Contract* began with the words, "Man was born free and is everywhere in chains." Painters also gave less attention to forms and rules in their work, and they sought to express upon the canvas not a copy of reality but the impression that reality had made upon them. Their paintings were an interpretation of nature rather than a portrait of it. Idealistic philosophy also emphasized the volitional and emotional side of man's nature. Kant built his arguments for God, the soul and immortality upon the sense of the right that man had within his nature. Men also became interested in the past history of their various states. All of these expressions of Romanticism, which held sway in Europe from about 1790 to 1850, strengthened the hold of religion upon man. Particularly did the colorful, ritualistic, sensuous religion of the Roman Catholic Church give rein to religious imagination and sentiment.

The Jesuits, who had been disbanded by papal action in 1773, were reconstituted by a papal bull issued by Pius VII in 1814. They immediately began their work of education and missionary activities, although they interfered less with the political activities of states than they had earlier in their history.

The political disabilities that had kept Roman Catholics in Britain from voting and filling any public office were removed in 1829 by the Catholic Emancipation Act, the result of the work of Daniel O'Connell. The Anglican Church was disestablished in Ireland in 1869 by Gladstone so that the people of Ireland no longer had to pay tithes to support the Anglican Church as well as supporting their own Roman Catholic clergy by voluntary gifts. The Oxford movement in the Anglican Church also helped the Roman Catholic Church both directly and indirectly. In 1845 Henry Edward Manning and John Henry Newman, leaders in the movement, joined the Roman Catholic Church, and by 1862 about 625 important individuals — soldiers, professors, members of Parliament — and nearly 250 Anglican clergymen became Roman Catholics. Indirectly, the movement aided Rome by restoring in the High Church section of the Anglican Church a view of the Communion not too far removed from transubstantiation, monasticism, ritualism in worship, and a sense of the importance of the Church in man's life. Many made an easy transition from the High Church party of the Anglican Church to the Roman Catholic Church.

Pius IX, who occupied the papal chair between 1846 and 1878, lost no opportunities to strengthen the Roman Catholic Church. In 1854, after consultation with the bishops of the church, Pius proclaimed the doctrine of the Immaculate Conception of Mary, that is, that Mary was conceived without "any taint of original sin." All of the faithful were henceforth to accept this doctrine as a part of the dogma of the Roman Catholic Church that one must believe in order to be saved.[2]

Shortly after this event the pope began to take note of the thought of the day that seemed hostile to the Roman Church, and in 1864 he issued the *Syllabus of Errors*.[3] In this he condemned such new forms of philosophy as idealism, with its tendency towards pantheism, toleration in religion, separation

[2] H. Bettenson, *Documents of the Christian Church* (New York: Oxford University Press, 1947), pp. 380-381.
[3] *Ibid.*, pp. 381-383.

of the Church and state, socialism, Bible societies, secular school systems, the view that the pope had no temporal power, civil marriage, and Biblical criticism. He believed that such thinking was destructive of the best interests of the church of which he was pontiff. In spite of this declaration, a movement favoring Biblical criticism made considerable gains among the Roman Catholic clergy. Pius X in 1907 issued a syllabus opposing all forms of Modernism that were expounded by such men as Alfred Loisy and George Tyrrell.

The declaration of papal infallibility in the decree of the Vatican Council in 1870 marked the peak of the work of Pius. The declaration was approved in 1870 by 533 of those who were present. Two voted against it, and a minority of nearly 100 had stayed away from the council that day. Evidently the heavy peals of thunder and the terrific flashes of lightning of the storm that raged outside were not reflected inside. The idea that when the pope speaks *ex cathedra*, that is, as the head of the Church on earth, concerning either faith or morals, whatever he says is infallible and must be accepted by the faithful as dogma to be believed if one is to enjoy salvation — that is the essence of the statement accepted by the council.[4] The doctrine made church councils unnecessary in the future because the pope was now the final authority concerning faith and morals.

III. THE PAPACY LOSES GROUND

The declaration of papal infallibility and the loss of political power were not far separated in time. Almost immediately after the declaration in 1870 the papacy began to experience anti-clerical hostility that brought losses in many countries. In 1870 the Italian armies took Rome when Louis Napoleon had to withdraw the French garrison protecting the papacy in order to meet the threat of the Franco-Prussian War, and the pope lost all of his temporal possessions except the immediate area of the Vatican buildings. But the pope would not come to terms with the new national Italian constitutional monarchy despite the generous offer held out in the Law of the Papal Guarantees of 1871 by the Italian government. This law offered him an annual sum of $645,000 in perpetuity to compensate him for the loss of his temporal possessions; it allowed him to keep his possessions in the Vatican; it provided for freedom of self-government in that area, and no interference from

4 *Ibid.*, p. 383.

the state. The pope refused to accept this settlement, issued an order forbidding Roman Catholics to vote or hold office in the Italian government, and retired to a self-imposed imprisonment in the Vatican from which a later pope was only rescued by an agreement with Mussolini's government in 1929.

The Church of Rome also faced trouble in Germany with the Iron Chancellor, Bismarck. Bismarck thought that the internationalism of the Roman Catholic Church stood in the way of full unification of the people of the new German Empire, which had been proclaimed in 1871 in the Hall of Mirrors in the Palace of Versailles. He thought that this "Black Internationale" was as much a threat to German national unity as the Red Internationale of socialism. In 1872 he expelled the Jesuits and in 1873 had the Falk or May Laws approved. These laws secularized education, put vital statistics under the control of the state, commanded civil marriage and forced the clergy to be educated in state universities. Bismarck, who remembered Canossa where Henry IV had been humiliated in 1073, said he would not go to Canossa as Henry had done. However, he did have to give up his battle by the end of the decade and to repeal some of the disabilities placed upon Roman Catholics because he found that the Roman Catholic Church was a valuable ally in the battle against socialism.

Anti-clerical feeling was strongest in France in this period. In 1901 religious orders of nuns and monks were excluded by law from educational activities, but the severest blow came in 1905 with the passing of the Separation Law by the French Chamber of Deputies. The clergy were to be no longer paid by the state, and all church property was to be taken over by the state. Churchmen had to form themselves into associations in order to get permission to use the property for religious purposes. The state would no longer recognize any faith in a special manner. Thus the Roman Church lost the privileged position that had been created by the Concordat of 1801. The pope denounced the new law, but his denunciation had no effect upon the carrying out of the law.

Such were the fortunes of the Roman Catholic Church between 1789 and 1914 in the major countries of Europe. Since 1914 the Church of Rome has found itself in increasing difficulties because of the expansion of Communism and the disorder

[428]

that two world wars in the twentieth century have created. It has fought back with every weapon at its disposal because defeat in the battle with Communism would bring about its destruction.

BIBLIOGRAPHY

History of the Papacy in the 19th Century (London: The Macmillan Co., 1930) by John B. Bury has helpful discussions of the *Syllabus of Errors* and the Vatican Council.

Chapter XXXV

RELIGION AND REFORM IN THE BRITISH ISLES

English religious life during the nineteenth century was characterized by a practical manifestation of the forces of revivalism in the Anglican and Nonconformist churches, by ritualism in the Anglican Church and by liberalism. The first produced a movement that fostered missionary activity and social reform; the second, a strong liturgical movement within the Church; and the last produced a liberal element in all of the major denominations. The pattern in Scotland was one of the reunion of diverse groups that had split off from the Church of Scotland. In Ireland the unjust double load of supporting the established Anglican Church by taxes and the Roman Catholic Church by voluntary giving was eased by the disestablishment of the Anglican Church.

I. English Religious Life

A. In the Anglican Church.

1. THE EVANGELICALS. The French Revolution made the ruling Tory party in England fearful of a similar revolution in Britain. From 1790 to 1820 the rising tide of reform was halted until religious and humanitarian liberal forces cooperated to force many reforms through the English Parliament between 1820 and 1852. The religious forces, generated by the Wesleyan and later Evangelical revivals, produced such practical fruits of social reform and missionary zeal that Latourette, the great modern historian of missions, has called the nineteenth century "The Great Century" of missionary effort. Personal piety and devotion to Christ and the Bible were also stimulated.

The Wesleyan revival of the early eighteenth century had been most influential in bringing personal religion to the workers and farm people of England. Not until the end of the century, however, was the upper class in the Established Church affected by revival. Between 1790 and 1830 the influence of revival was felt in the Anglican Church. The careless living of the Enlightenment gave way to personal piety, to faith in Christ and to philanthropic and social activity.

The early Evangelicals served as rectors in parishes scattered throughout England. One such was John Newton (1725–1807), the young infidel, who sank so low that he became the slave of a slave-trader. He was converted and, after a period of training, was ordained to the ministry. Becoming the minister at Olney, he was soon recognized as a spiritual leader, and his help was sought by many even outside Olney. His influence inspired the shy, sensitive invalid, William Cowper, to write his great hymns, such as "There is a Fountain Filled With Blood." Newton's successor, Thomas Scott, wrote a Biblical commentary that was widely used by Evangelicals.

The Evangelical movement also had such scholarly leaders as Isaac Milner (1750–1820) and Charles Simeon (1759–1836), who made Cambridge University the center of the Evangelical forces and who produced the Calvinistic theology that guided the group in its work and life.

The so-called Clapham Sect, made up of wealthy individuals who had their homes in Clapham, provided many of the lay leaders in social reform under the leadership of their godly rector, John Venn. This group of laymen often met in the great oval library of Henry Thornton, a wealthy banker who gave the greater part of his large income for philanthropy each year. Charles Grant, the chairman of the East India Company, William Wilberforce, who led in the fight for the emancipation of slaves, James Stephen, whose son, as head of the Colonial Office, gave so much aid to missionaries in the colonies, and other leading Evangelicals lived in this fashionable suburb which was just three miles from London.

Evangelical influence was also exerted on government through what was known as the Exeter Hall group. Exeter Hall in London was the building where most of the missionary societies held their annual meetings. These meetings so influenced Evangelical public opinion that the government was often forced to act favorably on matters of interest to the missionaries. John Philip, who served as the capable superintendent of Congregationalist missions in South Africa from 1819 until his death, used Exeter Hall influence to win favorable legislation to protect the Hottentots of Cape Colony from exploitation. This influence was always exerted to prevent exploitation or oppression of natives by white settlers and traders.

The Evangelicals were not so much interested in polity and doctrine as in the practical expression of Christianity in a redeemed life of piety that gained its inspiration from Bible study and prayer. William Wilberforce's widely read book, *Practical View* (1797), expressed the evangelical interest in the atonement as the only regenerating force, in justification by faith, in Bible reading under the illumination of the Holy Spirit, and in practical piety that would result in real service to society.

Followers of Adam Smith and the Philosophical Radicals, who looked to the writings of Jeremy Bentham and John Stuart Mill for inspiration, promoted political reform because they believed in the dignity of rational human personality, but the Evangelicals promoted social reform because they believed that man was a spiritual being who was either a potential or an actual son of God. Most of the social reforms between 1787 and 1850 were the outcome of Evangelical effort.

William Wilberforce (1759–1833), who had led a dissipated life in the company of such distinguished persons as the younger Pitt, was converted in 1784 through Isaac Milner's efforts. He then dedicated his life to the abolition of slavery in the British Empire. In 1787 a court decision made the ownership of slaves impossible in England. In 1807 Parliament passed an act that banned Englishmen from participating in the slave trade. Evangelical public opinion, working through the English delegate to the Congress of Vienna in 1815, was able to bring about the outlawing of the slave trade by most European states. This was at great cost to the English taxpayer because Spain and Portugal gave their consent only when they were promised 700,000 pounds from the English treasury. Slavery was ended in British possessions by an act passed just before Wilberforce's death in 1833. The act provided nearly 100,000,000 dollars to compensate the owners who freed 700,000 slaves. These achievements would have been impossible without the work of Wilberforce and his Evangelical friends in Parliament.

Another Evangelical of the second generation, Lord Shaftesbury (1801–1885), was the son of a socialite mother and a drunken politician. Having been led to Christ by his nurse, an Evangelical, Shaftesbury dedicated himself to the service of the poor and oppressed at the age of fourteen. He always marshalled his facts carefully so that he would have an unshakable case when he asked the House of Commons for reform legislation. He refused high offices in order to carry on his work without compensation, although others on the same commission were paid by Parliament. In 1840 he secured the passage of a law that kept boys under sixteen from the arduous and dangerous work of a chimney sweep. In 1842 he succeeded in getting legislation passed that barred women and boys under ten from working in the mines. His work resulted in laws in 1845 that protected the insane in such asylums as Bedlam where it had been the custom to charge a fee to admit the public to see the antics of the crazed. Crowded lodging houses, where disease and immorality abounded, became a thing of the past through his successful efforts in getting beneficial legislation.

Another Evangelical, John Howard, a Nonconformist who had been influenced by the Wesleyan revival, devoted his life and fortune to prison reform. Before his death in 1790 from jail fever, which he caught while inspecting a vile prison, he traveled fifty thousand miles and spent thirty thousand pounds of his own money in prison reform. Through his efforts jailers were paid salaries and given budgets for food, so that they no longer needed to extort money from the prisoners to keep the prison going. Prison sentences were emphasized as a corrective rather than as a punishment for crimes against society.

The Sunday school movement, introduced by Robert Raikes in 1780 to give children religious training and elementary instruction in reading, writing and simple arithmetic, was taken up by the Evangelicals and introduced into the Established Church. The Religious Tract Society, founded in 1799, and the British and Foreign Bible Society, founded in 1804 with Lord Teignmouth of the Clapham Sect as its first president, were practical expressions of the interest of the Evangelicals in the spread of the Gospel through the printed page. The Evangelicals were also the ardent supporters of the powerful missionary movement of the century.

2. THE BROAD CHURCH MOVEMENT. If the Evangelicals represented the spiritual force of revival, and if the Oxford movement represented the ritualistic segment, the Broad Church movement represented the social and the liberal or modernistic element in the Anglican Church. The Broad Church movement began about 1830 and continued to attract followers during

the century. These Latitudinarians, as they were often called, owed much to the Kantian idealism which Samuel Taylor Coleridge, poet and preacher, introduced into England at Oxford. They emphasized an intuitive consciousness of God and the immanence of Christ in man who was looked upon as a son of God. The Fall and the Atonement were either ignored or minimized.

One segment of the movement, led by F. D. Maurice (1805–1872) and Charles Kingsley (1819–1875), a clergyman and novelist, founded a Christian socialist group. This group originated the social gospel in England and had some influence upon Walter Rauschenbusch, the American formulator of similar ideas. It sought to bring the kingdom of God upon earth by social legislation that would give men economic and social as well as political democracy.

Another part of the group held ideas similar to those of Bishop Colenso of Natal, Africa, who was led to question the Mosaic authorship of the Pentateuch when he could not satisfactorily answer the questions of a native. Deposed in 1862 by the Archbishop of Capetown, Colenso was later reinstated by higher authorities. Thomas Arnold, the famous headmaster of Rugby, a private school for boys, and Henry Milman, the dean of St. Paul's, were of the same group to which Colenso belonged — the group that adopted the theories of the German Biblical critics. These two wings of the Broad Church movement thus fostered both liberalism in theology and a social gospel.

3. THE OXFORD MOVEMENT. The Oxford Movement, which was linked with Oxford University, emphasized the importance of the Church and ritual in the religious life of the individual. Shortly after 1830 its leaders began to publish *Tracts for the Times* in which they called attention to the importance of apostolic succession, baptismal regeneration, and the importance of ritual in the worship. Numerous Anglican churchmen accepted their ideas.

The movement was partly a protest against the domination of the church by the state. The grant of complete religious freedom to Nonconformists and Roman Catholics by acts of Parliament in 1828 and 1829 and the grant of the franchise to the middle class in 1832 made many churchmen fear that the Anglican Church might in time be disestablished by a Parliament dominated by dissenting forces. The Romantic movement, with its emphasis upon the glories of the Gothic past and its love of beautiful ritual that would stimulate the aesthetic emotions in worship, contributed to the ritualism of the movement. In another respect the movement was an outcome of what the Puritans thought of as an incomplete "purifying" of the Church of England at the time of the Reformation. Men became interested in the history of rites and vestments and sought to restore more of the color of the past to the service. The group symbolizing these forces in the Anglican Church has been known variously as the Oxford movement, the High Church movement, the Anglo-Catholic movement, the Puseyite movement — after one of the leaders, Edward Pusey — and the Tractarian movement because of the *Tracts for the Times.*

In 1827 John Keble (1792–1866) wrote a work called *The Christian Year.* This work, consisting of hymns in praise of the Church and the value of Communion, made Keble the virtual author of the Oxford movement. And his sermon on "National Apostasy"[1] on July 14, 1833, in Oxford, roused widespread interest in his ideas. Keble emphasized the real physical presence of Christ's body and blood in the Communion and maintained that the Communion was only valid when administered by ordained ministers in the apostolic succession.

John Henry Newman (1801–1890) became the leader of the Tractarians after he issued the first of the *Tracts for the Times* in 1833. Newman, the son of a London banker, brought up under Calvinistic doctrine, went through a period of liberalism at Oxford before he joined the men of the Tractarian group. While he is perhaps better known for his hymn, "Lead, Kindly Light," he was the real leader of the Oxford movement until he became a Roman Catholic in 1845. He wrote over twenty of the *Tracts.* The last of the *Tracts, Number Ninety,*[2] consisted of remarks upon the Thirty-nine Articles and the Prayer Book. In this tract Newman argued that these documents were not anti-Roman Catholic but simply condemned the abuses in that church. His friend Edward Manning and nearly 875 others, of whom nearly 250 were ministers or theological leaders at Oxford and Cambridge, followed him into the Roman Catholic Church between 1845 and 1862. Newman's greatest work was his *Apologia Pro Sua Vita,* an autobiographical account of his

---

[1] H. Bettenson, *Documents of the Christian Church* (New York: Oxford University Press, 1947), pp. 433-436.
[2] *Ibid.*, pp. 436-441.

life and work. Late in his life he was made a cardinal of the Roman Catholic Church.

After Newman's defection to Rome, Edward Pusey (1800–1882), who was a professor of Hebrew in Oxford, became the leader of the movement until his death. The Oxford men were interested in upholding the spiritual nature of the Church and its freedom from control by the state. They wanted to develop a middle position between an infallible ecclesiastical body and rampant individualism in the Church. They emphasized both the real presence of Christ in the elements of the sacrament and baptismal regeneration. They came very close to the Roman Catholic exaltation of the sacraments as important factors in justification.

By advocating the use of crosses and lights the movement brought a renewed stress on the importance of colorful ritual in the liturgy of the Church. Gothic architecture, too, was favored as an aid to worship. The ascetic tendency created by the group found expression in the founding of monasteries and convents for men and women who wanted to pursue an ascetic life of worship and service. The Cowley Fathers was one such organization for men.

The movement also deepened the gulf between the Anglican Church and the Nonconformist churches by its emphasis on the sacramental nature of the mass and apostolic succession. It also created a new party within the Anglican Church which was at odds with the Evangelicals. But it should be given credit for the service that its exponents rendered to the poor and the unchurched. To many it offered an appealing compromise between Roman Catholicism and the strong evangelical position, and it reminded Anglicans of their universal Christian heritage.

B. *Among the Nonconformists.*

While these three movements were agitating or rejuvenating the Established Church, new developments were taking place among the free churches. The Salvation Army was organized in 1878 by William Booth (1829–1912), a Methodist minister, to reach the down-and-outs by open-air evangelism and social work, which Booth started about 1865. The name Salvation Army was applied to the organization in 1880, when Booth organized it along military lines with an autocratic, hierarchal organization and uniforms. It is now world-wide.

John Darby (1800–1882), a lawyer who became a curate in the Church of Ireland, organized the groups known as the Brethren about 1830 in Dublin. The Brethren emphasized the priesthood of believers and the direct guidance of the Holy Spirit to such an extent that they did not accept an ordained ministry. They were, and still are, earnest students of the Bible and continue to manifest a practical piety in their lives. George Muller, the founder of a large orphanage in Bristol, and Samuel Tregelles, a great student of lower criticism — the study of the text of the New Testament — were both members of this group. The name Plymouth Brethren is often given to the group because Plymouth was the early chief center of the movement.

Edward Irving (1792–1834), a Scotch Presbyterian minister, believed that the Church should enjoy the gifts of the Holy Spirit that it had had in the Apostolic era. His followers emphasized "speaking in tongues" and the imminent return of Christ. They became known as the Catholic Apostolic Church about 1842.

George Williams founded the Young Men's Christian Association in 1844 to meet the need of young men in the city for exercise, social life and lodging in a Christian environment. The organization appeared in the United States in 1851. Its sister organization, the Young Women's Christian Association, was founded to provide similar services for young women in the cities.

II. English Protestant Missionary Effort

Protestant churches did not do much missionary work during the era of the Reformation because all of their energies were absorbed in the work of organization and the struggle to exist. During the Counter Reformation the great missionary work was done by the Jesuits and other orders in the Roman Catholic Church. But a combination of forces, beginning with the work of William Carey in 1792, led to such great missionary effort in the nineteenth century that the nineteenth has been called the "Great Century" in Protestant missionary effort.

This missionary enthusiasm was the result of revivalism among the Pietists and Methodists, and among the Evangelicals of the Anglican Church. People wanted to convert others to the same joyous religious experience that they had had. The gaining of empires by such Protestant nations as Holland and England acquainted Europeans with the spiritual need of people in other lands. Such missionary explorers as Livingstone, Grenfell, and Rebmann and Krapf, revealed the extent and needs of Africa to the world. The Reformation concept of the importance of the individual's relation to God provided a final motivating force for such work.

India was opened to missionary work after 1813 when the East India Company was forced to admit missionaries. China was forced to accept missionaries by the 1858 Treaty of Tientsin which ended the second Opium War. It is paradoxical that the war to force China to admit opium into her land should have resulted in opening China to missions.

Numerous missionary societies were organized after 1792. The Baptist Missionary Society was founded at Kettering, England, with an initial fund of a little over thirteen pounds, as a result of the vision of William Carey (1761–1834), the cobbler who taught himself several languages. Carey went to India in the employ of the East India Company in order to get into the country, but he made missionary work there his first interest. Grenfell was the Baptist Society's greatest missionary explorer. He, rather than Stanley, should be given the credit for mapping the Congo River and its tributaries between 1880 and 1890. A letter from Carey resulted in the founding of the London Missionary Society of the Congregationalists in 1795. John Philip, David Livingstone, Robert Moffat and John Mackenzie, the man who persuaded the British government to annex Bechuanaland to protect the natives from exploitation by the Boer colonists, were among its greatest missionary statesmen. The Scottish Missionary Society and the Glasgow Missionary Society were founded by Scotch Presbyterians in 1796 and 1797 respectively, and the Church Missionary Society was founded by the Evangelicals in 1799. The latter's greatest missionaries were Pilkington, the missionary translator of Uganda, and Tucker, the missionary bishop who was largely responsible for bringing Uganda under the British crown and for instituting the progressive policies that have made that country one of the finest in Africa. The Methodists founded the Wesleyan Missionary Society in 1817. Other societies were founded in rapid succession, and missionaries were sent out to all parts of the world.

William Carey, whose motto was "Expect great things from God; attempt great things for God," went to India where he became a leader in the translation of the Bible into the tongue

of the people, although nominally he was a chaplain of the
East India Company. After India was opened to missionaries
in 1813, such men as Henry Martyn, who was inspired to missionary effort by reading Brainerd's *Autobiography*, began missionary work. American missionary effort was joined to British
effort after the first American missionary society was founded
in 1810.

The London Missionary Society followed the Moravians into
South Africa and did excellent work among the natives, though
not without considerable friction with the Boer settlers. John
Philip protected the rights of the natives by persuading the
British government to grant them civil liberties. Moffat translated the Scriptures into the language of important tribes of
South Africa. Livingstone expanded geographical knowledge
of Central Africa and fought the Arab slave trade, which destroyed potential village preaching centers, as means to promote missionary effort. The Scotch Presbyterians took up Livingstone's challenge to work in the region of the great lakes
of Central Africa. The Evangelical Church Missionary Society
provided the martyrs who started work in Uganda.

It was Robert Morrison who studied the Chinese language
and who provided a Chinese dictionary and a Chinese translation of the Bible that could be used as soon as missionaries
were granted access to China after 1858.

The results of missionary work have been tremendous, not
only in the salvation of natives but also in many cultural accomplishments. Missionary explorers were often the first to inform the world of geographic conditions. Many names of missionaries are on the roster of the Royal Geographical Society
of Britain because of their work as explorers. Others, such as
Alexander Mackay and James Stewart, built the first roads in
Uganda and Nyassaland respectively. Missionaries have opened
academic and industrial training schools, introduced new crops
and stimulated trade so that the natives could raise their own
standard of living. Others have been empire builders because
they thought that the British government would better protect
the interests of the natives than the colonists who wanted the
land. Such men as Moffat, Morrison, Pilkington and Carey were
used of God to give the natives of their adopted lands the Scriptures in their own tongue. The missionary movement was in
some respects the ancestor of the modern ecumenical movement

[439]

because, as natives could not understand the divisions among Christians, missionaries of many denominations began to work together.

This advance has not been without struggle. Nationalism in the Far East and the unfortunate linking of the missionaries with Western imperialism have created problems in China and other countries. Communism and Catholicism have often opposed Protestant missionary effort. Liberalism among many of the missionaries has become an increasing problem in our own time. In spite of these handicaps, however, any unbiased historian will admit the great contribution that the Church has been able to make to the world through its missionary effort.

III. DIVISION AND REUNION OF THE SCOTCH CHURCHES

After the Scotch Church had rid itself of control by Rome by 1567, it faced the further problem of how to maintain the Presbyterian system of polity and the Calvinistic theology that it had adopted. From about 1567 until 1689 the Scotch opposed the attempts of Laud and others to force the espiscopal system of government upon them. Not until James II fled from England and William and Mary took the English throne was the Presbyterian Church securely established in 1690 as the national Church of Scotland.

From 1690 until 1847 the Scotch Church was plagued with divisions over the question of lay patronage. Lay patronage meant that the crown or landlords could dictate the choice of a minister for a congregation. Patronage was made official by act of the English Parliament in 1712. Many divisions occurred as the sturdy Scotch fought for the right to choose their own ministers. Ebenezer Erskine (1680–1754) was deposed by the General Assembly of the Church of Scotland because he upheld the right of a congregation to choose its own minister. In 1733 he and others founded the Associated Presbytery, which in 1740 became the Secession Church. This Church split again in 1747 into two groups, but by 1820 the two groups merged as the United Secession Church.

The problem of lay patronage also resulted in the founding of the Relief Church by Thomas Gillespie in 1761. The Relief Church and the United Secession Church united to form the United Presbyterian Church in 1847 because of the similarity of their stand against lay patronage.

A more important schism occurred when Thomas Chalmers

(1780–1847), a great mathematician, preacher and theologian, led a group in the founding of the Free Church in 1843 over the issues of the right of a congregation to choose its own minister and of the growing spirit of revival stimulated by the Evangelical Revival in Scotland. Nearly a third, 474, of the ministers of the state church withdrew. The Free Church became an aggressive evangelistic and missionary body. It united with the United Presbyterian Church in 1900 to form the United Free Church. A small minority, known as the Wee Frees, refused to unite and continued to exist as a separate group. The United Free Church combined with the Church of Scotland in 1929 to form the Kirk of Scotland because the right of lay patronage, the main cause of division, had long since disappeared with the abolition of patronage by act of Parliament in 1874. Today the Church of Scotland is the major church of Scotland.

Liberalism was also a problem in the Scotch churches. Professor William Robertson Smith, who was deposed from his chair in the Free Church college in Aberdeen in 1881, was largely responsible for the spread of German critical ideas in Scotland and for the rise of liberalism.

IV. The Church in Ireland

Racial antagonism and the natural hatred of the conquered for the conqueror were embittered at the time of the Reformation because the English accepted Protestantism while the Irish remained Roman Catholic. When he became King of England, James I deepened the division by settling Northern Ireland with Scotch settlers.

From a religious viewpoint, there were two major events in Ireland between 1689 and 1914. The first was the migration of thousands of Scotch-Irish of Northern Ireland to America. There they became the backbone of American Presbyterianism.

The second major event was the disestablishment of the Anglican Church in 1869. Until that time Irishmen had to pay church taxes for the support of the Anglican Church and to give voluntarily to the support of the Roman Catholic clergy whom they accepted as their real ministers. They had been given civil rights earlier in 1829 by the Catholic Emancipation Act which opened up all positions in local and national government to Roman Catholics except for the throne, the lord-lieutenancy of Ireland, and the positions of chancellor and the

THE CHURCH OF SCOTLAND, 1560 - 1929

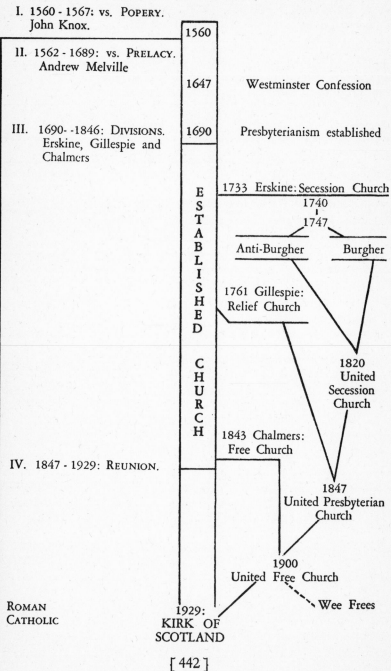

I. 1560 - 1567: vs. POPERY.
John Knox.

1560

II. 1562 - 1689: vs. PRELACY.
Andrew Melville

1647   Westminster Confession

III. 1690- -1846: DIVISIONS.   1690   Presbyterianism established
Erskine, Gillespie and
Chalmers

E
S   1733 Erskine: Secession Church
T   1740
A   1747
B   Anti-Burgher   Burgher
L
I
S   1761 Gillespie:
H   Relief Church
E
D   1820
C   United
H   Secession
U   Church
R
C   1843 Chalmers:
H   Free Church

IV. 1847 - 1929: REUNION.   1847
                              United Presbyterian
                                   Church

                                   1900
                              United Free Church
                                        Wee Frees

ROMAN   1929:
CATHOLIC   KIRK OF
            SCOTLAND

[442]

archbishop of Canterbury. Although these changes helped to relieve bitterness, religious hostility between English and Irish has persisted into the twentieth century.

BIBLIOGRAPHY

Ernest Howse has given an authoritative and useful account of the private life and social activity of the upper-class Evangelicals of the Clapham Sect in his *Saints in Politics* (Toronto: University of Toronto Press, 1952).

A History of the Evangelical Party (London: Longmans, Green & Co., 1911) by G. R. Balleine is an excellent account of the Evangelical Revival and its results in the Church of England.

Wilberforce, A Narrative (Oxford: Clarendon Press, 1923) by Reginald Coupland is an excellent account of that Evangelical's attempts to end slavery.

J. Wesley Bready in his volume, *Lord Shaftesbury and Social Industrial Progress* (London: G. Allen & Unwin Ltd., 1926), has a well-developed evaluation of Shaftesbury's life and work.

One wishing to understand John H. Newman's work as a leader of the Oxford movement can gain much from a reading of his *Apologia Pro Sua Vita* (London: Longmans, Green, Reader & Dyer, 1873), an autobiographical account of his life.

There are many fine biographies and autobiographies of the great missionary leaders of the nineteenth century.

Dr. H. A. Ironside has traced the development of the Brethren movement in his *A Historical Sketch of the Brethren Movement* (Grand Rapids: Zondervan Publishing House, 1942).

Chapter XXXVI

FOES OF THE FAITH

During the nineteenth century several movements appeared which threatened the faith that the Church has endeavored to hold throughout the ages. Biblical criticism grew out of the rationalistic, individualistic and humanistic climate produced by the Renaissance. This development was reinforced by the rationalism and individualism of the eighteenth century and the historical outlook of the Romantic movement and German idealistic philosophy. The preoccupation with material goods, engendered by the higher standard of living made possible by the Industrial Revolution, also helped to turn men's minds from the absolute authority of the Bible as a standard for faith and life. The biological dogma of evolution, when applied to the Bible by analogy, made Christianity the product of a system of religious evolution. The denial of the authority of the Bible was a logical outcome.

I. Criticism

Men have usually followed one of three approaches to the Bible. Pietists have approached it from an experimental viewpoint in which the application of truth to daily life is the criterion. Others have approached it as a source book of doctrine in the manner of the leaders of the Reformation. Still others have adopted an historical approach, which results in the conception of the Bible as an ethical guidebook only. This latter approach became the fashion in the nineteenth century because of the influence of German idealistic philosophy. When the historico-critical approach was combined with the application of the theory of evolution to religious phenomena, the background for a system of Biblical criticism was completed.

Discussion between one who accepts the critical approach to the Bible and one who is a believer in the inspiration and the integrity of the Bible is difficult because each has a different

[444]

set of basic ideas. The radical critic of the Bible assumes that the Bible is merely a work to be judged by the canons of literary criticism just as any other literary work would be; that there is an evolution of religion; and that natural explanations of Biblical phenomena should replace supernatural explanations. Such individuals look upon the Bible as a book that has been written by human authors. They ignore the function of the Holy Spirit in the inspiration of the writers of Scripture.

A. *The Philosophic and Theological Background of Biblical Criticism.*

The idealistic philosophy of Immanuel Kant (1724–1804), when combined with the views of Schleiermacher, Hegel and Ritschl, created a philosophic background favorable to a critical approach to the Bible. Kant accepted Locke's emphasis upon sensation and Descartes' stress upon reason as the keys to knowledge concerning the phenomena of nature, but he argued in his *Critique of Practical Reason* (1788) that man could not know God or the soul, both of which he classed as data of the world of "noumena," by the senses or reason. His pietistic background led him to the assertion that the sense of moral obligation or conscience in man, which he called the "categorical imperative," should be the starting point for religion. Because man has a moral sense, Kant argued, there is a God who has provided that sense. The postulates of the soul and immortal life become essential, if men who obey the dictates of conscience are to be rewarded, because often the good receive no temporal reward in this life.

Because Kant denies that man can know the world of noumena, there is no place in his system for an historical and objective revelation of God in the Bible. To him it is only a man-made book of history, to be subjected to historical criticism just as any other book. There is no place for Christ, the God-man, in Kant's system. Man with his free will and his immanent sense of what is right becomes the creator of a religion in which he develops the morality inherent in himself. There is a logical line of continuity between Kantian idealism and modern liberalism with its insistence upon the "spark of the divine" within each of us, which liberals insist, we need only to cultivate to achieve good moral conduct and eventual immortality. In this fashion Kant helped to provide a philosophical framework for both Biblical criticism and modern liberal theology.

Unlike Kant, who found the starting point for religion in man's moral nature, Friedrich Schleiermacher (1768-1834) made feelings or the emotions the element out of which religious experience develops. Schleiermacher was trained in the schools of the Pietists at Halle and owed the subjective nature of his philosophy to them and to Romanticism. To him religion was not a set of beliefs and obligations based on the authority of the Church, but it was the result of man's feelings of absolute dependence in a majestic universe in which he is but a small entity. Christianity best brings man into harmony with God as man passively realizes his dependence upon God. Religion thus becomes a mere subjective apprehension of Christ, who serves as the mediator to reconcile man to the Absolute who is immanent in the universe. Thus man is freed from dependence upon an historical revelation of the will of God and needs only to cultivate the feeling of dependence to enjoy a satisfactory religious experience.

George W. F. Hegel (1770–1831) also had a marked influence upon both theology and the critical approach to the Bible. Hegel identified being with thought. God was the Absolute, who was seeking to manifest himself in history by a logical process of reconciliation of contradictions which Hegel called thesis and antithesis. The synthesis or reconciliation created a new pair of contradictions that were again merged in a new reconciliation or synthesis. Hegel thus held to philosophical evolution as the way in which the Absolute was manifested. His dialectic or logic was taken over by Marx, and his emphasis upon the state as a manifestation of the Absolute was borrowed by Hitler and Mussolini in order to glorify both the state and the dictator who headed it.

Albrecht Ritschl (1822–1889) was influenced by Schleiermacher's acceptance of religious feeling as the foundation for religion, but he insisted that religion was the consciousness of dependence upon the part of the Church rather than upon the part of the individual. Christ brought the practical revelation of sin and salvation to the individual. The Bible is simply the record of community consciousness, and it should therefore be subjected to historical investigation in the same manner as any other book. Thus Ritschl, as well as the other philosophers, made religion subjective and opened the way for extreme critical study of the Bible. He also promoted the social approach to religious problems that was an inspiration to later adherents of the social gospel.

B. Biblical Criticism.

Rationalism of the Enlightenment and idealistic philosophy of the Romantic era were thus the parents of a criticism of the Bible that tries to destroy the supernatural nature of the Bible as a revelation and that makes the Bible the record of the subjective evolution of religion in human consciousness. Opposition to such destructive criticism should not lead the reverent student of the Bible to reject all Biblical criticism. Higher criticism, or, as it is sometimes known, introduction, which has come to be associated with the above destructive views, is simply the careful study of the historical background of each book of the Bible, and lower criticism is the study of the text of the Bible in an attempt to ascertain whether the text that we have is the one which came from the hands of the writers. Lower criticism has resulted in the granting to the text of the Bible a high degree of accuracy so that we can be sure that we have the writings of the original authors of the Bible. Thus no doctrine or ethical teaching of Scripture can be called into question by the most radical critic. It has been the radical higher criticism rather than the lower criticism that has destroyed many persons' faith in the divine revelation in the Bible.

The beginning of higher criticism is associated with the name of Jean Astruc (1684–1766), an eighteenth century French doctor, who in 1753 divided the book of Genesis into two parts. He assumed the use of two documents as sources because he found the name Elohim (God) used in some places and Jehovah (Lord) in others. Johann Eichorn (1752–1827), another critic, who laid down the dictum that the Bible was to be read as a human book and tested by human means, gave such studies the name of higher criticism. Eichorn noticed other literary characteristics as well as the use of the names for God which led him to believe that not only Genesis but the Hexateuch (Genesis to Joshua) were composite documents. Hupfeld in 1853 was the first to claim that the Pentateuch was the work of different authors rather than a narrative composed from many sources by Moses. Graf and Wellhausen developed a well-elaborated theory, known as the Graf-Wellhausen theory, which has been adopted by the higher critics. According to this theory, the sections in which the name Jehovah is used is the earliest document; another part by another author is known as E; still another in Deuteronomy as D; and P. In this fashion the unity of the Pentateuch and its Mosaic authorship are denied.

Later critics divided Isaiah into at least two parts and lowered the date of Daniel to the Maccabean period so that it became history rather than prophecy and history. The development of doctrine in the Bible was explained along evolutionary lines. Critics emphasized the development of the idea of God from the primitive storm god of Mt. Sinai to the ethical monotheistic God of the prophets. The work of Biblical archaeologists has forced many critics to abandon their former radical positions and has tended to confirm conservative views of the Bible.

The beginning of higher criticism of the New Testament is usually associated with the name of Hermann Reimarus (1694–1768), who taught Oriental languages at Hamburg. In his *Fragments* (1778) he denied the possibility of Biblical miracles and advanced the idea that the writers of the New Testament with their stories of miracles were pious frauds. Gotthold Lessing (1729–1781), who published Reimarus' *Fragments*, argued that the Scriptures served man as a guide during the primitive phase of his religious development but that reason and duty were sufficient guides in the more advanced state of religion.

Ferdinand Baur (1792–1860), who borrowed Hegel's logic, argued in 1831 that in the early Church there had been a Judaism that emphasized the Law and the Messiah. This earlier approach can be observed in the writings of James. Paul developed an antithesis in such books as Romans and Galatians in which the emphasis was upon grace rather than upon law. The Old Catholic Church of the second century represented a synthesis of Petrine and Pauline views. This synthesis is revealed in such books as the Gospel of Luke and the Pastoral Epistles. Baur then proceeded to date the books of the New Testament in this Hegelian framework as either early or late according to the manner in which they reflected Petrine, Pauline, or synthesizing tendencies. Historical data gave way to philosophical presupposition in ascertaining the chronology of the books of the New Testament.

Later New Testament criticism centered upon the question of the order of writing of the synoptic Gospels (Matthew, Mark and Luke) and the extent to which one was dependent upon another or upon even earlier sources. The latest approach, which is known as *formgeschichte,* teaches that the Gospels contain truth about Christ that can only be found after one peels off the layers of tradition and form in which the truth is hidden.

Some theologians, who adopt critical views of the New Testament, consider that the essence of the Gospel is in the ethical teachings of Jesus and that Paul changed the simple ethical religion of Jesus into a redemptive religion. Destructive higher criticism has led many to deny the inspiration of the Bible as a revelation from God through men inspired by the Holy Spirit and to minimize or to deny the deity of Christ and His saving work upon the Cross of Calvary. *The Life of Jesus* (1835–1836) by David Strauss combined all of these views. Strauss denied both the miracles and the integrity of the New Testament as well as the deity of Christ.

Germany, once the home of the Reformation, became the land in which criticism developed. The history of modern Germany well illustrates the lengths to which men will go when they deny God's revelation in the Bible and when they replace revelation with reason and science as the authority for thought and action.

II. Commercialism

Another movement or viewpoint that threatened the Faith during the nineteenth century, and that still threatens it today, was commercialism. More subtle perhaps than higher criticism, commercialism may be defined as the practice in modern society of emphasizing the material values of a high standard of living. To the extent that man's attention is concentrated upon this life, he will neglect the spiritual values of eternal life. The abundance of goods, which has made a high living standard possible, is an outcome of the Industrial Revolution which came first in England between 1760 and 1830. Machine power was substituted for hand power so that great amounts of goods could be produced cheaply. Nowhere has this emphasis upon a high material standard of living been greater than in America. Many nations have the impression that Americans respect only material values. A person who has an abundance of this world's goods can just as easily forget his spiritual obligations as the rich man of Christ's story, who built bigger barns so that he could enjoy his wealth but who forgot that God could require his soul of him at any time. Both Walter Rauschenbusch, the founder of the social gospel in America, and Karl Marx emphasized in their systems what they thought was the primary importance of material goods in life. Those who lay such stress upon the distribution of material goods forget that "man does not live by bread alone."

III. Evolution

If philosophical, literary and historical criticism of the Bible destroyed faith in it as a revelation from God, and if the commercialism induced by the Industrial Revolution created indifference to a future life, the views of Charles Darwin (1809–1882) and his successors created the idea that there was no such thing as sin or that sin was merely the remnant of animal instinct in man. Evolution as a philosophical doctrine goes back to the time of Aristotle, but Darwin was the first to put it on what seemed to be a scientific basis.

Darwin spent some time in studying medicine and theology before he developed his inclinations to become a naturalist. A voyage around the world on the *Beagle* between 1831 and 1836 convinced him that differences between living animals and fossils, on the mainlands and those on the islands that he visited, could only be accounted for by biological evolution. He published his book, *Origin of the Species,* in 1859 after finding that Alfred Wallace had independently arrived at similar conclusions. In his book Darwin argued that the struggle for existence kept the population of the various species constant in spite of the fact that reproduction is geometric and that many more are produced than are essential for the survival of the species. In this struggle some individuals develop characteristics favorable to survival through a process of adjustment or adaptation to environment. These characteristics are passed on by sexual selection in which the favored males and females mate. Thus only the fittest survive. He thought that such a similarity as that of the body structure between man and animals substantiated his theory, but he forgot that this and other similarities might be evidence of design on the part of the Creator who gave His creatures similar body structures because of the similarity of their environment. Darwin applied his theory to man in *The Descent of Man* (1871) and argued that man was linked with animal life by common ancestral types.

Darwin's idea of continuity between man and animal has

been summarized as "descent with change." This view is opposed to the Biblical concept of special creation by God with fixity in the groups thus created. In emphasizing similarities between man and animals Darwin ignored the uniqueness of man's larger brain, his power of speech, his use of the opposable thumb, his memory, conscience and concepts of God and the soul. He admitted that the last three were problems for his theory. No missing link that would conclusively identify man with animals has been discovered; in fact, crossbreeding between many groups is impossible. The use of the Hebrew word *bara* for the act of creation is only used of the heavens and the earth, mammals and man (Genesis 1:1, 21, 27). God is said to have made the different groups reproduce "after his kind."

Although the theory of evolution denied the direct creation of man by God, the greatest damage came from the application of the theory to the development of religion. God and the Bible were looked upon as the evolutionary products of man's religious consciousness, and the books of the Bible were dated accordingly. The Biblical eschatology, in which perfection would only come in this world by the direct intervention of God through the return of Christ, was replaced by the evolutionary view of a world that was being increasingly improved by human effort. Because man was not guilty through original sin, there was no need of Christ as Saviour. Tennyson gave poetic expression to evolution in his autobiographical poem, *In Memoriam* (1850).

Evolution was also used to justify the idea of race superiority because that idea seemed to fit in with Darwin's concept of the survival of the fittest. It has also been used to justify having no absolute foundation or norm for ethics. Good conduct is merely those actions deemed suitable by each generation for the proper conduct of society. The doctrine of evolution has also been used to glorify war as the survival of the fittest.

All of these conclusions have been reached by the application of a biological theory to other fields through an unwarranted use of the argument from analogy.

IV. COMMUNISM

The Church has also faced the enmity of socialism in the twentieth century. This movement had its roots in the materialistic philosophy of Karl Marx (1818–1883). He and Friedrich Engels developed the major outlines of his view in the pamphlet, *The Communist Manifesto* (1848). Marx had been attracted to the philosophy of Hegel, but he substituted materialism for Hegel's Absolute Being. Reality, he maintained, was material rather than spiritual. Upon this foundation he built the idea that all the religious, social and political institutions of society are determined by the way men make a living. In this making a living class struggle takes place because the capitalist takes the surplus value or profits. Marx argued that the profits belong to labor because, he believed, it is only labor that can create value. The progress of this struggle Marx charted by the application of Hegel's logic to it. Capitalism generated its antithesis, the proletariat, which would destroy it and set up a classless society after a temporary dictatorship of the proletariat or workers. Lenin provided a set of aggressive tactics by which this system could be worked out. He emphasized the idea that a devoted, highly disciplined, small party of Communists could infiltrate democratic organizations, such as labor unions and government, and use a time of crisis or war to seize power. Stalin successfully combined this program and technique in the Russian state.

Marx and his followers believe that "man shall live by bread alone." They ignore human sin, which will always upset their ideal order unless they resort to brutal regimentation — which Communists have everywhere done. They also oversimplify human problems. There is no place for God, the Bible, or absolute standards in their system. They have always insisted that "religion is the opiate of the people." While the emphasis upon the importance of the economic factor has been an aid to the historian, recent history has demonstrated the fundamental hostility of Marxism to all forms of religion. While the continuance of the Christian religion and the Church is not dependent upon any particular political or economic system, it must be recognized that socialism as practiced by the Communists can never come to terms with the Church.

Criticism of the Bible, Darwin's theory of evolution, and other social and intellectual forces created religious liberalism in the late nineteenth century. Liberal theology has been greatly devoted to the scientific method and has applied evolution to religion as a key that might explain its development. It has insisted upon the continuity of man's religious experience to such an extent that the Christian religion has become the mere product of a religious evolution rather than a revelation from

God through the Bible and Christ. Christian experience has been emphasized much more than theology. These views of liberalism which conservative Christianity has fought and the movement associated with the name of Karl Barth has opposed.

BIBLIOGRAPHY

More information concerning the history of criticism may be found in Edward J. Young's *An Introduction to the Old Testament* (Grand Rapids: Wm. B. Eerdmans Publishing Co., 1949), in Henry S. Nash's *The History of Higher Criticism of the New Testament* (New York: The Macmillan Co., 1906) and in Marvin R. Vincent's *A History of the Textual Criticism of the New Testament* (New York: The Macmillan Co., 1903).

The mass of texts of the Greek Bible are described, and their general confirmation of the integrity of the text of the Bible is clearly presented by Frederic C. Kenyon in *The Text of the Greek Bible* (London: Duckworth, 1937).

Chapter XXXVII

THE AMERICAN CHURCH IN THE NATIONAL ERA

By 1789 the influence of the Great Awakening had been largely dissipated by the Deism that had been brought over to the colonies by British army officers during the French and Indian War and by the import of deistic literature, and by the influence of the French Revolution. Yale illustrates the decadent religious spirit in this period. Few students professed regeneration; gambling, profanity, vice and drunkenness were the order of the day among students, who prided themselves upon being infidels. The Second Awakening, which improved this depressing picture, was the first of many revivals during the nineteenth century.

I. THE SECOND AWAKENING

In 1786 a revival movement began at Hampden-Sidney, a little college in Virginia. The revival, which grew out of concern by the students for their spiritual condition, spread to Washington College, and, from there, throughout the Presbyterian Church in the South.

The New England Congregational phase of the revival began at Yale in 1802 under the leadership of President Timothy Dwight (1752–1817), whose earnest scholarly chapel messages on infidelity and the Bible destroyed the shallow infidelity of the students. About a third of the student body professed conversion during the revival, which later spread to Dartmouth, Williams and other colleges. Still another awakening at Yale came in 1812.[1]

Revival also spread to the frontier, where great numbers of people had migrated. One-quarter of the population resided outside the thirteen original states by 1820. Whisky became a curse in these new settlements and was the cause of most frontier social and moral problems. The Presbyterians were

[1] P. G. Mode, *Source Book and Bibliographical Guide for American Church History* (Menasha, Wisconsin: George Banta Publishing Co., 1921), pp. 339-342.

the most influential in propagating revival on the frontier, the camp meeting originating among them. The most famous camp meeting was the one held at Cane Ridge in August, 1801.[2] It was marked by strange physical phenomena, such as falling, jerking, rolling, dancing and barking. But there could be no question concerning the desirable results of the revival. The frontier areas of Kentucky and Tennessee were all helped by it. The frontier revivalism was much more spectacular than the quiet spiritual awakening brought about by the preaching of the Word in New England.

As was the case with the Great Awakening, one of the results of revival was division within the churches. Division came among the Presbyterians when Cumberland Presbytery ordained men without the proper educational qualifications to minister to the increasing numbers of churches on the frontier. This division resulted in the formation of the Cumberland Presbyterian Church in 1810. Its use of the camp meeting and the circuit system, and its advocacy of revival made it one of the strong churches of the frontier.

Another division was made by Thomas Campbell, a Scotch-Irish, Anti-Burgher Presbyterian who came to America in 1807. When his church refused to permit him to administer Communion to those outside of his own group, he decided to preach a non-creedal faith based upon the Bible. He soon gained numerous followers among the Baptists; and, after his son Alexander came to America, he organized churches that practiced baptism by immersion. By 1826 these churches separated from the Baptists and were known as Disciples. In 1832 the Disciples united with the followers of Barton Stone to form the Disciples or Christian Church.

The Second Awakening indirectly helped to precipitate the rise of the Unitarian Church in New England. The first Unitarian Church in America had been formed in 1785 when members of King's Chapel, Boston, had voted to omit all mention of the Trinity from the service. Then in 1805 Henry Ware was appointed to the Hollis chair of divinity at Harvard in spite of his Unitarian views. Andover Theological Seminary was founded in 1808 by orthodox Congregationalists in protest against this appointment. In 1819 William E. Channing preached a sermon in Baltimore in which he developed Unitarian doctrine.[3] This

2 *Ibid.*, pp. 336-339.
3 *Ibid.*, pp. 404-407.

[455]

sermon became the basis of faith for over one hundred Unitarian churches that soon appeared in Boston and throughout New England. These churches opposed both orthodox Christianity and the revivalistic movement. The American Unitarian Association, which came into being in 1825, held the doctrines of the goodness of man, salvation by character culture, the unity of God, the humanity of Christ and the immanence of God in the human heart.

A second major result of the revival was the improvement of morals on the frontier. Drunkenness and profanity gave way to godly conduct as the Methodists and Baptists increased in number. Although the revival had begun among the Presbyterians, the Methodists and Baptists won more followers because they did not insist so strongly upon an educated ministry and made extensive use of the camp meeting technique which the Presbyterians ceased to use. In three years over ten thousand joined the Baptist churches in Kentucky.

From this time the midweek prayer meeting became an important institution in American Christianity. The American Sunday school was also started at this time. As early as 1786 Sunday school was held in a home in Virginia, and in 1790 it was introduced into a church in Philadelphia. Since then it has been an integral part of religion in America and enables a church to educate the young in Biblical truth. Higher education was strengthened by the founding of over a dozen new colleges between 1780 and 1830 by the Presbyterians and Congregationalists in order to meet the need for more trained ministers. Andover Seminary was founded in 1808 to meet the threat of Unitarianism in Harvard. Others, such as Princeton Seminary (1812), Auburn and Bangor, were founded soon after.

Missionary endeavor at home and abroad was another outcome of the revival. The founding of the American Board of Commissioners for Foreign Missions was in part the result of the "haystack prayer meeting" of Samuel Mills and other students at Williams College. Later, other denominational boards were created until missionary work by Americans swelled into a mighty tide by 1900. To aid this effort at home the American Tract Society was founded in 1825, and the American Bible Society was organized in 1816. Beginning with the *Boston Recorder* in 1816, numerous denominations began to publish weekly religious papers for their people.

Revivalism did not end with the Second Awakening. Charles

G. Finney (1792–1875), a lawyer who was converted in 1821, soon became a great revivalist. He had many conversions in his meetings in New England, New York, Pennsylvania and Ohio. After years of successful evangelism he became professor of theology at Oberlin in 1835. Another great revival among laymen, which grew out of a noonday prayer meeting in New York, occurred in the North in 1857 and 1858. The Confederate Army experienced a great revival between 1863 and 1865. Later revivals were led by such men as Dwight L. Moody, R. A. Torrey and other great revivalists of the nineteenth century. Revivalism has been a continuing characteristic of American Christianity.

II. Social Reform

The Church in America was also interested in social reform during the nineteenth century. Revivalism created an atmosphere antagonistic to the prevalent practice of dueling with pistols or swords. The tragic death of Alexander Hamilton in a duel with Aaron Burr, coupled with propaganda from the pulpit, soon brought the practice to an end. The interest of the Church in social reform also slowly brought about the abolition of imprisonment for debt and promoted prison reform.

During the nineteenth century, and earlier, the Church became interested in the problem of liquor. In 1785 Dr. Benjamin Rush exploded the theory that intoxicants were beneficial to the body and called upon the churches to support a temperance movement based upon total abstinence. The Methodists, who have always had a keen interest in social problems, demanded that their members neither sell nor use intoxicants. Presbyterians and Congregationalists soon followed suit. Before long numerous temperance societies were formed to promote abstinence and to battle the liquor interests. The Anti-Saloon League (1895), a federation of temperance agencies, was the most important of these. After World War I the realization that liquor incited crime, that liquor and modern machinery would not mix safely, and that thirty-three states had state prohibition, aided the work of the League. The adoption of the Eighteenth Amendment in 1919 was the outcome of all these forces. From 1919 America was officially prohibitionist until the repeal of the Eighteenth Amendment in 1933.

During the first half of the nineteenth century, slavery became a serious problem that the churches had to face. As early as 1769 Congregationalists in Rhode Island spoke out against slavery. John Woolman's *Journal* (1756–1772) describes the devoted efforts of that godly Quaker to persuade others to emancipate their slaves. About 1833 Lane Seminary in Cincinnati became the center of an anti-slavery movement led by a student, Theodore Weld. When the seminary authorities attempted to ban the movement, the students migrated to Oberlin College. The American Anti-Slavery Society was founded in 1833. Inspired by such people as the editor of the *Liberator*, William L. Garrison, poet John G. Whittier, educator Jonathan Blanchard, and by author Harriet Beecher Stowe (*Uncle Tom's Cabin*), the abolitionist movement grew rapidly. At the same time slavery was becoming an apparent economic necessity in the South in order to produce cotton for the increasing number of textile factories in New England and England.

Attempts to end slavery by religious persuasion split several denominations. The Wesleyan Methodist Church was organized in 1843 on the basis of no slaveowning membership after many withdrew from the Methodist Episcopal Church. A Southern Baptist Convention was organized in 1845 because of the opposition of Northern Baptists to slavery. In the same year the Methodist Episocpal Church, South was founded. Southern Presbyterians from both the Old and New School groups split in 1861 and 1863. They united to form the Presbyterian Church in the United States in 1863. The churches created by these schisms over slavery have not all yet reunited with their Northern brethren, although there have been recent overtures for reunion. But despite the schisms one should remember that the Church conscientiously faced the slavery issue as a social problem to be solved. When the Civil War came, churches on both sides of the line did their best to bring aid to the needy and suffering.

III. FRONTIER AND URBAN SECTS

In addition to the new denominations, such as the Cumberland Presbyterians and the Disciples or Christians, heterodox sects appeared on the American frontier and in American cities during the nineteenth century. The Mormons and Adventists appeared on the frontier, and Christian Science emerged in New England.

Joseph Smith (1805–1844) maintained that in 1827 he dug up a book of thin golden plates on a hill near Palmyra, New York. After three years spent in translating, he published the book as the Book of Mormon.[4] Attracting many followers, he

[4] *Ibid.*, pp. 491-499.

made Kirtland, Ohio, the headquarters for the organization between 1831 and 1837. Independence, Missouri, became the chief center until the Missourians drove the Mormons out in 1839. Nauvoo, Illinois, became the next center, but opposition to polygamy, which Joseph Smith sanctioned by revelation in 1843,[5] resulted in the death of Smith at the hands of his enemies and in the migration of the Mormons under the leadership of Brigham Young to Utah between 1846 and 1848. Salt Lake City is still the center of the largest group of Mormons. Aggressive missionary work has won thousands of converts all over the world. This body of nearly a million members is known as the Church of Jesus Christ of Latter-day Saints. A second group of about 145,000 repudiated polygamy and, led by Joseph Smith, the son of the original founder, built up a strong organization with headquarters in Independence, Missouri. This group is known as the Reorganized Church of Jesus Christ of Latter-day Saints.

The Mormons accept the Book of Mormon as well as the Bible as Scripture. They look for an earthly Zion and do not give Christ His rightful place as Lord and Saviour in their theology.[6] Baptism of living persons for dead persons is practiced by the Mormons. Until it came under federal ban, polygamy seemed to have been widely practiced among the Mormons as a means of having a large posterity in the future world.

Another frontier sect, the Seventh-Day Adventists, was founded by William Miller (1782–1849), a farmer who studied the Bible assiduously. Study of Daniel and Revelation convinced Miller that Christ was going to return to earth 2300 years (Daniel 8: 14) after Ezra's return to Jerusalem in 457 b.c. This gave him the date of 1843 as the year of Christ's return. Many thousands accepted his idea and began to prepare for the coming of Christ by selling their property to others at low rates, by making ascension robes, and by ascending high hills at the expected time to be nearer to the heaven from whence they expected Christ to come. They later explained the non-appearance of Christ in 1843 and 1844 by the theory that the sanctuary to which He came in that year was a heavenly rather than an earthly sanctuary. Although there are several Adventist denominations, most of them believe that the Sabbath (Saturday)

[5] *Ibid.*, pp. 499-501.
[6] *Ibid.*, p. 491.

is the correct day of rest, that the soul sleeps between death and the resurrection and that the wicked will be annihilated.

Spiritualism also had its beginning in America in this period. In 1848 strange knocks and other noises occurred in the bedroom of six-year-old Kate and eight-year-old Margaret Fox of Hydesville, New York. Both are reported to have confessed years later that the noises had been the result of childish pranks. But overnight they became a sensation and attracted numerous followers who later organized themselves into a Spiritualist Church. Spiritualist mediums purport to communicate with the dead. Spiritualism has made a strong appeal to those who have lost loved ones by death and has received vigorous support following the losses of war. Such influential people as Sir Arthur Conan Doyle and Ella Wheeler Wilcox accepted Spiritualism as an authentic religion.

Christian Science, which appeared first in Boston in the post-Civil War era, was an urban sect. It was the brain child of imaginative, moody Mary Baker (1821–1910). After the death of her first husband, Glover, she became increasingly subject to spells of hysteria. In 1853 she married Patterson, a dentist whom she divorced in 1873. She later married Eddy in 1877. All through this marital career she was seeking help for her neurotic tendencies. In 1862 she met P. P. Quimby who emphasized healing by mental assent to truth that denied the reality of both illness and matter. She set herself up as a practitioner of this "New Science," which she apparently gained from Quimby's manuscripts, and won many followers to whom she imparted the secret of her method in a series of lessons. In 1875 she published *Science and Health*. This work now has an equal position with the Bible in all Christian Science churches. The Christian Scientists Association was formed in 1876, and in 1879 the Church of Christ (Scientist) was given a state charter. The First Church of Christ, Scientist, of Boston became the finest and most important of all the churches and is known as the Mother Church.

Mrs. Eddy denied the reality of matter, evil and sickness and held that these were merely delusions of the senses. God is all and all is God. One has but to realize one's identity with God or good to be freed from both evil and sickness.[7] This emphasis upon healing has made the movement appealing to many sick people. Both New Thought and Unity are similar in their ap-

7 *Ibid.*, pp. 653-655.

proach to the problems of health and prosperity, and no doubt they owe a good deal to Mary Baker Eddy who, in turn, owes much to P. P. Quimby.

IV. THE PROBLEMS OF URBANIZATION

The increased industrialization of the nation during and after the Civil War and the expanded immigration from Southern and Eastern Europe after 1890 to provide unskilled labor for the mills, mines and factories of a developing America brought about an astonishing growth of great cities, such as Chicago and Detroit. This growth of urban communities created many new problems for the Church in America during the nineteenth century, and these problems continue to confront the Church in the twentieth century.

Many rural churches lost so many of their young people to the city that their existence was endangered. These youths in the cities often neglected their religious life because the city provided them anonymity. Immigrant laborers settled in congested areas, and the native groups moved to the suburbs along with their churches. Because most of the immigrants after 1890 were Roman Catholic, the problem of the relations between that church and the dominant Protestant churches was raised. Immigrants brought with them loose ideas concerning the observance of Sunday. Material success also in many cases created an indifference to spiritual life that could only be characterized as secularism. The tendency of city life toward secularity was reinforced by the widespread acceptance of evolution and all the naturalistic ideology that went with that theory.

To meet the challenge of these problems was the task of the Church after the Civil War. As early as 1850 city rescue missions were founded to meet the physical and spiritual needs of the down-and-out of the city. The Water Street Mission of New York, opened in 1872, became the most famous of these missions under the leadership of its founder, Jerry MacAuley, who had been saved from a wasted life through the work of another New York mission. Aid to tenement families, aggressive opposition to gambling, drinking and vice centers, physical care for the outcast, and aggressive evangelism to reclaim souls were the major elements in MacAuley's program.

In 1864 the New York Protestant Episcopal City Mission became the arm of that church for social service. Orphanages, missions, hospitals, homes for the aged and other agencies were developed to meet the needs of the poor, the homeless and the diseased.

The Young Men's Christian Association first appeared in Boston in 1851 to meet the social needs of young men in the cities. The movement grew rapidly as it provided lodging, exercise, Bible study and social activities for such men. The Young Women's Christian Association was organized in 1866 to meet similar needs of young women in the cities. Both these movements became agencies through which Christians of various denominations might cooperate in social service.

Social settlements, of which Hull House in Chicago under the leadership of Jane Addams was the earliest, carried out social work similar to that of the institutional church, but they did not emphasize religious education. The dynamic behind the settlements was humanitarian and social; that behind the social work of the institutional church was primarily religious.

The institutional church itself was still another agency to meet the challenge of urban problems. Thomas K. Beecher's Park Church in Elmira, New York, seems to have the honor of being the first institutional church. The institutional church attempted to provide for the entire life of the individual. Numerous churches of this type were organized by the various denominations after the Civil War. Gymnasiums, libraries, dispensaries, lecture rooms, social rooms, sewing rooms, auditoriums and other necessities for meeting the physical, social, mental and spiritual needs of people were usually a part of these churches. St. George's Episcopal Church in New York became an institutional church in 1882 in order to serve the people in its own area. The various types of work were carried on in the adjoining parish house. Temple University in Philadelphia developed from Russell H. Conwell's Baptist Temple, which adopted institutional practices in 1891.

The Goodwill Industries, originated in Edgar J. Helms' church in Boston shortly after 1900, were an attempt to provide employment for the poor and aged by having them repair discarded articles that could be sold cheaply to the needy. Thus the needs of both the unemployed and those who could not afford to pay for new articles were met. Religious and social activities were also provided. Between 1905, when the movement was incorporated, and 1953 it grew to include over 100 factories supplying 350 retail stores which had sales of nearly $14,000,000. The Salvation Army also met social as well as religious needs of people in cities. It began work in America shortly after its founding in England. Street meetings, social settlements, homes, nurseries and many other techniques were devised to meet the needs of the neglected poor and the outcast.

The social gospel was an attempt to get at the causes of the evils that some were attempting to meet by the means mentioned above. It was felt that measures which dealt with the symptoms of economic maladies were not sufficient because they left the causes untouched. Organized labor rose as one answer to the challenge of the capitalist who seldom considered the welfare of the consumer and worker in his mad desire for profits. Thinkers began to study the social teachings of Christ to see if there were not some way in which economic injustice might be righted. Basing their work upon the theological dogmas of the Fatherhood of God and the brotherhood of man, many turned their attention from the salvation of the individual to the application of the teachings of Christianity to the economic life of the state.

Washington Gladden, a Congregationalist minister in Ohio, emphasized the need for applying the principles of Christ to the social order by using, if necessary, the force of the state to intervene for the well-being of society. The popular work, *In His Steps* (1896), written by Charles Sheldon, showed in fictional form what the social outcome might be if everyone tried to act as Christ did in daily life. Walter Rauschenbusch (1861–1918), a German Baptist minister who taught church history at Rochester Theological Seminary, became the foremost American apostle of the social gospel as a result of his studying social ethics in the Bible and reading Utopian books. His books, *Christianizing the Social Order* (1912) and *The Theology for the Social Gospel* (1917), spread the social gospel widely. He emphasized the necessity of economic as well as political democracy as the way by which the kingdom of God could be realized on earth. He supported unions, government intervention and a mild socialism as means which might accomplish that end. He argued that because labor was not a commodity, men should have the right to organize and bargain with the employer for better hours of labor, better wages and better working conditions. He urged profit-sharing as a good way to give labor a fair return for its work. He was opposed to a *laissez-faire* type of capitalism which emphasized competition above cooperative action in society. These views were predicated upon the idea that the Church must realize the kingdom of God upon earth rather than to talk about a future millennial kingdom. At the beginning of the present century the social gospel was widely accepted by the liberal churches. The Federal Council of Churches was its main sponsor.

V. THEOLOGICAL LIBERALISM IN AMERICA

The development of Darwinian evolution, the appearance of Biblical criticism upon the American scene through theological students who studied in Germany and Scotland, and the importation of German idealism brought to American churches in the nineteenth century, liberalism. Mention has already been made of Rauschenbusch's social gospel, which was merely the application of liberal theology to the social and economic spheres of life. Liberal theology emphasized the ethical message of a humanized Christ and the immanence of God in the human heart. Thus experience rather than the Scriptures was normative. Liberals were also greatly devoted to the scientific method and to natural law to explain miracles but were opposed to supernaturalism, original sin and Christ's vicarious atonement. Many of the ministers trained by liberal teachers in the seminaries popularized these ideas from their pulpits.

Liberalism has had an impact upon the great movement for Christian education in the churches through the work of such a man as Horace Bushnell (1802–1876), the Congregationalist minister of North Church in Hartford. After completing the study of law, Bushnell turned to theology. In 1846 he published his book, *Christian Nurture,* in which he emphasized the idea that the child merely has to grow *into* grace in a religious environment. Holding to a defective view of original sin and to the moral influence theory of the Atonement, Bushnell did not believe that the experience of conversion and growth *in* grace, as taught by the evangelical church, was necessary for the child. He wanted the child to grow up as a Christian so that the child would never know himself as being other than a Christian. He emphasized divine love at the expense of divine justice and bitterly opposed the revivalism of his day.

These ideas influenced Christian education in the Church. Uniform Sunday school lessons were developed in 1872 as a result of the work of John H. Vincent. The grading of the lessons became a part of this work as the idea of the progressive development of the child in Christian truth was adopted from the ideas of Bushnell. A Religious Education Association was formed in 1903, out of which developed the International Council of Christian Education in 1922. Unfortunately, this movement, dedicated to ideas of Christian education similar to those of Bushnell, fell under liberal control.

VI. INTERDENOMINATIONAL COOPERATION

Cooperation with each other in various interdenominational endeavors was another activity of American churches during the nineteenth, and early twentieth century.

The Young Men's and Women's Christian Associations were the result of the cooperation of people of various denominations to meet pressing social needs in the new urban society of the day.

In 1881 Francis E. Clark, a minister of Portland, Maine, organized the first Christian Endeavor Society. This Society speedily became an interdenominational organization, enlisting the interest of young people of various denominations. By 1886 over eight hundred societies were organized. These provided ethical, social and religious training for young people. Later, denominational organizations along similar lines were set up to keep the movement within each denomination. The Epworth League of the Methodist churches is an illustration of this type of organization.

The Student Volunteer Movement, which began under Moody's auspices at Northfield, Massachusetts in 1886, provided an interdenominational agency under the leadership of John R. Mott to recruit missionaries by the stimulation of interest in missions. It has since come under control of liberal forces and is no longer the dynamic missionary movement it was in its early career. Denominations also cooperated in missionary activity along interdenominational lines after the founding of the Foreign Missions Conference of North America in 1893. A Laymen's Missionary Movement was organized in 1906[8] to interest laymen in missionary activity.

Interest in new social problems and theological liberalism, and a desire for interdenominational cooperation and unity coalesced in the founding of the Federal Council of the Churches of Christ in America. The Council provided for cooperation among the denominations through a council made up of the representatives of autonomous churches. In 1905 the constitu-

8 *Ibid.*, pp. 675-676.

tion of the Federal Council was drawn up at a meeting in Carnegie Hall in New York. It was accepted by thirty-three denominations at a meeting in Philadelphia in 1908.[9] The Federal Council has always been characterized by a strong interest in social problems and the application of the ethical principles of Christianity to the solution of those problems. Unfortunately, it fell under the influence of liberal leadership and at times seemed to subscribe to collectivism as the ideal economic order.

This survey of the history of the Church in America between 1789 and 1914 has revealed the diversity of the problems and the variety of solutions that the Church adopted to meet them. It is to be regretted that some of the churches in meeting many of these problems took positions that were hostile to the teachings of the Bible.

BIBLIOGRAPHY

The bibliographical references in Chapter XXXII also cover the era discussed in this chapter.

The Confusion of Tongues (Garden City, New York: Doubleday, Doran & Co., 1929) by Charles W. Ferguson is an interesting critical, but somewhat satirical, account of the history and dogmas of the major American cults.

Chaos of Cults (Grand Rapids: Wm. B. Eerdmans Publishing Co., 1944) by Jan K. Van Baalen is a useful history of the cults that compares their doctrines with the teachings of the Bible.

Freedom's Ferment (Minneapolis: University of Minnesota Press, 1944) by Alice F. Tyler contains detailed discussions of social reform in America.

Aaron I. Bell has given an account of the way in which Protestantism met the challenge of the city in *The Urban Impact on American Protestantism 1865-1900* (Cambridge: Harvard University Press, 1943).

The multi-volume set by William W. Sweet, with the general title of *Religion on the American Frontier*, has interesting source materials concerning the work of the Baptists, Presbyterians, Congregationalists and Methodists: Vol. I, *The Baptists* (New York: Henry Holt & Co., 1931); Vol. II, *The Presbyterians*, 1783-1840 (New York: Harper & Brothers, 1936); Vol. III, *The Congregationalists* (Chicago: University of Chicago Press, 1939).

Although it is written from a liberal viewpoint, *Religion in Our Times* (New York: Round Table Press, 1932) by Gaius G. Atkins gives much helpful information concerning modern American Christianity.

Winfred Garrison's *The March of Faith* (New York: Harper & Brothers, 1933) is another interesting survey of American Christianity since 1865.

[9] *Ibid.*, pp. 669-671.

THE CHURCH AND TWENTIETH CENTURY PROBLEMS

Chapter XXXVIII

THE CHURCH AND THE SECULAR STATE

The Church now has to cope with the increasing encroachment of the state upon what the Church had formerly considered to be its rights and privileges as well as its responsibilities. This growth of the power and functions of the secular state has been stimulated by the increase in social welfare legislation. Such legislation had its beginnings in England when the state was forced to give aid to those monks who had been dispossessed of their monasteries when the monasteries were broken up by 1539 and was forced to help those whom the Church had formerly served through the charitable work of the monks. The increasing political power of labor has forced the passage of legislation for its benefit, the administration and enforcement of which legislation has increased the power of the state. Two total wars in the twentieth century brought complete regimentation of all the human and material resources of states to win victory. These necessary wartime powers have increasingly been extended into the postwar era. Above all, the exaltation of the state in totalitarian Germany, Italy, Japan and Communistic Russia has created the all-powerful secular state, which in many cases will brook no opposition nor permit a division of allegiance on the part of its citizens. The threat to religion from the powerful secular and, in some cases, hostile state is the greatest problem the Church now faces.

I. The Churches in Two World Wars

During the nineteenth, and early twentieth, century aggressive movements that fostered the idea of world peace arose. Liberal theology and the social gospel with their emphasis upon the Fatherhood of God and the brotherhood of man helped to promote this tendency to work for world peace. Pacifistic groups also threw their weight behind the peace movement. The American Peace Society (1828) united many state peace societies into a larger national unit to work for world peace.

The Society condemned any war but that for self-defense and supported the negotiation of treaties of arbitration so that nations could settle their problems peacefully. By 1914 American secretaries of state had negotiated nearly fifty such treaties. International peace conferences, supported mainly by the churches, were held annually from the time of the first important meeting in Paris in 1889 until 1913. One of the more notable peace conferences was held at The Hague in 1899. That conference founded a court for the arbitration of international disputes. Then in 1910 the Carnegie Endowment for International Peace was founded by Andrew Carnegie.

The position of the American churches was summed up by an editorial in the May 7, 1898 issue of the *Outlook*. The churches after they had determined whether the war was righteous, were to strengthen national morale, to relieve suffering and to work to prevent the usual postwar decline in morals.

Optimism concerning peace was somewhat dampened by the coming of war in 1914, but the American churches supported Wilson's declaration of neutrality. They held Germany and her allies responsible for the war, but at the same time they believed that general European mammonism, immorality and neglect of things spiritual had contributed to the coming of war. While pity and aid were to be extended to sufferers through the Red Cross, America was to remain isolated from the war and even from the peace.

As propaganda increasingly interpreted the war in spiritual terms, as a struggle to save the Christian civilization that the "Huns" were trying to destroy, religious opinion gradually changed. A poll of American Presbyterian ministers in 1916 indicated that a large majority favored armament for self-defense. A strong America, it was believed, could help to extend democracy when peace came. By the beginning of 1917 churches were beginning to put the national flag in the churches along with the Christian flag and to give it the place of honor on the right.

American churches supported the declaration of war by the President in the spring of 1917 and sought in every possible way to help the state win the war. The attitude of hostility to war and of neutrality speedily changed to one whereby the churches sanctified the war and became agencies of the government. Notable clergymen gave their blessing to the bayonet as an instrument to bring about the kingdom of God. The churches provided chaplains for the armies that were coming into being. They supported the Red Cross by contributions and by such work on the part of the women as rolling bandages. Many preachers actively recruited young men for the army by expounding from the pulpit the religious nature of the war in Europe. Some ministers even sold war bonds in church services. Churchmen also spread atrocity propaganda. One outstanding minister even called German soldiers such names as "rattle-snakes" and "hyenas." Even German classical music was under ban during the war. Conscientious objectors and defenders of free speech were attacked for daring to oppose the war effort. In short, the Church blessed and supported the war.

With the failure of the nations to secure peace after World War I, the growth of nationalism, and the later repudiation by European states of their debts to the United States, the churches in America became disillusioned with war. Many ministers and laymen became pacifists. In fact, in a poll taken in 1931, over twelve thousand of about twenty thousand American clergymen of all denominations who replied to the poll stated that the Church should neither sanction nor support any future war. However, the task of aiding the impoverished churches of the Continent was not neglected by the churches of the victorious allies, and large sums were contributed for relief and recon-struction. The churches also supported disarmament and the outlawing of war between 1919 and 1939.

Even before World War II churches in such totalitarian coun-tries as Germany were forced to keep silent concerning political issues and to concentrate on the spiritual message of Christi-anity, to syncretize totalitarian dogma with the Christian faith, or to oppose the totalitarian state and accept the resulting per-secution. Many German churchmen led by Niemoller adopted the last course and suffered for their stand. Christians in these countries could well appreciate the plight of Christians who were persecuted by the Roman state in the early days of the Christian faith.

World War II found the churches much more cautious in their approach to war than they were in 1914. There was no attempt as in 1914 to make it a "holy war." The Church re-sisted the hate appeal. Many Christians in countries such as Norway and Holland, which were occupied by the Axis powers, suffered for their faith. Conscientious objectors were given more aid by the churches than they had been given in World War I. Reluctant support of the war was based upon the idea of the survival of the nation rather than upon any idealistic aim. A sense of the unity of all Christians, irrespective of which side of the battle front they were on, was maintained throughout the war. At the end of the war, the major Protestant American denominations pledged themselves to raise over $100,000,000 for relief and for the reconstruction of churches that were destroyed during the war in Europe.

Although the Church in World War II did not surrender its conscience to the state as it did in World War I by sanctifying the war, but maintained the essential unity of all Christians everywhere and resisted the tendency to hate, the Church did nevertheless provide chaplains for the armed forces and warmly supported the Red Cross. It also put greater efforts into serving the needy and suffering during the war and into the reconstruction of churches after the war. John Foster Dulles helped to integrate efforts of the American churches and the State Department to plan for a just peace.

II. THE ROMAN CATHOLIC CHURCH

The Roman Catholic Church has always insisted that it, speaking through the pope, is the final authority in matters of faith and morals. It has also claimed that the papal hierachy can give or withhold salvation through the sacraments which the hierarchy alone can dispense. This authoritarian, hierarchal and sacramental system is by its very nature totalitarian in its demands upon its people. Allegiance to the pope ideally precedes any other allegiance, but in practice Roman Catholics in such countries as the United States have modified this position. Insistence upon a prior allegiance to the church, as well as a tendency to interfere in politics, has brought the Roman Catholic Church under persecution in leftist totalitarian states, such as Russia and her satellites. Because totalitarian Russia is basically antireligious and because Rome demands complete allegiance to the church, both realize there can be no peaceful coexistence. For this reason, the pope has used every possible weapon he can against aggressive Communism and has also sought to enlist the support of powerful anticommunistic states. To that end the Roman Catholic Church in the United States has acted as a unit to promote national policy in line with the pope's objectives and to permeate American culture through the press, radio, motion picture and television.

One should realize that Roman Catholic hostility to totalitarian Russia is not hostility to totalitarianism as such. Where the state will recognize the rights of the papacy, the papacy will cooperate with that state even though it is totalitarian. This fact can be demonstrated by the recent history of the papacy in Italy. Pius IX, after the Italian state incorporated the Papal States and Rome into the nation (1870), retired to voluntary "imprisonment" within the Vatican and forbade Roman Catholics to cooperate with the democratic monarchial state in Italy either by voting or holding office. Not until 1929 in the Lateran Accord with the dictator Mussolini did the papacy relax its hostility to the Italian state. Mussolini permitted Pius XI to set up a new Vatican State to receive and to send ambassadors, and he recognized the Roman Catholic religion as the "only religion" of the state. In return, the papacy permitted the faithful to support the totalitarian state. The papacy has also supported the dictatorships of Franco in Spain and Salazar in Portugal. It also came to terms with Hitler in Germany in 1933. Only when the totalitarian state claims to have an international antireligious message and seeks to spread it will the Roman Catholic Church oppose totalitarianism. It has cooperated with any state, no matter how black its record concerning liberty, that will give it the status of a privileged or established religion of that state.

Recently the Roman Catholic Church has suffered great losses all over the world except in the Latin countries of Spain and Portugal and in Quebec and the United States. The Nazi dictatorship in Germany weakened the Roman Church of that land despite the 1933 concordat. The Communist revolution in 1917 eliminated any influence that the Roman Church had had in some parts of Russia. The acquisition by Russia after World War II of the satellite states of Estonia, Latvia, Lithuania, Czechoslovakia, Poland, Hungary, Bulgaria and Romania and the more recent Communist domination of China has resulted in the persecution of the leaders of the Roman Church in an effort to break their hold upon the people. In many Latin American countries the intellectuals have deserted the church and become indifferent to religion. The workers and farmers are stirring in revolt against the social, political and economic exploitation that they have undergone during the centuries. Because the Roman Church is associated with the rulers of the state, people may also turn against it as they become educated and see that it has sided with their exploiters. The nationalistic government of Mexico in its desire to create a higher economic standard of life has severely limited the power of the Roman Catholic Church and has sought to eliminate its political influence. The Roman Catholic Church seems to be losing its centuries-old religious monopoly in Latin America.

To offset this loss of communicants, the Roman Catholic Church has endeavored to strengthen her position in the United States and in other democratic countries whose aid she can enlist in the battle against Communism. She knows that the United States must now assume responsibility for the maintenance of world order. The attempt to secure an American ambassador to the Vatican and the increase in the number of American cardinals in the consistories of 1946 and 1953 seemed to be aimed at winning the support of American Roman Catholicism.

Early in the 1940's an attempt was made to have the United States' State Department refuse passports to Protestant missionaries seeking to enter South American lands, on the ground that they were endangering the Good Neighbor Policy. This move was defeated by aggressive action on the part of the Protestants. The power of the Roman Catholic Church in the United States is demonstrated by the way in which Hollywood avoids antagonizing the Roman Catholic Legion of Decency when the Legion objects to immoral or anti-Roman Catholic films. The Legion theoretically has the power to ban over twenty-five million American Roman Catholics from the theaters. Seldom does any publicity unfavorable to the Roman Catholic Church appear in the American press; on the contrary much favorable publicity, beyond its numerical strength in the population, is accorded to the Roman Church by many sections of the press. Over two hundred Roman Catholic colleges and as many seminaries are located in the United States. The Roman Catholic Church in the United States and elsewhere has also courted labor much more assiduously than the Protestant churches have done. It leans toward a syndicalist or corporate state similar to that which Mussolini built up in Italy. In such a state members of the legislature would be elected to represent economic groups, such as employers and employees in an industry, rather than to represent a geographical area.

In order to hold its people, the Roman Catholic Church has reinterpreted the theology of Thomas Aquinas in the light of modern scientific knowledge. It has also proclaimed a new dogma, which all its people must accept if they wish to be saved. In November, 1950, Pius XII declared that Mary's body was taken to heaven after her death. Known as the Assumption of the Virgin Mary, this dogma complements the dogma of the Immaculate Conception.

Continued attempts on the part of the papacy to foster stronger ties between the government of the United States and the Vatican may be expected as the papacy seeks the aid of the United States to defeat its archenemy, Communism. Through the American hierarchy, which is subject to the papacy, it can continue its efforts to mold public opinion and to secure legislation and governmental decisions favorable to its plans. However, as the Roman Catholic laity in the United States becomes aware of the aggressive nature of the plans of the Roman-controlled hierarchy, it may force some change in these activities that would be more in keeping with the role of a denomination in a state where either a privileged position for any church or its establishment as a state church is forbidden. Persecution of Protestants in lands where the Roman Catholic Church has power, such as in Italy and Columbia, and the furore over the attempt to have an American ambassador sent to the Vatican has made many American Roman Catholics uneasy concerning the activities of their church. The strong Protestant opposition to such persecution of Protestants and to the attempt to have an ambassador sent to the Vatican has been a matter of concern to others.

III. COMMUNISM AND CHRISTIANITY

Communism is a greater threat to organized Christianity than war or the modern blight of secularism and materialism that blasts so much of Western civilization. The opposition of the Roman state to the early Church and the spread of Mohammedanism at the expense of Christianity in the Mediterranean area during the seventh and eighth centuries are the only comparable threats that the Church has faced. Communism is dangerous because it is essentially a faith or a materialistic religion with an international scope and because it claims to have the only solutions to the problems of modern civilization. Its recent conquest of China has made its menace more apparent.

Communism is hostile to Christianity because of the materialistic atheism that underlies its philosophy. To a Marxian, religion is an "opiate" that makes the exploited content with their present hard life because they have the hope of a brighter life in the hereafter. Russian Communism has been antagonistic to religion also because the Russian Orthodox Church in the days of the Czars was linked with the oppressive policies of the state. When the Communists destroyed the Czarist state, they tried to destroy the Orthodox Church because it was a part of the system that they hated.

Because the Communists, through their leader, the Politburo and about six million members of the Communist Party, are able to control about two hundred million Russians for their own ends, the attitude of the Communists in Russia toward organized religion is of importance. In 1917 over one hundred million people in Russia belonged to the Orthodox Church, which was controlled by a wealthy bureaucratic hierarchy.

The Communists seized power in the revolution of November, 1917, and from that time until the beginning of 1923 they attacked the Church directly, even though the constitution of 1918 guaranteed freedom to proclaim both religious and antireligious propaganda. In 1918 the property of the Orthodox Church was confiscated and made state property without any compensation to the Church. The state permitted the use of churches only for worship. In that way the Church lost its means of support. Clergymen and monks were deprived of the privilege of the franchise, which often meant that they could not get work or ration cards for food. Religious instruction in any school was banned, except for seminaries for adults in which only theology could be taught. Marriage ceremonies were to be performed by state officials.

The economic failure of pure communism by 1921 forced the state to reinstate some features of capitalism in order to keep production going. This also helped to bring about a change in religious policy. The policy of direct attack gave way in 1923 to a policy that emphasized propaganda to discredit religion. Antireligious carnivals, in which objects used in worship were held up to ridicule, were organized. A Militant Atheists League was founded in 1925 to circulate atheistic propaganda.

Neither the ridicule nor the atheistic propaganda of the 1923 to 1927 program was successful, so the Russian government adopted a program that included strangling Christian culture, direct attack and antireligious education. It was carried out between 1928 and 1939. The few remaining churches were only permitted to hold services of worship and were deprived of the right to teach or persuade others to become Christians. Over fourteen hundred churches were closed in 1929 and used by the government for secular purposes. No one could go to church unless Sunday corresponded with the sixth rest day. The constitution of the state was amended in 1929 to provide "freedom of religious worship and antireligious propaganda." This meant that any attempt to win others to Christianity was banned, but atheism was given full rights to propagandize adults and the young in the schools.

The failure of militant atheism to eradicate Christianity, the persistence of belief in God, which seventy per cent of the Russian people expressed in the 1937 census, and the threatening international situation dictated the need for a strategic retreat after 1939. Churches were reopened, the antireligious carnivals were dropped and the teaching of atheism in the schools was abandoned. In 1943 Sergius was permitted to function as the patriarch of Moscow and all Russia. The seven-day week was restored, seminaries were permitted to reopen, and the Orthodox Church was freed of many burdensome restrictions. From the viewpoint of the government, the wisdom of making these concessions was shown when the Church supported the government at the time Germany invaded Russia in 1941. Because of the essential hostility of Communism to all forms of religion, the historian may be pardoned for doubting whether these concessions will be lasting. At the most, the Russian Church has toleration but not full freedom of religion.

Russian Communism emerged from World War II with great new additions of territory in Europe and Asia. The three Baltic republics, Poland, Czechoslovakia, Hungary, Rumania and Bulgaria have all come under Communist control. In each state the Church has been persecuted. The persecution in some instances had the support of the people because the clergy had a bad record of clerical oppression of the people. Even the nationalistic brand of Communism in Titoist Yugoslavia persecuted the Church. The Church in China is facing persecution from the Communistic authorities who want to eliminate religion.

No Communist government can come to any lasting agreement with Christianity in any form because Communism denies the spiritual nature of personality and demands complete ideological and political obedience from its followers. Concessions such as those made in Russia during the war are a matter of an expediency that is part of Communist tactics. The basic program and philosophy has been and will likely remain hostile to religion.

The Christian world must realize the nature of this new political faith by a study of its ideas so that people can discern the difference between truth and Communist propaganda. The Church must support measures to end the evils that help to create Communism. Communism flourishes best where there is poverty and suffering which it can promise to alleviate. The Church must not let itself become the tool of any particular group and sanctify wrongs in society. While recognizing that it can flourish best in a free-enterprise, democratic society, it should preach and live the Gospel rather than permit itself to become identified with any particular political or economic order. Above all, a consistent Christian life on the part of her members, whatever their status in society, is the most effective answer of the Church to Communism or to the secular state.

BIBLIOGRAPHY

Preachers Present Arms (New York: Round Table Press, 1933) by Ray H. Abrams contains much information on the role of the American churches in World War I.

Ray H. Abrams in "The Churches and Clergy in World War II" in *The Annals of the American Academy of Political Science*, 256:110-119 (March, 1948) discusses the role of the Church in World War II.

Paul Blanshard in his *American Freedom and Catholic Power* (Boston: Beacon Press, 1949) has written a well-documented survey of the activities of the Roman Catholic Church in the United States.

Harold E. Fay's series of articles in the November 29, 1944 to January 7, 1945 issues of *Christian Century*, "Can Catholicism Win America?" presents evidence of the many ramifications of Roman Catholic ecclesiastical machinery in the United States.

G. P. Howard presents a clear picture of the place of the Roman Catholic Church in Latin America in his *Religious Liberty in Latin America* (Philadelphia: The Westminster Press, ca. 1944).

John S. Curtiss has provided a well-documented account of the history of the Church in Russia since 1917 in *The Russian Church and Soviet State 1917-1950* (Boston: Little, Brown and Company, 1953).

Nicholas Timasheff has developed with adequate documentation the struggle between the Church and state in Russia in his book, *Religion in Soviet Russia* (New York: Sheed & Ward, 1942).

Alfred M. Rehwinkle in *Communism and the Church* (St. Louis: Concordia Publishing House, 1948) has ably discussed Communism and the means by which Christians can develop a positive approach and program to meet its threat.

Chapter XXXIX

RELIGIOUS DEVELOPMENTS SINCE 1919

There has been a growing tendency to turn from the subjective immanental theology of liberalism, which denied the deity of Christ, original sin and salvation by faith, either to a conservative theology, often called Fundamentalism, or to Neo-orthodoxy, which has developed from the teachings of Karl Barth. Supernatural and absolutist theology seems to be slowly replacing the relativistic theology of liberalism. In some respects the return is to the traditional Calvinism of many Protestants. There has also been a rediscovery of the idea of the universal Church, and this has promoted the cause of unity among the churches. This trend to unify the Church is known as the ecumenical movement.

I. The Revival of Theological Absolutism

The roots of liberal theology in America may be found in the importation of German idealistic philosophy to America early in the nineteenth century, in Biblical criticism, which was mediated to America from Scottish seminaries where Americans studied theology, and in the doctrine of evolution formulated by Charles Darwin. Liberal theology replaced a Calvinism modified by the influence of revivalism. By the beginning of the twentieth century the liberal ideas of the Fatherhood of God and the brotherhood of man had been carried from the seminaries to the laity as ministers, trained under liberal theologians, took over the pulpits of the land.

Liberalism denied the full inspiration of the Scriptures by an assertion that the Scriptures only contained the Word of God. The deity of Christ was rejected for an emphasis upon Him as a semi-divine being who preached an ethical gospel. The doctrine of original sin gave way to the doctrine of the essential goodness of man. The prophetic view of Christ's second return was replaced by the idea that it was the task of the

Church to create the Kingdom of God by social action. A poll of five hundred ministers and two hundred seminary students in Chicago in 1929 revealed that the only point upon which all were unanimous in belief was the existence of God. That the Bible was an absolute and infallible authority for faith and belief was denied by twenty-three per cent of the ministers and sixty-seven per cent of the seminary students. About half of the ministers accepted the doctrine of special creation, but ninety-five per cent of the students accepted evolution as the method of creation. The poll demonstrated the extent to which the dry rot of liberalism had penetrated the seminaries.

The fight between liberalism and conservatism was most furious in the Presbyterian Church, U. S. A., shortly before 1900. Union Seminary in New York became a leading center of liberalism. Charles A. Briggs' book, *Biblical Study,* became the issue that resulted in his expulsion from Union Seminary and the Presbyterian Church, U. S. A. in 1893, and the separation of that seminary from that church in 1905. Harry Emerson Fosdick has been one of the foremost exponents of liberalism in the twentieth century.

A. *The Fundamentalist Controversy.*

The conflict between Fundamentalism and Liberalism was focused by the Scopes trial in Dayton, Tennessee, in 1922. John T. Scopes had defied a state law against the teaching of evolution in the schools by teaching evolution in his science classes. William Jennings Bryan, an eloquent Presbyterian elder and three times a candidate for the Presidency, led the prosecution, and Clarence Darrow defended Scopes. Scopes lost his case in 1925, and similar laws banning the teaching of evolution appeared on the books of other states.

The divergence in the Presbyterian Church was demonstrated again when J. Gresham Machen and several students withdrew from Princeton Seminary in 1929 and founded Westminster Seminary, Philadelphia. In 1930 they formed their own denomination, the Orthodox Presbyterian Church. Other denominations had similar situations arise as the conservative and liberal forces clashed for control of the denomination. The above case has been used as an illustration because it was so widely publicized.

Since 1900, conservative forces have also engaged in positive attempts to counteract liberalism. Bible conferences have been and are being used to train people and leaders in Biblical doctrine. One of the early Bible conferences was sponsored in New York by A. J. Gordon. Another, held at Niagara in 1895, formulated five points of sound doctrine: an inerrant Bible, the Virgin Birth and the deity of Christ, the substitutionary Atonement, the physical Resurrection, and the physical Second Coming. These Bible conferences promoted practical piety as well as doctrinal orthodoxy.

The evangelicals also met liberalism with a strong literary apologetic. In 1909 Lyman and Milton Stewart, California millionaires, supported the publication of a set of twelve paperbound books called *The Fundamentals.* About three million copies were circulated widely among ministers and students. Because the articles in them were scholarly essays by recognized evangelical scholars, they served to strengthen the faith of many wavering ministers and students. The books were edited by A. C. Dixon, who had the help of R. A. Torrey and the $300,000 of financial backing from the Stewarts. J. Gresham Machen wrote many popular books, such as *Christianity and Liberalism* (1923), and scholarly works, such as his *The Virgin Birth of Christ* (1930).

Education in Bible schools and Christian colleges was another answer of the conservative in the churches to the liberal movement. The Nyack Bible School, founded by A. B. Simpson in 1882, and Moody Bible Institute, founded in 1886 by Dwight L. Moody, were among the first of these schools to give an education that emphasized the use of the English Bible as a textbook. The Christian education movement has grown until now there are scores of Bible schools in all countries of the world. Nearly forty Bible schools were founded between 1930 and 1940. Christian colleges, such as Wheaton College at Wheaton, Illinois, and Calvin College at Grand Rapids, Michigan, have sought to provide higher education that is, at the same time, scholarly, evangelical, Biblical, and God-centered.

B. Neo-orthodoxy.

The liberals' contest with the conservatives became a three-cornered struggle with the emergence of Neo-orthodoxy or, as it often is known, the theology of crisis. Neo-orthodoxy is usually associated with the name of Karl Barth. Emil Brunner was also an exponent of similar ideas until he disagreed with Barth as to whether, as he contended, one could know God through His creation (natural theology). Both to Barthians and conservatives, liberalism appeared to be a sentimental system with weak theological foundations.

Karl Barth, who was born in Basel, Switzerland, in 1886, received most of his advanced theological training in Germany. After his ordination he served for a short time as a religious writer for a liberal German magazine. He then became a pastor in Swiss churches until he was made professor of Reformed theology at Gottingen in 1921. From Gottingen he went to Munster in 1925 and Bonn in 1929. In both of these universities he was professor of theology. His opposition to Hitler's religious policy forced him to return to his homeland. He now teaches theology at the University of Basel, writes and often preaches. His dynamic presentation of Christianity has drawn students from all over the world to his classes. His spiritual pilgrimage has led him from liberalism to his present position in opposition to liberalism.

Both Barth and Brunner accept the principles and results of higher Biblical criticism. This means that they cannot accept the Bible as God's objective, historical revelation that is infallibly inspired. To them the Bible can only be a human witness to God's revelation as the Holy Spirit reveals God to the human heart. Until that moment of crisis it is merely another book that has no real meaning for the soul. Because of this viewpoint Barth is critical of orthodox Christianity, which accepts the plenary inspiration of the Bible.

Barth's whole system, which is reminiscent of Calvinism, is centered in God as the ultimate reality. God is holy, absolute, sovereign, eternal, and other than man and nature, both in essence and attribute. This view of a transcendent and sovereign God is opposed to the immanental subjective view of God held by liberal theologians since the days of Schleiermacher and Ritschl. Because there is discontinuity between God and man and history, man cannot know God by reason or sensation. Man, a finite human being under the bondage of sin, is utterly unable to help himself in the matter of salvation. Salvation therefore can only come through the miraculous supernatural piercing of history by God Himself in the person of His Son, Jesus Christ, the Word of God. It is in the crucified and resurrected Christ alone that man can find salvation. Grace mediated by the Holy Spirit through the Word can relate man to God. Only when the soul is confronted by God in Christ can there be salvation from the world. Only God can come into human affairs and cleanse the earth after judgment at the end of the age. Thus there is both a personal and global crisis. Barthian ethics are based entirely upon grace and not upon human effort.

Many have left the liberal camp in order to adopt Barth's or Brunner's views. Though the conservative regrets that Barth has not seen fit to found his system on the unassailable authority of the Bible, he hails Barth's repudiation both of liberalism and the social gospel and his assertion of the holiness of God and sinful man's need of divine grace. Barth's ideas have had a tremendous influence both upon the Continent and in America. They have also stimulated the development of Biblical theology.

C. *Roman Catholic Neo-Thomism.*

The Roman Catholic Church also suffered from the rise of liberalism. The French scholar Loisy and the English thinker G. Tyrell were the major Roman Catholic exponents of liberalism. The pope condemned the liberal movement in a papal encyclical in 1907 and a little later that year expelled Tyrell from the church. These scholars held, in common with Protestant liberals, the idea of an immanent God and the dogmas of Biblical criticism.

The challenge of idealistic philosophy and liberal theology was taken up in 1879 when Pope Leo XIII issued the bull *Aeterni Patris* in which he stated that "the precious wisdom" of Thomas Aquinas would be a sufficient answer to liberalism. This call for a return to absolute and authoritative theology was reinforced by the tragedy of the breakdown both of nations and morals in World War I. Cardinal Mercier (1851–1926), the primate of the Roman Catholic Church in Belgium, led in the revival of Thomistic studies at the University of Louvain. The French scholar Jacques Maritain is the present leader of the Neo-Thomists. The Neo-Thomists wish to recall the Church of Rome to absolutism in theology as developed by Thomas Aquinas, but they wish to rethink his theology in terms of the problem created by the rise of science and the secular state, so that Thomism will reconcile science and theology now as Aquinas reconciled Greek philosophy and theology in his day. The natural revelation of science is to be synthesized with the supernatural revelation of the Bible.

[483]

D. New Cults.

Many unhappy souls who were dissatisfied with the lack of authority in liberalism and who did not find refuge in the Roman Catholic Church or conservative Protestant churches turned to the message of theological or ethical absolutism proclaimed by various cults, many of which have arisen since World War I. A sect is the result of a heresy adopted by a minority of Christians who have split with the majority in order to form their own group, but cults are the result of an invention by some individual who gathers followers around him. The doctrines of cults are developed outside of the pale of the Church, and the leaders of cults seek to win converts from the Church by proselyting and by meetings, home visitation, or correspondence courses. All of the cults not only claim to have final or absolute answers to the problems of health, sorrow, popularity and success, but they offer an authority that the hungry soul cannot find in liberal Protestant churches. Cults provided an optimistic answer to the pessimism of the period between the two world wars.

Cults such as Spiritualism, Theosophy, New Thought, Unity and Christian Science oppose materialistic interpretations of the universe and assert its unity and spiritual nature. Spiritualism in particular grew fast after World War I because those who had lost loved fathers, husbands, or brothers in the war sought to communicate with them through mediums. Both Unity and New Thought were developments of the Quimby process of mental healing that Mrs. Mary Baker Eddy had used to good advantage in building up Christian Science. Charles Fillmore, who had been a cripple from infancy, and his wife Myrtle, who had had tuberculosis, developed the idea of their unity with God so that illness and poverty could have no hold upon them. Their group has grown so much that the leaders of the movement are building Unity City near Kansas City, Missouri.

The Russelites or, as they prefer to be known, Jehovah's Witnesses, were founded in 1872 by Charles T. Russell, whose avid study of the Bible led him to oppose the churches and ministers as tools of the Devil and to preach the doctrine of Christ's return and the participation of the "witnesses" in that event. Because they claim that their only allegiance is to God, members of Jehovah's Witnesses will not salute the flag, nor will they serve in the armed forces. Their leaders were not recognized as ministers in World War II. Judge Rutherford, a Missouri lawyer, became the leader upon Russell's death in 1916. The movement, which was incorporated as the Watch Tower Bible and Tract Society in New York in 1939, distributes millions of books and tracts. It is estimated that there are about five hundred thousand adherents in the United States and about three million in the world.

The Oxford Group or Buchmanites do not constitute a particular organization but seek to work in the churches somewhat after the fashion of the Pietists who desired to rejuvenate Lutheranism in the sixteenth century. Frank Buchman, the leader, was a Lutheran minister in Pennsylvania who was dissatisfied with his spiritual experience. He tried to reach the well-to-do and educated through his gospel of the changed life, "sharing" or confession to the group, guidance, and the four absolutes of honesty, purity, love and unselfishness. House parties for personal witnessing and public confession have been the method of operation adopted by the group. It has won many notable converts and even sought in Moral Rearmament, its new name, to prevent the coming of World War II by winning the leaders of states to Christianity. It has helped the educated and rich whom the Church often fears to challenge with the claims of Christ lest it lose their support. Two weaknesses of the Group are that the lack of a sound theology may lead to the substitution of the feeling of release, after one has "shared" sins, for real regeneration, and confession may be directed only to man rather than to God.

Neo-orthodoxy, Fundamentalism and the cults seem to have arisen to meet the need for a religious message with authority. To some extent, such movements are attempts to fill the spiritual void created by the theological bankruptcy of liberalism with its shallow message of a vague Fatherhood of God and brotherhood of man. Liberalism taught morality but neglected the religious dynamic of the Cross, which alone can energize a life so that it conforms to Christian ethics.

II. The Rise of the Ecumenical Movement

Until the formation of the Greek Orthodox Church in 1054 and the emergence of the Protestant churches during the Reformation, the Church was united in organization, if not in spirit. Ever since the Reformation many have desired to restore unity to the Church on earth. Unfortunately, in many cases this unity has been merely an organizational unity on the basis of the lowest common denominator of theology.

Four stages may be traced in the history of the attempt to unite the visible Church. Interdenominational cooperation began in the last century in such organizations as the Bible societies. There have been several organic reunions of denominations in the present century. Federation on a national and international scale has been carried out. Within recent years the ecumenical movement to unite all denominations on an international level has been the objective of proponents of unity.

A. *Interdenominational Cooperation.*

The founding of the British and Foreign Bible Society in 1804 and of the American Bible Society in 1816 offered an opportunity for the various denominations to cooperate in a work in which they could all participate without endangering their particular doctrinal emphasis. The founding of the Y.M.C.A. in England in 1844 and its coming to the United States in 1851 furthered cooperation among the denominations in the worthwhile work of the "Y." The Christian Endeavor organization, founded in 1881, brought the young people of various denominations together in a cooperative experience of worship and service. The Student Volunteer Movement, founded in 1886 with Moody's aid, united students of all denominations in thought and action concerning the challenge of missionary service. These and many other organizations brought churchmen of various denominations together in common worship and service. Many churchmen became interested in the idea of closer cooperation.

B. *Organic Reunion.*

Organic reunion occurs when groups give up their identity as separate bodies in order to form a new organization. It has been easier to have organic reunion of denominations with similar backgrounds of theology and rite. The Cumberland Presbyterians, who had separated from the Presbyterian Church in 1810 over the licensing of partly trained preachers after the Second Awakening, reunited with the Presbyterian Church, U.S.A., in 1906. The Methodist Protestant, the Methodist Episcopal Church, South, and the Methodist Episcopal Church united to form the Methodist Church in the spring of 1939 in Kansas City, Missouri. The act of union, performed by a conference of nine hundred delegates, brought together over eight million people. Several mergers have also taken place among the Baptists and Lutherans.

Union of different denominations has also taken place. The United Church of Canada, which includes the major part of the Presbyterian, the Methodist and the Congregational churches of Canada, came into being by a union of these three groups in 1925. The polity of the new church combined elements of the polity of each of the constituent bodies, but the theological statement, which included most of the elements of the Reformed theology, was not binding upon the ministers of the new church. The United Presbyterian and the Free Churches of Scotland combined in the United Free Church in 1900. The United Free Church reunited with the established church in 1929 to form the Kirk (Church) of Scotland. Other attempts to unite different denominations took place in Germany, Southern India, Japan and China.

C. National and International Ecclesiastical Federations.

In any system of ecclesiastical federation thus far developed, the cooperating units maintain their sovereignty but cooperate to achieve ends of common interest to the participating groups. Various denominations have set up international organizations in which the same denominations in various nations can work cooperatively to advance the interests of that denomination throughout the world. Ever since 1867 Anglicans throughout the world have met every tenth year in what is known as the Lambeth Conference to consider matters of common interest to Anglicans. The World Alliance of Reformed Churches Holding the Presbyterian System was organized in 1875 and held its first meeting at Edinburgh in 1877. The International Congregational Council held its first meeting in 1891. The Baptist World Alliance came into being in 1905 to consider matters of interest to all Baptists. The decision of these councils are merely advisory and may or may not be put into effect by the member groups. The Lutheran World Federation has met several times since its inception in 1923. The Methodists also have an Ecumenical Methodist Conference. These conferences, which bring together nationals of like faith from many countries, have given men a new sense of their unity in faith and practice, and they have strengthened the idea of ecumenical federation of all denominations.

Different Protestant denominations have set up national federations so that they can cooperate in service. In 1905 the Protestant churches of France created the Protestant Federation of France. The Swiss Federation of Churches came into being shortly after World War I. But the most important illustration of national federation of different denominations is the Federal Council of the Churches of Christ in America, which is now known as the National Council of the Churches of Christ. The former came into being in 1908 when the assembled delegates of thirty denominations approved the constitution that had been drafted at an earlier meeting in 1905.[1] The words "divine Lord and Savior" constituted the only statement of theology in the constitution. The major interest of the Federal Council has been to have the churches cooperate in social action. The Social Creed of the Churches adopted by the Council urged the churches to support such things as abolition of child labor, a minimum living wage and arbitration in industrial disputes. Various commissions were set up to carry out these and other programs. Because of this social emphasis and weak theological foundation, liberals have been able to seize and hold the reins of leadership firmly since the inception of the Council.

On November 29, 1950 the Federal Council ceased to be, and the National Council came into being. The International Council of Religious Education, the Foreign Missions Conference of North America, the Home Missions Council and various other interdenominational boards united with the Federal Council in the new organization. Missionary, educational, social and other activities were coordinated under this larger organization. Twenty-five Protestant and four Orthodox denominations became a part of the Council. Many of the liberal leaders of the Federal Council became prominent leaders of the new organization. The National Council has moved further than the Federal Council in the direction of a national superchurch.

The conservatives have not been behind the liberals in the development of interdenominational cooperation by federation. The American Council of Churches was organized in September, 1941, to dispute the claim of the Federal Council to speak for all Protestants. Churches which are in any way related to the National Council are not eligible for membership. The American Council has been led by Carl McIntire, who has not hesitated

---

[1] P. G. Mode, *Source Book and Bibliographical Guide for American Church History* (Menasha, Wisconsin: George Banta Publishing Co., 1921), pp. 669-671.

to oppose the National Council in the pages of *The Christian Beacon.* This Council claims to represent about two million Protestants.

The National Association of Evangelicals, which is more irenic than the American Council but no less true to the historic faith of Christianity, came into being in Chicago, in May, 1943. The delegates accepted the provisional constitution, which had been drafted at a meeting of 170 evangelicals in April, 1942. The organization has an evangelical statement of faith, but it will accept for full membership evangelicals and evangelical churches even though their denomination may belong to the National Council. The American Council will not permit this because it believes that the National Council is "apostate" and socialistic. The N.A.E. has commissions at work on various projects involving such matters as missions, education, evangelism and social action. Its periodical, *United Evangelical Action,* gives regular reports concerning its activities that are of common interest to the several million members that the organization claims to represent.

In many countries of the world these national Protestant federations have been formed to provide an agency for interdenominational cooperation. Each of them has stimulated the demand for an ecumenical council that will embrace the Protestant orthodox churches of the world.

D. *The World Council of Churches.*

Not since the days of the ecumenical councils at Nicaea, Constantinople and Chalcedon in the fourth and fifth century has there been such a wave of cooperation among churches as there has been in recent years. Founded in London in 1846, the Evangelical Alliance had a definite theological statement, but it was one that made many liberals dissatisfied with it. Consequently, the Alliance became inactive about 1900 as other organizations to promote interdenominational and international cooperation came into being. But it marked the first step in the development of a modern ecumenical body. The accompanying chart shows the development of the World Council of Churches.

The World Council of Churches owes much to the various international missionary conferences that began in 1854 in New York. At the New York meeting in 1900 the word "ecumenical" was used for the first time to describe the nature of the meet-

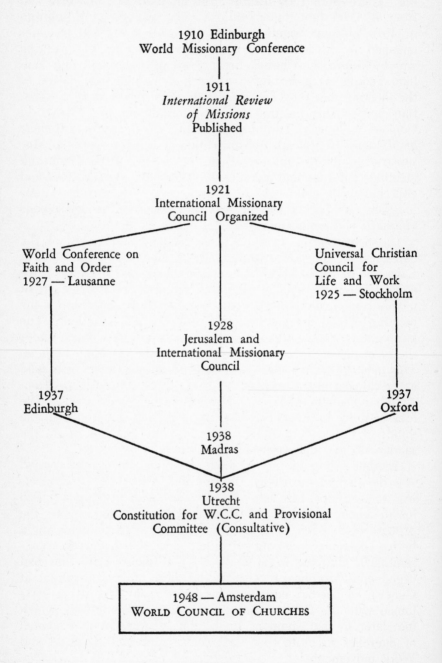

1910 Edinburgh
World Missionary Conference

1911
*International Review
of Missions*
Published

1921
International Missionary
Council Organized

World Conference on
Faith and Order
1927 — Lausanne

Universal Christian
Council for
Life and Work
1925 — Stockholm

1928
Jerusalem and
International Missionary
Council

1937
Edinburgh

1937
Oxford

1938
Madras

1938
Utrecht
Constitution for W.C.C. and Provisional
Committee (Consultative)

1948 — Amsterdam
WORLD COUNCIL OF CHURCHES

ing. There were 1500 leaders from all parts of the world and from all Protestant denominations. The meeting at Edinburgh in 1910 brought together 1200 delegates from 160 societies engaged in missionary work. Representation at the meeting was by countries. Charles Brent, Nathan Soderblom and William Temple were so impressed with the ecumenical nature of the meeting that they dedicated their lives to the task of Christian unity. This meeting laid the foundation for the World Council of Church. The publication of the *International Review of Missions* in 1911 and the formation of the International Missionary Council in 1921 were important results of the Edinburgh meeting. International meetings of missionary organizations and churches were again held in Jerusalem in 1928 and in Madras in 1938. At Madras, for the first time, some of the indigenous churches had representatives.

The first meeting involving the theology and polity of the churches was the World Conference on Faith and Order held at Lausanne in 1927. Bishop Charles Brent of the Protestant Episcopal Church of the United States, financed by a large gift of money from J. Pierpont Morgan, was largely responsible for the meeting of 450 delegates representing 90 denominations. The participants were conscious of their unity in one Church under the headship of Christ and urged that another meeting be held. This meeting, which also dealt with Faith and Order, was held at Edinburgh in the summer of 1937. Over 400 delegates from 122 churches and 43 lands conferred on theological issues. The idea of unity in diversity seems to have been uppermost in the minds of the leaders as they discussed the common faith, the sacraments and the nature of the Church.

Another group of international meetings during this period was devoted to the theme of Life and Work. The first meeting to consider Life and Work was held in August 1925 in Stockholm through the efforts of Nathan Soderblom, the primate of Sweden. The program was devoted to plans for a better economic and political order. The 500 delegates, representing 91 churches in 33 lands, did not adjourn until they had urged consideration of the creation of a universal council at Geneva. A second equally large meeting at Oxford in 1937 joined with the Faith and Order meeting at Edinburgh, which met later in that summer, to call for an international council of churches to unite the Faith and Order and the Life and Work movements.

The meeting of 80 leaders at Utrecht in the spring of 1938 resulted in the development of a provisional constitution,[2] a plan of organization for the World Council of Churches and the creation of a Provisional Committee to bring it into being. Between August 22 and September 4, 1948, over 350 delegates, representing about 150 churches from 44 countries, met at Amsterdam. This meeting completed the task of creating an ecumenical council. The Southern Baptists of the United States, the Roman Catholic Church, Missouri Synod Lutherans and the Russian Orthodox Church were not represented at the meeting, although they had been invited to attend. William Temple's dream of an international ecclesiastical organization came to pass as the delegates discussed "Man's Disorder and God's Design." Some friction occurred when the meeting wanted to condemn captitalism and communism equally for man's disorder, but it finally condemned a *"laissez-faire* capitalism," a type of capitalism that did not exist anywhere in the world at that time. Many of the major backers of the project were Americans who were also involved in the Federal Council of Churches. The major result of the meeting was the formation of the World Council of Churches with its headquarters in Geneva. The World Council is composed of an Assembly, which meets every five years, a Central Committee, which meets annually, an Administrative Secretariat and various Commissions that work on major problems facing the organization.

Both the American Council of Churches and the National Association of Evangelicals answered the attempt by the liberal forces to create an ecumenical church by creating conservative international organizations. The International Council of Christian Churches was founded in Amsterdam in 1948 two weeks before the meeting described above in order to oppose liberalism and to develop evangelical world spirit. At a meeting in Holland in August, 1951 the World Evangelical Fellowship came into being to provide fellowship and to coordinate the work of the N.A.E. with that of evangelicals throughout the world. Both these organizations and the Roman Catholic Church oppose plans of the World Council. Rome will only consider ecumenical unity on the terms of complete submission to the papacy.

As one objectively reviews this movement towards world ec-

---

[2] G. K. A. Bell, ed., *Documents on Christian Unity* (London: Oxford University Press, 3rd. series, 1930-1948, 1948), pp. 292-297.

clesiastical unity, one is constrained to wonder whether Christ had unity of the organizational type described above in mind when He spoke of the unity of His Church, or whether He had in mind a spiritual unity that believers in the invisible Church, the Body of Christ, have through Him as their Head. The true Church will always be a living organism, and no human organization or machinery should ever be a substitute for this spiritual unity that makes the Church the only true international body in the world. Such a unity of spirit will never endanger orthodox doctrine.

BIBLIOGRAPHY

An excellent detailed survey of the various unions and federations up until 1929 is given in the book, *Christian Unity* (New York: E. P. Dutton & Co., 1929), by Gaius J. Slosser.

Walter M. Horton describes the important twentieth century ecumenical meetings, including the Amsterdam meeting in 1948, in his book, *Toward a Reborn Church* (New York: Harper & Brothers, 1949).

The little work by Rene Pache, *The Ecumenical Movement* (Dallas: Dallas Theological Seminary, 1950), is an excellent survey of the rise of the World Council from an evangelical viewpoint.

The work by Stewart G. Cole, *History of Fundamentalism* (New York: Harper & Brothers, 1931), is a good account, although from a liberal viewpoint, of Fundamentalism.

Conclusion

PROBLEMS AND PROSPECTS

Problems are no new thing in the history of the Church, but the scope and intensity of problems that face the Church today seem to be as great as at any previous time in the history of the Church. Many Christians, who become pessimistic in the face of these problems, forget that the prospects of Christianity are bright when the Church depends upon her Lord.

I. PROBLEMS

A. *The Problem of Communism.*

Communism looms in the eyes of Christians all over the world as the greatest problem that the modern Church faces. Communism is not only a political and economic system; it is also a religion that attracts youth with its message of men unitedly striving for a better order, the coming of which is as inevitable, in the minds of the Communists, as is the coming of each sunrise. Communism holds sway over about one-third of the world's population, although millions of these people are the helpless slaves of a small minority whose clever use of modern techniques of revolution has enabled them to gain and hold power. According to the best estimates, there are not more than seven million Communists in Russia. This number controls a population of approximately two hundred million people. Communism has never won any country by a free election; it has always seized power through a minority of Communist nationals backed up by the Red Army. Communism holds sway today from the Elbe to the Pacific coast of Asia and from the Baltic to the Adriatic in Europe and to the borders of Iran and India in Asia.

Because of its basic materialistic premises, it has presented a uniformly hostile front to Christianity wherever it has obtained power. Opposition to Christianity in China by the Communist forces under Mao-Tse Tsung has been demonstrated by the expulsion of the missionaries and the persecution of the Chinese churches in various open and more subtle ways. The Communist Party in countries that are still democratic seeks in every way possible to subvert Christianity. The Church must reckon with this dynamic force, whether in Communist lands or in lands still not under the heel of Communism.

B. The Problem of Missions.

The threat of Communism is closely related to the problem of missions because where Communism has gained control missions have been ended. But Communism is only one of the forces that make effective missionary work increasingly difficult. Nationalism, as a reaction against the imperialism of the past century, has offered increasing opposition to missions in Asia and Africa. The Treaty of Tientsin in 1858, which forced China to open her doors to missionaries, has always been associated in the Chinese mind with Western imperialism and the Second Opium War which that treaty ended. The Boxer Rebellion of 1900 was an early manifestation of that nationalism upon which the Communist leaders of China are now capitalizing. The problem is just as acute in Africa where the slogan "Africa for the Africans" is uniting the various tribes of Africa against their European overlords. Libya became an independent nation in 1952. Many states in Asia, such as India, Pakistan, Burma, Ceylon, the Philippines and the United States of Indonesia, have become independent states since World War II. Nationhood has made these countries question the admission of missionaries who are still linked in their minds with the imperialism from which they have just escaped. Mohammedans in the Arab nations have been using nationalism as a tool to keep missionaries from offering effective competition to their faith.

The American Catholic hierarchy made efforts in 1942 to prevent Protestant missionaries from getting passports to South American countries on the grounds that their presence endangered the Good Neighbor Policy in Latin America.

Liberals have also opposed conservative missions. In 1931 an interdenominational group set up the Laymen's Foreign Missions Inquiry which visited missions in India, Burma, China and Japan in that year. Their report, *Re-Thinking Missions*, put out in 1932 under the leadership of William E. Hocking, a Harvard professor of philosophy, suggested the continuance of missions along liberal lines that would emphasize social effort, through

[495]

medicine and other techniques, apart from evangelism. Missionaries should seek, they wrote, to link their faith with whatever common features they find in pagan religions. They also recommended greater unity in missionary activity. Any reading of the report reveals that the conversion of men and women to Christ is not, according to the authors, the primary aim of missions.

The severe depression of the thirties and wartime population shifts coupled with high taxes, high national debts and inflation, which leaves less extra money available for religious use, have all hampered missionary work. Although national incomes have gone up, support of missionary effort has not gone up proportionately.

C. *The Problem of Catholicism.*

Catholicism, too, has become an increasing problem, which persons of all shades of Protestant theological opinion are beginning to recognize. Where Rome has been in power politically, persecution of Protestants has resulted. Persecutions of Protestants in Columbia is an illustration of this. Rome has also sought to influence the government of the United States through efforts of Roman Catholics to secure political help for the papacy against Communism. Attempts to appoint an American ambassador to Rome give evidence of this tendency of the Roman Catholic Church to engage in politics for her own ends.

D. *The Problem of Moral Decline.*

Moral decline, which always follows war, has become an increasing problem for the spiritual forces of the nations. An increase in sexual immorality, drunkenness, divorce, and the low moral tone of many radio and television programs threaten the stability of the family, which is the basic unit in the nation. Even the Russian Communists, who at first permitted easy divorce, had to tighten laws to protect the family. The average age of criminals has lowered till most crimes in the United States in 1949 were committed by youths between the ages of twenty and twenty-four. An increasing number of women are also becoming a part of the army of crime. About 750,000 Americans are classed as alcoholics; nearly 3,750,000 are rated as habitual drunkards. Clever advertising by the liquor industries calls for moderate drinking or otherwise pictures temperate social drinking as something that is the correct and sophisticated thing to do. The Kefauver Committee, which investigated gambling, revealed the connection between local and national politics and criminal forces in the United States.

E. *The Problem of Shifting Population.*

The shifts in population in recent years in most countries, particularly in the United States, and the gradual alienation of labor from the Church offers a challenge to ecclesiastical statesmanship. People in the cities have been moving to the suburbs in great numbers and have often neglected their spiritual life. Neglected rural areas call for ministers. Only 23.5 per cent of the people of the State of Washington were affiliated with a church in the early part of the forties. The Church has had to found new churches in these areas in order to reach these unchurched people. A new interest in applying the Gospel to social and economic problems of modern society as well as to the matter of personal salvation is being manifested by the churches.

F. *The Problem of Institutionalization.*

Another problem and danger is the tendency to institutionalize the Church as the Roman Catholic Church was institutionalized during the Middle Ages, when the Church of Rome degenerated into a superorganization with top heavy machinery and a bureaucracy. These and many other problems constitute the challenge faced by the Church of Christ today.

II. PROSPECTS

What are the prospects for the Church faced with this dark picture? The student of church history will remember other eras when it seemed as if the Church would go down before her enemies. The collapse of the Roman Empire presented the Church with the task of winning the Teutonic tribes who swept across the Rhine into the Empire, but the Church met this challenge by winning these people to Christianity. When it seemed as if Mohammedanism would overrun Europe in the seventh century, the Church responded to that challenge.

A. *The Prospect of Revival.*

One is impressed with the perennial recurrence of revival in the Church at times when her problems seem insurmountable. Although recent years have not produced revival on the scale of the Wesleyan movement in England or the Great Awakening in the Thirteen Colonies, there are many evidences of revival forces which taken together constitute a mighty influence for

[497]

God in our day. Such an evangelist as Billy Graham demonstrates the interest in and response to the Gospel even in mass evangelism. The enthusiastic response to the work of the Gideons and the various national Bible societies in the distribution of the Scriptures gives evidence of a hunger for the life-giving Word of God. Groups such as the Inter-Varsity Fellowship and the Foreign Missions Fellowship challenge college students with the claims of Christ and missions. Movements to promote evangelism have been and are being developed and put into effect by major Protestant denominations. Young Life workers seek to make Christ known to high school students, and Youth for Christ International has been a potent force in the task of world-wide evangelism of youth. These and many other agencies demonstrate that the statement that revivalism is disappearing is not founded on fact.

B. *The Prospect of Revival of Biblical Theology.*

Another encouraging prospect is the revival of Biblical theology. Part of the credit should go to Karl Barth who has again called men back to meet the claims of a personal and transcendent God. This new interest in Biblical theology should develop a teaching ministry that emphasizes the importance of theology as a base for Christian belief. Bible institutes in large numbers are now flourishing. Christian colleges are increasing in number and are raising their standards of scholarship as they seek to give a Christ-and Bible-centered education. The book, *Christian Education in a Democracy* (New York: Oxford University Press, 1951), edited by Frank Gaebelein, shows the interest of educators in a Christian philosophy of education.

C. *The Prospect of Ecumenicity.*

While some might wonder whether the ecumenical movement represented by the World Council of Churches will result in anything but a unity based upon organization and machinery, there are encouraging notes that lead many to believe that Evangelicals throughout the world are beginning to realize their unity in the only truly international body, the Body of Christ. Any sound ecumenical movement must be built upon a unity of spirit, based upon an experience of Christ as Saviour from sin and upon the Bible as the fully-inspired, infallible source of faith and conduct. The National Association of Evangelicals is an encouraging development when considered from this viewpoint. It and allied movements are seeking not only to win men to Christ but also to make the Gospel socially relevant without depriving it of a theological and spiritual foundation in the way so many of the exponents of the social gospel have done. Cooperation of evangelical denominations in various fields of endeavor is beginning to bear fruit.

D. *The Prospect of Missions.*

There are still fields open to the proclamation of the Gospel by missionaries. Japan has been a fruitful field during the period of the American occupation, and it is hoped that now that she is again independent she will still welcome missionaries. The presence of many wealthy and influential Chinese in the various lands of Asia outside China is a challenge that the Church is beginning to meet. Missionaries who know the Chinese language and culture and who have been driven out of the Chinese mainland are beginning to reach these people. The Church has also been willing to adopt new techniques. Radio Station HCJB in South America has been broadcasting the Gospel over shortwave radio to all parts of the world for many years. Other stations are being developed in the Far East and Africa to do similar work in those areas. The airplane has speeded up missionary travel and has removed many of the rigors faced by pioneering missionaries. Medical work, educational activity through schools of various kinds, and agricultural work have been the religious "Point Four" that has been used as means to win the native population to Christ.

The student of church history, who has observed the operation of the transforming power of the Gospel over the span of the centuries in remaking the lives of men and nations, can see the problems that have been discussed only as challenges to renewed effort in the power of the Holy Spirit. He realizes that God is in history as Providential Sustainer of the universe and as Saviour through the work of Jesus Christ upon the Cross. Both history and the end of history are in the capable hands of His Son. With serene confidence in her risen Lord, the Church shall rise to meet the challenges of the present as she has met the challenges of the past.

INDEX

The references are to pages. The numbers in italics refer to the main entries.